— you will now find a muddled Cabinet happening beyond about as the minority Report of its Labour members! Then Mr Leonard also told me with [struck] pompous solemnity that they were all agreed — & that there was no prospect of any minority Report — and we had to keep all the term over it talk! had been putting the last touches to it that very morning! Certainly the persons with having a independent means may have a restful time in the post of permanent secretary or fly on it else.

Altogether our present life is delightful. Love, health, ease, freedom, friends' all the good things of life in abundant measure. Sometimes one feels guilty of this abundance of happiness — as if of a monopoly. Sometimes I feel that the ease & comfort of our lives is stolen from others & that we ought to be more ascetic. We work hard it is true — but myself for myself — but then

The Diary
of
BEATRICE WEBB

Volume Two
1892–1905
"All the Good Things of Life"

The Diary
of
BEATRICE WEBB

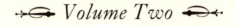 *Volume Two*

1892–1905

"All the Good Things of Life"

Edited by
Norman and Jeanne MacKenzie

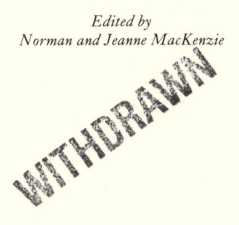

THE BELKNAP PRESS OF
HARVARD UNIVERSITY PRESS
CAMBRIDGE, MASSACHUSETTS
1983

Printed in Great Britain

Library of Congress Cataloging in Publication Data

Webb, Beatrice Potter, 1858–1943.
  "All the good things of life," 1892–1905.

  (The Diary of Beatrice Webb; v.2)
  Bibliography: p.
  Includes index.
  1. Webb, Beatrice Potter, 1858–1943. 2. Socialists—Great
Britain—Biography. I. MacKenzie, Norman Ian. II. MacKenzie,
Jeanne. III. Title. IV. Series: Webb, Beatrice Potter, 1858–1943.
Diary of Beatrice Webb; v.2
HX243.W383   1983 vol. 2   335'.14'0924   83–63
ISBN 0–674–20288–0

Contents

v

Illustrations

Cover

Beatrice Webb 1907 (Passfield Papers, London School of
    Economics and Political Science)
Bernard Shaw c. 1901 (Radio Times Hulton Picture Library)
A.J. Balfour 1898 (Radio Times Hulton Picture Library)
Sidney Webb 1894 (Mansell Collection)
Bertrand Russell date unknown (Barbara Halpern)

Between Pages 176 and 177

Beatrice and Sidney Webb shortly after their marriage (Nicholas
    Meinertzhagen)
Beatrice and Sidney Webb c. 1898 (Passfield Papers)
Beatrice and Sidney Webb, photographed by Bernard Shaw date
    unknown (London School of Economics and Political Science)
Beatrice Webb date unknown (Nicholas Meinertzhagen)
Cartoon of Sidney Webb c. 1895 (Passfield Papers)
Beatrice Webb, photographed by Bernard Shaw c. 1904
    (Passfield Papers)
Mrs and Mrs Joseph Chamberlain date unknown
    (Mansell Collection)
Cripps' family group date unknown (Cripps family)
Family group at Standish c. 1893 (Niall Hobhouse)
The Potter sisters on the same occasion (Kitty Muggeridge)
The Argoed 1982
'The Platform Spellbinder' by Bertha Newcombe 1893 (Mansell
    Collection)
H.G. Wells with his wife Jane 1895 (Wells Collection, University
    of Illinois)

vi

Lawrencina Heywo[...]
1821–18[...]

Catherine — Leonard
1847–1929   Courtney
             1832–1918

Georgina — Daniel
1850–1914   Meinertzhagen
            1842–1910

Bla[...]
1851–1[...]

William
b. 1878

Lawrencina — Robert Holt
1845–1906   1832–1908

Daniel
1875–1898

Blanche
(Julia)
1879–19[...]

Richard — Eliza Wells
1868–1941   1868–1951

Barbara — Bernard Drake
(Bardie)   n.d.
1876–1963

Standish
1881–19[...]

Catherine — William
1871–1952   Dampier-Whetham
            1867–1952

Richard — Annie Jackson
1878–1967   n.d.

Richard
1882–19[...]

Robert — Alice Graves
1872–1952   n.d.

Margaret — George Booth
1880–1959   n.d.

Rosie
1885–19[...]

Elizabeth — Edward Russell
(Betty)   d. 1917
1875–1947

Frederick — Florence
1881–1962   Maxwell Barnes
            n.d.

Henry
b. 1887

Philip — Phyllis Palmer
1876–1958   n.d.

Lawrencina — Hubert
1883–1976   Warre-Cornish
             n.d.

Edward — Christabel
1878–1955   de Vere Allen
            n.d.

Katherine — Robert Mayor
Beatrice   1869–1947
(Bobo)
1885–1977

Mary — John Russell
(Molly) d. 1958
1880–1955

Louis — Gwynedd
1887–1941   Llewellyn
            n.d.

Lawrence — Evelyn Jacks
1882–1961   d. 1978

Mary — Alexander
1889–1943   Wollaston
            1875–1930

Georgina — Ralph Neale
1890–1948   n.d

Mary — Arthur Playne
1849–1923   1845–1923

William — Manuella
1870–1935   Meinertzhagen
            n.d.

hard Potter
7–1892

Villiam Cripps
850–1923

'era Pring
.d.

'homas Faulder
.d.

Mary Ashley
.d.

Beatrice Hart
..d.

Hilda Pring
..d.

Beatrice – Sidney Webb
1858–1943   1859–1947

Margaret – Henry Hobhouse
1854–1921 | 1854–1937

Stephen – Rosa Waugh
1881–1964   1891–1970

Rachel – Felix Clay
1883–1981   1871–1941

Eleanor
1884–1956

Arthur – Konradin
1886–1965   Huth Jackson
1896–1964

Esther
1891–1893

John – Catherine
1893–1961   Brown
n.d.

Paul
1894–1918

Rosalind – (1) Arthur
1865–1949   Dyson Williams
1859–1896

Noel
1889–1918

– (2) George
Dobbs
1869–1946

Patrick – Muriel Ware
1900–1981   n.d

Leonard – Elaine
1901–1942   Cantaloube
n.d.

Kathleen – Malcolm
(Kitty)   Muggeridge
b.1903   b.1903

Richard – Phyllis Leon
1905–1980   n.d.

William – Ruth Dobbs
b.1906   n.d.

Theresa – Charles
1852–1893 | Alfred Cripps
1852–1941

Seddon
1882–1977

Ruth – Alfred Egerton
1884–1978   1886–1959

Frederick – Violet Wilson
1885–1977   n.d.

Leonard – Miriam Joyce
1887–1959   1892–1960

Stafford – Isobel
1889–1952   Swithenbank
1891–1979

Introduction

The Diary

THIS SECOND VOLUME of Beatrice Webb's diary covers the years between her marriage to Sidney Webb in 1892 and her entry into public life in 1906. It is curiously irregular. Sometimes she wrote every day, and at length. Sometimes she let days, weeks or even months go by without making an entry. Sometimes she seems to deal with trivia and to pay no attention to events she might well have discussed. She makes only a passing reference, for instance, to the prospect of the twentieth century, though that millennial date set everyone talking about the future. She says nothing about the row over the Boer War which convulsed and nearly wrecked the Fabian Society, or about the interesting dining club (called The Co-Efficients) which she and Sidney founded in 1903 to promote their idea of a new political party dedicated to the goal of national efficiency. It is clear from the tone of the entries that she was more likely to write when she was excited or depressed, less likely to find time for comment when she was very busy or felt contented. But in one of the rare remarks she makes about her habits as a diarist she gives a far more significant explanation of such irregularity of interest.

Three months had passed with 'neither the desire nor the opportunity' to write in her diary, she noted on 16 October 1904 after a long holiday in Scotland.

> When Sidney is with me I cannot talk to the 'Other Self' with whom I commune when I am alone – 'it' ceases to be present and only reappears when he is absent. Then the Old Self, who knew me and whom I have known for that long period before Sidney entered my life, who seems to be that which is permanent in me, sits again in the judgement seat and listens to the tale of the hours and days, acts, thoughts and feelings which the Earthly One has experienced.

It is precisely this double-visioned quality which reveals what Beatrice called her 'duplex personality', and the unending dialogue between its parts. She was well aware of her paradoxical nature, in which powerful physical feelings were at war with her moral convictions, in which an instinctive mysticism struggled with an educated desire for a positive science of society, and in which individual conscience was uneasily matched with a belief in the collective regulation of behaviour – temperamental conflicts that broke out into long bouts of depression and anorexic ill health. And in the painful struggle to resolve them, as she herself remarked, she made the diary her psychic partner just as she made Sidney her working partner and life's companion. All through the fourteen years covered by the present volume the conflicts of her nature recurred to plague her, so that her private troubles provide a nagging counterpoint to her public success and enjoyment of 'all the good things of life' that came with it. That was Beatrice's cross, and she carried it without a word of complaint to anyone except the Other Self who listened in the pages of this diary.

Beatrice kept her diary, which runs to nearly three million words in all, in barely legible handwriting in a series of fifty-seven exercise-books. Each of these books corresponds to one of the volume numbers which appear at approximately yearly intervals, and at the time of her marriage, when this book begins, Beatrice was in the middle of Volume 14. Both the manuscript and a typed version of the diary were published in microfiche in 1978, but this is the first comprehensive though condensed edition prepared for the general reader. There has been silent correction of punctuation, capitalization and other points of style, following the lead given by Beatrice when she prepared passages for publication, and the text has been cut to publishable length. Otherwise the diary appears as she wrote it, with the addition of introductions to each part and prefatory notes where the context or content of an entry requires them. There have in fact been fewer cuts in this volume than in the first: in the prime of her life Beatrice wrote more easily and to the point, for she had now mastered the skills of the diarist. Some long summaries of books she was reading have gone, some character sketches of minor politicians have been left out, and other entries have been shortened (each brief ellipsis is indicated by three dots and longer excisions by four) but nothing of great significance has been lost in the editing.

The explanatory notes about individuals, included at the first significant mention, can be found by reference to the index, which also indicates whether a person has been mentioned in the previous volume. Organizations are a different matter, since Beatrice was prone to use initials for bodies familiar to her but not to modern readers. Where clarification is most needed these initials have been expanded where they occur, but for convenience a list of the most common is given below.

The Charity Organization Society (C.O.S.) A philanthropic body which sought to systematize alms-giving in London and to prevent benevolence 'demoralizing' the beneficiaries.

The Fabian Society (F.S.) Founded in 1884 by a small group which sought to combine self-improvement with social reform, by 1893 it had become the most influential (and also the most respectable) of the small socialist societies. It was known for its moderate and anti-Marxist views, and for its distinctive 'Fabian' tactic of permeating other organizations with its ideas.

The Independent Labour Party (I.L.P.) Founded in 1893 to promote parliamentary candidates in the labour interest, and to campaign for trade union support of this policy, its philosophy was an amalgam of ethical socialism and class consciousness. It was one of the groups which (with the Fabians and a number of trade unions) formed the *Labour Representation Committee* (L.R.C.) in 1900, and until 1918 it was the usual means through which individuals joined a Labour Party (L.P.) dominated by affiliated trade unions.

The Liberal Imperialists ('Limps') The group of Liberal M.P.s, especially H. H. Asquith, Edward Grey and R. B. Haldane, who, together with Lord Rosebery, inclined to imperial expansion abroad and social improvement at home. Distinct from the Radical and predominantly Nonconformist faction of pacifist inclinations which formed the left of the Liberal Party.

The Liberal Unionists The large group of Liberal M.P.s who followed Joseph Chamberlain when he broke with his party in 1886–87 in protest against Gladstone's proposal to give Home Rule to Ireland. They formed a coalition with the Conservatives under Lord Salisbury, and then under Arthur Balfour. A few returned to the Liberal Party when Chamberlain began to campaign for protective tariffs, but the majority were absorbed into the Conservative Party.

The Local Government Board (L.G.B.) The civil service department responsible for the central administration of the Poor Law (P.L.), for the reorganization of local government that began with the creation of county and county borough councils in 1888, and for relations between Whitehall and these local authorities.

The London County Council (L.C.C.) First elected in 1889, the Council soon brought municipal reform to a capital city that had been singularly ill-governed. In its early years the Council was dominated by the Progressive Party (Progressives), which was a loose electoral alliance of Liberals, philanthropists and administrative reformers such as Sidney Webb. The Moderate Party (Moderates) was a local variant on Conservative politics, though the organization included some independently-minded persons who could be induced to support particular improvements. After 1903 it became responsible for elementary, secondary and further education in London, and was given a supporting role in higher education as well.

The London School of Economics and Political Science (the L.S.E. or 'the School') Founded by Sidney and Beatrice Webb in 1895, it grew rapidly from very modest beginnings to be a centre of social science research and teaching that attracted students from all over the world.

The Social Democratic Federation (S.D.F.) Established as the Democratic Federation in 1881 (with a change of name in 1883), it was the first Marxist party in Britain. It was doctrinaire and schismatic, but it played a significant part in the unemployed marches of the 1880s and in the great dock strike of 1889.

The Technical Education Board (T.E.B.) This body, chaired by Sidney Webb and including both elected members of the L.C.C. and representatives of the main educational interests, grew out of the *Technical Education Committee* (T.E.C.) which was originally set up to allocate the 'whisky money' or liquor tax which the government had decided should be used to promote technical education. The T.E.B. was the means whereby Sidney Webb won control of secondary, and then elementary education away from the independent *London School Board* (L.S.B.) and gave invaluable help to the London School of Economics and the reorganized University of London.

The Trades Union Congress (T.U.C.) A confederal body of affiliated trade unions which held an annual conference in September. Successive attempts to win a majority for the independent representation of labour culminated in the motion which led to the creation of the Labour Representation Committee in 1900. The Parliamentary Committee of the T.U.C. (P.C.) was the body which traditionally expressed the political interests of organized labour. A stronghold of Liberal supporters, with a scattering of Conservatives, it was consistently hostile to socialist attempts to win trade union support.

The editors reaffirm their thanks to those mentioned in Volume I and add Barbara Strachey, Peter Rose, Julia MacKenzie, Paul Thompson, Birmingham Public Library, the Library of the House of Lords, the Public Information Service of the House of Commons, the Baker Library of Dartmouth College, the *New Statesman*, the Salvation Army and Professor Robert Webb, of the University of Maryland, who has kindly read the text as it has been prepared and made most helpful suggestions.

Acknowledgements and thanks for the illustrations are due to the individuals and institutions listed in parentheses on pages vi–vii.

PART I

The Ideal Life

August 1892–March 1898

Introduction to Part I

'QUEEN VICTORIA was like a giant paperweight that for half a century sat upon men's minds,' H. G. Wells wrote as he looked back on the long reign that ended in January 1901, 'and when she was removed their ideas began to blow about all over the place haphazardly.' Wells was himself a notable example of that liberating shift of mood from the Victorian to the Edwardian age, in which a whole generation was swept along by the changes that had already begun to transform Britain by the end of the century.

There were great improvements in the comforts, convenience and pleasures of everyday life. The safety bicycle, motor car, the flying machine, the telephone, radio and domestic electricity were about to develop from interesting novelties into the elements of a second industrial revolution. A new world was emerging. There were new kinds of art, architecture, domestic furnishings and music, new newspapers and magazines to cater to new publics. In 1901, in London alone, there were nineteen morning and ten evening papers and dozens of weekly and monthly magazines profiting from the seller's market in popular journalism. New publishers continually sprang up and new authors came forward to meet the demand. The roll-call of novelists, romancers and short-story writers at the beginning of the new century was a remarkable muster of talent. Meredith, Hardy and James were in their prime; Wells had already achieved a reputation for his tales of space and time; Conrad had made his mark; Rider Haggard, Conan Doyle, Marie Corelli and Hall Caine were household names, Bennett and Kipling about to become so; and Pinero, Ibsen and Shaw were challenging the received morality and style of the stage.

These years are still remembered as a time of excitement, freedom and gaiety. Yet they were also years of stress and strain, in which

3

Britain came to depend upon her factories, mines and foreign trade, letting her agriculture flounder into such a long depression that land seemed the outstanding social problem almost to the end of Victoria's reign; years in which the industrial towns doubled in size, and doubled again, and manufacturers had to accept that trade unionism had come to stay; years of an increasingly assertive imperialism abroad and a matching jingoism at home, which culminated in the wretched and divisive war against the Boer settlers in South Africa. They were years, too, of significant political change. Between 1880 and 1905 the Liberal Party fell apart on the Irish issue, divided again on the Boer War, and stumbled back to office with a huge majority that concealed the fatal flaws in its organization and policy. The Irish themselves became a disciplined force in the House of Commons, able to make and unmake governments. Socialist agitation not only induced organized labour to create a parliamentary party of its own, but was part of a more general reaction against individualism and *laissez-faire* and towards collectivism – an alteration in public consciousness which accompanied the rise of an efficient civil service, the extension of municipal enterprise, a growing concern with the causes and consequences of poverty, and an overdue attempt to remedy the deficiencies that marked all levels of English education.

On 11 August 1892, five days before this volume of Beatrice Webb's diary begins, Gladstone took office for the fourth time at the age of eighty-two. With a slim parliamentary majority he had little chance of settling the Irish question – his one aim – let alone implementing the programme of reform which had been agreed at the Newcastle conference of the Liberal Party in October 1891. The Condition of England was the emerging question and the Webbs were to spend their lives trying to find answers to it in a partnership which began soon after they met in January 1890.

It was a most unlikely partnership. Beatrice Potter, born on 22 January 1858, was the eighth of the nine daughters of Richard Potter and Lawrencina Heyworth. Her father and mother both came from self-made Lancashire business families of Radical persuasion, and after losing his first fortune in a financial panic her father made himself wealthy again as a timber merchant and railway promoter. He was a man of enlightened views, with many intellectual friends, and all Beatrice's elder sisters 'married well', to businessmen and politicians of whom he approved. It was a busy, intellectually stimulating household, and yet Beatrice was lonely and withdrawn. Her mother was not overly affectionate and she was never intimate with her sisters. The eldest, Lallie, had married Robert Holt, a wealthy Liverpool merchant, when Beatrice was a child. Kate left home to do social work in the East End of London, where she worked until she married the Liberal M.P. Leonard Courtney. Beatrice went on a grand tour with her sister Mary and her husband Arthur Playne, a prosperous mill-owner in Gloucestershire, but they did not get on well and it was not until later in life that Beatrice appreciated Mary's qualities. Georgina married the banker Daniel Meinertzhagen when Beatrice was fifteen but she, like Mary, was unsympathetic to Beatrice's bookish ways. Blanche, who married the fashionable surgeon William Harrison Cripps, was eccentric and artistic. Beatrice travelled in Italy with Theresa, who returned to marry another member of the Cripps family, Charles Alfred, a successful lawyer. It was only with her sister Margaret – Maggie – that Beatrice enjoyed anything approaching an intimate relationship, when they went off for a holiday together in the Lake District, but they grew apart after Maggie's marriage to Henry Hobhouse, a West Country landowner and politician. Then Beatrice was left at home with Rosy, whom she called her 'problematical' younger sister, and after the death of her mother took on the task of hostess for her father and companion for Rosy.

On the face of it there seemed no reason why Beatrice should not marry as her sisters had done, within the social conventions of her class and time. She was, after all, handsome, talented and an heiress in a modest way, and she had a number of suitors. But there were two difficulties. Beatrice was anxious to have an occupation of her own which was intellectually satisfying and socially useful. She was repelled by the boring self-indulgence of Society life, and her struggle to separate herself from it, and to find instead a craft and a creed, is described in Volume I of the diary. Her ambitions were further complicated by her passionate attachment to Joseph Chamberlain, the Radical leader who was said to be the most eligible widower in public life. She suffered years of conflicted feelings which she recorded in a succession of tormented entries in her diary. This episode left her with a strong antipathy to marriage, which she scathingly described as 'an act of *felo de se*'. By 1890 she had made up her mind that she would remain part of the 'working sisterhood' of celibate professional women and pursue her vocation as a social investigator.

In January of that year, while she was trying to complete her first book (on the Co-operative Movement), she met Sidney Webb, a civil servant of great ability – Bernard Shaw called him the cleverest man in England – who had become the strategist of the Fabian Society with ambitions to make a career in politics. Although Beatrice was impressed by his knowledge, his capacity for work and his passionate commitment to self-improvement and public good, she found him physically unattractive, with his large head, small body and nasal Cockney accent. Sidney had been attracted to her from the first, but although Beatrice agreed that he was the ideal collaborator for the work she had in mind, she continued to rebuff his proposals for over a year. The disparities of status and style between her family and the aspiring Cockney socialist made the affair seem 'an absurdity'. Eventually Sidney's patience, good nature and reforming zeal, added to her own loneliness and increasing pleasure in his companionship, led her to give way, and they were married in July 1892.

Beatrice clearly experienced her life with Sidney as something very different from the physical passion for Joseph Chamberlain that she described so movingly in the first of these volumes. Chamberlain had, she said, 'absorbed the whole of my sexual feeling,' and it was many years before she properly recovered from this attachment. 'I shall never quite free myself of the shadow of past events,' she wrote in April 1896, and she admitted that she would 'always be subject to relapses'. Although Beatrice and Sidney apparently enjoyed a limited physical relationship – her dislike of enforced celibacy, her frank avowal of sexual passion, her desire for motherhood, all show the strength of her physical feelings – the emphasis of their life was on self-denial and work for the public good. Beatrice paid a price for this self-denial, and in times of strain she would fall back upon reveries about the might-have-beens of life. She called them 'castles in the air'. The distress which she experienced around 1901 suggests such an acute sense of emotional deprivation that she could only overcome it by a punitive self-discipline which verged on anorexia.

For all this heartache the marriage, surprisingly, proved to be immediately and enduringly rewarding. Writing to her friend Graham Wallas from Glasgow in September 1892, when she and Sidney were still combining a honeymoon with research on their history of trade unionism, she said: 'We are very happy – if that be the end of human life'. And nine years later, noting that their joint work had greatly prospered, she came back to the point she made repeatedly through life. 'We are still on our honeymoon and every year makes our relationship more tender and complete.'

The Webb partnership, as Beatrice observed when she was drafting her autobiography almost half a century later, began with certain assets.

> An unearned income of £1,000 a year, and a liking for the simple life, ensured unfettered freedom in the choice of a career. We were in the prime of life and in good health; we felt assured of loving companionship without end, a confidence which proved singularly well founded; we shared the same faith and practised the same craft; we enjoyed laughing at ourselves and at other people.

But such domestic felicities were merely incidental to the peculiarly complementary division of talents between husband and wife. Beatrice was well aware of it. Sidney had a 'unique aptitude' for the paperwork of research, she noted, and 'an amazing capacity for memorizing facts and developing, in logical sequence and lucid phrase, arguments and conclusions'. While he cared little for interviews and had no art in conversation, she was an experienced hostess and a crafty talker with men who were not accustomed to taking women seriously. 'Skill in social intercourse was my special gift,' she wrote; and Bernard Shaw was not far from the point when he wrote jestingly after her marriage to suggest that 'Madame Potter-Webb' should start her own political *salon*. She soon did so, to great effect, as many entries in her diary reveal.

During their courtship, when Sidney was trying to persuade Beatrice that by working together they could do far more for the public good than they could hope to achieve separately, he had repeatedly pointed out the differences in temperament and capacity that could be turned to good account, and the virtues of their division of labour were evident as soon as they were married. Beatrice's ingenuity and imagination, their first research assistant said, were matched by Sidney's 'executive power and driving force'. A. G. Gardiner, an outstanding contemporary journalist, said there was constant controversy among those who knew them 'as to which of the two is before or after the other', though he thought this an idle argument, 'for you can never tell where one ends and the other begins – how much you are yielding to the eloquence of Mrs Webb, and how much to the suggestion of Mr Webb.' One wove the spells and the other forged the bolts.

There seems to have been a remarkable equality in their relationship, at least in intellectual matters, for Beatrice spoke of 'the extreme happiness' of writing together when 'every statement and argument has been thought out by two minds'; and in many ways Sidney deferred to her speculations and impulses, like a well-trained civil servant who will take instructions about policy if he is able to draft the documents. Yet there were clearly moments of strain, especially in the first years of marriage. In April 1893 Beatrice wrote to the secretary of the Fabian Society, now at the peak of its public influence as a group of gradualist reformers, declining an invitation to speak at a May Day meeting. 'Not only does my vow of courage fail me,' she added, 'but the hidden masculinity of Sidney's views of women is discernible in his decided objection to my figuring among the speakers. See how skin-deep are these professions of advanced opinion, with regard to women, among your leaders of the forward party!' And though Sidney was too deeply and admiringly in love with Beatrice ever to express any criticism of her whims and wishes there is some evidence that she quashed his parliamentary ambitions when they married – preferring to keep him at hand for their joint research and considering him more suited to the work of the London County Council than to the House of Commons; and there is a lingering note of condescension in her remarks about him that shows how hard it was for her to shake off the patronizing habits of her well-to-do family. 'From early childhood I had lived in the atmosphere of political parties and the conflict of classes,' Beatrice wrote when she was planning the second and incomplete volume of autobiography she called *Our Partnership*, and she recalled that both her grandfathers had been prominent Radical M.P.s, that her father had become a committed Conservative, and that among her eight brothers-in-law she numbered both Liberal and Tory politicians. That background was a great help when, to advance the policies which she and Sidney devised, she took to entertaining the Prime Minister, members of several governments, bishops and great financiers, as well as trade union leaders and socialist propagandists. But it had also left its mark in the form of a social vanity for which she scolded herself in her more sober moods, knowing that the modest Sidney rather disliked wooing grand people on their own terms and by their own methods. He was, Beatrice said, 'too absorbed in disentangling questions and promoting causes to have intimate friendships', and women bored him. 'The plain truth is that his emotional life – all his capacity for personal intimacy and for over-appreciation of another's gifts – has been centred in his wife and partner, and his wife just because she is his partner.'

By the time Beatrice wrote this retrospective comment she was well aware of the impoverishment of feeling which made other people find the Webbs dedicated, calculating and arid personalities. In 1903, when they took a cycle tour of Normandy with Bertrand and Alys Russell, Russell complained that they always seemed to be measuring cathedrals rather than enjoying them; and for all the impish malice in the gibe there was some truth to it, as Beatrice herself conceded. There were, she wrote in a frank passage of memory,

> disabling gaps in our knowledge of Victorian England . . . of sport, games and racing . . . foreign affairs, generally speaking, were a closed book to us . . . owing to our concentration on research, municipal administration and Fabian propaganda, we had neither the time nor the energy, nor yet the means, to listen to music and the drama, to brood over classical literature, ancient and modern, to visit picture galleries, or to view with an informed intelligence the wonders of architecture. Such dim inklings as we had of these great human achievements reached us second-hand through our friendship with Bernard Shaw. Our only vision of the beautiful arose during our holiday wanderings, at home and overseas, sometimes walking, sometimes cycling, by river and field path, over plains and mountains in mist, cloud and sunshine.

Beatrice judged herself a little too harshly. Unlike Sidney, who was a materialist agnostic, she never wholly lost her sense of mystery about life or her capacity for finding comfort in its difficulties from the habit of prayer. But she had found work 'the great anodyne' when she was struggling to subdue her infatuation for Chamberlain, and she had schooled herself to turn its disciplines from satisfying a private need to serving the public good.

The work was all to the same point – in general to develop a science of society which, like the natural sciences, would give mankind 'an ever-increasing control of the forces amid which it lived', and in particular to do so by transforming the production and distribution of wealth

9

from the 'anarchic industrial profit-making' of an individualist society to the 'regulated social service' of collectivism. The Webbs believed that they had come to their maturity at a time of transition between these two systems, and they were bent on doing all they could to hurry on that change. Beatrice put their hopes for reconstructing society very clearly in a letter she wrote to Charlotte Payne-Townshend (who was shortly to marry Bernard Shaw) in June 1896. 'For the last twenty years,' she explained, in a phrase which revealed her continuing debt to her mentor Herbert Spencer,

> I have had a fixed idea that if we are to progress quickly and safely *we must apply the scientific method to social questions*. The present politicians of all parties are Quacks – sometimes they hit on the right idea and sometimes they do not. . . . Of course, it is a stupendous task to convert politics into a science – it is possible we may only succeed in laying the foundations. But then, on the whole, it is better to try to do a big thing than to fritter one's brains or one's money away in accomplishing small things.

Holding such opinions, and believing that there was nothing much to choose between one politician or one party and another, Beatrice was prone to see them all as potential instruments of 'the right idea'; by a combination of persuasion and pressure they might be induced to take up proposals designed by the Webbs to sail before the strengthening wind of collectivism. Like the Positivists, to whom they owed a great deal, they could well be described as political cuckoos who laid their eggs in any convenient nest.

For the Webbs were rationalists who thought that any reasonable man or woman could be moralized into supporting reforms, and educated by social science into choosing those which were most likely to come to the desired result. It was this conviction, which found its clearest expression in the Fabian doctrine of permeation, that led the Webbs into a succession of tactical (and sometimes tactless) alliances. Nominally socialist, though they preferred to call themselves collectivists, they in fact had very little to do with the socialist sects after 1893, or with the Independent Labour Party founded in that year, or even with the important Radical and Nonconformist factions in the Liberal Party. They chose instead to attach themselves to the small group of Liberal Imperialists popularly known as the 'Limps', to woo the indecisive Lord Rosebery as the potential leader of a government dedicated to national efficiency, to consort with Arthur

Balfour, the most intellectual of Tory prime ministers, to help design two Conservative Education Acts and to spend their leisure lobbying bishops and wire-pulling to make sure that they were implemented. 'Politics are very topsy-turvy just now,' Beatrice wrote to her sister Georgina in December 1903. 'One never knows who is to be one's bedfellow.'

The Webbs certainly achieved a good deal by working through well-placed and influential individuals, some politicians and some the talented public servants whom they saw as the trained élite that a successful 'housekeeping state' would require. But Beatrice admitted that their methods brought results rather than popularity, and in the longer run the price they paid for the various manipulations Beatrice describes in this volume was an increasing isolation from the real centres of power in a parliamentary democracy. By 1906, they were at odds with almost all the politicians swept into office by the landslide Liberal victory, and they played virtually no part in the programme of reform which followed. 'It is the sleuth-like pursuit of their purposes that makes them so powerful and so often distrusted,' A. G. Gardiner wrote at the time.

> There is nothing that men dislike so much as being 'managed'. And Mr and Mrs Webb are always 'managing' you. They sit behind the scenes, touching buttons, pulling wires, making the figures on the stage dance to their rhythms. To their modest table come the great and the powerful to learn their lessons, and to be coached up in their facts. Some fear to enter that parlour of incantations, and watch the Webbs with unsleeping hostility. A mere suspicion that they are prompting behind the curtain is enough to make them damn the most perfect play.

To be fair to the Webbs, the process of permeation which reached its peak between 1895 and 1905 was not merely a matter of temperament and conviction: it also fitted the peculiar political circumstances of a decade in which the two-party system was broken and all sorts of new alignments seemed possible in the ensuing confusion. By 1894 the Webbs had concluded that nothing useful could be expected from the Liberal Party. Soon to give way to a Tory government that lasted for the next ten years, too decentralized to be captured by any faction, and too fragmented to offer any hope of effective leadership or an agreed programme, it sprawled across the parliamentary landscape like a ruin that could neither be properly

11

used nor demolished. Though they had hopes of Rosebery and the little clique of Liberal Imperialists, especially their close friend and fellow manipulator Richard Burdon Haldane, the 'Limps' had no prospect of office unless the Liberals somehow managed to win an election or became the nucleus of a new party. As late as 1903 the Webbs still hoped some new deal might follow the shuffling of the old party cards, but they had made the best of the Tory governments headed by Lord Salisbury and his nephew Arthur Balfour; and permeation had been the only means to influence national policy or legislation.

Local government was another matter, for the creation of county borough and county councils had encouraged experiments in what came to be called 'gas-and-water socialism'. Chamberlain had shown in the seventies what could be done in Birmingham, which had become a model of municipal enterprise, and by the end of the century London and other big cities had followed with the provision of public transport, gas and electricity supplies, with museums, libraries, parks and baths, with health regulations and a network of maintained schools. Sidney Webb, sitting on the London County Council from 1892 to 1910, and drafting many of the tracts in which the Fabians argued for these practical reforms, became such a noted spokesman for civic improvement that (Beatrice privately dissenting) he was often compared to Chamberlain. 'If Mr Webb could only have spoken as well as he could write pamphlets, amass information, and act as a political guide,' the *New Age* declared on 12 March 1896, 'the likeness between himself and Mr Chamberlain would have been much more evident than it is.' The tactics of permeation, indeed, paid some handsome dividends in local politics, where party lines were not so sharply drawn as at Westminster, and the growth of the towns in the late Victorian age had provided both challenges and opportunities. Much of Beatrice's diary for the years around the turn of the century describes the wire-pulling arrangements whereby the Webbs contrived the necessary alliances to put their favoured measures into effect.

It also shows how much they enjoyed themselves in the process. Beatrice said that they were leading 'the ideal life', combining politics and research in a partnership whose 'extreme happiness' was in marked contrast to the dismal subjects they studied, the pessimism with which they regarded the future if there was too little reform and it came too late, and the bitter feelings provoked by the Boer War, which divided their Fabian friends as sharply as it divided the country. When Beatrice and Sidney met in 1890 they were both what Bernard Shaw called 'intellectual proletarians'; hard-working, self-denying and earnest, they sought to improve themselves and to change the world for the better.

After a long working honeymoon in Ireland and Scotland, interviewing trade union officials and scouring their archives for the fresh material that made *The History of Trade Unionism* a landmark in social research, the Webbs returned to their Hampstead flat in Netherhall Gardens. Beatrice told Sidney that she found it 'delightful to get back to our "dovecot", and to be again with my darling old boy – who twists his strong-minded wife around his little finger, by soft sounds and kisses'. The pleasures of domesticity came sweet to a woman who had married late, and who unexpectedly found both affection and intellectual satisfaction in the match.

But the Webbs were soon to move from Hampstead to 41 Grosvenor Road on the Westminster riverside, finding it more convenient for the London County Council offices in Spring Gardens, off Trafalgar Square, and for the centres of national politics in Parliament and Whitehall. And in this austere ten-roomed house, rented for £110 a year, they settled quickly into the style of life that lasted for the next thirty years – modest yet comfortable, with a couple of maids and a research assistant to cater for their various needs, with lunches and dinners for useful guests, and little energy wasted on gadding about, with Sidney making his public work a full-time occupation, and what would have been leisure for others devoted to their articles, pamphlets and books.

The house, as Beatrice described it, was as much like a small research institute as a home.

> Our workroom on the ground floor, which served also for meals, a long narrow room running east to west, in early morning and late afternoon welcoming sunshine, was lined with books and blue-books. . . . On the half-landing the secretary's office: oil-clothed floor, large deal writing-table, from floor to ceiling shelved with pamphlet boxes. . . . Not less utilitarian in its furnishing was the conventionally shaped sitting-room on the first floor; long seats fitted into alcoves and, under the western window, an escritoire, a table heaped with books, three easy

13

chairs but no sofa: all designed to accommodate the largest number of guests standing or sitting.

It was, Beatrice admitted, a 'harsh interior', redeemed by the beauty of its outlook over the Thames to Lambeth Palace.

In the first years of marriage Beatrice had a notion of 'making our little home the intellectual headquarters of the labour movement'. She had come to know many of the leading personalities when she was writing her book on the Co-operatives, and the research for the trade union history had widened that acquaintance. Believing that their task was 'the precise observation of actual facts' the Webbs had written a fine narrative account of the rise of the trade unions, only to discover at the end that they had 'no systematic theory or vision of how trade unionism operated, or what it effected'. They therefore planned another book, which they called *Industrial Democracy*, in the hope of extracting 'a clear, comprehensive and verifiable theory' from the mass of material they had so painstakingly collected. By then, however, they had also discovered that they had little sympathy and less in common with the socialist enthusiasts, such as Tom Mann and Keir Hardie, who were agitating for the New Unionism of the unskilled and the independent representation of all working-men in the House of Commons, or with the defensive narrow-mindedness of the old guard on the Parliamentary Committee that ruled the Trades Union Congress. All the same, they still kept in touch with them. Sidney was to draft Tom Mann's Minority Report for the Royal Commission on Labour in 1894, and to do the same for Henry Broadhurst for the Royal Commission on the Aged Poor a year later. Yet before the Webbs could finish *Industrial Democracy*, which Beatrice repeatedly complained had become a wearing 'grind' at analysis, Sidney's commitment to the L.C.C. had turned their practical interest towards local government, especially its educational aspects, and their research towards the massive history of manors, parishes, roads, prisons and the Poor Law which they only completed in 1929.

The L.C.C. was still a novelty when Sidney Webb was elected as a Progressive member for Deptford in March 1892. Even after the creation of the L.C.C. in 1888 the City of London had remained independent, and it was some years before the metropolitan boroughs were brought in to replace the archaic vestry system which served the larger parishes and groups of the smaller ones. But by 1892 the

Progressive Party, which was a coalition of Liberal politicians, philanthropists and municipal reformers, had begun to make the Council an effective force in the nation's capital, and from that year Sidney was to play a notable part in its work. Though he sat on half a dozen committees, and was considered to be a brilliant tactician both within and outside the Council chamber, his chief opportunity came with the chairmanship of the Technical Education Committee and the Technical Education Board (T.E.B.), which he devised to succeed it. He was perhaps the only man in London who could have made such a seemingly dull and unrewarding post the means to real reforms and an enduring reputation.

Unlike the usual council committees the T.E.B. was a mixed body, on which twenty Council nominees sat with fifteen representatives of such other educational interests as the London School Board, the City livery companies which had secondary schools of their own, the teachers and trade unionists; and it enjoyed unusual freedom in its policies and finances. If there had been no such meeting-place of interests, and decisions on educational issues had been made by party votes in the Council, the battle to modernize London education would have been even more confused and bitter, and Sidney would never have been able to engineer the changes which in just over a decade made the L.C.C. the largest and most comprehensive education authority in the world.

Sidney had almost stumbled into this chance. He had hitherto shown relatively little interest in education. Neither his best-selling Fabian tract, *Facts for Socialists*, nor the *London Programme*, which he wrote with the 1892 elections in mind, made any reference to the subject. But he had been associated with a group of scientists and politicians who had formed the National Association for the Promotion of Technical Education, which was drawing attention to the deficiencies of English education and the efficiency of German technical schools and institutes. Soon after the new county councils and county boroughs had been created they were given the proceeds of a tax on beer and spirits, generally known as 'whisky money', to spend on technical education. This was fortunately defined in very broad terms. After Sidney had enquired what subjects could be encouraged by government grants he was jubilant. 'We can now lawfully teach anything under the sun except ancient Greek and Theology,' he is supposed to have said as he left the Department of Education; and he certainly worked in the spirit of that remark.

15

There was an obvious conflict of interest between the new authorities and the school boards, set up all over the country after the 1870 Act to fill the gaps left by the church and voluntary schools. For in the last years of the century the school boards were seeking to move on from elementary to secondary level work; and because they were often dominated by Nonconformists and representatives of the teachers they saw such an extension as a way to take advanced education away from denominational control and raise their own status at the same time. The conflict was particularly sharp in the capital, where the powerful London School Board (L.S.B.), which served half a million primary pupils and employed 10,000 teachers, was unwilling to surrender secondary education to the T.E.B., let alone acquiesce in the 1903 Education Act which abolished it and transferred its schools to the L.C.C. Led by the eminent Baptist preacher Dr John Clifford, the Nonconformists in the Progressive and Liberal parties campaigned so fiercely against government grants to church schools that they nearly wrecked both the Act and the L.C.C. The saving of both, as Beatrice makes clear, was largely the work of the Webbs, in a struggle that was politically complex, much embittered, and always fraught with intrigue.

Sidney Webb's control of the T.E.B. was the decisive factor in this victory, but it had also been vital in the early days of the London School of Economics and Political Science. On 26 July 1894 a Derby solicitor named Henry Hunt Hutchinson shot himself. An active though crotchety member of the Fabian Society, he left about half of his estate of £20,000 to be spent on 'the propaganda and other purposes' of the Society. When the Webbs learned of this legacy they at once decided that they would not let the money be squandered on running forlorn-hope candidates for Parliament, or on publicizing 'the shibboleths of collectivism'. They preferred to found a School of Economics 'which would train experts in the task of reforming society' and encourage *hard thinking*', though this decision was a running cause of difficulty with those Fabians who thought Sidney had diverted money from their political purposes to his own educational ends. A year later, in 1895, when the L.S.E. had actually been founded, and the first students were about to be admitted, Bernard Shaw was still complaining that Sidney was guilty of 'atrocious malversation', and telling the Webbs that if the money was spent on the L.S.E. there should be no pretence at unbiased research: 'the collectivist flag must be waved and the *Marseillaise* played.'

Sidney took no notice. He knew that the School must be genuinely independent and academically respectable if it was to survive, and that it would soon come to depend more on grants from the T.E.B., and from business sources, than on Hutchinson's quirky inheritance. That money had simply given the Webbs the courage to launch their venture. In any case, only half of it was ever received by the L.S.E., and the rest went to support Fabian lectures and publications. The T.E.B. not only paid for approved classes: Sidney also persuaded the L.C.C. itself to provide a site for the School when the Aldwych area was being cleared and rebuilt, and to give regular subsidies through its general subvention to the University of London.

The decision to divert half the Hutchinson fund to teaching and research, rather than to 'endow socialism', was a turning point for the Webbs. It followed logically from the idea of permeation, and from their belief that education rather than agitation was the 'best way of building up a new party on the basis of collectivism'; and it came at a time when the Liberal government elected two years before was clearly doomed. Rosebery had succeeded Gladstone in 1894 but was incapable of revitalizing a party in such disarray. He achieved little and annoyed everyone. The Radicals were disillusioned by his failure to press reforms. The pacifists and free-traders distrusted his imperialist sympathies. And the Nonconformists were antagonized by his patrician style of life and his addiction to horse-racing. 'The rot has set in,' R. B. Haldane told Beatrice. 'There is no hope now but to be beaten and then to reconstruct a new party.'

That hope was to tease the Webbs for the next ten years. But in the short run they were afraid that the impending collapse of the Liberals would give the new Independent Labour Party the chance to establish itself, and that Fabians who sympathized with its combination of ethical socialism and labour electioneering might use the Hutchinson bequest to support Keir Hardie, Tom Mann and James Ramsay MacDonald, the able young Fabian who had just decided to abandon the Liberals and join the party he was eventually to lead. The Webbs made a half-hearted attempt to collaborate with the I.L.P., when they met to discuss a joint campaign for the L.C.C. elections in March 1895, and Beatrice's account of the embarrassing evening shows just how far the two sides were from a meeting of minds or temperaments.

In the course of 1895, indeed, the political tide set so strongly towards the Tories that progressives of all kinds were demoralized and prepared for a long spell in the wilderness. Only the Webbs

17

found some comfort in defeat. 'From our point of view the field had to be cleared,' Beatrice declared after the general election in which she and Sidney had 'held aloof'; and looking at the incoming Tories she felt assured that 'the affairs of the nation are in the hands of an exceptionally able set of men who have been elected as trustees of the *status quo*.' In three years of marriage the Webbs had moved from principle to permeation, and they did not shirk the political consequences.

The Webbs were married in London on 23 July and spent their honeymoon in research for *The History of Trade Unionism*, published in 1894. Eaton Park was part of the Duke of Westminster's estate, whose notable Eaton Hall had been remodelled ten years earlier. Henri Frédéric Amiel (1821–81) was a Swiss writer whose *Fragments d'un Journal Intime* (1883) had been translated by Mrs Humphry Ward in 1885. Afraid of practical life, Amiel devoted himself to the life of thought, believing man to be saved by love and duty. The Irish lawyer was Sir Horace Curzon Plunkett (1854–1932), son of the Irish peer Lord Dunsany, M.P. for Dublin 1892–1900 and the promoter of Irish Co-operatives. The Liberal politician Leonard Courtney (1832–1918) had married Beatrice's sister, Kate, in 1883. Professor Leonard Alston (1875–1953) wrote on religious, constitutional and political subjects.

VOLUME 2

∽ 1892 ∾

16 August. Glasgow [6 Blythwood Square]
The ceremony over, a 'bewildering' time at pretty little Chester – Sunday spent on walls in Cathedral and Eaton Park – reading at intervals Amiel's *Journal* by way of relieving the preoccupation of the first hours of married life. Then Dublin – lodgings, depressing climate, unsuccessful investigation into that ramshackle race and its affairs as regards trade organizations; now remaining only memories of huge, dirty, so-called 'rude' hovels in back streets lined with tenement houses with Irish urchins sprawling in the sun in the hot August weather. Halls surmounted with coats of arms and date of the old Protestant guild, from which their modern Catholic combination of journeymen claim descent (the whole Irish nation being descended directly from its Kings). Charters, purloined or picked up, hoarded away and shown to us – English 'tourists' – as proof positive that they had evolved from old Protestant corporations established by Protestants to prevent Papists from gaining an honest livelihood. Pathetic people – with their high pretences and low purposes! Unfit to be yoked with other races.

Then two delightful days of real honeymoon in the Wicklow Hills, escorted there by a brilliant Irish lawyer and good-natured friend. Hence to Belfast. Here we did some serious work. Courtney's introduction served us well with employers, Harland and Wolff, large shipbuilders. . . All Belfast anxious to prove to casual tourists, not the descent from Irish kings, but its capacity for turning 20s into 30s in marvellous short time. Veracity reigned here – no discrepancy

19

between employer and worker account of wages for the simple reason that employers were in primitive stage of money-getting and had not yet developed social compunction. Told us complacently the low price they paid to labour, were proud they could get female flesh and blood and bone for 5s a week (or less) and male ditto for 11s a week. That fact equally satisfactory as the low rent or cheap potatoes or any other of Professor Alston's glories! Energy, conduct, piety, a hideous hypocrisy in some cases, quite unselfconscious as yet.

General fact about Ulster: well-mannered and well-paid skilled labour, low-paid unskilled. This its only similarity with Dublin. . . .

In little quiet Shaftesbury Hotel received levies of trade unionists every night – Sidney and I interviewing in different corners. Then there was the daily excitement of the papers and the long chats over politics, as at present and to come. Altogether happy there working on our holiday task. Now for Scotland.

Sir Charles Dilke (1843–1911) had been one of the Radical leaders in Parliament before he was politically ruined by a sensational divorce case in 1885, when a Mrs Crawford named him as co-respondent. In a series of legal actions, in which Dilke claimed he was the victim of a conspiracy, he failed to clear his name. He returned to the House of Commons in 1892. Although he later took part in world affairs, he never regained his old position. In 1885 he had married Emilia Frances Pattison (1840–1904), a distinguished journalist and chairman of the Women's Trade Union League, who was the widow of Mark Pattison, Rector of Lincoln College, Oxford.

17 September. [6 Blythwood Square, Glasgow]
I should sum up my general opinion of Glasgow as the quintessence of individualism on its good and its evil side. The employers I have interviewed are hard-headed, original-minded men, a large proportion self-made; the working-men are cautious, suspicious, difficult to lead and very careful of the pence. The officials of the union are rather a poor lot. Seemingly the best men do not care for the job, preferring to advance themselves and push out a higher class. . . Ugly certainly are the banks of the Clyde, and very hideous are the results of enormous earnings by certain sections of men, brutalized by want in bad times and long hours of work during the spells of prosperity. The Clyde is the home of piece-work and contract work, of poverty, drunkenness, cupidity and competition. . . .

The Congress was entertaining. Sir Charles and Lady Dilke were the genii of the scene, entertaining the Congress wholesale to lunch, tea and dinner. . . The hopeful side of the labour movement seems to me to lie in the growing collectivism of the Miners' Federation and of the cotton operatives. Here, at last, we are on solid ground and among men who, if they take a thing up, do it with the intention and capacity to carry it through. But all said and done, the labour movement has its seamy, I would almost say its disgusting side, quarrels between sections, intrigues among individuals, and it is this side which is uppermost at a Trades Union Congress.

Auberon Herbert (1838–1906) was an old and intellectually eccentric friend of Beatrice who had been a Liberal M.P. before he retired to farm in the New Forest. He had a holiday home on Loch Awe. Richard Burdon Haldane (1856–1928), a lawyer who was and remained one of Sidney's closest friends, became a Liberal M.P. in 1885 and Secretary of State for War in 1906. His family home was at Cloan in Perthshire. 'The Souls' were a group of Society men and women who were interested in literature and art. They met at their country houses for weekend parties, and emphasized their distinction from conventional upper-class circles. Herbert Henry Asquith (1852–1928) was also a lawyer. He became a Liberal M.P. in 1886, Home Secretary in 1892, Chancellor of the Exchequer in 1906 and Prime Minister 1908–16. He and Haldane were two of a small group of Liberals who came together in 1886 and later formed the nucleus of the Liberal Imperialist or 'Limp' faction. The other members were Sir Edward Grey (1862–1933), who became Foreign Secretary in 1906; Sir Arthur Acland (1847–1926), who sat in the 1892 Cabinet as vice-president of the Committee of the Council on Education; Ronald Munro-Ferguson (1860–1934), who became Governor-General of Australia; and Sydney Buxton (1853–1934), Under-Secretary for the Colonies 1892–95 and Postmaster-General in 1906. Alfred Lyttelton (1857–1913) was a lawyer who became a Liberal Unionist M.P. in 1895. His wife Edith was a member of the Balfour family.

19 September. [6 Blythwood Square, Glasgow]
Exactly four weeks at Glasgow – the last ten days a rush of work, Sidney working the whole day on documents except the hours he has spent trudging out to the far suburbs after trade union secretaries. Out of the four weeks we have had two holidays – a Sunday on Loch Awe with Auberon Herbert and a weekend visit to Haldane.

Auberon Herbert was as mad and as delightful as ever. Sidney thought the whole scene – the rickety little cottage overlooking the lake, the scrambly meals, handsome girls, and the 'on the spot' talk – a very mad mixture. A very pleasant afternoon sitting in his tent and talking 'shop'.

Then back to Glasgow, long drive and tourist steamer. Sunday with Haldane was more remunerative. He is now an influential man, willing to stand in the background, to counsel the minorities and act as go-between. Talked incessantly about the possibilities of re-organizing the Home Office as the Ministry of Labour, perfecting the Factory Department, ending in his pressing us to write a memo for Asquith (a request since repeated from Asquith). Three-quarters wrote it the other day but stress of work has made us keep it over till Edinburgh. Haldane not hopeful of the future – 'constituencies not converted to collectivism – at least not in Scotland'.

Sunday afternoon a fair bevy of 'Souls' came over to tea – Haldane priding himself on hovering between a fashionable 'paradise' represented by the 'Souls' and the collectivist state represented by the Fabians. 'Souls' good to look on and very gushing and anxious to strike up an acquaintanceship with an unconventional couple. A charming pair – the Alfred Lytteltons – graceful, modest, intelligent and with the exquisite deference and ease which constitutes good breeding. But to me the 'Souls' would not bring the 'peace that passeth all understanding' but a vain restlessness of tickled vanity. One would become quickly satiated.

I leave Glasgow with no regrets. The working-men leaders here are an uninteresting lot, without enthusiasm or much intelligence. The Scotch nature does not lend itself to combination – the strong men seek to rise and provide for themselves and not to serve others. And apparently the Co-operators have absorbed the finer intelligence and warmer hearts among the Scotch working-men of the official cast.

Frank W. Galton (1867–1952) was an engraver who abandoned his trade in 1892 to become research assistant to the Webbs on a salary of £100 p.a. He was secretary of the Fabian Society 1920–39. William Harrison Cripps (1850–1923) was a fashionable surgeon who was married to Beatrice's sister Blanche. Beatrice had worked with Charles Booth (1840–1914) on his pioneering survey of London life and labour: he was married to her cousin Mary Macaulay (1847–1939). Graham Wallas (1858–1932) was a prominent Fabian who later became a notable professor of politics at the London School of Economics. At this time he was a member of the London School Board, employed as an Extension lecturer, and he was working on a biography of the early Radical, Francis Place. Alice Stopford Green (1847–1929), widow of the historian J. R. Green, was one of the few friends of Beatrice who had encouraged her relationship with Sidney.

1 December. 10 Netherhall Gardens [Hampstead]
Gloomy November weather finds us settled three hundred feet above the sea in a cosy little flat in South Hampstead. Our life an even tenor

of happiness. In the last two months engaged on indexing and arranging our material or wading through Stonemasons and Compositors [union records] and writing a brief skeleton of the first volume of our book. Each morning we begin work about 9.30 (breakfast and reading papers and letters take an hour), Galton joins us about 10 and we three drive through material until 1 or 1.30. Then four days out of six Sidney hurries off to London and gives the remainder of his day to the London County Council. Meanwhile Galton goes on steadfastly. I spend a couple of hours either walking on the Heath or travelling into London on shopping errands. At 4 o'clock Galton and I have a cup of tea and a chat and again set to work until 6 or 6.30. At 7.30 Sidney returns full of the doings of the L.C.C. of carrying back news of an interview with a Cabinet Minister on some proposed reform. A simple meat supper, cigarettes and then an evening of peaceful happiness, either him reading to me or working at L.C.C. matters, or we entertain working-men friends and so forth. But we mostly spend our evenings alone. Dinner-parties we have resolutely eschewed, I finding that I cannot keep a clear brain for work with talk exciting the evening. But as usual in November my brain has been half torpid: I have not done my full measure of work. Perhaps also the calm of married happiness deadens, in the first instance, one's intellectual energies. Why work when one is happy; and when he is working it is a silent excuse for physical torpor.

On the other hand Sidney is working well. I see with satisfaction that every day gives him a more complete grasp of L.C.C. work. He is one of that little circle of a dozen committee [chairmen] who practically run the L.C.C. for the simple reason that they do the work; and he is the trusted confidant and helpmate of the great officials of the Council – the chairman, vice-chairman and deputy chairman. And as chairman of the Technical Education Committee he has his own independent work creating a new organization.

Beyond this he is steadily acquiring influence with the official Liberals, regarded every day more as a man who must be listened to, and, if possible, complied with. I doubt whether he will ever be a 'leader', that is, an acknowledged chief. What he is rapidly becoming is the *chief instigator* of policies, the source of Liberal doctrine. He is a kind of indescribable influence which cannot be measured – sometimes it is denied, at other times grossly overestimated! So far as I can tell our life will be, or rather my life will be, that of a recluse, with Sidney as an open window into the world. The distance from London

23

and preoccupation in work, three-quarters strange opinions – all combine to isolate us from our own class. With my own family I am on friendly terms (except Willie Cripps who has practically cut us!) though, as there is nothing in common, we do not seek to meet. The friendship with the Booths is practically broken, through Mary's covered hostility. For Charlie Booth I have a warm strong regard but, for one reason or another, Mary has deemed it better to cut off all real intimacy, and I, having struggled for years against it, refusing to believe that she meant it, have finally succumbed and accepted the situation.

It is only fair to admit that matters have not been mended by Sidney's instinctive dislike and distrust of Mary Booth, a dislike too thorough to counterbalance even his very strong admiration for Charlie. So ends the friendship. We may become again friendly acquaintances; we can never again be friends. I often brood over it with keen and painful regret. One frank word might have saved it. But Mary's polish was impenetrable. Other friendships remain steadier. Graham Wallas is a constant visitor for Sunday midday dinner and walks on Hampstead Heath. Alice Green and others appear now and again, like meteors in our life. But our comradeship with one another is so complete that in the perfection of the new relationship we do not seem to need friends. Possibly that is a reason for our partial isolation. I look forward with wonderful happiness to the coming year. Creative work is always delightful to me, and the stress and strain of writing a big book will be incalculably lightened by his help and loving kindness. Who knows how long I may have a large share of his life, how soon he may not belong body and soul to the nation.

Arthur James Balfour (1848–1930) was the nephew of Lord Salisbury, whose influence led him to give up philosophy in favour of politics. He entered Parliament in 1874, and in 1892 he was the Conservative leader in the House of Commons. He was a keen member of 'The Souls'. The Royal Commission on Labour, chaired by the Duke of Devonshire, was appointed in 1891 to consider the relations between employer and employed. A Minority Report, signed by the Labour members of the Commission (and drafted by Sidney) created a stir when it was presented on 15 March 1894. Gerald Balfour (1853–1945), brother to A. J. Balfour, had been elected as a Tory M.P. in 1885. Sir Frederick Pollock (1845–1937) was a distinguished judge, and was the current editor of the *Law Quarterly Review*. Alfred Marshall (1842–1924) was professor of economics at the University of Cambridge. Beatrice had met him early in her career as a social investigator. Balfour, Pollock, Marshall and Courtney were all members of the

Royal Commission. Mrs Alice Dugdale (1843–1902) was the sister of Sir George Otto Trevelyan (1838–1928), who had been Chief Secretary for Ireland 1882–84.

24 December. [Hampstead]

How gloomy other Christmas Eves have been! – always the low-water mark of a year's despair, at the best an arid time of family gossip, overeating, preparation for heartless winter gaieties. Now I have won a vantage ground of wonderful happiness, and even when physical energy ebbs low, I still feel fundamentally happy. And Sidney also has found a resting-place; no need now to struggle for personal happiness or success; all energy can be given to work. We have actually begun the book but after writing the greater part of the first chapter we are reading at the B.M. to get a fresh idea of the eighteenth-century industry. It is still to be proved – the experiment of writing a book together; sometimes our ideas clash and we fall between the rival ideas, but on the whole we get on. My only complaint is that I can work such short hours compared to him that I feel a mere dilettante, but when spring comes I shall feel better.

Have seen something of politicians – Haldane and Asquith to dinner, Sydney Buxton and Acland coming later on, but seen something of by Sidney. All the young men in the government hard at work introducing administrative reforms, yet uncertain whether the old gang will not dictate a policy of evasion to all legislative proposals. No leader to the reform movement, a mere upheaval in favour of doing something, not the tight sitting on the part of the provincial Liberal capitalists. And when they do give way, they give way on the wrong points and as likely as not skedaddle in face of some preposterous demand while refusing even to consider some quite sound scheme. And the result is that the political world is simply chaotic at present, at least on the reform side. Men like Balfour know well enough what they are playing for, a success in having a compact party in the state. If chaos continues, they will lead a still larger mass of voters. The people above all want guidance.

Royal Commission on Labour a gigantic fraud. Made up of a little knot of dialecticians, plus a carefully picked parcel of variegated labour men, and the rest landlords and capitalists, pure and simple. The dialecticians – G. Balfour, Fred Pollock, Marshall and Courtney – have had it their way. They have puzzled the workmen with economic conundrums, balked inconvenient evidence by cross-questions, and delivered themselves of elaborate treatises on

25

economics, history and philosophy to bewildered reporters, equally in the form of questions. Spent a somewhat painful day there – the first day of Sidney's examination. He was aggravated with the bad faith of the Commission, and treated them to a little of their own game. His answers read well and were richly deserved, but his manner was objectionable and pained me. Also the Booths, K. Courtney, Mrs Dugdale and others of that set were sitting listening to him, and, as they agreed with the dialecticians, they showed their disapproval markedly. However, the next day the dear boy made a pretty apology and bore the cross-examination with perfect good humour. It ended in an amicable discussion between him and Gerald Balfour for 1½ hours on abstract economics – pleasant to listen to, but fit for an after-dinner talk, and not the sort of question and answer to be delivered at public expense. Utter waste of time to all concerned except that it woke us up to the harm the Commission might do if their report is to be taken in good faith. . . .

∿ 1893 ∾

10 March. [Hampstead]
Three chapters finished, beginning to read for the fourth. How hard it is to tell whether one is doing one's level best or becoming complacent with a low level of exertion! A certain apathy overtakes me, a disinclination to exertion which seems to me a new feature in my life. I am happy *not working*, from which state I suffer spasmodic reverse. Nevertheless I work pretty regularly – certainly I don't 'play' when I don't work. I vegetate!

There is nothing to tell nowadays! No interesting extracts of gloom and light, no piquant relationships, all warm flat midday sunlight – little excitement and no discomfiture. I tell Sidney laughingly that I miss the exciting relationships with marriageable or marrying men, that I feel 'hemmed in' by matrimony. Truly I am too happy to seek excitement, too satisfied to look for friendship. Fortunately I have a bit of solid work in hand. I doubt more than ever whether I could have been long satisfied with a life in which intellectual effort were not the main or rather the most prominent part.

Sidney for his part is enthusiastically happy. He seems to have settled down to the L.C.C. administrative work. Parliament seems farther off than ever. We are content for the present with the prospect of intellectual study and the more humble role of a county councillor. But we are watching eagerly the course of politics. Personally, I think more is to be done by administrative experiment on the one hand, and educating the constituencies on the other, than by entering into the political game carried on in Parliament. We have visions of a good lecturing tour some two or three years hence – to teach the provincials 'progressive' principles and collectivist economics. Meanwhile we will work ourselves and observe others.

Theresa Cripps, the sixth of the Potter sisters, died suddenly after a throat infection at her home at Parmoor on 22 May at the age of forty-one. In 1881 she had married Alfred Cripps (1852–1941), an immensely successful barrister who was a Conservative M.P. from 1895 to 1914, when he was created Lord Parmoor. An opponent of war, he eventually held office in the Labour governments of 1924 and 1929. They had four sons and one daughter. The eldest, Seddon, was eleven when his mother died, and the youngest, Stafford – nicknamed 'Daddy' – was four. Stafford later became as notable an advocate as his father, a most active socialist and leading member of the 1945 Labour government. Theresa was attracted to spiritualism and published a book with messages she believed had come to her by means of automatic writing.

22 May. [Parmoor, Henley-on-Thames]
We were in the midst of the Bristol Co-operative Congress when the telegram arrived that our dear sister, Theresa, had died after a few hours' illness. The shock was inexpressibly painful, subordinated only to the thought of poor Alfred's agony and the children's irretrievable loss.

Our dear sweet sister – the artist, now the 'spiritualist' (used in its true sense) of the family – gifted with an ardent imagination, extraordinary vivid sympathy with all forms of life. Perhaps the best loved of the sisters, for she was open-minded, more ready to believe, without reserve, in the good intentions and high ideals of others than the rest of the hard-headed, matter-of-fact family. Her home was the most gracious and graceful – there was an atmosphere of caress of love and light. And the marriage was absolutely happy – except that Alfred's companionship, able and warm-hearted man that he be, left unsatisfied the 'spiritual' needs of Theresa's nature. . . . Weariness, possibly physical weariness, was one of the notes of Theresa's married life. It was an *occasional* note, not a continuous one. The burden of her life was love given to, and taken from, husband and children,

27

friendship generously yielded to all unfortunates and all whom the world misunderstood.

It was this quality of friendship in Theresa that was beginning to bring me nearer to her these last months. All my sisters have acted in a sensible and kindly way towards my marriage. They had not, however, attempted to understand it. But the last times I have seen Theresa she has really tried, not simply to be kind, but to understand and realize what we are aiming at. And she has done this with such touching grace that I have wondered whether she and I could become more than sisterly acquaintances. . . . No sister of the nine stands perhaps so friendless as I do. No sister so independent of the opinion and approval of her family. Again it is proved that you cannot gain the advantages of all courses. I chose to live apart, so that while living in the very centre of the family, I might yet live my own life. My sisters no longer know me; they know only the shell with which I covered myself. To me this death is, in some ways, horribly tragic. Tomorrow, after the funeral, I shall come back to my husband and my work. Looking back through the years, I shall not be able to recall *one single word of intimacy* from me to her, the memory of this gifted and precious nature, anxious and willing to be loved, will seem like a far-away dream, a picture and not a reality.

And now that I am talking about relationships, let me tell quite frankly that this tragic death, except as it affects others, seems of slight personal consequence to me beside the loss of an old friendship. The utter breakdown of the friendship between me and Charles and Mary Booth has been an ever-open wound. That friendship was the stay of my life during the real struggle of it. It seemed as if this friendship was so tempered that no force could snap it asunder. And yet when I strained it, I should have thought slightly, it broke, or rather, I found that *it was already broken*. Even today I have not recovered from my amazement and wonder at this fact. I can never cease to regret it.

See the Potter Sisters family tree on pp. viii–ix. Lawrencina (Lallie) was Beatrice's oldest sister. She was married to Robert Durning Holt (1832–1908), a prosperous Liberal merchant and shipper in Liverpool. Georgina was married to Daniel Meinertzhagen (1842–1910), a wealthy banker. Rosalind, the youngest sister, had married Arthur Dyson Williams (1859–96), a lawyer whose career was blighted by his failing health. Mary married Arthur Playne (1845–1923), a mill-owner from a well-known Gloucestershire family, who owned an estate of more than five hundred acres at Longfords, near Stroud. Box House, where Richard Potter spent his last years, was on the estate. Margaret was married to Henry

Hobhouse (1854–1937), a politician from an old Liberal family which had lived at Hadspen House, near Castle Cary in Somerset, since the late eighteenth century. Georgina lived at Mottisfont Abbey in Hampshire. She wrote a poem to mark Theresa's death. The last verse ran:

> Let the life of each be a light to the others,
> As the life of our dear one torn from her home.
> Let each one give a hand to his brothers,
> Nor leave them in trouble to bear it alone;
> Till the last may go in the blaze of a sun,
> That setteth at evening with sorrow for none.
> So close the ranks, my sisters dear,
> When lives are passing, God is near.

21 June. [Hampstead?]

A month after Theresa's death, we all met (except Lallie) at Georgie's house – seven sisters – all of us haunted by the idea of the dismal blank. We talked and laughed with the brothers-in-law as of yore, but all of us felt the empty place. The *irretrievable loss*, the absolute extinction of the dear one. Georgie looked the saddest of the sisters – to her, life has had little charm, though on the surface so prosperous; her marriage a big mistake. Poor little Rosalind with her miserable husband, an egotistical invalid, looked depressed but sweet and loving. Mary, Margaret, Kate, all happy women. Blanche too madly noble and nobly mad to be disturbed by death. All and each of us going on our own way, saddened and softened by the common loss, perhaps even drawn together by the fear that others might drop down too. But family relationships are like to a strange dream – real and yet unreal – always disappointing and disquieting whether in shortcomings or in excess of affection without intimacy. Possibly this death will bring us closer to each other, will close up the ranks, as Georgie says so sweetly. But I doubt it. I doubt whether there can ever be companionship without a common faith. Theresa stood apart from the family – lived her own hidden spiritual life. . . And so we go on in life – eight sisters – bound together yet not combining.

Meanwhile my husband and I grow nearer to each other each hour of the day. A beautiful pact, marriage. Personal love and tenderness, community of faith, fellowship in work, a divine relationship. The one and only drawback – a doubt whether happiness does not stupefy life with its inevitable self-complacency. As days and months fly by and little is done, one wonders whether one is unduly apathetic or simply lazy. . . .

Beatrice now refers to her infatuation for Joseph Chamberlain (1836–1914) which had disturbed so many years of her young womanhood and was still capable of teasing her emotions. He was still on the fringe of her private life. She enclosed in her diary a letter dated 17 August 1893 from Kate, who wrote: 'Mr Chamberlain dined here last night – expressed a wish to meet you and your husband. I will ask him when you come back if you like. He stays to the bitter end and no one knows how long that will be. He is villainously full of fight, rather too much so for my more moderate-tempered mind.' At this time Gladstone was trying to get his last Home Rule Bill through Parliament – yet another attempt to meet the Irish desire for independence by granting a substantial measure of self-government. Chamberlain was its most vehement opponent, for this was the issue on which he had broken with the Liberals seven years earlier. It had passed a second reading in April but after a stormy progress in Parliament was finally rejected by an overwhelming vote in the House of Lords in September.

Lord Cowper (1834–1905), who had been an active Liberal politician, was chairman of a Commission considering the future of the University of London. Its report in 1894 stressed the need for specialist institutes of higher education, such as the École Libre des Sciences Politiques, which was to provide one of the models for the foundation of the London School of Economics. Lord Rosebery (1847–1929) was Gladstone's Foreign Secretary in 1886 and 1892–94, when he became Prime Minister for thirteen months. He served as the first chairman of the L.C.C. in 1889–90. He was a keen sportsman – his horses won the Derby in 1894, 1895 and 1905. Benjamin Francis (Frank) Costelloe (1855–99) was a barrister, a Progressive member of the L.C.C., a Fabian and a personal friend of Sidney Webb. His wife, Mary Pearsall Smith (1864–1945), after years of marital unhappiness, deserted him for the American art critic Bernard Berenson (1865–1959) whom she married after Costelloe's death. Her daughter, Ray Costelloe, married Oliver Strachey, the brother of the critic Lytton Strachey, and wrote a number of works including *The Cause* (1924), which remains a pioneer work on the women's movement. The younger daughter, Karin Costelloe, married Adrian Stephen, the brother of Vanessa Bell and Virginia Woolf. Sir John Williams Benn (1850–1922) was a prominent Progressive member of the L.C.C. from 1889 until his death, chairman in 1904, and a Liberal M.P. 1904–10. John Burns (1858–1943), an engineering worker who was active in the Social Democratic Federation and leader of the London dock strike in 1889, was a member of the L.C.C. and Independent Labour M.P. for Battersea 1892–1918. He held Cabinet rank as president of the Local Government Board in the Liberal government of 1906–14. Beatrice had great hopes of him, as the first working-man to achieve Cabinet rank, but her diary reveals her increasing disappointment as he proved to be the victim of his egotism and the prisoner of his permanent officials.

Richard Potter had acquired The Argoed in 1865 as a holiday home, not far from Tintern in the Wye Valley. It was kept by the family for a few years after his death, and Beatrice greatly enjoyed staying there.

30 July. The Argoed

Alone here awaiting Rosy Williams and Sidney. Here we intend to spend our holiday – six weeks of quiet and country.

A lovely breezy summer day, the absolute stillness of this high land tempered by the summer wind rustling in the sycamores. The calm lines of the hills over the Wye picked out by sunlight and cloud so that they seem within walking distance and almost invite you to visit them. Why is it sad to visit these old scenes of childhood, youth and struggling womanhood? Why that wondering melancholy as visions of the old life come trooping back – the happy child in its holiday haunt (the visits here were the one spot of brightness in my childhood), the ardent brainworker elated with first feelings of intellectual creation, the woman overtaken with passionate feeling wrestling with the demon of passion for her very soul, the resigned worker on the threshold of achievement – all those states of my old self rise up before me, and all, whether bright or sullen, force me to regret that they are no more. How strange these subdued moanings over dead states. . . .

This day too has its own associations. It is strange, I wonder that I, a happy wife, should brood over the thought of this day six years ago. It was Sunday 29 July 1887 that Chamberlain spent here – it was on this day that five long-drawn-out years of passionate feeling reached their climax. Since that day we have not met. But he is always there: year in and year out I watch him struggling in the political prize fight – for a cause? or for personal supremacy? Only a few days since I saw him speaking in the House, leading up to those disgraceful scenes of Thursday. Each year brings out in stronger relief his extraordinary personality – every political event gives occasion for a display of his marvellous agility, whilst it uncovers his limitations and defects. As a political prize-fighter he easily throws all his rivals; as a man he becomes steadily more vulgar; as a political thinker more shallow and ill-informed. And yet he loses neither his interest nor his charm, at least not to one of his humbler fellows. How will history sum up this man? A great statesman or a maligned orator? More likely than either, a *pre-eminent parliamentarian, ill-equipped with knowledge, and damaged by an irretrievable vulgarity of method and ideals.*

I still believe in the old habit of a periodical searching of heart, a testing of the worth of past months' work. How have these months passed, what has been done and left undone? With Sidney's life I am more than satisfied. He has worked hard and well this spring. . .

Every morning he writes hard from three to four hours, either the book or, if I am indisposed, letters, memos or inspired 'pars' for besieging editors. Five afternoons of the week he is engrossed in committee work. . . Kind friends tell me he is an extraordinarily clever chairman of a troublesome board of experts and obstructioners. Besides this – his special work – he has had to draw up the plans to be submitted to the Unification Commission. . . . This rush of work for him has made it essential to live nearer Spring Gardens – hence our new home at Grosvenor Road. . . . The work he is doing – creating machinery for collective action – is the work I desired to see him do and the fact that his work is unostentatious, that it cannot be seen or estimated except by his fellow workers, makes it all the finer both in itself and in the effect on our lives. And in spite of this finely administrative effort, he still finds energy to think, to reconstruct past history, to disentangle ideas. . .

With my own effort I am less satisfied. Whether it be London life, whether it be the preoccupation of marriage, I do not seem to get either the same quality or quantity of work out of myself. I am so often below the level of real work. I sometimes wonder whether I work at all or whether I simply watch Sidney work. And then I wonder whether the *construction* of this book, for which I am mainly responsible, is not really inferior to what I have before done. I am no longer 'possessed' by the plan of a chapter or even of a paragraph like I used to be – it all seems mechanical labour to me now. Further I know that my thoughts are constantly trivial, that I no longer live in a world of ideas, that I tend to live in a world of persons. This holiday high up in the solitude of these hills, I intend to see if I cannot raise myself on to a higher plane, physical and mental. . . .

Many times I wonder whether the great want in my life – perhaps in our lives – is not 'spirituality', whether I ought not to cultivate my own soul to keep it perforce holy, tender and impersonal. There is such 'dross' in one's thoughts and feelings, unworthy vanities, useless anxiety, conscious self-congratulations, silly castles in the air.

I need prayer, or the substitute for prayer, whatever that may be – a deliberate tuning of one's thoughts and feelings by the deeper and higher tones of life. To the man, with his fully occupied intellectual faculties (with Sidney these faculties are devoted to the good of others) with his adoration of the Woman – the spiritual life seems unneedful. His nature seems more fully satisfied and absorbed in his work and his human affections. With the woman, her delicacy and her incapacity leaves her consciousness more the prey of irresponsible undirected ideas. Spiritual life alone fills her being with the inspiration needful to keep her thoughts on a high plane. If only one could kneel down and pray each morning for noble effort, every evening for pure peaceful rest. But one seems, for lack of this faith, to sink into ruts of small fears and mean wishes, out of which one only raises oneself by some intellectual concentration or by some loving concern for the Beloved. One ought to think and to love, but one ought also to *aspire*.

This lack of spirituality is the one large need of my life without which I think my effort will be degraded. This spirit of prayer, this yearning for personal holiness, I must again attain. There are other wants, some of a lower character, others apparently inconsistent with our lives. I long sometimes for a wider culture, knowledge of other and higher forms of intellectual effort. All the world of art and literature is closed to me. But I do not see how with such slight and intermittent intellectual energy I could well spare any portion of it from my own work. Here I fear I narrowed Sidney's life. He has sufficient energy to use his few spare minutes for other forms of intellectual activity, but I dare not join him so he gives it up to be with me. Then again the same applies to companionship with men and women of more polished minds or workers in different fields of investigation. Again I have no energy to spare, and here again I fear I limit Sidney. The basic desire for social distinction I gladly note as futile – 'Society', however brilliant and distinguished, seems to eat out the hearts of men and women if it does not sterilize their minds. But it is not pardonable, the longing to be more loved and needed by my relations and my old friends. This *want*, this longing to see old times strengthened, not this pain to see them rudely snapped asunder, is the one and only sacrifice on the altar of my love for Sidney and my faith in the cause he has at heart.

The London County Council looms large in our life because it takes up so much of Sidney's energies. Every day he comes home he tells me about his various committees and gives me glimpses of the internal working of the machine. Let me see whether I can sum up some of the impressions he leaves on my mind.

First, the L.C.C. consists of the Progressive portion of it. The Moderates as a party are simply out of it. Individual Moderates become chairmen of committees but only because in those particular departments they are more progressive then the Progressives. Indeed the conversion of the abler Moderates to different portions of the

Progressive programme is one of the notable features of the County Council and a token of the triumph of the idea of public administration as against private enterprise. That is, of course, the whole significance of the L.C.C. – the growing faith in and enthusiasm for public service. It is not that the L.C.C. does so much more than its predecessor, the Metropolitan Water Board, but that it does all its work with efficiency and zeal with a view to increasing and not diminishing its functions.

There is no one man in the L.C.C. who dominates the organization. I imagine in the last Council Lord Rosebery took a pre-eminent part. But though Lord Rosebery continues a member he seldom attends, and his sweeping down on them with regard to a proposed site the other day was much resented. The Council is really run by various groups of county councillors circling round the three officials – the chairman, vice-chairman and deputy chairman – of the Council. Of these the most prominent are the group who direct the parliamentary and political policy of the County Council – Costelloe, Sidney, Benn. Then come the chairmen of the non-political committees such as Housing, Parks, Asylums etc., all of whom are in touch with the chairman [of the Council]. John Burns occupies a quite unique position; owing not to his committee work, but to his powerful personality and labour following outside the Council. His influence, however, is diminishing since he has become an M.P.

It is perhaps a sign that the County Council is still young that the whole direction of the administration is still in the hands of the councillors and not relegated to the paid servants. There are twenty or thirty men who make a profession of the Council – in the sense of spending their whole energies on its work. This of course means that the L.C.C. is a middle-class body, composed of men of sufficient means to work for nothing. And even those working-men who are on it contribute little to its government; they speak in the weekly meetings of the Council but they take little or no part in committees.

The weekly Council meetings are perhaps the least important part of the Council's proceedings. The great aim of the able chairman of a committee is to pass his reports through the Tuesday meeting without raising contentious questions. It is only the badly managed committees that get their actions talked about and their policy discussed. The Council is a machine for evolving committees, the committee a machine for evolving one man – the chairman. Both alike are machines for dodging the democracy (in a crude sense) by introducing government by a select minority instead of the rule of the majority.

George Bernard Shaw (1856–1950), who had been a friend and political collaborator of Sidney Webb since they first met in 1879, shared the effective leadership of the Fabian Society with him. Shaw had so far earned a precarious living as a music and theatre critic. His attempts to make a career as a novelist had failed in a welter of rejection slips. His first play, *Widowers' Houses*, had been given a few performances at the Royalty Theatre in December 1892, and while he was staying with the Webbs at The Argoed he was writing *Mrs Warren's Profession*. He was very close to the Webbs in the first years of their marriage, and remained a lifelong friend.

17 September. The Argoed
Seven weeks here – heavenly weather, delightful holiday just flavoured by a few hours' work a day. The first fortnight, alone with Rosy, we spent finishing the sixth chapter of our book. Then Graham Wallas came on the scene, read our first chapter, severely criticized the form of it. He made me feel rather desperate about its shortcomings, so I took it and wrestled with it, writing out a complete new syllabus of it with a quite different arrangement of the subject. This Sidney 'wrote to' with my help.

Bernard Shaw came ten days after, and has stayed with us the remainder of our time, working almost every morning at our book. The form of the first chapter satisfied him, and he altered only words and sentences, the second chapter he took more in hand, and the third he is to a large extent remodelling. Sidney certainly has devoted friends, but then it is a common understanding with all these men that they use each other up where necessary; that is the basis of the influence of the Fabian Society in contemporary political thought. The little group of leaders are practical communists in all the fruits of their labour.

While Bernard Shaw was working on the book, Sidney and I set about different tasks, I attempting to write a lecture on the Sphere of Trade Unions, he at work on Tom Mann's Minority Report. My attempt proved to be a hopeless fiasco. I struggled in vain among my great mass of information . . . the stuff overwhelming me. After five days' work I read to Sidney what I had written. He looked puzzled, and suggested that he should write it out. Then we had a little bit of a tiff. For when my miserable meanderings appeared in his clear hand it was all obviously out of place for a lecture, and that mortified me. I was in a devil of a temper. Next morning he sat down patiently to recast it, and we worked four days together and made a rough draft. Now I am working it up into lecture form. But my failure made me feel a bit of a parasite. So much for our holiday tasks.

All the afternoons we have spent out of doors, taking long excursions, forced out of our natural indolence by Graham Wallas's and Bernard Shaw's energy. Have I ever described either of these men? Here is a brief outline.

Graham Wallas, six foot with a slouching figure, good features and genial open smile, utterly unselfconscious and lacking in vanity or personal ambition. Without convictions he would have lounged through life – with convictions he *grinds*; his natural sluggishness of nature turned by his social fervour into a slow grinding at anything that turns up to do. In spite of his moral fervour, he seems incapable of directing his own life and tends to drift into doing anything that other people desire. This tendency is accentuated by his benevolence, kindliness and selflessness, which almost amounts to a weakness. Thus, while his intimate friends love him and impose on him, superficial strangers of poor character often actually despise him. To some men and women he appears simply as a kindly dull failure, an impression which is fostered by a slovenliness of dress and general worn-out look. He preaches too, a habit carried over from his life as an usher and teacher of boys. To his disciples he appears a brilliant man, first-rate lecturer, a very genius for teaching, a suggestive thinker and a conscientious writer. It remains to be seen what else he will become beyond a skilful propagandist and an admirable and most popular University Extension lecturer. He has two books on hand, but owing to his constant running off on other people's business they stand a poor chance of being finished for a year or so. If enthusiasm, purity of motive, hard, if somewhat mechanical, work will make a man a success, then Graham Wallas has a great career before him. He has plenty of intellectual ability too – what he lacks is deliberate concentration and rapid decision, what to do and how to do it. A lovable man.

Bernard Shaw I know less well than Graham Wallas, though he is quite as old a friend of Sidney's. Marvellously smart witty fellow with a crank for not making money, except he can make it exactly as he pleases. Persons with no sense of humour regard him as a combined Don Juan and a professional blasphemer of the existing order. An artist to the tips of his fingers and an admirable *craftsman*. I have never known a man use his pen in such a workmanlike fashion or acquire such a thoroughly technical knowledge of any subject upon which he gives an opinion. But his technique in specialism never overpowers him – he always translates it into epigram, sparkling generalization or witty personalities. As to his character, I do not understand it. He has been for twelve years a devoted propagandist, hammering away at the ordinary routine of Fabian Executive work with as much persistence as Wallas or Sidney. He is an excellent friend – at least to men – but beyond this I know nothing. I am inclined to think that he has a 'slight' personality – agile, graceful and even virile, but lacking in *weight*. Adored by many women, he is a born philanderer – a 'Soul', so to speak – disliking to be hampered either by passions or by conventions and therefore always tying himself up into knots which have to be cut before he is free for another adventure. Vain is he? A month ago I should have said that vanity was the bane of his nature. Now I am not so sure that the vanity itself is not part of the *mise en scène* – whether, in fact, it is not part of the character he imagines himself to be playing in the world's comedy. A vegetarian, fastidious but unconventional in his clothes, six foot in height with a lithe, broad-chested figure and laughing blue eyes. Above all a brilliant talker, and, therefore, a delightful companion. To my mind he is not yet a *personality*; he is merely a pleasant, though somewhat incongruous, group of qualities. Some people would call him a cynic – he is really an *Idealist* of the purest water (see his *Quintessence of Ibsenism* and his plays).

These two men with Sidney make up the Fabian Junta. Sidney is the organizer and gives most of the practical initiative, Graham Wallas imparts the morality and scrupulousness, Bernard Shaw gives the sparkle and flavour. Graham Wallas appeals to those of the upper and educated class who have good intentions. No one can doubt his candour, disinterestedness, enthusiasm, entire moral refinement. Sidney insinuates ideas, arguments, programmes, organizes the organism. Bernard Shaw heads off the men of straw, men with light heads, the would-be revolutionists, who are attracted by his wit, his daring onslaughts and amusing parodies. He has also a clientele among the cynical journalists and men of the world. What the Junta needs to make it a great power are one or two personalities of *weight*, men of wide experience and sagacity, able to play a long hand and to *master* the movement. If John Burns would get over his incurable suspicion, if he could conquer his instinctive fear of comradeship, I know no man who could so thoroughly complete the Fabian trio and

37

make it thoroughly effective. If Burns would come in and give himself away to the other three as they do to each other, the Fabians could dominate the reform movement. Burns, in some respects, is the strongest man of the four, though utterly ill-equipped, in his isolation, for leadership. But that contingency, I fear, is past praying for. Collectivism will spread but it will spread from no one centre. Those who sit down and think will, however, mould the form, though they will not set the pace or appear openly as the directors.

The wallpapers, textile designs and furniture of the socialist writer and artist William Morris (1834–96) became very fashionable in the last years of the century.

[Early October?] *41 Grosvenor Road*
Three weeks' incessant work at furnishing, though still in a muddle here about furniture buying. Have wearied and excited my poor little brain to get the furniture attractive and the home as beautiful as we can make it with my limited cash and still more limited taste. Have deliberately spent money on it because I do not wish it to be thought that simplicity of daily life means ugliness and lack of order and charm. The ideal to be aimed at is strict economy in weekly expenditure, no self-indulgence and show, but beautiful sur-roundings – i.e. the best tack and the best workmanship in those things you have. So I have gone to Morris's for papers and furniture and spent days over my curtains and in looking up charming old bits of furniture in second-hand furniture shops. All of which causes the enemy (i.e. my sisters) to blaspheme, saying 'They do not see much socialism in that.' It is, in fact, a hopelessly difficult problem of how much one should spend on one's own house. Efficiency only demands plenty of nourishing food, well-ordered drains, and a certain freedom of petty cares – it is somewhat softening to contend that you *need* beautiful things to work with. It *may* be desirable to have them, but it requires a lot of proving! Of course it is easy to take one's stand to the outsider and boldly declare that personal expenditure, when you have proved property, is a question of conscience, that there is no rule by which it can be judged. It is still easier to deceive yourself, to cheat your conscience, as doubtless we *do* cheat it from time to time. Altogether, though I have deliberately (I say it again) spent this extra £100 in buying prettier and better things than were absolutely necessary, yet I am not altogether at rest about it. At any rate, as Sidney

says, we must work harder in order to deserve it. Next week I hope to begin.

John Burns collected early trade union documents and books on labour history. Tom Mann (1856–1941) was another skilled engineer and early member of the S.D.F., who had worked with Burns during the dock strike, and was active in the campaign to organize the unskilled in the new type of trade union. He was a man of vigorous and unstable personality, who played a useful part in the first phase of the Independent Labour Party, became a syndicalist, and was one of the founders of the Communist Party. James Keir Hardie (1856–1915) was a Scottish miners' organizer who became the chief advocate of the direct representation of working-men in Parliament, the founder of the I.L.P. in 1893, and its leader for many years. He first entered Parliament in 1892.

12 October. [41 Grosvenor Road]
Spent the whole morning with John Burns looking over the trade union documents he has.

Our relation to John Burns has never been a cordial one – it promises to be more so in future. I began with a prejudice against him – at the Newcastle Congress he seemed to me an intriguer who suspected everyone else of intrigue. His unfriendly attitude towards Tom Mann also displeased me. Possibly he heard of my dislike, for he treated me with very marked suspicion. Of Sidney he has, until lately, been jealous and was anxious that he should not come on the L.C.C. But, for one reason or another, this unfriendliness has much lessened. On my part, I have long since seen reason to alter my opinion of him as a public man. His capacity, straightforwardness, and power of reason has given him a permanent position, which poor Mann has forfeited by his light-headed change of fronts on all questions human and divine. Sidney has always had a high opinion of him. Burns, on his side, sees now that Sidney does not seek to play the rival Labour leader, that his influence (Burns's) will not be diminished by Sidney's presence on the L.C.C. If Sidney went into Parliament it might be that old jealousy would revive.

For jealousy and suspicion of rather a mean kind is John Burns's burning sin. A man of splendid physique, fine strong intelligence, human sympathy, practical capacity, he is unfitted for a really great position by his utter inability to be a constant and loyal comrade. He stands absolutely alone. He is intensely jealous of other Labour men, acutely suspicious of all middle-class sympathizers, while his hatred of Keir Hardie reaches about the dimensions of mania. He is a born ruler of barbarians, impressing his followers with his will and

39

determination, not guiding them by reason. And yet he is essentially an intellectual man – one of his finest qualities is the constant testing of questions by intellectual methods rather than by sentimental considerations. All said and done, it is pitiful to see this splendid man a prey to egotism of the most sordid kind, an egotism that seeks not so much to fill the world with its own doings as to debase all other reputations in order that his own work may stand out in relief.

The Fabian manifesto called 'To Your Tents, O Israel!' was an article written by Webb and Shaw, published in the *Fortnightly Review* on 1 November 1893. It was a sustained diatribe against the Liberals, prompted in part by their failure to implement the reforms promised by their Newcastle Programme, in part by Shaw's belief that unless he and Webb satisfied 'the legitimate aspirations of the ardent spirits' among the Fabians they would be discredited as mere hangers-on to the failing Liberal Party, and in part because independent labour representation was gaining sufficient support for the Fabians to show some interest in it. The manifesto proved to be only a brief flirtation with the I.L.P., in whose creation in January Shaw and the Fabians had played a marginal role. Both Shaw and Webb were temporarily drawn back to the notion of permeating the Liberals when Rosebery succeeded Gladstone. But this sharp and clever article did not please the enthusiasts of the I.L.P., who rightly suspected that Webb and Shaw were at best lukewarm about their cause, and it greatly annoyed some of their Liberal friends. 'The manifesto is a heavy blow to us,' Haldane wrote to Beatrice. 'It hurts *us* more than the old gang.' Henry William Massingham (1860–1924), the campaigning Liberal journalist who edited the *Daily Chronicle*, the *Star* and then the *Nation*, was even more exasperated, calling the article 'a mere freak of mischievous tomfoolery' and resigning from the Fabian Society in protest. Mrs Thompson had been the nurse who cared for Beatrice's father in his last illness. Dyson Williams died two years later. He and Rosalind had one son, Noel Dyson (1889–1918), who was killed in the First World War. Hubert Llewellyn Smith (1864–1945) had worked with Beatrice on the Booth survey, co-authored the history of the 1889 dock strike, and drafted the report on London education which had led to the creation of the Technical Education Board. In 1907 he became Permanent Secretary to the Board of Trade and the organizer of the system of labour exchanges. Ella Pycroft had worked with Beatrice in managing Katherine Buildings, a 'model' tenement near Tower Bridge in London's East End, and she was now making a career of domestic science teaching.

Christmas Day. The Argoed

Here with Sidney, Graham and Shaw. Writing the last chapter of the book and just sending part of it to the press.

The autumn has gone quickly. I have worked well in the mornings at the book and recast large portions of it. Our house exactly suits us and as yet there is no chance of our being disturbed by too many acquaintances. We entertain much more than we are entertained, having a constant succession of 'professional' friends to dinner, sometimes to lunch, all for some purpose – either to help us or to be helped into the right line themselves.

The excitement of the autumn has been the issue of the Fabian manifesto (*Fortnightly Review*) which for a week or so loomed large to us. Shaw's manufacturing out of Sidney's facts. It boomed in the press – the Tory Democratic papers quoting it freely, the Radical papers denouncing it, and only such standard respectables as the *Spectator* and the *Standard* refusing to notice it out of sheer perplexity how to treat it. I am not sure whether, after the event, I altogether approve of it. There is some truth in Graham's original objection that we were rushed with it by fear of being thought complacent and apathetic by the Labour Party. Whether it is wise to do anything simply from fear of being left behind? But that was not the whole of the motive. All through the spring Sidney and Shaw have been feeling the need of some strong outspoken words on the lack of faith and will to go forward manifested by the majority of the Cabinet. They could hardly go on supporting the Liberals if these were deliberately fooling the progressives with addled promises. Perhaps the Fabian Junta chose the right time to speak – anyway they said only what they thought. They spoke to the world exactly what they had been saying in private. So far the manifesto was justified.

Another chicken hatched here last summer – Tom Mann's Minority Report – has not yet come off, though he has accepted it cordially and all promises well. Sidney has spent quite three weeks on it, one time or another, but, though we think it is of importance, we cannot help regarding it as a practical joke over which we chuckle with considerable satisfaction. Poor Labour Commission, having carefully excluded any competent Socialists from its numbers, having scouted the idea of appointing me as a humble assistant commissioner, will now find a detailed collectivist programme blazoned about as the Minority Report of its labour members! Poor old Leonard, who told us with pompous superiority that they were all agreed, and that there was no prospect of any Minority Report, and we had it all the time lying on the table! – had been putting the last touches to it that very morning! Certainly persons with brains and independent means may have a rare good time in the part of permeator or fly on the wheel.

Altogether our personal life is delightful. Love, health, capacity, freedom, friends, all the good things of life in abundant measure.

Sometimes one feels guilty of this abundance of happiness, as if of a monopoly; sometimes I feel that the ease and comfort of our lives is stolen from others and that we ought to be more ascetic. We work hard, it is true – Sidney especially – but this work is what we like and we deny ourselves nothing that we really desire. We are – at any rate I am – self-indulgent, more self-indulgent than we ought to be. But somehow or other when one wants a thing one never finds time to deny it to oneself.

Sad scenes at the Williams's. Dyson becoming a hopeless morphia and chloroform drunkard, the little boy nervous and ailing, Rosy a slave to her husband, trying to recoup herself by having her own way in the management of her child. Mrs Thompson suited them as nurse to both husband and child . . . . Poor Rosebud, the 'unfortunate' one of the family.

She is the only sister of whom I see much – many afternoons I walk along the Embankment and call in, partly to cheer up Mrs Thompson. Six years I spent with that woman and always found her a true friend and wise counsellor. . . .

The sisterhood is scattered – many of us are becoming strangers with no interest in common. Of Mary Playne, with whom I used at one time to be intimate, I have seen nought since my marriage; Georgie and Blanche mere formal visits from time to time; Lallie too far off; Kate and Maggie rather more, for Rosy is a common source of anxiety. But none of the brothers-in-law care to see much of Sidney (Alfred is hardly now a brother and will in time cease to be an acquaintance). Willie, Leonard and Arthur positively dislike my husband; Daniel is indifferent; Robert chaffingly affectionate, but as I have never been intimate it makes little difference. The Booths, too, retire more completely into the background; we meet rarely and then only on terms of distant and formal comradeship. We are not without friends. Graham Wallas, L. Smith, Bernard Shaw, Haldane, Ella Pycroft (now working as an L.C.C. organizer for technical education under Sidney). Alice Green and all my host of 'labour' friends are there in their different degree of relationship. But friends are not changeable quantities – another friend however true and tender is no substitute for a lost one. The Booths have no successors.

I must not break off on this minor key. All said and done I am triumphantly happy. I am getting back my intellectual *zest* which I seemed to lose last autumn. Construction is again a pleasure to me. Now for the next three weeks I have to set to and construct the last

chapter of our book – 'The Trade Union World'. Welcome New Year
1894.

✑ 1894 ∿

   Henry Broadhurst (1840–1911), General Secretary of the Stonemasons'
Union, was a Liberal M.P. 1880–86 and 1894–1906. Although he was a
vigorous and effective labour leader and a dominant figure in the Trades Union
Congress, he strongly opposed the New Unionism and its socialist advocates. He
was a member of the Royal Commission on the Poor Law, set up in 1892 by the
Liberal government as a response to Chamberlain's suggestion of an insurance
scheme covering old age and infirmity. The Commission did not examine
immediate labour problems and no attempt was made to modify the law to meet the
case of the unemployed. Nor did it represent the new labour forces. Its only labour
members were men of the old school like Joseph Arch and Broadhurst. John Burns
declined to serve on it. When the Commission reported in April 1895 it advocated
further enquiry; and more than ten years were to pass before the Liberals
introduced a system of old-age pensions. James Mawdsley (1848–1902) was a
Conservative trade unionist who led the Lancashire cotton spinners. He was a
member of the Royal Commission on Labour, which reported in April 1894.
James Knowles (1831–1908) was for many years editor of the *Nineteenth Century*.

2 March. [41 Grosvenor Road]
Getting our work through the press, dawdling between batches of
proofs, considering the form of an article promised to Knowles on the
Royal Commission, lecturing casually in London and Oxford.
Sidney slaving at proofs, L.C.C., and now writing Broadhurst's
Minority Report for the Poor Law Commission. Seen a good deal
lately of trade union leaders – Burns, Broadhurst, Mann and
Mawdsley. Burns excessively friendly, relying a good deal on the
Fabians for advice. From all accounts the Parliamentary Committee
[of the Trades Union Congress] is torn asunder by jealousy and
suspicion of the leading members. . . Altogether the trade union
movement has at present no leader or group of leaders. Trying hard to
persuade Burns to take the position. . . But he is at present suffering
from severe disillusionment with labour and an equally excessive
admiration for the brainworking class. That is the worst of these
working-men: from the standpoint of thinking every man is as good as
another, they jump at one bound to a position of cynical contempt for
the common lump of men and an altogether extravagant appreciation
of the able man of affairs. They forget that the middle-class

43

brainworker is made to order exactly as the engineer or carpenter, and that the greater part of his superiority is simply knowledge of the tricks of the trade – the acquired habit of brainwork. No sign yet of any real leader, either in the labour movement or the Radical ranks.

On 3 March 1894 William Ewart Gladstone resigned as Prime Minister owing to failing health, political differences with his colleagues and the defeat of Home Rule by the House of Lords. Rosebery then formed a new Liberal administration. George John Shaw-Lefevre (1831–1928) had been a Liberal M.P. since 1863 and had held other Cabinet posts before being appointed president of the Local Government Board (L.G.B.) by Rosebery. George William Russell (1853–1919) was a Liberal M.P. and L.C.C. alderman who became Under-Secretary at the Home Office. Henry Labouchere (1831–1912), Liberal M.P. from 1880, was an anti-collectivist Radical. Sir William Harcourt (1827–1904) had been the obvious successor to Gladstone, but he was not liked by his colleagues. He retained his post as Chancellor of the Exchequer and introduced death duties in his Budget for 1894. John Morley (1838–1923) was an editor and man of letters who became a Liberal M.P. in 1883 and Chief Secretary for Ireland in 1886 and 1892–95. He was a strong supporter of Gladstone and of Home Rule. Sir Henry Fowler (1830–1911), who had been at the Local Government Board, became Secretary of State for India.

12 March. [41 Grosvenor Road]
Thursday last I was settling to work after breakfast when Haldane was announced. 'I have come to see you and Webb about the political situation,' he began, looking grave and put out. I called Sidney in and we both sat down feeling that we were expected to condole with some grievance but not quite certain which. 'There are really four appointments,' he continued. 'Shaw-Lefevre is fatal at the Local Government Board – couldn't be worse. George Russell at the Home Office too.' And then Haldane unburdened his soul to us. He described how the last ten days had been in reality a pitched battle between the old and the new Radicals. The common lump of Liberal members were strongly in favour of Harcourt, the little gang of collectivist Radicals (excluding Asquith, Acland, Sydney Buxton and Grey) had forced Rosebery on the Parliamentary Radicals with the aid of such outside forces as London Progressives, and the [*Daily*] *Chronicle.* John Morley had joined them from personal dislike of Harcourt so that the hand of the Labouchere lot had been forced by the threat of retirement of the most vital part of the ministry. But the old gang had had their revenge. They had promoted Fowler, forced into L.G.B. Shaw-Lefevre (Fowler and Harcourt's nominee) and

effectively barred the way to Haldane's entry into the Cabinet. It was natural enough that poor Haldane, having sacrificed himself by incurring the hatred of the rank and file by his successful Rosebery intrigue, should not be satisfied with the result. He had come to us to suggest that the *Chronicle* should be more critical in its attitude towards the new government and that the Progressives generally should not give themselves away. It was a quaint episode when one remembered his grave remonstrance of our hostile attitude last autumn that he should be instigating us to be independent. I saw, however, that it was more the *Chronicle* that he was after than ourselves, so I arranged that he should meet Massingham here on Sunday night and talk it over.

Massingham came and before Haldane arrived, confirmed his account of what had taken place. Asquith and Haldane, he says, are hated by the House of Commons Radical, who feels the ground slipping from under him without knowing why. Haldane incited Massingham to keep the *Chronicle* an independent force – they and Sidney more or less determined on a plan of campaign to oust the old gang from the party. 'It is war to the knife now,' said Haldane impressively, 'either they or we have to go down!'

But what amused me was the way in which the present crisis had completely healed the strained feeling aroused between Sidney and Massingham and to some extent Haldane by the Fabian manifesto. Massingham who had told us solemnly that he would never work with us again! was now taking counsel about his conduct of the *Chronicle* and his ultimatum to the nominal editor that he would stand no interference in the political editorship. It shows how right we were to treat his angry outburst of private and public abuse with imperturbable good temper, and turn our left cheek when he struck our right! I like Massingham immensely. I like him more than I respect him. His excitability, impressionableness, his quick appreciation of anything you say and clever reproduction of it – all this is attractive. But one feels that to be safe with him one ought to keep him very much in tow – to that extent he resembles Tom Mann; he needs ballast.

Our little plan for writing the Minority Reports of the two Commissions seems to be coming off all right. Tom Mann hands his elaborate manifesto and programme in tomorrow. Broadhurst swallowed the bait quite complacently and Sidney has prepared him an excellent document on old-age pensions and Reform of the Poor

Law. But we tremble lest some misadventure should spoil our pretty little game and Sidney's work would be wasted. But these sort of risks one has to run with these labour men. They are not *efficient*. . . Whether we shall succeed in making our little home the intellectual headquarters of the labour movement depends a good deal on the success from the point of view of the two men concerned in these Minority Reports. If it becomes generally known among the working-men leaders that Sidney is always ready to give them their 'stock in hand' and that no discredit comes to them from accepting his help, then we shall be able to direct the aims and methods of the popular party on those questions which we understand. This 'behind the scenes' intellectual leadership is, I believe, Sidney's special talent if he can get the opportunity to use it to the full. For a popular leader his personality is not sufficiently striking and attractive for real 'direction' and 'mediation'. His intellectual grasp, his resource, ingenuity, quickness and lucidity of expression, above all his quite extraordinary freedom from personal vanity or the vulgar form of ambition, render him an admirable instrument. It is my business to see that he has the material to work upon in so far as hospitality, discretion and tact can bring it. It will be discretion that I shall lack most!

Michael Austin (1855–1916), an Irish nationalist and trade unionist, became a Liberal M.P. in 1892 and a member of the Royal Commission on Labour. William Abraham (1842–1922) was a Methodist preacher and a pioneer of trade unionism among the Welsh miners. He was elected as a Liberal M.P. in 1885, and was also a member of the Commission on Labour.

13 March. [41 Grosvenor Road]
Amusing afternoon. Mann came in the morning to say that he was bringing Mawdsley, Austin and Abraham to discuss the Minority Report at 5 o'clock, the excuse being that he had left it with Sidney to look over from a legal point of view. We were both rather taken aback, thinking that Mawdsley, whose adhesion was most important, would not only refuse to swallow it but would perhaps join the rest of the Commission in trying to keep it out altogether. We could not imagine Mawdsley, a staunch Conservative, adopting it 'all of a heap'. When Mawdsley turned up early to write his copy for the *Factory Times*, I was relieved to find that he was supremely discontented with the Majority Report and felt in a fix as to what he should do. Sidney took the matter in hand, and asked leave, as a

lawyer, to give the others the gist of Mann's Report. Standing in front of the fire, he began reading out all the parts which would affect Mawdsley most, Mann playing into his hand by suggesting more advanced statements, Sidney supporting Mawdsley in many of his criticisms. As he read on Mawdsley expressed his approval and was apparently delighted with the practical and detailed character of the suggestions. It ended by Mawdsley considering the Report his own! and taking it on himself to announce to the Commission that they were drawing up a Minority Report and would present it in a couple of days. The only alteration he insisted on was the omission of the word 'Socialism', though he agreed to the substitution of the words 'public administration, national and local'. So much in a word.

VOLUME 15

Beatrice's article, 'The Failure of the Labour Commission', was published in the *Nineteenth Century* in July 1894.

30 April. Grosvenor Road

Our book comes out tomorrow, the Minority Report of the Labour Commission has been handed in corrected, ditto of P.L.C. [Aged Poor Commission] handed in as memo, the article for the *Nineteenth Century* demolishing the Labour Commission has been written, so that now we feel free to go off for a real holiday of three weeks. It is the first complete break in our work that we have had since those happy days in Norway three years ago. Of course, I have had days and weeks of 'lazing' from sheer incapacity to work, but I think I have used up all my energy during the last three years in work. I have never had sufficient over to enjoy anything but a somewhat depressed rest. The last weeks I have slacked off so that I may have plenty of spirits for our holy-day. We need to rid ourselves of the turmoil of life here during the last three months, so as to set to our next bit of work with a clear hand and clean conscience!

Sir Lawrence Alma Tadema (1836–1912) was a much admired Victorian painter of glossy marbled interiors. Lt.-Gen. Sir Richard Strachey (1817–1908) was a distinguished officer and administrator. His wife wrote poetry and memoirs. They were the parents of the biographer and critic Lytton Strachey.

21 May. Grosvenor Road

Back from a delightful three weeks' holiday. Nine days in Venice. Charming rooms overlooking an Alma Tadema court, with canal and bridge between us and it and old marble gateway and well, whither Venetian women with their soft-coloured clothes went to draw water. Our days were spent on the water with an old gondolier whom we engaged by the day, and in St Mark's Piazza and in St Mark's itself – that vision of sumptuous beauty which it is a glory to recall. Very sweet hours of companionship – not thinking, but simply feeling the beauty around us – a true honeymoon of love and common enjoyment. Then to Como (Menaggio) where we met the Richard Stracheys – the General, an old experienced Indian administrator, and Mrs Strachey, a strong, warm-hearted, enthusiastically literary woman. But though our evenings were spent with them, smoking cigarettes and sipping coffee on the terrace, our days were spent together wandering over the hills and in the lovely gardens of the Villas. Then a long journey back, and we are again in our little house, beautifully cleaned up by our two maids, and with Galton keenly anxious to be at the next volume. The holiday has been just what we needed; it has swept away all the cobwebs of secret Minority Reports and all the tatters of the last bit of work, so that we can begin fresh and clear, a new subject. One day spent over our correspondence and this morning I started off to plan the new volume. . . . It will be a difficult and delicate piece of work and need a great deal of hard hammering to weld it into anything like form. But we are encouraged, if indeed such a labour of love needs encouragement, by the appreciation of our labour and patience in the first volume. . . .

A Local Government Act was passed in March 1894, after considerable opposition in the Commons (led by Joseph Chamberlain) and the Lords. It set up a new system of democratically elected urban, rural and parish councils, and gave qualified women the right to run as candidates. In London the Conservatives wished to abolish the L.C.C., giving some of its powers to a new group of metropolitan boroughs and returning others to a revived Metropolitan Board of Works. This 'indirect' body, set up in 1855, had dealt fairly effectively with drainage, slum clearance and the construction of the Thames Embankment, but it had been discredited by cases of corruption and its responsibilities had been transferred to the L.C.C. in 1888. Lord Salisbury (1830–1903) had been the leader of the Conservative Party since the death of Lord Beaconsfield (Benjamin Disraeli) in 1881. He became Prime Minister in June 1885, and again in July 1886–92. He resumed office in 1895 until he resigned in favour of his nephew Arthur Balfour in July 1902.

20 June. Grosvenor Road

Haldane has just been here: says that the Unionist [the expected Tory-Liberal Unionist coalition] government will make a determined attack on the L.C.C. and attempt to break up London into separate municipalities. That this has been in the mind of Chamberlain, Balfour and Salisbury is clear from their recent utterances. But Sidney says it is an impossibility; you could not divest the L.C.C. of the great bulk of its powers though, of course, it would be possible to change its constitution and reinstate the Metropolitan Board of Works. . . . Cannot help thinking that Chamberlain is leading his party very wrong and that he will knock his head against a blank wall, both on the London question and on that of the trade unions. It looks like sheer political idiocy to throw the trade unions and the London Progressives into the arms of the Liberals – but I suppose he thinks he sees his game! Personally, one would regret being forced into the fight, as we shall both be if the attack is serious. It is so much pleasanter to investigate and write rather than organize and speak. Just now our life is so perfect; it might easily become strained and dissipated in mere manipulation. But one thing is clear: we must live the plainest, most healthful life in order to get through the maximum amount of work, and one must economize on all personal luxuries in order to have cash to spend on anything that turns up to be done. With so much love and personal happiness, one ought to be able to do much for others.

10 July. Grosvenor Road

Not getting on with our book. It is a horrid grind, this analysis – one sentence is exactly like another, the same words, the same construction, no relief in narrative. . . . I sometimes despair of getting on with the book. I feel horribly vexed with myself for loitering and idling as I do morning after morning, looking on while poor Sidney drudges along. London, too, is beginning to get on my nerves, with the heat and the continual noise and movement and the distraction of seeing one person and another. When we get to the country it may be better: we must make an effort! -

Sidney is discouraged about the political situation. Absorbed in the L.C.C. administrative work and in the book, he has little time for wire-pulling. He feels that there is a backwardation. The Conservative Unionist party is now fully alive to the issue of individualism and property as against collectivism and labour legislation, and is making preparation to fight hard, whilst the Liberal Party, though vaguely collectivist, is not led by collectivists and has even among its leaders the most bigoted individualists. We have to some extent roused our natural enemies without having secured our natural allies. The Independent Labour Party with its lack of money, brains and, to some extent, moral characteristics, is as yet more a thorn in the side of the Liberals than an effective force on our side. . . .

I sometimes wonder whether I am right in inclining Sidney *not* to go into Parliament. Hardly a month passes but some constituency or other throws out a fly for him, but so far he resolutely refuses to consider it, and that largely because I discourage him. Personally, I feel that he is doing real work on the L.C.C., work which is not only useful to London, but useful to him, in that it gives him problems of administration to think out instead of pure wire-puller's work. Is there any distinction? Is not all administrative work wire-pulling – with a clear conception of your ends? Perhaps the distinction is that in administration your ends must be practicable and desirable; in political wire-pulling, you may be highly successful in your machinery but have altogether misunderstood the object of it. I do not feel confident that he would be a big success in the House; I do not think the finest part of his mind and character would be called out by the manipulation and intrigues of the lobby. And then a parliamentary career would destroy our united life: would cut at the root of a good deal of our joint effort. Perhaps that is why I distrust my dislike of his going into Parliament – it would take so much away from me personally, would add so many ties and inconveniences. Sooner or later I suppose he will have to make the sacrifice, but better later than sooner.

The Webbs made a habit of renting houses for a long summer retreat. Borough Farm was not far from Godalming, standing alone in the heathlands towards Milford.

25 July. Borough Farm, Surrey
Overlooking a little country lane with heather-covered moorland on one side and a thicket of young trees behind, stands the farmhouse we have taken for three months. The farmer and his wife, hard-headed, somewhat grasping folk, who make us pay more than London prices for all their produce and whom I rather suspect of taking toll on our groceries! and a grim old labourer who serves them and does menial

offices for us and whom we meet in the late evening with a coat puffed out with concealed rabbits, are our co-occupants of the substantial red brick old-fashioned house. Though only one hour and a few minutes by rail from London, it is too remote for postal delivery and we have to fetch our letters some 1½ miles from a village! But this and other drawbacks are outweighed by the exceeding charm of the country. . . .

Spent two days (while Sidney was in London) alone with Graham Wallas. Long walks after dinner on the moorland in the clouded twilight of this stormy summer season – with the yellow of the setting sun peering on the horizon between thick black clouds. Poor fellow, he is in a dreary mood just now, overworked with organizing the Progressives for the next School Board election – and himself standing for Hackney – besides making his livelihood by lecturing. Like many men who live alone and work hard he is a joyless being who has to some extent lost his manners and capacity for agreeable intercourse in the daily grind of devoted work for others. We are probably his nearest and dearest friends with whom he feels perfectly at ease, able to come and go as if our house were his rightful home. He will be with us, off and on, the whole three months, finishing his book on Francis Place. But friends, however dear, are no substitute for a beloved partner who would share evil and good days with him. And Wallas has not Shaw's light-heartedness, nor Shaw's witty observations of men and things, which gives an intellectual zest to life and makes a man welcomed wherever he goes. Then Shaw lives in a drama or comedy of which he himself is the hero – his *amour propre* is satisfied by the jealousy and restless devotion of half a dozen women, all cordially hating each other. Graham Wallas grinds on, making no personal claims, impersonal and almost callous in his manner, an English gentleman in his relations with women to whom a flirtation, let alone an intrigue, would seem underbred as well as unkind and dishonourable. All the same, he is not positively unhappy, only perpetually overworked and living in a grey cloudland of dutiful effort.

25 July. [Borough Farm]
An exquisite still evening, cloudless, each leaf on the tree which grows close to the house standing out, with all its own delicate individuality against the blue green of the twilight sky. During my lonely walk (Sidney is away in London, Graham at Oxford) this afternoon, I have

been meditating on womanhood – and the perfection of it – what sort of being a woman should be. First and foremost I should wish a woman I loved to be a mother. To this end I would educate her, preserving her health and vigour at all hazards, training her to self-control and to capacity for sustained intellectual work so far as health permitted and no further. From the first I would impress on her the holiness of motherhood, its infinite superiority over any other occupation that a woman may take to. But for the sake of that very motherhood I would teach her that she must be an intellectual being, that without a strong deliberate mind she is only capable of the animal office of bearing children, not of rearing them. It pains me to see a fine, intelligent girl, directly she marries, putting aside intellectual things as no longer pertinent to her daily life. And yet the other alternative, so often nowadays chosen by intellectual women, of deliberately forgoing motherhood, seems to me to thwart all the purposes of their nature. I myself – or rather we – chose this course on our marriage, but then I had passed the age when it is easy and natural for a woman to become a child-bearer; my physical nature was to some extent dried up at thirty-five after ten years' stress and strain of a purely brainworking and sexless life. If I were again a young woman and had the choice between a brainworking profession or mother-hood, I would not hesitate which life to choose (as it is, I sometimes wonder whether I had better not have risked it and taken my chance).

I do not much believe in the productive power of woman's intellect; strain herself as much as she may, the output is small and the ideas thin and wire-drawn from lack of matter and wide experience. Neither do I believe that mere training will give her that fullness of intellectual life which distinguishes the really able man. The woman's plenitude consists of that wonderful combination of tenderness and judgement which is the genius of motherhood, a plenitude springing from the very sources of her nature, not acquired or attained by outward training. To think of the many hours in each day which I idle and mope away simply because I can only work my tiny intellect for two or three hours at the most, whereas I could be giving forth tenderness and judgement to my children hour after hour and day after day without effort or strain. It is this over-abundance of affection which the woman who is simply a brainworker, even though she be also a loving comrade to her husband, deliberately wastes by forgoing motherhood. And what is perhaps equally sad, with the sacrifice of the function she sacrifices, to a great extent, the faculty.

But what will be the solution of the woman's question? We collectivists are apt to say that the time is not ripe to deal with it. No thoughtful person wishes to see the old regimen of economic and personal dependence preserved from the attacks of the modern woman's movement for complete freedom and emancipation. But most of us distrust the reform as much as we dislike the evil. We do not believe that the cry for equal opportunities, a fair field and no favour, will bring woman to her goal. If women are to compete with men, to struggle to become wealth producers and energetic citizens, to vie with men in acquisition of riches, power or learning, then I believe they will harden and narrow themselves, degrade the standard of life of the men they try to supplant, and fail to stimulate and inspire their brother workers to a higher level of effort. And above all, to succeed in the struggle, they must forgo motherhood, even if, in training themselves for the prize fight, they do not incapacitate themselves for child-bearing. And what shall we gain? Surely it is enough to have half the human race straining every nerve to outrun their fellows in the race for subsistence or power? Surely we need some human beings who will watch and pray, who will observe and inspire, and, above all, who will guard and love all who are weak, unfit or distressed? Is there not a special service of woman, as there is a special service of man? The man is paid directly or indirectly by the community to create commodities in return for his subsistence. We collectivists believe that it is best that he should be enlisted and paid directly by the community, so that he may feel himself enrolled as a servant and minister of society. We believe that only by this direct and recognized enrolment can we ensure that he is producing and not destroying, that he is working for his fellows and not warring against them or living on them. Should not women, too, be enrolled as servants of the community, creators of something more precious than commodities, creators of the nation's children? And as man with his unremitting activity and physical restlessness seems fitted to labour, direct and organize, so woman, with her long periods of passive existence and her constantly recurring physical incapacity, seems ordained to watch over the young and guard over the rising generation and preserve for all the community the peaceful and joyful home.

All this points to the endowment of motherhood and raising the 'generation and rearing' of children into an art through the elaboration of science. Sometimes I imagine how the men and women of a hundred years hence will wonder at our spending all our energy and thought on the social organization of adult men and women, and omitting altogether the vastly more important question of the breeding of the generation that is to succeed them. . . . But, for all that, we cannot take up the woman's question. We cannot hope to attack individualism or, as we prefer to call it, anarchy, in its stronghold of the home and the family, entrenched behind current religious morality and custom, before we have replaced it by deliberate collective rule in the factory, the mine – in the whole machinery of wealth production, where anarchy stands condemned by the great bulk of the people as meaning oppression and gross injustice between man and man. Possibly too, woman will have to go through the same social stages as the labourer, on her way to freedom; she will have to exchange the servitude of *status* for the servitude of *contract*, to rise out of personal dependence before she gains social protection and recognition. We can but leave this problem reverently to our children, preparing their way by cutting at the roots of prejudice, superstition and rotten custom. . . . How far, I wonder, will the collectivist principle carry us? The thinkers of fifty years ago believed as firmly in individualism as we believe in collectivism – probably more uncompromisingly, for the men and women of today distrust general principles even though they are prepared to use them. And yet it is easy to see now that the settled conviction of the individualists, that government should be limited to keeping the ring clear for private individuals to fight in, was based on the experience of a one-sided and corrupt participation of the government in industrial organization, and not on any necessary characteristic of state action. Face to face with the government action of their own day, they were to a large extent right. Is it not possible that it is the same with collectivism? Public administration is the alternative to private enterprise, and since private enterprise is corrupt and selfish, we propose to supersede it by democratic control. But it is, on the face of it, as unlikely that the collectivist principle will apply all round as that the individualist principle would solve all the social problems of fifty years ago. I do not think that we Fabians believe in more than a limited application of the collectivist principle, though, as practical politicians, we think that we are as yet nowhere near the 'margin of cultivation', that we can cultivate this principle vigorously for all that it is worth, in all directions without exhausting its vitality. But of one thing I feel certain; the controversy which seems to us now so full of significance and import will seem barren and useless to our great-grandchildren.

They will be amazed that we fought so hard to establish one metaphysical position and to destroy another. And that is why I value diagnosis so much more highly than controversy and propaganda. . . . One must be content to work for one's own day.

30 July. Borough Farm
Another day alone. Yesterday tropical rain deluged the country, the lane in front of our gate becoming a rushing stream of water. Early this morning the thick clouds gave way, a steaming mist arose from the moor to be dispelled at midday by the sun which blazed out in full summer splendour. Oh, the luxury of these hours alone with nature. . . .

10 August. Borough Farm
Either the Surrey climate is enervating or I am no good at this analytical deductive work which goes to make up our second volume. . .

Geoffrey Drage (1860–1955) was the secretary to the Royal Commission on Labour. He became a Tory M.P. in 1895. The trustees of the Hutchinson bequest (described in the Introduction) were Hutchinson's daughter Constance, Sidney Webb, and three other prominent Fabians – Edward Pease (1857–1955), who had been one of the founders of the Society and was its secretary for many years, William de Mattos (b. 1851), its lecture secretary, and William Clarke (1852–1901), a journalist on the Fabian executive.

21 September. Borough Farm
Cannot say that I have been working well this summer. The task is very difficult. I have been in poor health, and this climate, not at any time invigorating, has been especially depressing this damp summer. For the last fortnight we have had during one day after another dank white mist from early morning to the close of evening, with rain in the night. And until ten days ago I did not discover that I was suffering from a bowel disorder that needed a strict diet and proper treatment. Now I have taken to a rigid diet – discarded fruit, sugar, alcohol and most vegetables – and I feel wonderfully better.

In the meantime I have been foolishly upset by Geoffrey Drage's reply to my article on the Labour Commission. I fear this is very womanish, to resent being hit at when one has hit hard oneself without personal provocation. Perhaps what really distresses me is that I was persuaded by my menkind – Sidney, Graham and Shaw – not to answer it, and now that it is too late I find that other persons expect me to reply to his accusations of inaccuracy! . . . What I need is a little intellectual regimen – to take my brain in hand as I have my stomach and absolutely refuse entrance to thoughts that are morbid and worthless. Somehow or other my intellect is becoming less strenuous than before my marriage. I must wrestle with this tendency to become parasitic on Sidney's effort. I must do myself *an honest day's work* and not give way to this desire to shirk my share of the hard labour. . . .

An odd adventure! A few weeks ago Sidney received a letter from a Derby solicitor informing him that he was left executor to a certain Mr Hutchinson. All he knew of this man (whom he had never seen) was the fact that he was an eccentric old gentleman, member of the Fabian Society, who alternately sent considerable cheques and wrote querulous letters about Shaw's rudeness, or some other fancied grievance he had suffered at the hands of some member of the Fabian Society. 'Old Hutch' had, however, been a financial stay of the Society and the Executive was always deploring his advancing age and infirmity. When Sidney heard he was made executor he, therefore, expected that the old man had left something to the Fabian Society. Now it turns out that he has left nearly £10,000 to five trustees and appointed Sidney chairman and administrator – all the money to be spent in ten years. The poor old man blew his brains out, finding his infirmities grow upon him. He had always lived a penurious life and stinted his wife and by no means spoilt his children, and left his wife only £100 a year (which Sidney proposes should be doubled by the trustees). The children are all provided for and do not seem to resent the will.

But the question is how to spend the money. It might be placed to the credit of the Fabian Society and spent in the ordinary work of propaganda. Or a big political splash might be made with it – all the Fabian Executive might stand for Parliament! and I.L.P. candidates might be subsidized in their constituencies. But neither of these ways seem to us 'equal to the occasion'. If it is mainly used for the ordinary work of the Fabian Society, then it will really save the pockets of ordinary subscribers or inflate the common work of the organization for a few years beyond its normal growth. Moreover, mere propaganda of the shibboleths of collectivism is going on at a rapid rate through the I.L.P.; the ball has been set running and it is rolling down the hill at a fair pace. It looks as if the great bulk of the working-men will be collectivists before the end of the century. But reform will not be brought about by shouting. What is needed is *hard thinking*. And the same objection applies to sending nondescript socialists into Parliament. The Radical members are quite sufficiently compliant in their views: what is lacking in them is the leaven of knowledge. So Sidney has been planning to persuade the other trustees to devote the greater part of the money to encouraging research and economic study. His vision is to found, slowly and quietly, a 'London School of Economics and Political Science' – a centre not only of lectures on special subjects, but an association of students who would be directed and supported in doing original work. Last evening we sat by the fire and jotted down a whole list of subjects which want elucidating – issues of fact which need clearing up. Above all, we want the ordinary citizen to feel that reforming society is no light matter, and must be undertaken by experts specially trained for the purpose.

Rusland Hall in Cumberland had been a rented holiday home for the Potters, Richard Potter having business interests at nearby Barrow-in-Furness. Bertha Newcombe, a professional artist and a Fabian, had an unrequited attachment to Bernard Shaw. Alfred Taylor (1869–1945) was a philosopher and fellow of Merton College, Oxford.

9 October. Borough Farm
It is some years since I have watched summer turn into autumn and felt the first breath of winter creeping over the country. This year the summer left us early, the sky closing over with cold grey clouds, only now and again they break and the sun slants out and lights up the sombre blues and browns of the landscape. Perhaps it is the rich tones of the heath and bracken which recall some of those lovely Rusland autumns, for, as I stand and watch the clouds drifting across the moor and try to fathom the glorious depths of colour of land and sky, memories of old days jostle each other and seem to take me back to the thoughts and feelings and daily life of struggling girlhood – the inevitable melancholy of the autumn months, the brooding over books, the long walks with Father, afternoon tea in the little hall at Rusland after a trudge in the mist, Mother's bright welcome to Father, her keen relish of her cup of tea before she went to her boudoir to study her grammars, or settled herself down to a talk with Father over his business affairs and the family prospects – all the strange medley of good and evil one lived through as a girl. But in chewing the cud of these old memories, I am impressed not with the *past-ness* of the old life but with the perfect continuity of the present and the past: these

autumn months of years ago were always devoted to study, were always stimulated by a restless desire to conquer new strands of thought. After nearly twenty years of adult life, I am still living the same daily life, still using my whole energy in unravelling ideas and attempting to clear issues – the practical affairs which occupy most people's middle life are no more now than they were then – at least not during our three months' holiday. There is an inexpressible delight in this consciousness of continuity, in feeling that those hours of lonely and painful study are linked on to the settled occupation, perhaps one might almost say the settled profession, of a productive brainworker. If one could only have foreseen that this daily intellectual effort would one day be set in a frame of loving companionship and constant sympathy, one would have been less restless and morbidly self-conscious. . . what light love brings to the daily task: it turns that black despair of the over-strained brainworker into calm quiescence. When first I was married, I feared that my happiness would dull my energies and make me intellectually dependent. I no longer feel that; the old fervour for work has returned without the old restlessness. Of course my life in London, with its other claims, leaves me with less physical energy, but this I think is almost counterbalanced by the absence of any waste through mental misery. On the whole, then, I would advise the brainworking woman to marry – if only she can find her Sidney!

Beyond Shaw, Wallas and Bertha Newcombe and Rosy Williams we have seen few people here. Rosy and Noel have stayed some three weeks. Rosy is like a shade from the old family life. She is now the only one of my sisters I see anything of. She likes being with us; the three men make a pet of Noel and are kind to her, and she is not oppressed with our superiority in wealth and successfulness as with the other sisters. And I am glad to pay off old scores of neglected duty to that poor child – I made an ignominious failure with her, a failure which I now recognize. Mrs Green, attended by her devoted Irish lawyer – Taylor – flew down here for three days on her way to a round of fashionable visits. She is, I fear, disillusioned about us, her disillusionment taking the form of an almost irritable criticism of our ways of life, with our sordid simplicity, lack of culture and general lower-middle-class-ness. . . If she cared to go on seeing me I should still like to be friendly with her, for she is an open window to other ways of thought and feeling, to other emotional and intellectual interests, new outlooks which amuse and entertain and rest me. But unless we speedily become 'distinguished', that is, thought well of by London Society (a fate which is not likely to befall us) I fear we shall see little more of Alice Green. . .

The parish councils had just been established under the Local Government Act of 1894.

11 October. Borough Farm

Tomorrow we leave. Sidney has trudged across the moor to meet the few village Radicals to advise them as to the parish councils election, and I turn to my old friend the diary for companionship. First, let me correct the libellous account I gave of our host and hostess. The woman turns out to be a fine, honest creature, working from early morning: the man, honest and genial enough, but abjectly lazy, willing to chat, to smoke, to drive us about the country – to do anything but work. If one were to generalize from the three farms we have had dealings with – the women are the wealth producers, the men do the ornamental and social side of life, varying this with the boozer's torpor. The countryside, in its social aspect, is depressing enough: the labourers a low, dishonest lot, the farmers idle and incapable, except for the wives, mere parasites on the land, the tradesmen servile dependents on the great Tory landlords who dominate the neighbourhood, and a floating 'foreign' summer population of middle-class holiday-makers like ourselves and East End tramps in search of odd harvest jobs. Parish councils will hardly turn the inhabitants of these parts into citizens!

For all that I leave this quaint little home with regret. The last months I have pulled myself together and done some hard thinking. We have roughed out four or five chapters of our book. I am beginning to see that if we can only put enough work into it this volume will be far more instructive than the *History*, a far bigger achievement. . . . I must, in order to be able to work, resolutely refuse to *worry*. Otherwise I shall not do my share of the labour and shall be a source of fatigue and not rest to Sidney. The next six months, with the vestry and L.C.C. elections added on to all the administrative business, seems likely to be somewhat trying for My Boy.

The vestries, based upon an archaic jigsaw of parishes, were London's traditional form of local government, and there were over five thousand elected places to be filled. They were soon to be swept away, but the Webbs in the meantime made an effort to improve the Progressive representation on the Westminster

Vestry, making their house the campaign headquarters and themselves running as candidates. The contest for the London School Board, to which Graham Wallas was re-elected, was held at the same time. The L.C.C. elections were due in the following March.

1 December. Grosvenor Road

Galton's little study turned into the central office of the Progressive candidates for the Westminster Vestry elections. Certainly, we have created our organization and selected our ninety candidates with singularly little trouble. . . The Westminster Radicals, a poor downtrodden lot, perpetually licked at all elections, hardly know themselves with their ninety candidates. Sidney has drafted the address, Galton is acting as election agent, and the working-men candidates are doing the canvassing and even the clerks' work. If by some marvellous chance we get returned today fortnight, we shall have our work cut out to drill them into working shape.

Altogether we have been living in the atmosphere of elections. Graham's candidature for the School Board gave us a personal interest in the fight. . . . It is very curious that both Sidney and Graham, though very advanced in their views, are better liked by the Moderates on the L.C.C. and the L.S.B. than other members of the Progressive Party. 'Wily Webb', as Sidney is called on the L.C.C., is always colloguing with the more sensible of the Moderates with a view of getting them to agree to things *in detail* which they could hardly accept in bulk. That seems also to be Graham's policy which he is carefully beginning at L.S.B. The truth is that *we want the things done* and we don't much care what persons or which party gets the credit. We are pretty confident that, if it comes to a fight, we know the arts of war as well as our enemies; but between the battles our cause may be advanced by diplomacy, even by a frank alliance with our former enemies if they be willing to take one little step forward in our direction. The Fabians are still convinced believers in the policy of permeation.

Meanwhile the book hangs fire. With both Sidney and Galton completely absorbed, I feel helpless. Moreover, as a candidate myself for the Vestry, I have caught a little of the election fever and am growing excited and perturbed. The L.C.C. elections, upon which so much depends, are looming in the distance. It might be better to give myself up frankly to electioneering and use these weeks as an opportunity for observing how elections are fought and won. It is all part of our subject-matter – democracy. Surely we shall end by constructing the great Webb Chart of the Modern Democratic State!

Angela Burdett-Coutts (1814–1906), heiress and philanthropist, had built St Stephen's, Westminster, and other churches; and endowed many charitable institutions.

[?] *December*. [41 Grosvenor Road]
Crushing defeat at Westminster Vestry elections; only five Progressives out of ninety-six! . . . apparently the slums of Westminster are as completely Tory as the palaces. I do not think there has been any lack of energy or even of skill in engineering such forces as we had. But it is obvious that our attempt to collar the constituency with three weeks' work – mostly amateur – was a fiasco which we ought to have expected. Against us we had a perfect organization with a permanent staff, a local paper and unlimited money. We had all the wealthy residents, nearly all the employers of labour and the whole liquor interest – no fewer than ten publicans and five other persons connected with 'the Trade' – running as Conservative candidates. We had a Register from which every known Liberal had been knocked off, year by year, without a protest from the feeble flickering little Liberal Association. Behind all this, we had Burdett-Coutts's charities and churches. And to fight these potent powers, Galton stood single-handed with a mob of working-men and small tradesmen candidates – some of them good talkers, but like most Labour men full of gassy optimism, caring only to foregather in the rooms of the Liberal Association and talk big of the victory they are going to win. . . Deeply rooted distrust of entrusting business to a lot of 'small folk' of no standing operated, too, against our candidates. Working-men, other things being equal, prefer an employer to a fellow worker as a candidate. Other things were in this case unequal, to our disadvantage. Add to these causes the perfectly legitimate grudge the Westminster ratepayers have against the Progressives for the 6*d* extra imposed by the Rate Equalization Bill. . . .

28 December. [Parmoor]
Spent our Christmas at Parmoor with Alfred Cripps, the children, the Courtneys and various Cripps nieces.
Alfred's home is strangely attractive, with a dash of sadness in it, especially to Theresa's sisters. A charming house, designed largely by Theresa, the soft luxurious colouring, the quaintness of the furniture, the walls covered with her portraits, all bring back to me the memory

of her gracious personality, so full of sympathy, wit and vivid imagination. And yet the home seems complete without her – the children revel in high spirits and health, the servants are contented. Alfred himself has regained all the light-heartedness of his charming disposition. . . . He is again the young man, unattached, absolute master of his own life. And he is in the full tide of great prosperity. An enormous professional income (he told Arthur [Playne] that he made £1,000 a week during the session) has enabled him to buy the family estate and sit down in front of a promising constituency. Doubtless he sees before him a brilliant career. Dear old Father used to call him 'the little jewel of an advocate' – a term which just fits him. There is something jewelled in his nature, intellectual skilfulness raised to the highest degree, a perfect deftness in execution, a loving disposition, unruffled temper, a cheery optimism – all these bright qualities set in a solid determination that all things shall fit in with his view of what is desirable for himself and others. He is a delightful father – the children obeying him implicitly with no consciousness of being ruled or regulated, a charming host, seeming to place his whole establishment at the service of his guests, a most indulgent master and landlord. And yet for all that, he gets his own way in life, and takes a very large share of the good things of the world both material and spiritual. With this disposition he could hardly be a reformer. He has become of late years more and more a Conservative opportunist, bent on keeping the soft places of the world for his own class, but ready to compromise and 'deal' whenever his class would lose more by fighting. He has almost a constitutional dislike of economic or social principle. . . . With his skill and charm he will succeed in politics as he has succeeded at the Bar – he will 'make money or its equivalent' and that is all. For all that, he remains an essentially lovable man. And without doubt he will one day find another mate, and then we shall lose sight of him.

It is curious to see the three brothers-in-law together. Each one has, for the opinions of the other two, tolerant contempt. Leonard Courtney likes Alfred far better than he does Sidney, thinks him a pleasant, attractive fellow with all the antecedents of a gentleman and a scholar. But for his opportunist Toryism, his demagogic anti-democratic attitude, he has, I think, an even greater intellectual contempt than for Sidney's collectivism. . . . To Leonard the means whereby you carry through a proposal, the arguments with which you support it, are as important as the end itself. And to do Leonard justice he is a democrat at heart, in that he honestly desires that the government of that country should be the reflection of the free desires and views of the whole body of the people. Possibly he is more of a democrat than we are ourselves, for we have little faith in the 'average sensual man'; we do not believe that he can do much more than describe his grievances, we do not think that he can prescribe the remedies. It is probably exactly on this point that Leonard feels most antagonistic to our opinions. We wish to introduce into politics the professional expert, to extend the sphere of government by adding to its enormous advantages of wholesale and compulsory management, the advantage of the most skilled entrepreneur. Leonard agrees with us, I think, in believing that the happiness of the mass is the end to be aimed at, but he has no faith in our methods because he holds a radically different economic creed. Alfred, on the other hand, refuses seriously to discuss with us, because he recognizes at once that we desire different ends. Leonard he holds to be a cranky faddist who cannot make up his mind which side of things he is really going to support. The attitude of the three brothers-in-law may therefore be described thus: Alfred looks on Sidney as a traitor to the brainworking and propertied class, Sidney looks on Alfred as a 'kept' advocate of the *status quo*, Leonard looks on Alfred as a somewhat selfish, thoughtless and superficial conservative, on Sidney as a shallow-minded self-complacent half-educated democrat, whilst both Sidney and Alfred have much the same opinion of Leonard – an upright but wrong-headed man dominated by a worn-out economic creed and shackled by lack of sympathy and quick intelligence. To some extent all opinions are equally true – as a summing-up of each individual they are all equally false.

∽ 1895 ∾

The London Reform Union, nominally non-party, was the electoral body which combined various reforming groups and individuals to run Progressive candidates for the L.C.C. The London Liberal and Radical Union was the other electoral organization of the Progressives. Webb was an active member.

12 January. [41 Grosvenor Road]
Both 'Front Benches' are throwing all their strength into the L.C.C. fight. On our side the collectivist Ministers, Asquith, Acland, Grey

with Lord Rosebery as a London county councillor, have spoken or are about to speak at great demonstrations. Sidney is in constant request, advising them as to what they are to say; supplied Asquith with his facts for his November oration and saw Acland today who sat and took notes from him. Nothing in fact can exceed the cordiality of the official Liberals to the Progressives of the L.C.C. in general and to Sidney in particular. On the other hand, the Unionists, stimulated and led by Chamberlain, are laying siege to every constituency. . . . Chamberlain has insisted on their putting forward what appears to be a most advanced programme – thoroughly demagogic in tone – the anti-immigration laws, old-age pensions, merchandise marks Act – all to act as gilt to the scarcely veiled attempt to reconstitute a sort of Metropolitan Board of Works in the place of a directly elected central Council. . . . Chamberlain is a nasty enemy and is going to make it a hot fight for us. . . . Odd that he and Sidney should be pitting their brains against each other – he overtly leading and directing the Moderate forces, Sidney, behind the scenes, drafting leaflets for both the Progressive organizations – L.R.U. and L.L.R.A. – and coaching official Progressive speakers. Wonder whether they will ever become face-to-face opponents!

Sir Edward Hamilton (1847–1908) was private secretary to Gladstone and became a senior official in the Treasury 1885–1907. In 1894 (after the early death of his first wife) Asquith married Margot (1864–1945), the clever and eccentrically outspoken daughter of Sir Charles Tennant (1823–1906), a rich Liberal baronet. She was one of the most active members of 'The Souls'.

20 January. [41 Grosvenor Road]
Haldane utterly discouraged with condition of Liberal Party, says there is now no hope that the Cabinet will pull themselves through. With the exception of Acland, none of the Ministers are doing any work. Rosebery sees no one but Eddy Hamilton, a flashy fast Treasury clerk, his stud-groom and various non-political fashionables. Sir William Harcourt amuses himself at his country place and abroad, determined to do nothing to help Rosebery. Even Asquith, under the dominance of his brilliant but silly wife, has given up attending to his department and occupies his time by visiting rich country houses and learning to ride! 'Rot has set in,' says Haldane. 'There is no hope now but to be beaten and then to reconstruct a new party. If only you Progressives can hold your own at the L.C.C.

elections, you would be a plank saved from the wreck upon which we could build a new combination.'

The same strains from Massingham – now much under Haldane's influence. He spent three or four hours here the other day being coached for the *Daily Chronicle* on the L.C.C. election. Urged Sidney to go into Parliament and become one of the leaders of the reconstruction party. But Sidney will bide his time. At present, the L.C.C. is a better platform from which to bring about collectivism than the House of Commons.

James Ramsay MacDonald (1866–1937), a poor-born Scot, made an exiguous living as a journalist and lecturer before his marriage, in 1896, to the daughter of a distinguished scientist. He and the Webbs were mutually incompatible, and this became a significant factor in the differences between the I.L.P. and the Webbs. He became the leader of the emergent Labour Party, and Prime Minister of the Labour governments of 1924 and 1929. By then the personal antagonism had eased, and he appointed Sidney to both his Cabinets. Frank Smith (1854–1940), who for a time held a leading position in the Salvation Army, was a journalist who became an I.L.P. member of the L.C.C. in 1892. The Democratic Federation, founded by H.M. Hyndman (1842–1921) in 1881 and renamed the Social Democratic Federation [S.D.F.] in 1883, was noted for its sectarian views and tactics.

23 January. [41 Grosvenor Road]
Last night we had an informal conference with the I.L.P. leaders. MacDonald and Frank Smith (who are members both of the Fabians and the I.L.P.) have been for some time harping on the desirability of an understanding between the two societies. To satisfy them Sidney asked a little dinner of Keir Hardie, Tom Mann, Pease and Shaw and the two intermediaries. I think the principals on either side felt it would come to nothing. Nevertheless, it was interesting. Keir Hardie was reserved, and merely reiterated the burden of his speech at the Fabian. But Tom Mann gushed out his soul. The practical issue before us was the action of the I.L.P. at the L.C.C. elections. Tom Mann, with the concurrence of Keir Hardie, advised the I.L.P. to abstain from voting. The Progressives on the L.C.C., he said, were not convinced Socialists, and even those who were, chose to run as Progressives and not as purely Socialist candidates. Therefore, the I.L.P. should be hostile to their return. He would not support John Burns (or presumably Sidney), 'because Jack played to get the vote of the mere Liberal.' No one should get the votes of the I.L.P. who did not pledge himself to the 'Nationalization of the Means of Production

and *who did not run overtly in opposition to all who were not socialists.'* He would accept no alliance. . . . It was melancholy to see Tom Mann reverting to the old views of the S.D.F. and, what is worse, to their narrow sectarian policy. Keir Hardie, who impressed me very unfavourably, deliberately chooses this policy as the only one which he can boss. His only chance of leadership lies in the creation of an organization 'agin the government'; he knows little and cares less for any constructive thought or action. But with Tom Mann it is different. He is possessed with the idea of a 'church' – of a body of men all professing exactly the same creed and all working in exact uniformity to exactly the same end. No idea which is not 'absolute', which admits of any compromise or qualification, no adhesion which is tempered with doubt, has the slightest attraction to him. And, as Shaw remarked, he is deteriorating. This stumping the country, talking abstractions and raving emotions, is not good for a man's judgement, and the perpetual excitement leads, among other things, to too much whisky.

I do not think the conference ended in any understanding. We made clear our position. The Fabians in no way competed with the I.L.P. We were a purely educational body, we did not seek to become a 'party'. We should continue our policy of inoculation, of giving to each class, to each person, that came under our influence the exact dose of collectivism that they were prepared to assimilate. And we should continue to improve and enlarge such machinery of government that came into our hands. Of course this slow imperceptible change in men's opinions and in the national institutions is not favourable to the growth of a revolutionary party. There is some truth in Keir Hardie's remark that we were the worst enemies of the social revolution. No great transformation is possible in a free democratic state like England unless *you alter the opinions of all classes of the community* – and even if it were possible, it would not be desirable. That is the crux between us!

1 February. [41 Grosvenor Road]
For the last three months an idea has haunted me that after we have ended our stiff work on trade unions I would try my hand at pure 'fiction' in the form of a novel dated 'sixty years hence'. It should not be an attempt to picture a utopia. It should attempt to foreshadow society as it will be eighty years hence if we go on 'evoluting' in our humdrum way. Two main ideas should run through it. The fully-fledged

woman engaged in a great career should be pictured just as we should now picture a man, and collectivism should be the orthodox creed carried out as a matter of course in moulding the institutions of the country. The truth is I want to have my 'fling'. I want to imagine anything I damn please without regard to facts as they are. I want to give full play to whatever faculty I have for descriptive and dramatic work. I want to try my hand at an artist's work instead of mechanics. I am sick to death of trying to put hideous facts, multitudinous details, exasperating qualifications, into a readable form. Doubtless when I discover that I have no artistic faculties I shall turn back to my old love and write with equanimity *The History of Municipal Institutions*. But before I can have this debauch I have a grind before me that must be got through, however little I like it.

10 February. [41 Grosvenor Road]
Three weeks off the L.C.C. elections. Sidney spending all his mornings writing articles for all sorts of papers, especially the religious organs such as the *Guardian*, the *Church Times*, the *Christian World*, *Methodist Times*, etc. We are, in fact, making a vigorous attempt to get the Church, the Catholic and the Nonconformist Ministers on our side. As all the 'sinners' are against us, we might as well get the saints to support us. Moreover we resolutely refuse to believe that any good person *properly informed* could be otherwise than a Progressive! If we are beaten — i.e. if a Moderate majority is returned, it will not be for lack of organization. We are better *organized* than our opponents — if they win it will show that the common opinion is against us. . . .

Though the L.C.C. election on 2 March produced a dead heat the Progressives managed to maintain overall control of the Council. Sidney's running-mate in Deptford was beaten.

5 March. Grosvenor Road
An anti-climax! After all the heat on both sides, after the blowing of both the big party trumpets, the calling to arms of saints and sinners by their respective champions, the rousing, on the one hand, of all the threatened 'interests', the appeals, on the other hand, to the forces of piety and democracy, London citizens send back an exactly even number of Moderates and Progressives, a bare half of registered electors taking the trouble to vote. In so many words, our constituents laugh in their sleeves and say 'tweedledee, tweedledum'. As far as

Sidney personally is concerned, it is 'as in 1892', his poll becoming fractionally higher, his majority fractionally lower. In a Conservative constituency he retains a Progressive majority of 1800 . . . .

[?] *March. Grosvenor Road*

Sidney low about the L.C.C. – brooding over the defeat . . . These times of physical want and mental despair are either the seed times of angry revolutionary feelings or of colourless despairing quietude. We forget that it was not until the dark years of 1881–85 were well over that *constitutional socialism* as distinguished from *revolutionary socialism* began to grow. It was no coincidence that the great Progressive victory came in the year of greatest prosperity. We must educate and wait for 'fat' years.

It has added to Sidney's discomfiture that the mercurial Massingham has turned against him. Massingham has had fits of admiration for Sidney of more or less duration – latterly they have been of less duration! But only the other day we heard him dilating on his greatness and asserting that any day he cared he could be in the Cabinet! All through the L.C.C. campaign he has been more than friendly, both publicly and privately. But the results of the fight have brought about a reaction against Sidney; and strangely enough it has been Sidney's personal success which seems to have tipped the balance. The fall in Burns's majority has angered Massingham, and the fact that Sidney, a middle-class collectivist, has not received the same snub from the multitude has made him still angrier. For Massingham has a hero-worship of John Burns. His excitable unstable nature has always been attracted by the boisterous vigour and immense self-conceit and assurance of our great labour leader. As a dramatic critic, he has infinitely preferred the stalwart demagogue, with his picturesque language and bracing personality, to Sidney's quiet, unpretentious little figure, with its even flow of statistics, arguments and diplomatic persuasiveness (or, as some would say, evasiveness!), and, like a good critic, he is sore and angry that the audience do not take his view and favour his favourite. For the rest, Burns has always disliked and suspected the pair of us and has instilled some of his prejudice into Massingham's mind. But Sidney will write a soft answer, and, in a few months, perhaps weeks, the tantrum will be over.

There is no use blinding ourselves to the setback to our ideas. Tom Mann said that the victory of the Progressives would redound to the glory of official Liberalism. Quite the contrary, it is our defeat which will give them secret joy. 'No more of your collectivism for us,' the Liberal capitalist will say; 'it cannot buy votes for our party.' It will doubtless harden the heart of the old gang, militate against the reconstruction of the Liberal Party on a collectivist basis. And, while it will delay permeation, it will also weaken the chances of an Independent Labour Party becoming any force in the land . . . .

Charles Harrison (1835–97) was a Liberal M.P. and vice-chairman of the L.C.C. Katherine Farrer was the wife of Baron Farrer, a vice-chairman of the L.C.C.; Charlotte Beachcroft was the wife of Sir Melville Beachcroft, a founding member of the L.C.C.

13 March. Grosvenor Road
Yesterday at the L.C.C. was an exciting scene. When we arrived at half-past two the entrance was crowded and all the galleries filled – the inside of the building leading to the Council chamber thronged with councillors and their immediate friends and relatives. By Charles Harrison's kindness I was passed on to the dais where I sat between Lady Farrer and Mrs Beachcroft on the 'Moderate' side of the Chair . . . . Certainly if the Progressives have accomplished no other good, we have made the L.C.C. the most distinguished, even the most 'aristocratic' local body in the world! A strange effect of the labour and socialist onslaught on London! And we must admit that the Moderate victories have raised the standard of good looks of the L.C.C. Slim aristocrats, well-fed and slightly dissipated-looking frequenters to London drawing-rooms and clubs, are, from a scenic point of view, welcome contrasts to the stunted figures of the labour representatives and the ungraceful corpulence of the 'Progressive' men of business. But the manners are as distinctly deteriorated. The 'gentlemen's party' are loud and insolent in their ways, an insolence which is possibly a reaction from their long term of servitude to an overwhelming Progressive majority. Our side was subdued, sitting tight and forcing their way through, by their bare majority, to the vice-chairmanship – thus retaining the three executive offices in their hands . . . .

Here Beatrice gives some pen portraits of some of the Progressive members of the L.C.C.: Sir John Hutton (1842–1903) chairman of the L.C.C. 1892–95; Sir John Benn (see entry for 30 July 1893); Sir William Collins (1859–1946), surgeon and county councillor who became chairman of the L.C.C. in 1897; and Sir

Willoughby Dickinson (1859–1943), a barrister and member of the L.C.C. in 1889–1907, who became its chairman in 1900 and a Liberal M.P. in 1906. At the beginning of March 1895, Speaker Peel resigned on grounds of health and Leonard Courtney was canvassed as his successor. Although Courtney had opposed the Liberals on Home Rule the government supported his nomination. The Tories, soon to come into office, opposed him but the decisive factor was the negative vote of Chamberlain and the Liberal Unionists.

19 March. [41 Grosvenor Road]

Poor dear Leonard diddled out of the Speakership by his own party. A mean and discreditable intrigue of Chamberlain's, who has had an animus against him ever since I can remember; first because Leonard was too much of a Whig, then because he retained too much of the Radical. Most likely, however, it has been all through a personal animus dating from Leonard's refusal fifteen years ago to enrol himself as Chamberlain's follower. It is only fair to say that Leonard has had a contempt for Chamberlain's intelligence and character, and Leonard is not a man to hide his opinions. Leonard's bad manners (in which include his supercilious depreciation of other people's claims and his lack of graciousness) have been Chamberlain's opportunity. We are grieved not only for his and Kate's sake but because we really believe we have lost the most democratic Speaker available. For, with all his faults, Leonard has an honest desire for the maximum *efficiency* in democratic machinery: and he judges each change on its own merits and not on what it may lead to. He has *faith in democracy*, a quality which covers many sins.

Beatrice Chamberlain (1861 – 1918) was the daughter of Joseph Chamberlain, and Beatrice [Webb] had been on good terms with her during the 1880s. Asquith, as Home Secretary, had introduced a Factory Bill in March 1895, making safety regulations and creating a number of women inspectors. George Joachim Goschen (1831 – 1907) was a Liberal Unionist and Chancellor of the Exchequer 1886 – 92.

26 March [41 Grosvenor Road]

Beatrice Chamberlain paid me one of her annual visits, and we had a long talk on politics, carefully avoiding the L.C.C. and the Speakership. She was anxious to know our opinion of the Factory Bill – was it a good bill, did it go far enough? I gather from her attitude that J.C. is friendly to regulation of private enterprise and has no prejudices in favour of 'free trade' in labour. I told her that the Bill was excellent so far as it went, but might easily be made better by certain amendments. I felt inclined to offer to send her the amendments but I am not sufficiently certain of Joseph Chamberlain's *bona fides* to be completely confidential. One great advantage of the Bill is that at last we get recognized the principle I have been fighting for for five years, the responsibility of the *giver out of work* for conditions of employment. My own pet invention – labour legislation – I am glad to see at last embodied in the black and white of a government bill.

Costelloe. An old friend of Sidney's: ten years ago he was a pushing young politician full of cleverness and ambition, just married to an exceedingly pretty American girl of family and means [Mary Pearsall Smith], stepping into the political arena as Radical candidate in the Chamberlain interest for Edinburgh in opposition to Goschen in 1885. Made friends with the Fabians and was the first person at all within the political world who hobnobbed with them. Since that time poor Costelloe has lived through a domestic tragedy and has largely failed as a public man. His wife has deserted him, leaving their two little girls on his hands, living for the most part abroad in close friendship with an American Jew [Bernard Berenson], but occasionally returning to see her children when her husband happens to be away from home. The case is complicated by Costelloe's fear that his little girls brought up as Catholics will be demoralized by the mother's free thought and anarchic ways – his struggle to be firm and even generous to his wife and yet to protect his children from her influence is pathetic. All this would have embittered most men, but though it has saddened Costelloe and increased the grouchiness of his manners it has not made any serious inroads into his self-complacency. I said that he was a failure in public life. That is hardly fair. He makes a good income at the Bar and journalism, he is one of the principal men on the L.C.C. But he has lost favour with the public just as he lost the affection of his wife. He starts with a most unpleasant personality. Lame and affected with a skin disease, he is physically disagreeable if not repulsive. Then he is curiously jesuitical, over-ingenious, affectedly diplomatic. Always debating, constantly posing, never wholly true to himself, he gives the ordinary man an uncomfortable feeling that he is being over-reached . . . .

W.A.S. Hewins (1865 – 1931) was a young economist at Pembroke College, Oxford, whom the Webbs had met by chance when they were researching in the Bodleian Library for their trade union history. He was not their first choice for Director of the London School of Economics, for Graham Wallas had already declined when Sidney wrote to Hewins on 24 March: Hewins was appointed five days later. Temporary premises were found at 9 John Street, Adelphi. The Hutchinson lecturers were supported by part of the legacy and the L.C.C. lecturers were paid out of T.E.B. funds. David F.Schloss was on the staff of the Labour Department in the Board of Trade. Sir William Acworth (1850 – 1925) was a barrister and railway economist. H.S. Foxwell (1849 – 1936), was a conservatively-minded professor of political economy at University College, London, who had built up a remarkable collection of books on economics that Webb hoped to acquire for the L.S.E. Charles Trevelyan (1870 – 1958) was a wealthy young Liberal who was close to the Webbs in his youth. He was elected to the London School Board in 1896, was a Liberal M.P. 1899 – 1918, and a Labour M.P. 1922 – 31. Herbert Samuel (1870 – 1963) was a Liberal M.P. who first held office in 1906: he shared the Webb interest in social questions and remained a personal friend.

9 April. [41 Grosvenor Road]
Settled down to work again. Finishing each chapter now as we go along ready to be typewritten and submitted to Shaw. Have settled down quite comfortably to work again, spending all our mornings over our book and Sidney at the L.C.C. in the afternoon. Re-elected chairman of Technical Education Board, and giving a good deal of time to that and the starting of the 'London School of Economics and Political Science'. Selected Hewins (a young Oxford don) as Director, engaged Wallas and Schloss as Hutchinson lecturers, and Acworth and probably Foxwell as L.C.C. lecturers. Also, in treaty with Chamber of Commerce and Society of Arts for rooms free of charge. Great good luck that Sidney happens to be chairman of the Technical Education Board – able to combine the two 'sources'; promises well just at present but impossible to tell whether the old gang won't wake up and cry out before the institution is fairly started which would delay, possibly balk, our plans . . . .

Sidney and I are both somewhat exhausted and we go tomorrow for a week to Beachy Head with a party of six – Graham Wallas and Bernard Shaw, Albert Ball (an old fellow traveller in the Tyrol), C.P. Trevelyan and Herbert Samuel (a wealthy young Jew with Fabian proclivities), and, as the only other woman beside myself, Bertha Newcombe, the Fabian artist. What fortunate people we are: Love, Work, Friends and Health, given holidays whenever we need it! An Ideal Life!

25 April. [41 Grosvenor Road]
A 'jolly' time at Beachy Head, learning the bicycle and sitting out chatting on the cliff. Sidney and I both felt better for the change, but

now down again, he with his usual cold in the head, I with my usual bowel trouble. Find it hard to do brainwork and keep well in London. Our plan is to work all the morning and then for Sidney to be at L.C.C. work the rest of the day, I meanwhile idling or attending committees. But whether it is the constant excitement of London life and the atmosphere of 'news' in which one lives or whether I am simply growing old, I do not find that I am strong enough for much real brainwork. I get a spurt on for two or three days and then I collapse with indigestion or other complaints and have to spend most of my day in open air and exercise and lying down to set me on my feet again. If it were only the book one had to think about! Two mornings a week at least we spend patching up other people's work, writing memoranda for politicians or answering conundrums from foreign and native socialists. Sidney believes in helping all and sundry, in always being ready with advice and suggestions, in giving himself away to the world at large . . . .

F.Y. Edgeworth (1845 – 1926) was professor of political economy at King's College, London; he had formed a forlorn attachment to Beatrice shortly before she met Sidney.

8 May. [41 Grosvenor Road]
The London School looks promising. Hewins has talked over the principal economists including Marshall and Edgeworth; we have squared Foxwell; the Society of Arts and Chamber of Commerce are giving us their rooms free; the Technical Education Board has voted the £500 a year; the trustees are amenable and apparently there is no hitch of any kind. I myself am anxious that the 'show' lecture side should not be too much developed, and that we should concentrate on getting *research really done.* For that object I should like to gather round us all the able young men and women who are taking to economics, free their minds of prejudices and start them with a high ideal of accuracy and exhaustiveness in work. If there is one thing I have believed 'from the beginning to the end', it is that no progress can be made except on the basis of ascertained fact and carefully thought-out suggestion. Despite our theory, bias, creed and prejudice, we are all equally wandering in the labyrinth, searching for the clue of true facts to bring us out on the right side of each particular problem. It is pitiful to see the narrow sectarian view most Socialists take, binding themselves hand and foot by a series of shibboleths. The working-

men are especially afflicted with the theological temperament, the implicit faith in a certain creed which has been 'revealed' to them by a sort of inner light. 'Why is it that I, a poor ignorant man,' said [H.W.] Hobart, one of the I.L.P., to me yesterday, 'have perceived *the truth*, whilst educated men with leisure and brains are still adhering to the old errors; unless I am right in saying they are mostly knaves?' Poor I.L.P., there will be a rude awakening and a disheartening collapse.

27 May. [41 Grosvenor Road]
A grey outlook in political situation. A heavy reaction setting in against the Liberal government – the Haves thoroughly frightened, the Have-nots unsatisfied. Within the Liberal Party each man complaining of the other, no comradeship or cohesion, all at sixes and sevens with regard to opinions.

Sir Hugh Bell (1844 – 1931) was a coal and iron master in the Tyne area, a director of Brunner Mond, Dorman Long and the London North Eastern Railway. He and his wife were interested in social problems. The Booths had seven children. The eldest, Antonia (called 'Dodo'), was born in 1873, the youngest, Charles, in 1886. Tom, the eldest son, born in 1874, became Colonel-in-Chief of the Gordon Highlanders. Charles Booth was still engaged on his many-volumed survey of London life and labour, but he was particularly concerned at this time with the aged poor. He was a member of the Royal Commission of 1905. In December 1891, in a paper to the Statistical Society, he had put forward the idea of state pensions for the old.

28 May. [41 Grosvenor Road]
The other night the Booths dined here to meet Hewins and Hugh Bell, and to be informed as to the London School. It was the first time Charlie had been in my house since our marriage (Mary has called periodically). Charles Booth has not changed one whit – he is still the sincere simple-natured man, with an aloof intellectual interest in human affairs, that I knew so well and cared so deeply for years ago. Of course he is now the acquaintance and not the friend. But surely it is not pure imagination that makes me see a change in Mary, a change so fundamental that even if we would we could not again be intimate. From the curiously unconventional little puritan living in almost eccentric simplicity, spending her whole day teaching her little ones and reading books, she has become the worldly-wise woman living in great style whose main preoccupation for the last year has been to get her eldest son into the smartest possible regiment.

After dinner, when she and I retired, I listened for some twenty minutes to her account of the unsuccessful struggles to get Tom into the Guards and the successful compromise of the Black Watch. She was smartly dressed, her hair twisted into the last new knot, her face and figure looking singularly young, bright and charming, resembling much more her portrait as a girl than the highly-strung, worn, dowdy 'mother, friend and wife' that I knew and loved so well for fifteen years. Is it possible that the husband's influence has been slowly killed by the children's? And that Mary has been 'demoralized' by these polished young persons she has taken so much pains to educate? For the family seems strangely incongruous – Charlie living most of the week in an artisan's house in a back street in Liverpool – not for the purpose of investigation but simply because 'it suits him' – Mary carrying on a great house in London and one in the country entertaining the smart young friends of her children. She told me much of Tom's social triumphs, was always recurring to their 'riding in the Row', to their parties, to this and that semi-fashionable friendship, until I became dazed with my attempts to fit in this Mary with the Mary I knew years ago, and fell into a silent fit of wondering whether it was I or she who had so completely transformed our point of view. She treated me with half-condescending kindness, but was full of her own affairs. Her expression I watched narrowly – she looked exceedingly happy. Compared to her old self, she looked as if some *weight* had been lifted off – as if she were breathing freer and living more according to her own will. Again I say, is it possible that her old self was largely a reflection of Charlie's noble nature and her old tastes a reflex of his simplicity, and that now her children have liberated her and she has rebounded to her natural position? I remember hearing of her when she was a girl as a socially ambitious and rather artificial woman and her portrait bore that expression. But I always regarded the portrait and the description as libellous and could not make out how persons could have so misunderstood her. Now I begin to think I was mistaken and that the dear sweet modest little woman, hating society and loving strenuous effort, was a beautiful distortion, all the fine qualities intensified, all the evil poor motives minimized by the constant companionship of a singularly fine and unique personality. Now her daily companionship is of a different order. For some reason or other, the children are common stuff – Tom a pleasure-loving self-indulgent lad, Dodo a self-complacent artificial woman and the others all commonplace. An interesting study – this possible deterioration of a parent through the influence of the children! Anyway, this change, probably a slow and silent growth, explains the whole alteration in her attitude towards me. Poor Mary! How irksome my friendship must have been to her for years before she shook me off, how complete and satisfactory the occasion for the final severance – my marriage to an undersized, underbred, and 'unendowed' little socialist! If I had only perceived this 'growth' I should have saved myself all the intense misery, I should have spared her all the extreme annoyance of my long and fierce struggle to keep the friendship. Anyway, I will keep the memory of it intact. After all, there remains the big fact that for the fifteen hardest years of my life they were my best and most helpful friends – Mary as well as Charlie.

12 June. Casthrop Farm, Derbyshire
Three or four days at a noisy, dirty railway hotel at Huddersfield, attending the Co-operative Congress. Lost much of its interest. I have no longer anything to learn from the Co-operators. I have measured with my particular gauge their movement; to other students it will no doubt reveal new aspects, for me its meaning is exhausted. . . .

The Liberal government was defeated on a snap vote on 21 June 1895, and in the election that followed the Conservatives were returned with a majority of 152. Harcourt and Morley were among the prominent Liberals who lost their seats, as did Keir Hardie. The new government under Lord Salisbury launched on a policy of expansive imperialism. Jesse Collings (1831–1920) was a Radical M.P. who had followed Chamberlain: he was a passionate supporter of smallholdings, and coined the famous slogan 'Three Acres and a Cow!' Joseph Powell Williams (1840–1904) was a Liberal Unionist M.P. for Birmingham, and Chamberlain's right-hand man. Austen Chamberlain (1863–1937) was the son of Joseph Chamberlain. Elected as a Liberal Unionist in 1892, he became Civil Lord of the Admiralty in 1895, Chancellor of the Exchequer in 1903, and held high offices in Conservative governments until 1931.

8 July. [41 Grosvenor Road]
On the eve of the general election. The Fabians are sitting with their hands in their laps. From our point of view no result can be satisfactory. The Liberals, even on the eve of dissolution, show no signs of grace, they go unabsolved to their grave – if anything, rather inclined to repent their good deeds, not to regret their lost opportunities. Lords, Home Rule and Local Veto are their battle-cries – Rosebery, Morley and Harcourt voicing each separately. The

I.L.P. is splashing about in a futile ineffectual fashion, the S.D.F. turning all its energies into a fanatical crusade against John Burns! We wish the Liberals to be beaten but we do not wish the Tories to win. A tie or something near a tie would suit us best. But it looks like a triumphant majority for the Tories. Nor does there seem much hope in the future. The Liberal Party is pledged to three measures which offend all the conservative instincts of the people – Home Rule, Local Veto and Church Disestablishment – without exciting the slightest enthusiasm among the advanced section of their party. Sometimes we think we are in for a long spell of strong Conservative rule, beginning with 1895, and lasting possibly for another twenty years with only short interregnums of weak Liberal governments. For the Liberals have no leaders inspired with a new faith. Asquith has been ruined by marrying a silly ignorant wife, and there is no other man who has at once capacity, character and conviction. The Labour men are mere babies in politics; judging from our knowledge of the Labour movement we can expect *no* leader from the working class. Our only hope is in permeating the young middle-class men, catching them for collectivism before they have enlisted on the other side.

Though the situation looks bad for our side of things, it is impossible not to be amused and interested in the political drama. Chamberlain is the Man of the Moment. He has kept the little band of Liberal Unionists separate and compact for ten years, and now, just before they must of necessity melt away, he has deftly used them to ride into power, dragging into the government the faithful Jesse [Collings], the servile Powell Williams, and the amiable youth, Austen. The humour of the situation is the fact that the majority of the Liberal Unionists in the House of Commons have been anti-Chamberlainites, more hostile in their hearts to 'Joe' than the bigoted Tories! It is a testimony to the marvellous force of Chamberlain's personality that he pervades this election – no one trusts him, no one likes him, no one really believes in him, and yet everyone accepts him as the leader of the united Unionists. His position in the Tory Party is, in fact, very similar to his position in 1885 in the Liberal Party. Is it equally unstable? Will he play again the role of the usurper to keep his seat on the throne – or does he believe sufficiently in his new party to serve it faithfully? I am inclined to think that, barring accidents from evil temper, the cause of 'property' is sufficiently attractive to Chamberlain's mind to keep him from wilful wrecking. I am inclined to think that on the whole Salisbury has got a fair consideration in the bargain of the last few days. But alas! for the poor dear Liberal Unionists – that little company of upright, narrowly enlightened well-bred men, who drifted away from the Liberal Party ostensibly on Home Rule, but mainly because of the shoddy social schemes 'Joe' had imposed on Gladstone. To be used as the ladder up which 'Joe' climbs into a Conservative government, waving aloft his banner of shoddy reform, then to be thrown ignominiously aside. A fit ending for a company of prigs! . . .

VOLUME 16

16 July. [41 Grosvenor Road]
Attended London Trades Council meeting last Thursday . . . the most astounding fact about this meeting was the total absence of any reference, or even a by-the-way allusion, to the approaching general election. It is almost inconceivable that a meeting of the representative working-men of London should be held within four days of the general election without taking apparently the slightest notice of it. It is another proof of the disastrous political incapacity of the present trade union leaders. The trade union world seems half para-lysed . . . the I.L.P. journals – *Clarion* and *Labour Leader* – have published no programme, have given no lead, except Keir Hardie's futile suggestion that I.L.P. voters should spoil their ballot papers by writing the name of some woman as candidate. Even the miners seem to be in a state of political suspended animation.

Of course this has meant a rout for the anti-Conservatives (really that is the only generic term wide enough to cover the numberless groups) all along the line – Sir William Harcourt being smashed at Derby and Keir Hardie at West Ham! The rout is quite indiscriminate – if the official Liberals have been extinguished, the Labour Party has certainly not won. Some dozen seats have probably been lost by Labour candidatures, but where the Liberal has stood aside, the Labour man has failed to win the place.

To us the result is not altogether unsatisfactory. From our point of view the field had to be cleared . . . The utter rout – the annihilation one might almost say – of the Harcourt faction, the hopeless discredit into which such reforms as Local Veto, Home Rule, Church Disestablishment have fallen, clears the field of a good deal of

cumbrous debris. On the other hand, the I.L.P. has completed its
suicide. Its policy of abstention and deliberate wrecking is proved to
be futile and absurd. Keir Hardie has probably lost for good any
chance of posturing as an M.P. and will sink into the old place of a
discredited labour leader. So long as the I.L.P. existed as an unknown
force of irreconcilables the more reasonable policy of permeation and
levelling up was utterly checkmated.

I do not mean to say that events have gone as we wished. Two years
ago we hoped not only to go on levelling up the great body of Liberals
but also to weed out of the party, by a reasonable and discriminating
Labour policy, the reactionaries; and thus possibly bring about a
small Tory majority. But directly we discovered the 'ruck-up' of
official Liberalism on the one hand, and the utterly unreasonable
attitude of the I.L.P. on the other, we saw plainly that *our* game was
up. *We* were beaten in the local elections of last autumn and this
spring. From the general election we held aloof, refusing either to
back the I.L.P. or support the Liberals. The rout of both therefore is
no defeat for us. It leaves us free, in fact, to begin afresh on the old
lines – of building up a new party on the basis of collectivism.
Whether the English nation desires the change, or can be brought to
desire it; whether, if it does desire it, it will have the patience to work it
out, is to my mind still an open question. In any case it will be a long
business, and mainly dependent on the levelling up of character and
intelligence in the mass of the people. Meanwhile the affairs of the
nation are in the hands of an exceptionally able set of men who have
been elected as trustees of the *status quo*. There is little danger of
reaction, either in administration or legislation. The Conservatives
are pledged up to the hilt to a policy of social reform, and the worst
they can do is to stand still.

'It is vile country for bicycling,' Shaw wrote to the actress Janet Achurch on 8
July, in one of several descriptions of his falls and scrapes in the Wye Valley lanes.
He was spending his holiday writing *The Man of Destiny*.

4 August. The Argoed
Settled again for the summer in the old home – Shaw, Sidney and I,
awaiting Wallas and Rosy and Noel to join us presently. Brought with
us our three bicycles (most absorbing new toys) and endless work
including an article on municipalization and one on state regulation of
women's labour, and our book. Sidney has settled down to his article.

I am trying to fashion our first chapter ready for him to execute, so that it may be typewritten for Shaw to look over, with the other two that are already done, during his stay here. In spite of the cold and the waterspouts and hailstorms we are very happy – the same delightful old combination of honeymoon, intellectual work and friendship that we have known these last three summers. Just these first days it is rather a struggle to work – the cold wet weather, the reaction from the rush of London and my monthly trouble all combining to make me sleepy and lazy. But this summer I am quite healthy, have fixed on a diet and found an exercise that suits me. Bicycling has brought some 'fun' or 'sport' into my life, an element that was rather lacking in our workaday and somewhat strained existence. We go plodding on with our book, with a childlike faith that some one will value its detailed and carefully wrought analysis. Most persons will think it 'much to-do about nothing'. We plod on in the faith that it will be a sample of political and economic research, a foretaste of what the 'New School' will do in other departments. . . .

9 September. [The Argoed]
Trades Union Congress. On Sunday week Sidney, Shaw and I left here about 10 o'clock on our cycles, rode through the exquisite valley of Raglan, Usk to Newport, thence along the coast to Cardiff, our first long ride (forty miles) arriving at the great Park Hotel hot, dusty and pleasantly self-complacent with our new toy and its exploits. It is certainly attractive – riding through the beautiful country, trundling slowly up hills and rushing down, with feet up, every incline. The only disadvantage being the intolerable thirst you suffer as a novice. One's 'bike' is a great addition to the pleasure of life – we have still to prove that it does not detract from one's desire, if not one's capacity, for work. . . .

William Pollard Byles (1839–1917) was the editor of the *Bradford Observer* and at the time of his election as Radical M.P. for Shipley he was a Fabian sympathizer. After he was chosen as a candidate Beatrice decided he was 'a poor creature' who was eager 'to conciliate the Gladstonians'. His wife was a stronger personality, inclined to Labour views. Bertrand Russell (1872–1970), philosopher and mathematician, had married, in December 1894, Alys Pearsall Smith (1867–1951), sister of Mary and Logan (1865–1946), man of letters. Their parents Robert (1827–98) and Hannah (1832–1911) Pearsall Smith were well-to-do American Quakers who had settled in England, living three doors away from the Webb house in Grosvenor Road and also renting a large establishment at

Friday's Hill near Haslemere. The Russell marriage broke up in 1911, though the Webbs retained a close association with both Bertrand and Alys for some years. Bertrand's father, Viscount Amberley (1842–1876), died before his father, the first Earl Russell (1792–1878). Arthur Pelham was the younger son of the Earl of Chichester. In 1883 he and his wife Evelyne had settled at Moorcroft, a neighbouring property to The Argoed.

25 September. Grosvenor Road

Back again at Grosvenor Road after a really effective holiday at The Argoed. The dear old place more beautiful than ever – the large rooms and general ease of the house a luxury, the absolute peace delightful. I have seldom been so lazy on a holiday – Sidney, too, for the first time, fully enjoyed the life. Shaw stayed with us the whole of the seven weeks: Graham came for a fortnight but was restless and not quite happy in our company. He is going through a crisis – wants to leave the Fabian Society and be free of all formulas and intellectual ties so as to give himself over, as he thinks, to empirical administration and 'untrammelled' thought. It is interesting to watch the struggle in his mind. He says, as I think truly, that he has not changed his mind and that he is still an economic collectivist of an empirical kind. And he admits that the Fabian Society has explicitly and implicitly declared its creed to be purely empirical or hypothetical. But he complains that some of the members and the greater part of the public identify the word socialist with a cut-and-dried formula held with theological fervour; that on the one hand he is treated as a traitor by the extreme section, and on the other hand as a fanatic by the outside public – that his position is misunderstood. Behind this are the facts; in his present life on the School Board and in his University Extension work he is constantly associating with cultivated sceptics, either with the purely practical or with the purely academic mind. To these men the socialists are either irritating or contemptible and Graham naturally resents the feeling he is arousing. He lacks patience to quietly persist and live the misunderstanding down; he wants to cut the whole thing away and start fresh in the world. Many long talks we had with him . . . . Poor Graham, he is one of those sensitive self-conscious men who will always be in trouble about his soul. Anyway his present attitude makes him restless and unsatisfied with us. He is lonely and overworked and wants a little mental coddling – and we are inclined to douche him with cold water! . . . I must see whether I cannot show more tact. I am horribly narrow and limited and Sidney and I are obviously self-complacent in our perfectly happy married life. I must rouse myself to more sympathy.

Bernard Shaw is a perfect 'house friend' – self-sufficient, witty and tolerant, going his own way and yet adapting himself to your ways. If only he would concentrate his really brilliant intellect on some consecutive thought.

The Byles (editor of the *Bradford Observer*) and the Bertrand Russells spent some days with us. Russell a young aristocrat – the son of old friends of our family, the Amberleys – a *very young* man with considerable intellectual promise, subtle and contentious but anarchic in his dislike of working in teams. Has married a pretty bright American Quakeress some years older than himself with anarchic views of life, also hating routine. The Pelhams were there – reminding one of old times – Mrs Pelham an adorer of Shaw's (Shaw's public is not of a solid sort – it is made up of dilettantes). Finished our holiday by a three days' ride in exquisite weather by Bath, Warminster, Stonehenge, Andover, arriving here dusty and hot early yesterday morning. Must now set to and work hard at the book. It is hanging somewhat heavily on our hands . . . . Hewins dropped in this morning [to talk] chiefly about the success of the School, which promises well.

Robert Charles Phillimore (1871–1919), the well-to-do son of a judge, was an active Fabian who served with Bernard Shaw on the St Pancras Vestry and was Sidney's L.C.C. running mate in Deptford 1898–1910. His wife, Lucy, known as 'Lion', was active in many progressive causes. Henry Macrosty, a civil servant who was a member of the Fabian Executive from 1895 to 1907, supported the Webbs in the internal disputes in the Society. John W. Martin, an early Fabian with special interests in education, also served on the Fabian Executive before emigrating to New York. Beatrice's old friend Dr Mandell Creighton (1843–1901), a distinguished churchman and historian, was to become Bishop of London in 1897. The National Union of Women Workers was established at Nottingham in 1895: it was not a trade union but a grouping of women interested in women's organizations. Beatrice's friend Louise Creighton (1850–1936) was the dominant personality. Beatrice later found that it was too much under the control of the wives of the bishops and she objected to the opening of meetings with prayers.

18 October. Grosvenor Hotel, Manchester
Sidney and I journeyed down here to cultivate Rochdale, Sidney speaking to the I.L.P. and I holding forth from the pulpit of a large Congregational church on the ethics of factory legislation. Rochdale, if ever Sidney thought of going into Parliament, is a possible

constituency, at present held by a Tory owing to a split between Labour and Liberal. But Parliament seems further off than ever. We are loath to give up our quiet life of thought and enquiry, and we are discouraged by the hopeless state of Progressive politics. Those who form the backbone of the Liberal Party, who dominate the party machinery, who own the wealth, who to a large extent monopolize the intelligence, have no convictions on all the questions that interest working-men. At the best they are timid empiricists, who if they are assured that collectivism is the 'coming creed' give it a faint-hearted support. For the most part they are secretly hostile – they dare not proclaim their hostility, so they remain dumb trying to evade the questions as outside 'practical politics'. These men would prefer to see a Conservative government in power than to allow the leaders of their own side to push forward 'social democracy' . . . . Now we collectivists have to assert ourselves as a distinct school of thought, taking up each question separately and reviewing it in the light of our principles. But the first need of a School of Thought is to *think*. Our special mission seems to be to undertake the difficult problems ourselves, and to gather round us young men and women who will more or less study under inspiration. At present we have a certain set of young people all more or less devoted to the Fabian Junta. Herbert Samuel, Charles Trevelyan, Bobby Phillimore, Bertrand Russell – all rich men of the upper or middle class, and MacDonald, Martin, Macrosty of the lower middle class. The London School of Economics should furnish others. But, in order to occupy this position, we must to some extent hold ourselves aloof, and, above all, we must be, and what is more or at least equally important, we must *appear* absolutely disinterested.

At present that position seems inconsistent with any attempt to push forward a political career. If Sidney goes into Parliament he must go as an 'independent', elected on account of his peculiar opinions and more or less the leader of a new party either within the Liberal organization or outside it. No other position would compensate to the Cause for his loss as an active thinker and administrator; no other position could make up for the personal sacrifice of giving up our joint work and life of learned 'leisure'! for the inconvenience, separation and turmoil of a political career.

Three days at the Women's Conference at Nottingham. This National Union of Women Workers sprang out of a sort of federation of philanthropic societies to befriend young girls. Louise

Creighton with great energy and considerable capacity has organized it into a somewhat incoherent federation of all societies of women dealing with industrial, philanthropic and educational matters. Its chief function is to hold an annual conference to which all women who work are invited to listen to papers on any conceivable topic and discuss. Hitherto it has been dominated by bishops' wives and deaconesses, is almost flagrantly non-political and distinctly religious in tone. Louise persuaded me last spring to be co-opted on to the Executive and this year to stand for re-election by the General Committee composed of the representatives of the various societies . . . Here I thought was an association which would bring me into touch with women all over the country, the silent good and narrow women who do so much to form the undercurrents of public opinion, women whom in one's secular and revolutionary set one never comes across . . . The conference consisted of about six hundred, mostly middle-aged well-to-do, but a good many hardworking professional philanthropists, guardians of the poor etc. A very fair assembly, well-meaning, with a slight tendency to 'cant' but sober and on the whole open-minded, thoroughly typical of provincial English middle class . . . . Altogether the Conference was promising; it opens out virgin soil to Fabians, possibly rather stony!

12 November. The Angel, Chesterfield
Away on one of my investigating tours. Attended a Derbyshire Miners council meeting . . . a stupid stolid lot of men characterized by fairmindedness and kindliness – but oh! how dense! . . . Is it the abnormal quantity of whisky these good fellows drink, without being drunk, that deadens their intelligence, or is it brainwork carried on by an uncultivated and untrained mind that exhausts all the intelligence? How can anyone fear anything but unmitigated conservatism from the English Democracy? . . . Of course there remains the fact that their real interests are on the side of economic collectivism, and sooner or later they will, I suppose, perceive it in a dim sort of way. But it will have to be dinned into them, and they will depend exclusively on middle-class leadership for years to come.

Leonard Trelawny Hobhouse (1864–1929), a cousin of Henry Hobhouse, later professor of sociology at the University of London, was currently fellow of Corpus Christi College, Oxford: his works included *The Labour Movement* (1893) and *Morals in Evolution* (1906). George Macaulay Trevelyan (1876–1962), who became a distinguished historian and Master of Trinity College, Cambridge, was the younger brother of Charles Trevelyan, who was translating *The Referendum in Switzerland,* published in London in 1898; Robert Calverley Trevelyan (1872–1951), poet and man of letters, was the third of the three brothers, and a helper in some of the Webb campaigns. Welcombe, near Stratford-upon-Avon, was the family home of Lady Trevelyan, though she and her husband normally lived at Wallington, their Northumberland mansion.

Christmas. Welcombe

On the whole a satisfactory autumn. Our own little bit of work, the Book, is slowly progressing . . . We have recovered from our feelings of depression at the widespread [political] reaction – we have turned our hopes from propaganda to education, from the working class to the middle class . . . Having been beaten back in our endeavour to make a London Progressive Party with a permanent majority, we are creating the London School of Economics and Political Science as a wider foundation than street-corner preaching. Hewins is making a success of the School – 200 to 300 students attending the different classes and lectures. It is honestly scientific, served indeed by more individualist lecturers than collectivists, because the individualists are still the better men. But collectivists are encouraged, and the younger men and women are brought under 'collectivist' influence. We are to some extent trying to gather the promising students round us. We are also trying our best to attract the clever men from the universities – Sidney and Wallas lecturing at Oxford and Cambridge – and letting it be known that anyone coming up who is interested in economics will have a warm welcome at Grosvenor Road. Leonard Hobhouse recruits for us at Oxford, the young Trevelyans at Cambridge. All this means a good deal of expenditure of time, sympathy and alas! money. One cannot keep open house and live economically.

Now we are spending a peaceful Xmas at Welcombe, the gorgeous mansion belonging to Lady Trevelyan. Charles Trevelyan asked us down here for a week – we, his brother George and a friend 'camping out' in one of the wings with one manservant and a due number of maids. The younger brother is a youth of great promise. Tall and graceful with a sensitive face, small intellectual head, dark rich colouring, expressive eyes, a keen conversationalist and sympathetic companion, he would be a singularly attractive youth if he were not so uncannily self-possessed and self-controlled. He is bringing himself up to be a great man, is precise and methodical in all his ways, ascetic and regular in his habits, eating according to rule, 'exercising' according to rule, going to bed according to rule and neither smoking, tea or coffee drinking, nor touching alcohol. Sport he indulges in with the deliberate object of cultivating the barbarian in himself, fearing the scholar's overwork and hypochondria. He is always analysing his powers and carefully considering how he can make the best of himself. In intellectual parts he is brilliant, with a wonderful memory, keen analytic power and a vivid style. In his philosophy of life, he is, at present, commonplace, but then he is young – only nineteen!

Charles Trevelyan (aged twenty-five) is a dear lovable boy – simple, direct, genuinely public-spirited. I am not sure about his future, for I have not yet made up my mind whether he has the capacity for sustained and serious work. Excellent common sense, sound instincts and sanguine happy temperament, he only needs real capacity for work and a dash of talent to make him a considerable politician . . . For him a good deal will depend on his wife to whom he will be devoted – George's wife will have to be devoted to him or she will have a bad time of it!

Sidney is very happy here discussing and arguing with these boys, correcting Charles's translation of the book on the Referendum, listening to George's historical essays and giving hints. It is a new and good experience to him to have young men of capacity and training seeking advice and, in doing so, testing his arguments and statements of fact. And he is singularly happy in his manner with them, drawing them out and appreciating all they say, and yet criticizing frankly. The perfect happiness of his own life has cured his old defects of manner, he has lost the aggressive self-assertive tone, the slight touch of insolence which was only another form of shyness, and has gained immeasurably in persuasiveness. Partly, no doubt, his administrative work as chairman of the Technical Education Board has taught him how to manage men and get them to adopt his views; partly also his standard of knowledge has undoubtedly risen and he no longer feels so cock-sure of his own position. But principally his improved manner is due to happiness – to the blessed fact of loving and being loved with a love without flaw or blemish.

✑ 1896 ✐

Stephen Hobhouse (1881–1964) was the eldest son of Henry and Margaret Hobhouse who had seven children in all. The two surviving daughters (Esther Margaret having died in infancy) were Rachel (1883–1981) and Eleanor (1884–1956). The other sons were Arthur (1886–1965), John (1893–1961) and Paul (1894–1918). Joseph Chamberlain, appointed Colonial Secretary when the Conservatives took office in July, had been encouraging Cecil Rhodes (1853–1902), Prime Minister of the Cape Colony, in a forward policy in South Africa. The crisis in the Transvaal was the abortive Jameson Raid, in which Dr Starr Jameson of the South Africa Company crossed the border into the Boer republic of the Transvaal with five hundred men on 29 December 1895. He was captured three days later.

5 January. Parmoor

Two other visits, and we are back tomorrow at our work. Five days at Hadspen – Sidney's first introduction to the Hobhouse household. For Henry he has always had an honest liking, admiring his public spirit and his refined view of life, and his painstaking industry. Henry's great lack is intellectual initiative and moral experience; he is narrow and limited – so to speak, blind to whole sides of life and quite incapable of unworthy motif. In this imperfect world these high and chivalrous qualities are admirable. Perhaps it has weighed with us that alone among my brothers-in-law he has welcomed Sidney with grave courtesy into the family, has always treated him with respect and friendliness, has apparently never felt that repulsion which most of my brothers-in-law have shown to him – either on account of his lack of social status or because of his opinions.

Maggie of course is the same high-spirited, rather vulgar and sharp-tongued woman, has cut her nature down to suit her husband's intellectual limitations without raising it to conform to her husband's moral standard. There is always therefore a jar in the house, Maggie protesting against Henry's quixotic principles, Henry silently resenting her plots and plans for social advancement and pecuniary saving. The family life suffers a little from this jar and loses in grace and charm. But this is only superficial. The two are honestly fond of each other, and Margaret is a capable and wholly devoted mother. Stephen, the eldest boy, now scholar at Eton, is a tall, lanky, ugly boy, unspoilt and simple-minded, with none of the public schoolboy's 'side' – industrious, discreet, and interested in men and things. No charm of body or mind except an unsullied honesty and purity of nature. The little girls are correct and well-mannered, bright and happy, very pleasant to look at and quite sufficiently intelligent . . . . The most marked general feature of all of them is the lack of that introspective morbid character that distinguished most of us. Neither Stephen nor the two girls show any curiosity about religion, they all conform and never ask questions . . . I should imagine that Stephen Hobhouse is destined by his character to be a civil servant, in which case we may hope to see something of this boy, to whom I feel drawn.

After five days at Hadspen we came on here . . . Alfred, after a brilliant professional career, is entering political life with all self-assurance and ambition of the man who has never failed. And what a contrast to Henry! With a wide though superficial knowledge of human affairs, with the typical advocate's temperament, Alfred has chosen his political party and means to abide by it . . . With infinitely more intelligence, knowledge and sympathy than Henry, he is far less capable of a sound political judgement . . . Having decided to stand by his class, being honestly (and no doubt justly) convinced that that class has everything to lose and nothing to gain by an alteration in the *status quo*, the one thing needful is to appeal to the popular suspicion, fear, prejudices and fallacies to keep back any further 'reforms' . . .

The whole mind of the country is at present absorbed in foreign politics. There has been a dramatic interest in the Transvaal events. 'Private enterprise' in international matters has I think been finally discredited so far as England is concerned. And the occasion has found the man. Joe Chamberlain is today the National Hero. Only a small section – the extreme Tories of the Alfred Cripps type – withhold their admiration for the swiftness and courage with which he has grappled with the crisis. Whether his Cabinet altogether appreciates the autocratic way in which he deals single-handed with every event is an interesting question of Cabinet politics. But his ways – his strong will, assiduity and reasonableness – have certainly given the nation confidence, not only in his administration of the Colonies but in the Conservative government. In these troubled times, with every nation secretly disliking us, it is a comfortable thought that we have a government of strong resolute men, not given either to bluster or vacillation, but prompt in taking every measure to keep us out of a war and to make us successful should we be forced in to it.

88

15 January. Birmingham

Came here last night on receipt of telegram from Ashton that I might attend Miners' Federation Annual Conference . . . .

Ben Pickard (1842–1904), a Yorkshire miner who played a leading part in the 1893 strike, was a Liberal M.P. 1885–1904.

16 January. Birmingham

Sitting for five or six hours in a 'stinking' room with an open sewer on one side and ill-ventilated urinals on the other is not an invigorating occupation. But in spite of headache and general depression I am glad I came. These two days' debate have made me better appreciate the sagacity, good temper and fair-mindedness of these miners than I could have done by reading endless reports. Their speeches, to which, by the way, there is no limit, are admirable – clear, to the point, and show a thorough grip of the subject. Of course the whole debate turned on minute technical points, exactly the questions which these officials are always dealing with and with which they are therefore thoroughly familiar . . . . I rather expected they would ask me to say a few words but Pickard evidently did not intend to, so I shook hands cordially with him and left just after the vote of thanks to the chairman. I hurried back to the hotel, packed up, and left by the first train from that damnable Birmingham for my own dear little home. Found Sidney only too glad to get me back . . . .

Herbert Spencer (1820–1903), the social philosopher, was an old friend of Beatrice and her family and his ideas had been a seminal influence in her youth. He made frequent long visits to Brighton and finally settled at 5 Percival Terrace in 1898. Carrie Darling had been governess in the Playne family and an early friend of Beatrice before she emigrated to Australia.

[?19 January]. *Brighton*

Two rites of friendship! Agreed some time ago to spend a week with Herbert Spencer. A few days before my visit a letter from Carrie Brown (née Darling) to say that she would be in England in a day or two and might she come straight to me. After two days at Grosvenor Road I brought her down here so as not to upset the old gentleman's plans. Here I am, then, spending my time in reviving these old and long unused friendships.

The old man is still living on his living death. He clings desperately to life, watches every symptom, seems devoured by an inward rage at his continual feebleness. 'If I were to be influenced by inductive reasoning I should long ago have believed in the existence of a Devil. For over fifty years I seem to have been pursued by demons.' And yet this old man of seventy-six lives in comfort, can afford to buy every luxury, has far above the average vitality, eats well, goes for months together to his club, continues to spin out his philosophy in volume after volume – has, so far as human observation goes, very little to complain of. But he is terribly exacting, claims from nature as his right a pleasant, agreeable life with the vigour of middle age. So, too, in all his relationships. Everybody must yield to him. He lies in his bed or on his sofa, when he is ill-disposed, and broods over his 'rights', exacts hard terms from his tradesmen, his housekeeper, his secretary, not because he grasps at money, but because he is possessed with this almost religious craze of getting his 'rights'. This temperament makes a visit to his house excessively irksome. He insists on doing his own housekeeping; consequently you get very indifferent food, for he has elaborate theories as to the amount every guest ought to cost him, theories which unfortunately, for you, do not square with the cook's views as to her perquisites! At every hour of the day you feel his presence in the house; you may be sent for or sent away according to whether his pulse goes a little quicker or slower. When you do get a chance of talking to him you feel instinctively that you must either amuse or flatter him – anything else will produce sleeplessness. So he lives on with so many slaves about him, a seedy discontented secretary, a decayed gentlewoman or two to read or play to him, and three other servants – any friends who come have to assume the same position. Poor old man. For all that he is a noble wreck.

Meanwhile I have caught up the threads of another friendship. Carrie Darling, when I was a young girl living in my own home, was my first intellectual friendship. She was the first 'professional' woman I had come across. Fresh from Newnham and full of the fervour and enthusiasm of those early pioneers, saved from priggishness and pedantry by having earned her livelihood from fifteen years of age, by being at least three times engaged to be married before she went to college at twenty-eight – with, in fact, all the charms of a bohemian and a highly trained professional – she captivated my imagination. Her friendship was of the utmost value to me: she stimulated all that was good in me – my love of learning and intellectual ambition, all my moral enthusiasm, and to some extent checked the vulgar materialism brought about by life in second-rate fashionable sets. Her personality had a certain distinction and charm. . . . All this charm is gone. . . For these thirteen years she has lived exclusively with inferiors. Eight years in a small Australian town with all its vulgarity and petty intrigues, five years in an Indian military station consorting with clergy and Eurasians, and, above all, five years' servitude to a husband who is her inferior in every respect – a mere elementary schoolteacher in training and a narrow evangelical prig by constitution. . . . She has practically fled from him. Poor clever Carrie! The whole week we spent in one long tale of married misery. To me the friendship is no longer invigorating. I have lived in some ways a more strenuously 'professional' life than she has, I am satisfied by love, and overburdened with friendships. But there is the supreme value of faithfulness. I hate to think that I have lost the Booths – to drop a friend or be dropped degrades life – makes life seem a horrid morass where anyone may be left to die uncared for. All ties should be made in their degree secure – to be broken only by mutual consent and for very sufficient reasons. The change from youth to age, from success to failure, is no reason. How I hate anarchism in all its forms!

1 March. [Oxford]
Two days at Somerville College. A charming vision of intellectual girlhood. The large quaint red brick building with its conventional garden, the girls' studies with their window-seats from which you can see the Oxford towers and hear the Oxford bells, the calm and peace, the atmosphere of studious leisure without either worldliness or domestic brawls – surely a delightful modern analogue to the convent. How different from the youth of our generation with its storm and stress of quarrelling households and competitive marriage markets! As I sat in the living-room allotted to me, toasting my feet and preparing my lecture for the evening, I felt almost a longing to retire to such a place and give body and soul to 'pure' learning. It is the complete absorption in the intellectual life that gives this college life its charm – the open and avowed cultivation of your intellect without fear of ridicule or abuse for selfishness. Some attractive types of womanhood among the students. It was pleasant, too, to have these young hearts and intellects clustering round me, eager to gain insight and experience and to get a word of counsel from the experienced and somewhat saddened traveller in life's ways. But I was impressed with the narrowness of the life, except to the quite young mind. The

women dons were old maids – the old type of boarding-school mistress. To my mind no woman should be accepted as a tutor who has not lived her life in the outside world. A man don is bad enough but nowadays dons are married, and even in old days they were not presumably 'celibates'.

Even without the excuse of delivering two lectures (one to the Women's Liberal Association, the other to the Somerville girls and their friends) I should have been glad of those two days' experience. It brought back the memory of my old enthusiasm for days spent in study – only instead of the ugly setting of my own girlhood, this beautiful new haven with its stimulating calm now open to the intellectual woman. If I had enjoyed good working health, how I should have revelled in such a life twenty years ago! How life slips away. An elderly woman among all these girls – infinitely their inferior in learning and cultivation but old in the knowledge of human nature and sad with the deepening sense of the complexity of social evil.

The separation of the Library from the L.S.E. as a teaching institution was a characteristic example of Sidney's ingenuity, for it enabled him to raise funds specifically for the Library; and by making the School the nominal tenant of premises occupied by the Library he was able to secure the reduction in rates which was enjoyed by libraries. The Webbs had hoped for a single large benefaction before they began to send out begging letters. John Passmore Edwards (1823–1911) was editor of the *Echo*, a short-lived halfpenny newspaper for which Sidney wrote, a philanthropist and a pacifist. He founded libraries and a settlement in East London, and not long afterwards gave £10,000 to provide the L.S.E. with its first building, on the Clare Market site off Aldwych. Sir Hickman Bacon (1855–1945), the premier baronet in Britain, was a wealthy man who supported some of the Webb projects.

28 March. Grosvenor Road

Our time, for the last five weeks, a good deal taken up with writing 'begging letters' for the Political Science Library. This winter the rapid growth of the School of Economics made new premises inevitable. But how to raise the money? The Technical Education Board which, under Sidney's chairmanship, subsidizes most of the lectures, could not be asked to find premises, and the funds of the Hutchinson Trustees are not inexhaustible. A brilliant idea flashed across Sidney's mind. We needed, for the use of the students, books and reports – why not appeal to the public to subscribe to a Library of Political Science? At first we thought we could get a millionaire to subscribe the whole amount on condition that he called it by his own name. In vain I flattered Passmore Edwards, in vain Sidney pressed Sir Hickman Bacon, in vain we wrote 'on spec' to various magnates. The idea did not impress them. So we decided to scrape money together by small subscriptions. Sidney drafted a circular, Hewins secured the adhesion of the economists and then began a long process of begging letter-writing. Sidney wrote to all the politicians, I raked up all my old ball partners, and between us we have gathered together a most respectable set of contributors, a list which is eloquent testimony to our respectability! Next week the appeal goes out for publication to the press. Even if we collect a comparatively small sum, the issue of the appeal has been a splendid advertisement to the School; and whatever we do get is so much spoil of the Egyptians. Not that we want to deceive the contributors. We are perfectly *bona fide* in our desire to advance economic knowledge, caring more for that than for our own pet ideas. And anyone who knows us knows our opinions, and all the money has been practically sent to *us* personally, so that the contributors are fully aware in whom they are placing their confidence.

All this has interfered with our book. I am fagged out – have no value left in me. And during these last months I have been weak and foolish and allowed myself to brood over old relationships. I am absolutely happy with Sidney – our life is one long and close companionship, a companionship so close that it is almost a joint existence. But I shall never quite free myself from the shadow of past events, or, rather, I shall always be subject to relapses. These broodings are the special curse of a vivid and vigorous imagination, unoccupied in my present dry work of analysis and abstractions. Perhaps a holiday on the Westmorland moors will clear these vain imaginings away. I must some day write that novel and work in all these brilliant scenes I am constantly constructing.

Enid Stacy (d.1913) was an effective speaker, who was one of the itinerant lecturers supported by the part of the Hutchinson legacy devoted to Fabian purposes, though even here Sidney had insisted that the money should not be spent on mere propaganda. She was an active member of the I.L.P. until her early death.

18 April. [High Borrans, Windermere]
Delightful holiday in sister Holt's comfortable house. The Holts absent the greater part of the time – Sidney and I enjoyed the moors alone – rode over to Rusland and up the Grisedale valley, over to

Thirlmere by Grasmere and Rydal. It was very sweet. Taking my boy to visit the beautiful Rusland valley, one of the seed places of my youth. And the air and the sights of those sublime little hills swept my mind clear of all its diseased rumblings. Now that one's mind is again free one is amazed at the mania.

Whilst we were at the Lakes, had furious letters from J.R. MacDonald on the 'abuse of the Hutchinson Trust' in the proposal to contribute to the Library of Political Science. J.R.M. is a brilliant young Scot, lately I.L.P. candidate for Southampton, whom we have been employing as Hutchinson Trust lecturer in the provinces. These lectures are avowedly socialistic, but from the first Sidney has insisted that both MacDonald and Enid Stacy should make them educational, should issue an elaborate syllabus of a connected course with bibliographies, etc. And apparently they have been extremely successful. But MacDonald is personally discontented because we refused to have him as a lecturer for the London School. He is not good enough for that work; he has never had the time to do any sound original work, or even learn the old stuff well. Moreover he objects altogether to diverting 'socialist funds' to education. Even his own lectures, he declares, are too educational 'to make socialists' – he wants an organizer sent about the country. 'Organize what?' asked Sidney. MacDonald dared not reply 'I.L.P. branches', which he meant, neither could he suggest organizing Fabian societies, as it has always been against the policy of the Fabians to 'organize' people, its function being to permeate existing organizations. The truth is that we and MacDonald are opposed on a radical issue of policy. To bring about the maximum amount of public control and public administration, do we want to organize the *un*thinking persons into socialist societies, or to make the *thinking* persons socialistic? We believe in the latter policy.

In 1895 Sir John Gorst (1835–1916) became vice-president of the Education Department. He was a Conservative M.P. who had been a member of Lord Randolph Churchill's abortive Fourth Party. The ill-fated Education Bill introduced in 1896, which was a complicated measure, disappointed the Webbs, who considered it a lost opportunity to give the county councils and county boroughs a comprehensive responsibility for education. The Bill, designed to harass the local school boards, marked the beginning of a bitter fight between the government and the Nonconformists because it proposed to provide public funds for church schools, and also to abolish the 'Cowper-Temple' clause in the 1870 Education Act which had prohibited denominational teaching. It was withdrawn after Balfour had casually accepted an amendment which would have made it unworkable. Sir Michael Sadler (1861–1943), a specialist in educational research, was a member of the 1894 Royal Commission on Secondary Education. Lord George Hamilton (1845–1927), a Tory M.P. elected in 1885, had just been appointed Secretary of State for India. He became chairman of the Royal Commission on the Poor Law set up in 1905. Sir Alfred Milner (1854–1925), a journalist and notable civil servant, was currently chairman of the Board of Inland Revenue. In 1897 he became High Commissioner for South Africa, where he played the key role in the events leading to the Boer War and became the dominant political figure in that campaign. Sir George Kekewich (1841–1921), was Secretary to the Department of Education 1890–1900. Sir Henry Cunynghame (1848–1936) was Assistant Under-Secretary at the Home Office 1894–1913. Before his marriage Sidney had been a senior clerk in the Colonial Office.

Whitsun. The Argoed
Came here with the Hewins yesterday, Sidney, Graham and the widowed Rosy arrive tomorrow – our Whitsun party.

A good working time since we returned from the north. Got on with the book. Sidney much enjoyed colloquy with Gorst, Sadler, Llewellyn Smith and others about Education Bill. On the whole he is favourable to the central idea of the Bill – that is, replacing *ad hoc* bodies by one set of representatives chosen to manage all the business of the locality . . . also not against helping voluntary or denominational schools in return for a measure of control, which is bound to grow. Other clauses enabling public authorities to subsidize private venture schools he looks upon as radically bad. He, however, recognizes that it is good *for him* to oppose the Bill – far better to appreciate the good in it and by appreciating it get some influence in amending it in our direction. And he is fortunately placed for this purpose. . . This work, and pushing the London School and Political Science Library, combine to force us more into political society on both sides. On Monday, for instance, we dined at the House with Haldane and Asquith and other Liberals, on Tuesday with Sir John Gorst and Lord George Hamilton, two Conservative Ministers. Becoming, too, every day more connected with the superior rank of civil servants such as Sir Alfred Milner, Sir George Kekewich, Henry Cunynghame and others. Sidney's old connection with the civil service stands in good stead – he knows the ropes of almost every office. All this is in a way pleasant (I do not hide from myself that I am pleased and flattered that my boy is recognized as a distinguished man!), but it means less intellectual absorption in our work. Still, we go plodding on with our analysis, making up our

95

minds on each separate subject as we go along, more than ever convinced that we must write a 'textbook of democracy', crisp and authoritative, as our next work. We are always abusing the Liberal Party for not knowing its own mind, it would be more to the purpose if we made it up ourselves. *We must create a new 'orthodoxy'.*

The Russells made extended visits to Europe and America after their marriage and then settled at The Millhanger, a little cottage near Friday's Hill where Russell started to write *Principia Mathematica* and Alys travelled round the country organizing and speaking for temperance and suffrage. She was the youth organizer in the British Women's Temperance Association run by Lady Henry Somerset. The Phillimores lived at Radlett in Hertfordshire.

20 June. [41 Grosvenor Road]
Spent last Sunday with Bertrand Russells. Rode from Guildford through the Milford country to Millhanger, the little cottage in which they have settled themselves. A workman's cottage with stuffy attic bedrooms, but with the inevitable decent size sitting-room added on to it by the Russells. Found the young Phillimores there. A typical nineteenth-century party – two young aristocrats, married, one to a charming American [Alys Pearsall Smith], the other to [Lucy Fitzpatrick] a bright talented Irish woman (reputed a drunken Belfast carpenter's daughter who worked her way up as a district visitor to Lady Henry Somerset's secretaryship, from that to a seat on the St Pancras Vestry and thence to a marriage with her fellow vestryman – the socialist, philanthropic and eccentric son of Sir Walter Phillimore) – both women a good deal older than their very young husbands, mere boys in age though old in thought and tastes. We six spent the Sunday lounging in the cottage garden talking metaphysics, politics, very slightly interspersed with literature and art. The Bertrand Russells live idyllic lives, devotedly attached to each other, living with somewhat disorderly and extravagant simplicity – the simplest result extravagantly achieved – as might be expected from an anarchic American with means of her own, Russell working some six or seven hours at his metaphysical book, Alys rushing up to town at short intervals to girls' clubs and temperance meetings and resting with her beloved the remainder of the week.

The Phillimores vary the life of love in a cottage (on the father's estates) by attendance on vestry meetings and committees and preparing themselves to write a 'textbook on London government'. So far as I can see there is only one serious criticism on the lives of the six persons gathered together in a Surrey cottage on this lovely June day – *no children* – all too intellectual or strenuous to bear children! Whether the omission is 'intentional' or 'inevitable' does not much matter from the community's point of view. There is obviously some flaw in these ideal marriages of pure companionship. Can we afford that these rather picked individuals shall remain childless? Is less highly-wrought material better to breed from? I, at least, can fall back with complacency on the thirty-seven nephews and nieces who are carrying on the 'Potter' stock and so far unperturbed with ideas or enthusiasm.

Came back and found the Education Bill practically dead, and Balfour disgraced as a leader by his incompetency. The discreditable failure of this complicated measure only another instance of how impossible it is nowadays to succeed in politics without technical knowledge of the great democratic machine. The last Liberal government went out discredited because their members were mere prigs thrust into office – the present government are going the same way. 'In these matters I am a child,' says Balfour! We do not want clever schoolboys at the head of our great departments. We want grown men – 'grown up' *in the particular business they take in hand,* doing their eight or nine hours' work for ten months in every year, whether in office or out of office, behaving towards their profession as the great civil engineer, lawyer or medical man behaves. In political life the standard of natural ability is remarkably high, the standard of acquirements ludicrously low. Who would trust the building of a bridge to a man who started with such an infinitesimal knowledge of engineering as Balfour or Gorst have of national education and its machinery? There seems to be a settled conviction that any clever man trained to any profession whatsoever will succeed in politics whether or no he knows anything about the details of public administration or the facts of the common life he has to attempt to reform. That impression we must try to destroy.

In May 1896 Leonard Courtney was suddenly afflicted with serious trouble in his right eye. He underwent a course of treatment with a German specialist but although he did not completely lose his sight he could never read again.

8 July. [41 Grosvenor Road]
Went to say goodbye to the Courtneys who leave for Germany tomorrow. A great calamity has overtaken them. At Whitsun

Leonard lost his sight for reading and writing – one eye nearly blind and with the other eye, which is slightly affected, he cannot see near objects. Meanwhile Kate's health has collapsed – she is weak and has lost her nerve. Neither of them show any rebound since the first shock a month ago. Leonard especially is struck dumb. From the melancholy and *humiliation* of his expression I gather that this sudden blindness has made him realize that his career is over and his work done. Outsiders can see that, however terrible the deprivation, he exaggerates the effect on his public life. First, alas, we lookers-on have realized that before this blindness his *active* career was at an end. After the events of last year no one could believe that Leonard had any chance of taking part in a government. He could only hope to fill the position of an outside critic. That position is not altered by his blindness: it may even be improved. But his blindness and consequent dependence comes to him as the symbol of the closing of his life. . . .

In the first session, 281 (eighty-seven of them women) had enrolled at the L.S.E., and the need to accommodate more staff and students led to a move to the nearby 10 Adelphi Terrace, taken at a rent of £360 p.a.

14 July. [41 Grosvenor Road]
Making arrangements to start the London School in its new abode at Adelphi Terrace in October. Engaged a bright girl as housekeeper and accountant. Advertised for political science lecturer – and yesterday interviewed candidates, a nondescript set of university men. All hopeless from our point of view. All imagined that political science consisted of a knowledge of Aristotle and 'modern' writers such as de Tocqueville – wanted to put the students through a course of Utopias from More downwards. When Sidney suggested a course of lectures be prepared on the different systems of municipal taxation, when Graham suggested a study of the rival methods of election, from *ad hoc* to proportional representation, the wretched candidates looked aghast and thought evidently that we were amusing ourselves at their expense. . . . Finally we determined to do without our lecturer – to my mind a blessed consummation. It struck me always as a trifle difficult to teach a science which does not yet exist. . . .

The London Congress of the Second International was preceded by an acrimonious debate within the Fabian Society on Tract 70 *(Report on Fabian Policy)* which Shaw had drafted for presentation at the meeting. It was a provocative defence of permeation, which annoyed the I.L.P. and its Fabian sympathizers; and Shaw took every chance at the meeting to contrast Fabian moderation with the Marxist hyperbole of the Continental delegates. Hubert Bland (1856–1914), journalist and founder member of the Fabian Society, was married to Edith Nesbit (1858–1924), the well-known author of children's books. Allen Clement Edwards (1869–1928) was a Fabian journalist.

14 August. Stratford St Andrew Rectory, Saxmundham
A whole fortnight wasted in illness – a rheumatic cold combined with general collapse. This must excuse the absence of the brilliant account which I looked forward to writing of the International Congress! To us, it was, as we expected it to be, a public humiliation. The rank and file of socialists, especially English socialists, are unusually silly folk – for the most part feather-headed failures – and heaped together in one hall with the consciousness that their every word would be reported by the 'world press', they approached raving imbecility. The confusion of tongues, of procedure, the grotesque absurdity of masquerading as 'nations' and you have all the factors for a hideous fiasco from the point of view of public opinion. The Fabians sat silent taking notes as reporters for the 'capitalist press', Sidney writing descriptive accounts for the *Manchester Guardian,* Shaw for the *Star,* Bland for a weekly paper, Clem Edwards for the *Daily News* and another Fabian for the *Chronicle.* The Fabians at any rate write history if they do not make it!

But though we were ashamed of the 'British nation' as represented by the callow youths and maidens of the I.L.P. and S.D.F., the socialists of other lands were exceptionally enlightening. The German Political Socialists are substantial persons, their intellects somewhat twisted by their authoritarian dogmatism, but with strong sterling character and capable of persistent and deliberate effort. . . . Among the French, Swiss, Dutch and Italians there are individuals who are really 'thinking': we felt, perhaps for the first time, how much the collectivist movement would gain by a quiet exchange of thought and experience between the cultivated and intellectual socialists of all countries. Such a conference will be one of our likely plans for the future.

Charlotte Payne-Townshend (1857–1943) was a rich Irishwoman who had spent her youth restlessly searching for an occupation. The Webbs made a conveniently profitable arrangement with her to let the upper part of 10 Adelphi Terrace at a rent which almost covered the cost of the whole building. They introduced her to Bernard Shaw on 29 January 1896, who distressed his friends by his philandering attitude to Charlotte. 'I am going to refresh my heart by falling in love with her,' Shaw told the actress Ellen Terry on 28 August. Shaw was working on his play *The Devil's Disciple.*

16 September. [Stratford St Andrew]

Last day of our stay in the Suffolk rectory. For first three weeks I was seedy, mooned and dreamed my life away chatting with our visitors or sitting in the little study watching Sidney work on with our chapter on Apprenticeship, or straining after the party on my bicycle, feeling all the time somewhat miserable and woebegone. The last four weeks we have worked well together and have really got within sight of the end of our book and the completion of our theory. Now that we have finished the elaborate technical analysis of each set of regulations, our own theory of trade unionism is emerging. It is exciting, this clearing up of one's own thought after two years of patient plodding. And as far as we can tell, the ideas we are evolving seem to be fruitful and likely to breed others. Out of our study of trade unionism we are developing a new view of democracy and I think quite an original set of economic and political hypotheses. For the first time since we began this book I am feeling intellectually keen and absorbed in my work.

Meanwhile a new friend has joined the 'Bo' family. ['Bo' was the Potter family name for Beatrice.] Charlotte Payne-Townshend is a wealthy unmarried woman of about my own age. Bred up in second-rate fashionable society without any education or habit of work, she found herself at about thirty-three years of age alone in the world, without ties, without any definite creed, and with a large income. For the last four years she has drifted about – in India, in Italy, in Egypt, in London, seeking occupation and fellow spirits. In person she is attractive – a large graceful woman with masses of chocolate-brown hair, pleasant grey eyes, 'matte' complexion which sometimes looks muddy, at other times forms a picturesquely pale background to her brilliant hair and bright eyes. She dresses well – in her flowing white evening robes she approaches beauty. At moments she is plain. By temperament she is an anarchist – feeling any regulation or rule intolerable – a tendency which has been exaggerated by her irresponsible wealth. She is romantic but thinks herself cynical. She is a socialist and a radical, not because she understands the collectivist standpoint, but because she is by nature a rebel. She has no snobbishness and no convention: she has 'swallowed all formulas' but has not worked out principles of her own. She is fond of men and impatient of most women, bitterly resents her enforced celibacy but thinks she could not tolerate the matter-of-fact side of marriage. Sweet-tempered, sympathetic and genuinely anxious to increase the world's enjoyment and diminish the world's pain.

This is the woman who has, for a short time or for good, entered the 'Bo' family. Last autumn she was introduced to us. We, knowing she was wealthy, and hearing she was socialistic, interested her in the London School of Economics. She subscribed £1,000 to the Library, endowed a woman's scholarship, and has now taken the rooms over the School at Adelphi Terrace, paying us £300 a year for rent and service. It was on account of her generosity to our projects and 'for the good of the cause' that I first made friends with her. To bring her more directly into our little set of comrades, I suggested that we should take a house together in the country and entertain our friends. To me she seemed at that time a pleasant, well-dressed, well-intentioned woman – I thought she should do very well for Graham Wallas! Now she turns out to be an 'original', with considerable personal charm and certain volcanic tendencies. Graham Wallas bored her with his morality and learning. In a few days she and Bernard Shaw were constant companions. For the last fortnight, when the party has been reduced to ourselves and Shaw, and we have been occupied with our work and each other, they have been scouring the country together and sitting up late at night. To all seeming, she is in love with the brilliant philanderer and he is taken, in his cold sort of way, with her. They are, I gather from him, on very confidential terms and have 'explained' their relative positions. Though interested I am somewhat uneasy. These warm-hearted unmarried women of a certain age are audacious and are almost childishly reckless of consequences. I doubt whether Bernard Shaw could be induced to marry: I doubt whether she will be happy without it. It is harder for a woman to remain celibate than a man.

William Jennings Bryan (1860–1925) was the unsuccessful Democratic candidate in the American presidential election of 1896. He campaigned for the unlimited coinage of silver, which he thought would reflate the economy to the advantage of farmers and workers. Bimetallism permitted free coinage of gold and silver, at variable commercial values, and it was generally considered a source of economic instability. Leopold Amery (1873–1955) was a journalist, briefly a Fabian, who had made his reputation in South Africa and went on to become a fervent imperialist and a prominent Conservative statesman. Beatrice noted later that when he visited the Webbs in 1897 'he advocated the sudden destruction of the German fleet, without notice.'

5 October. Grosvenor Road
The last fortnight we have been a good deal absorbed in preparing Adelphi Terrace for the opening of the School. Found Hewins in a

state of nervous collapse threatening severe illness, sent him away with his wife and child and took over the work of preparing for the coming term. Poor Sidney trudges over there directly after breakfast and spends his mornings with painters, plumbers and locksmiths, would-be students intervening to whom he gives fatherly advice, comes home to lunch and then off to the L.C.C. In the interval of arranging the details of the housekeeping at the School, I am getting on slowly with the book, preparing the ground for work with Sidney next week when Hewins is back. Obvious that this institution will take up much of our time for the next few years. We are convinced it is worth while, in spite of the harassing character of the work. We want to create a centre of intellectual work and comradeship from which our views will radiate through personal intercourse. It remains to be seen how we succeed.

Had to attend Manchester Conference of Women [National Union of Women Workers]. Usual large gathering of sensible and God-fearing folk, dominated by the Executive of bishops' wives, who give to the proceedings an atmosphere of extreme decorum and dignity. I have resigned from the Executive owing to their persistence in having prayers before all their business meetings which, I suggest, is wanting in courtesy to the Jewesses and infidels whom they wish to serve with them. Some of them agree but say that the Union would lose membership if it were not understood to be deliberately Christian. Very well; then I have no place on its Executive. I remain on sub-committees and will keep the Union straight on industrial questions. . . .

Louise Creighton now becomes – as wife to the Bishop of London – one of the great hostesses of London society. In spite of the fact that she is a fervent Christian and I an avowed agnostic, we have a warm respect for each other. She is an absolutely straight woman, who never swerves from what she believes to be right, is sometimes ugly in her brusque directness. She hides with difficulty her dislike or disapproval, and so has many enemies, or rather, persons who disparage her and call her 'bourgeois' and thick-minded. To Alice Green, with her tortuous mind and uncertain ways, Louise is anathema, though possibly now that she is the wife of the Bishop of London Alice Green may see 'quality' in her. . . .

One reason I am so fagged is the growth of the social side of our work. We are perpetually entertaining, and the opening of the School has added a long list of students whom we feel it our duty to see and talk to. The usual visit to Oxford – forty-eight hours talking – propaganda of collectivist views and the expediency of research – enjoyable enough, this bright discussion with young dons and undergraduates but oh! how exhausting. Sidney lectured twice and we both talked incessantly from the breakfast party to the last smoke late at night.

Leonard Courtney gave a remarkable lecture to the W.L.U.A. [Women's Liberal Unionist Association], to be repeated at the School, and published in the *Nineteenth Century* for January, on the issue of the Presidential Election in the United States. Summed up in favour of Bryan on all counts! An audacious challenge to orthodox public opinion of his own class. The tone of the lecture was admirable, strong and convinced yet impartial. The audience – mostly women of London Society – sat aghast, half afraid to clap and yet deeply impressed by his righteous indignation and calm assurance that 'such was the fact'.

I have no opinion on currency. But bimetallism must have reason in it, for it seems to awaken the believer's mind to all other good thoughts! It leads men to be more collectivist – the association of ideas I do not yet understand.

Introduced a brilliant Oxford Fabian, Amery, to Leonard as private secretary.

My old friend Carrie becomes an enthusiastic Board School teacher! We got her on 'supply', she worked her way through classes of eighty infants to the higher standards, had a month's work at a P.T.C. [Primary Training College] and is now taken on the permanent staff of a Board School while she works up for the Board's certificate. . . Sent her to our lawyer who has extracted from the husband £300 and arranged a judicial separation. Now she seems to have really made a new start and likely to have a life of influence before her.

Ada Webb (1865–1940) was Sidney's sister.

8 November. Cliftonville, Margate
Four days' outing here with Ada Webb to recover from a cold and give her a holiday.

School promising but not assured. Successful classes and lectures are those giving purely technical instruction to professionals – methods of statistics and railway economics – such subjects as commercial law and currency proving rather too abstract for the clerk to see in what way they make for his bread and butter. Pure learning and culture, such as growth of political theory, is at present a 'frost' except for the attendance of the full student who has paid his guinea and attends all the lectures. It is this class we want to encourage – until we have a regular clientele of three hundred full students our success will be problematic in the extreme. Hewins, who expected great things, has been depressed and irritable and it has taken all Sidney's good temper and tact to keep things going smooth. Hewins is a sanguine enthusiast, pulls hard and strong when he feels the stream with him, but I doubt whether he has the 'staying power' for bad times. And he has a small-minded little wife always whispering discontent into his ear, suggesting that he is being put upon and that the enterprise will not succeed, a little quiet mouse of a body with no influence in times of health and prosperity, but insidiously depressing when things are not going quite right. However, with the rise of the students to 220 Hewins's spirits have gone up and he is now again prophesying great things. But I see that this School, if it is to be made a permanent success, will mean a good deal of work and thought from Sidney and myself.

✍ 1897 ✍

18 January. [The Argoed]
Xmas with Alfred Cripps. Last year he was starting his political life: this year he is well on the road to office. He is in splendid spirits, talks with easy critical familiarity of Balfour and other leading Conservatives and gives one to understand incidentally that he is constantly consulted by them. He is rapidly becoming a sort of legal adviser . . . to the Conservative party. . . . He is still making a large income at the Bar and spending it lavishly on his constituency, home and children. The eldest boy, Seddon, is exhausting pleasures at a tremendous rate: this year his bicycle was discarded and he was driving about in the smallest dogcart covered with his initials, with rug, lamps etc. to match. Ruth has become more thoughtful and looks on rather wistfully – the mother in her is creeping into view. A year's school has made Leonard commonplace: a year's home has made 'Daddy' [Stafford] more exuberant than ever. The Playnes were

staying there: Arthur cross and uncivil, Mary extremely affable and uncomfortably anxious to be pleasant. Refused a half-hearted invitation to take in Longfords [the Playne house] on the way here.

Came on here for three weeks' work – over two weeks alone, Hewins with us for one week. The hill enveloped in cold mist. But it has been a splendid time for work: have written the best part of two chapters. Have worked both together and apart, Sidney reading through the thirty volumes we brought with us on abstract economics, and writing, with occasional suggestions from me, the chapter giving our synthesis of the higgling of the market. Then he and I would write it out clearly – he criticizing my ideas; sometimes we would get at cross purposes – but our cross purposes would always end in a shower of kisses. I doubt whether two persons could stand the stress and strain of this long-drawn-out work, this joint struggle with ideas, a perpetual hammering at each other's minds, if it were not for the equally perpetual 'honeymoon' of our life together. These three weeks, with the peaceful grey days and long evenings, the wanderings over the moorland and up and down dale, the cosy evenings by the log fire, he reading *Brandt* and *Peer Gynt* to me, have been a delicious holy-day, a relief from the noise, bustle and news of London. And as if to reward us for being so happy enshrouded in cold mist, the sun, the last three days, has come out gloriously shining in red splendour over the whitened landscape and followed at sunset by an equally glorious moon lighting up in an absolutely still air the long lines of highland, their night's shroud of white mist creeping stealthily up from the village. I am so well, and so blessedly happy. Again those morbid troublings of last autumn seem to me amazing!

Looking back on the year I am satisfied with our work. We are nearly through with our book – three months' more grind of our little minds and we shall have turned out all that they can yield on this subject. Of course the worth of our work will be only temporary: all our hypotheses will be either truisms or fallacies in a generation's time. Still I think we shall have left a solid substream of fact for others to reason on. Our descriptive analysis of special facts is, I believe, the best part of our work and likely to be most permanent.

The London School is progressing – Sidney has contrived to edge it in to any possible London University. It is still a substratum in money, students, and output but it promises well. And while we have been busy with our little affairs, the greater world of politics has not been doing so badly from our point of view. The Conservative government finds itself paralysed. Except for its sordid grant to landlords it has not been able to move backward or to move forward. The Liberal leaders are as feeble and half-hearted as ever. But neither party are putting forward any alternative policy to collectivism – neither party *dare* take any step or even make a proposal that contradicts this policy. The Conservative government is being dragged by its own arbitration act into regulating the condition of labour: it is being coerced by its promises into spending additional money on public education. It will presently have to confess itself bankrupt in proposals or accept the collectivist solution of employers' liability and old-age pensions. In all probability it will do nothing in these matters, and the Chamberlain programme of social reform will collapse, as it has done before. Social reform is becoming far too complicated for the actor-politician or the accomplished *littérateur*. That fact works our way: the collectivists alone have the faith to grind out a Science of Politics and I think they will prove to have the capacity.

1 February. [41 Grosvenor Road]
This extract from Chamberlain's speech interests me unusually.

> Why, gentlemen, I daresay that Mr Morley was thinking chiefly of our domestic controversy, and, if I might venture to say so, I would add that this is a mistake which the leaders of the Radical party are constantly making. They forget in the attention which they give to these domestic controversies, which, after all, whichever way they are settled, are all of minor importance, they forget the great part which this country has played, and is called upon to play, in the history of the world. *(Daily Chronicle*, 1 February 1897: 'Joseph Chamberlain at Birmingham'.)

It means many things in his development as a politician. First that social reform is from his standpoint 'no go'. This is partly because he is now irrecoverably a leader of the reactionary party; partly because he has found industrial problems, with his insufficient knowledge and untrained intellect, too difficult to unravel. It also means (by the light of Balfour's failure these two sessions) a definite and timely bid for the Tory Party's allegiance as distinguished from the Liberal Unionists. To myself, who knew him as a man in the prime of life apparently inspired by a passionate desire to better the conditions of 'the common lump of men', it reads like a pathetic confession of failure, not less pathetic because it is unselfconscious and is expressed in words of buoyant oratory. The intricate but insistent problem of *how best to use the machinery of political democracy to further the interests of the whole people* is far too complicated, far too abstruse to be solved by fervour or ambition. Patient persistent plodding both in propaganda and investigation are the only ways in which each generation will take a few steps forward to the desired state of social democracy. But it speaks volumes for the force of that silent pressure from the bulk of the people in a freely working democracy that in spite of lack of goodwill and lack of capacity in our statesmen of both parties they are perpetually stumbling forwards even when they secretly wish to step backwards! In England reaction is ashamed of itself and is inadequate in its methods. And happily the complexity of things is an even greater stumbling-block for those who wish to step backwards than for those who desire to go forwards.

The Duke of Devonshire (1833–1908) was Lord President of the Council. Henry Chaplin (1840–1923), a spendthrift landowner said to care more about hunting than politics, was president of the Local Government Board 1895–1900.

3 February. [41 Grosvenor Road]
Last night, being the second night of the Education Debate, Gorst entertained a lively party of young people at dinner, retiring afterwards to his private room where we laughed and smoked whilst division bells were ringing and count-outs were threatening. As we sat on the sofa Gorst became confidential in a curious spasmodic way. 'The newspapers say this is a humiliation for me, this Education Bill. But it's the Duke who is humiliated. Salisbury told me from the first that I was to be Under-Secretary and that the Duke would be responsible for the education policy in the Cabinet. The Duke is quite as much against this Bill as I am. He told the Cabinet so, and when they insisted he shrugged his shoulders!' From the Education Bill we passed to the general situation. I ventured to say that Balfour was discredited, at which Gorst looked pleased. 'He doesn't know anything,' he remarked contemptuously. 'We are on the eve of a crisis: there will be a revolt presently of the urban Tories. They can't go on watching their seats being taken from under them. As for social reform, all chance of that is gone. When first this government came into office they honestly intended to do something. I know as a matter of fact that Salisbury said to Chaplin soon after the government was

formed: "Chaplin, can't you do something for the unemployed?" At this my gravity gave way, and Gorst's eyes twinkled merrily, but when the others looked up at my laughter, he checked himself and became demure and began to talk Indian administration and colonial policy. Rhodes to be rehabilitated it seems.

6 February [41 Grosvenor Road]
A great gathering last night in Queen's Hall – nine hundred L.C.C. scholars receiving their certificates from the Prince of Wales. Sat close to H.R.H. [Edward, Prince of Wales] and watched him with curiosity. In his performance of the ceremony, from his incoming to his outgoing, he acted like a well-oiled automaton, saying exactly the words he was expected to say, noticing the right persons on the platform, maintaining his own dignity whilst setting others at ease, and otherwise acting with perfectly polished discretion. But observing him closely you could see that underneath the Royal automaton there lay the child and the animal, a simple kindly un-moral temperament which makes him a good fellow. Not an English gentleman, essentially a foreigner and yet an almost perfect constitutional sovereign. From a political point of view his vices and foibles, his lack of intellectual refinement or moral distinction, are as nothing compared to his complete detachment from all party prejudice and class interests and his genius for political *discretion*. But one sighs to think that this unutterably commonplace person should set the tone to London Society. There is something comic in the great British nation with its infinite variety of talents, having this undistinguished and limited-minded German bourgeois to be its social sovereign. A sovereign of real distinction who would take over as his peculiar province the direction of the *voluntary side of social life,* who could cultivate in rich and leisured society a desire to increase the sum of real intellectual effort and eminence – what might he not do to further our civilization by creating a real aristocracy of character and intellect. As it is, we have our social leader proposing in this morning's papers as a fit commemoration of his august mother's longest reign, the freeing of the hospitals from debt, the sort of proposal one would expect from the rank and file of 'scripture readers' or a committee of village grocers intent on goodwill on earth and saving the rates.

My boy spoke a few words to the nine hundred children at the end – worth all the rest of the speeches put together – urging them to remember that as London had helped them they must seek, in their future lives, to serve London.

Beatrice here contrasts the Greek landing on Crete to support the current insurrection against Turkish rule with the complicity of Cecil Rhodes in the Jameson Raid late in 1895. A select committee had been appointed in August 1896 to look into the British South Africa Company and the examination of Rhodes had begun on 16 February 1897.

23 February. [41 Grosvenor Road]
Horribly difficult to get on with the book in London – so many days I am hopelessly unfit – and Sidney refuses to go on without me. A flying visit to Cambridge to address the Newnham and Girton students – stayed with the Marshalls. Professor Marshall is more footling than ever. . . . For really when one talks to him and he advances his little subtle qualifications to his own slipshod generalizations, one gets irritated, almost as irritated as when, in order to controvert some 'popular' notion, he makes an astonishing assertion which bears no relation to fact. . . . But I was prejudiced against Marshall because of his dislike and fear of us. We have forced him into the position of an intellectual reactionary. He used to call himself a socialist. But the socialism he believed in was a revolt against the great industry and consisted in a faraway hope in the setting up of little Co-operative productive societies or even of individual producers, anything to get relief from the bureaucracy of the great industrial machine. We come along and accept that bureaucracy – only we wish to control it – and in controlling it to complete the transformation from individual to social production. And in our propaganda we appeal deliberately to economics and business principles against sentimentalism. Marshall has been forced, as an economist, to accept much of our destructive criticism of the old Co-operative ideal. As an idealist anarchist he enlists himself against the democratizing of the great machine, not because he is anti-democratic (be it said to his credit) but because he dreads and hates the great machine and fully realizes that it would be enormously strengthened by having a democratic basis. So he finds himself timidly and regretfully ranging himself on the side of pure reaction in its fight with democracy. It is a pitiable position and he knows we think it so.

Greece and Rhodes – two political raids – one heroic, the other sordid – absorb the attention of the political public. In both episodes the great English nation shows its meanest characteristics. In our foreign policy we are still guided by no intelligible principle – grab, scuttle or fence – according to the exigencies of the day. So far as there exists a community of nations, it is still in the early stages of barbarism in which force is only alternated by deception. England is more successful but no worse than other nations. . . .

Bertha Newcombe's portrait of Shaw – 'The Platform Spellbinder' – was lost during the Second World War. Shaw's fifth novel, first published as a serial in *To-Day* in 1884, was intended as the beginning of a 'vast work depicting capitalist society in dissolution'.

9 March. [41 Grosvenor Road]
As I mounted the stairs with Shaw's *Unsocial Socialist* to return to Bertha Newcombe I felt somewhat uncomfortable as I knew I should encounter a sad soul full of bitterness and loneliness. I stepped into a small wainscotted studio and was greeted coldly by the little woman. She is *petite* and dark, about forty years old but looks more like a wizened girl than a fully developed woman. Her jet-black hair heavily fringed, half-smart, half-artistic clothes, pinched aquiline features and thin lips, give you a somewhat unpleasant impression though not wholly inartistic. She is bad style without being vulgar or common or loud – indeed many persons, Kate Courtney for instance, would call her 'lady-like' – but she is insignificant and undistinguished. 'I want to talk to you, Mrs Webb,' she said when I seated myself. And then followed, told with the dignity of devoted feeling, the story of her relationship to Bernard Shaw, her five years of devoted love, his cold philandering, her hopes aroused by repeated advice to him (which he, it appears, had repeated much exaggerated) to marry her, and then her feeling of misery and resentment against me when she discovered that I was encouraging him 'to marry Miss Townshend'. Finally, he had written a month ago to break it off entirely: they were not to meet again. And I had to explain with perfect frankness that so long as there seemed a chance for her I had been willing to act as chaperone, that she had never been a personal friend of mine or Sidney's, that I had regarded her only as Shaw's friend, and that as far as I was concerned I should have welcomed her as his wife. But directly I saw that he meant nothing I backed out of the affair. She took it all quietly, her little face seemed to shrink up and the colour of her skin looked as if it were reflecting the sad lavender of her dress.
'You are well out of it, Miss Newcombe,' I said gently. 'If you had

married Shaw he would not have remained faithful to you. You know my opinion of him — as a friend and a colleague, as a critic and literary worker, there are few men for whom I have so warm a liking; but in his relations with women he is vulgar, if not worse; it is a vulgarity that includes cruelty and springs from vanity.'

As I uttered these words my eye caught her portrait of Shaw — full-length, with his red-gold hair and laughing blue eyes and his mouth slightly open as if scoffing at us both, a powerful picture in which the love of the woman had given genius to the artist. Her little face turned to follow my eyes and she also felt the expression of the man, the mockery at her deep-rooted affection. 'It is so horribly lonely,' she muttered. 'I daresay it is more peaceful than being kept on the rack, but it is like the peace of death.'

There seemed nothing more to be said. I rose and with a perfunctory 'Come and see me — someday,' I kissed her on the forehead and escaped down the stairs. And then I thought of that other woman with her loving easygoing nature and anarchic luxurious ways, her well-bred manners and well-made clothes, her leisure, wealth and knowledge of the world. Would she succeed in taming the philanderer?

The Webbs took a pretty house on the North Downs near Dorking as a holiday home. In May, Shaw was elected as a member of the St Pancras Vestry, and he divided his time that early summer between London and Surrey. 'I wonder what you would think of our life,' he wrote to Ellen Terry on 28 May; 'our eternal political shop; our mornings of dogged writing, all in separate rooms, our ravenous plain meals; our bicycling; the Webbs' incorrigible spooning over their industrial and political science; Miss P.T., Irish, shrewd and green-eyed, finding everything "very interesting"; myself always tired and careworn. . . .' He had just withdrawn *You Never Can Tell* from the Haymarket because he could not accept the producer's request for alterations.

1 May. [Dorking]
Retired for three months into the country to finish our forthcoming work. Our party consists of Charlotte Townshend (who shares the expenses), Bernard Shaw and ourselves, and we are enlisting a succession of visitors for Sundays. Already a month of our time here is past. I have been especially vigorous, completely absorbed in thinking out the last chapter of our book. To me the unravelling of a consistent theory of industrial regulation (in the chapter on the economic characteristics of trade unionism) has been extremely exciting. Now that we have found our theory every previous part of our analysis seems to fit in perfectly,

and facts which before puzzled us range themselves in their places as if 'by nature'.

We alternate from thinking that the Work will be as great in its effect on political and economic thought as Adam Smith's *Wealth of Nations,* to wondering whether the whole of it is not an elaborate figment of our imagination. . . The companionship over the book in these latter parts has been delightful, the constant testing of the thought by the two minds, the act of combined thinking in which the experience and the hypotheses of the two intellects become inextricably mingled, so that we are both unconscious of what we have each of us contributed, has been extraordinarily stimulating. But I doubt whether the English reading public will understand or be impressed – if there is to be a *succès d' estime* that appreciation will come from Germany. The background of our lives – the pleasant friendships, the beautiful spring, with all its sweet sounds, sights and scents, and the pretty house and garden, the long hours of leisure – is luxurious almost to a fault. One broods at times over the question whether our work is worth all the happiness and well-being we are extracting from the life of the community, and at times one feels uneasy lest we are taking more than our share. Happily the supreme luxury of love and close comradeship does not abstract from other people's chances of enjoyment. Our life at present is like the early summer, growth and the delight in growing, love and the delight in loving. We are getting middle-aged and yet we feel young in our intellectual life, always on the threshold of new discovery and almost childish in our revelling in each other's adoration and tenderness. How full and brimming over with happiness human life can be. How could this happiness become universal or nearly universal – that is the problem.

I am watching with concern and curiosity the development of the Shaw-Townshend friendship. All this winter they have been lovers – of a philandering and harmless kind, always together when Shaw was free. Charlotte insisted on taking a house with us in order that he might be here constantly, and it is obvious that she is deeply attached to him. But I see no sign on his side of the growth of any genuine and steadfast affection. He finds it pleasant to be with her in her luxurious surroundings, he has been studying her and all her little ways and amusing himself by dissecting the rich woman brought up without training and drifting about at the beck of impulse. I think he has now exhausted the study, observed all that there is to observe. He has been flattered by her devotion and absorption in him; he is kindly and has a cat-like preference for those persons to whom he is accustomed. But there are ominous signs that he is tired of watching the effect of little words of gallantry and personal interest with which he plied her in the first months of the friendship. And he is annoyed by her lack of purpose and utter incapacity for work. If she would set to, and do even the smallest and least considerable task of intellectual work, I believe she could retain his interest and perhaps develop his feeling for her. Otherwise he will drift away, for Shaw is too high-minded and too conventionally honourable to marry her for the life of leisure and luxury he could gain for himself as her husband.

In 1890 Haldane had been jilted by Valerie, the sister of his fellow 'Limp' Ronald Munro-Ferguson: she lampooned him in three novels before she died insane in an asylum in 1897. Haldane never married.

3 May. [Dorking]
Haldane here for a Sunday. Difficult to estimate what amount of influence that man exercises in public affairs. He has never held office, but during the last Liberal government he was the chief instigator of their collectivist policy, serving to carry information and suggestions from specialists like ourselves to the heads of departments. He was also responsible for many of their appointments. In this parliament he is in constant confidential intercourse with Balfour and other Conservatives over the many non-party questions dealt with by a government, and even in some purely political questions his advice is asked. He attracts confidence where he is at all liked; once on friendly terms, you feel absolutely secure that he will never use personal knowledge to advance his own public career to the detriment of any friend. The rank and file of his own party dislike him intensely, partly because he detaches himself from party discipline and acts according to his own inner light and partly because he seems dominated by some vague principle which they do not understand and which he does not make intelligible. His bulky awkward form and pompous ways, his absolute lack of masculine vices and 'manly' tastes (beyond a good dinner), his intense superiority and constant attitude of a teacher, his curiously woolly mind would make him an unattractive figure if it were not for the beaming kindliness of his nature, warm appreciation of friends and a certain pawky humour with which he surveys the world. And there is

pathos in his personality. In spite of the successful professional life, the interest and entertainment of constantly mixing with the most powerful minds and in the most stirring affairs, the enjoyment of luxurious living to a man with a first-rate digestion, he is a restless lonely man – in his heart still worshipping the woman who jilted him seven years ago. All the sadder that genuine affectionateness, pleasure in intimate and entirely confidential relations, a yearning towards some sort of *permanence*, is really the strongest side of Haldane's character. He was made to be husband, father and close comrade. He has to put up with pleasant intercourse with political friends and political foes.

When we are together we are constantly discussing hotly. He has been converted in a sort of vague metaphysical way to the principles of collectivism. But whether it is that his best brains are given to his professional work or whether it is that he is incapable of working out or even fully comprehending concrete principles, he never sees the right side of a question until you have spent hours dinning it into him. . . All the same, we two and he remain genuinely fond of each other.

8 May. [Dorking]
Silly these philanderings of Shaw's. He imagines that he gets to know women by making them in love with him. Just the contrary. His stupid gallantries bar out from him the friendship of women who are either too sensible, too puritanical or too much 'otherwise engaged' to care to bandy personal flatteries with him. One large section of women, comprising some, at any rate, of the finest types, remains hidden from him. With the women with whom he has *'bonne fortune'* he also fails in his object, or rather in his *avowed* object – vivi-section. He idealizes them for a few days, weeks or years, imagines them to be something utterly different from their true selves, then has a revulsion of feeling and discovers them to be unutterably vulgar, second-rate, rapscallion, or insipidly well-bred. He never fathoms their real worth, nor rightly sees their limitations. But in fact it is not the end he cares for: it is the *process*. His sensuality has all drifted into sexual vanity, delight in being the candle to the moths, with a dash of intellectual curiosity to give flavour to his tickled vanity. And he is mistaken if he thinks that it does not affect his artistic work. His incompleteness as a thinker, his shallow and vulgar view of many human relationships, the lack of the sterner kind of humour which

would show him the dreariness of his farce and the total absence of proportion and inadequateness in some of his ideas, all these defects come largely from the flippant and worthless self-complacency brought about by the worship of rather second-rate women. For all that, he is a good-natured agreeable sprite of a man, an intellectual cricket on the hearth always chirping away brilliant paradox, sharp-witted observation and friendly comments. Whether I like him, admire him or despise him most I do not know. Just at present I feel annoyed and contemptuous.

For the dancing light has gone out of Charlotte's eyes – there is at times a blank haggard look, a look that I myself felt in my own eyes for long years. But throughout all my misery I had the habit of hard work and an almost religious sense of my intellectual mission. I had always my convent to fly to. Poor Charlotte has nowhere to turn. She can only wander listless through the world, with no reason for turning one way rather than another. What a comfort to be a fanatic. It is Bernard Shaw's fanaticism to turn everything inside out and see whether the other side won't do just as well if not better; it is this fanaticism which gives him genuine charm. He has a sort of affectionateness too, underneath his vanity. Will she touch that?

William Pember Reeves (1857–1932) was a New Zealander who had resigned as Minister of Labour to come to England as the country's Agent-General. He and his wife Maud were active Fabians. In 1908 he became Director of the London School of Economics; she was interested in the theatre, and social problems, publishing a widely read book on low incomes called *Round About a Pound a Week*. Sir Maurice Sheldon Amos (1872–1940) was a lawyer who served in the Egyptian administration and later became professor of comparative law at University College, London. Marie Souvestre (d. 1905) was a freethinker, well known among English intellectuals; she ran a fashionable girls' school, first in Fontainebleau and then in Wimbledon. Shaw was tiring of regular theatre criticism for the *Saturday Review:* 'the ever returning Saturday windmill knocks me down,' he wrote to Ellen Terry on 28 May.

24 May. [Dorking]
Glorious summer days. In excellent working form. Long mornings spent in work, recasting some of the chapters, filling up crevasses and thinking out the last chapter and foreshadowing the preface. Sidney sits at one table and I at another: the sun streams in through the dancing leaves. As fast as I can plan he criticizes and executes, filling in his time with administrative work, but sacrificing everything to the book. Charlotte sits upstairs typewriting Shaw's plays. Shaw wanders

about the garden with writing-book and pencil, writing the *Saturday* article, correcting his plays for press or reading through one of our chapters. With extraordinary good nature he will spend days over some part of our work, and an astute reader will quickly divine those chapters which Shaw has corrected and those which he has not – there is a conciseness and crispness in parts subjected to his pruning-knife lacking elsewhere.

In the afternoon there is the interval for cigarettes, letters and the newspapers before the early cup of tea, and between 5 or 6 o'clock and 8 o'clock supper, a ride or a walk in this beautiful country. Our daily life is an earthly paradise. Absolutely the only ruffle, an uncomfortable feeling that my housekeeping is extravagant through carelessness of detail, a consciousness of waste. Some nights I wake up and worry about it and make all sorts of plans for reformation. But when the morning comes, my fully awakened mind turns to the book and refuses obstinately to consider the price of vegetables or the pounds of butter or meat. All sorts of sophistries sooth my conscience – that I cannot reform a bad system but must make the best of it, that my brains are better employed in unravelling problems – all the same, at the bottom of my heart I know that I am unnecessarily lazy about it and lacking in moral courage not to control my servants with more vigour. If it were not for this uneasy conscience I and they would probably do worse, and I should make Mary cry with my black looks. Sometimes no doubt she laughs in her sleeve at my *laissez-faire, laissez-aller*. I am fond of my two girls with their smart figures and pretty faces, and they, I think, are fond of us – it is now four years that these two sisters have been with us. But the relation between mistress and servant and private tradesmen is a bad one, thoroughly unsound in its capricious carelessness, lack of knowledge and supervision of buyer over the seller. All the spending of the world should, like its government and its production, be carried on by experts, not by untrained and indifferent amateurs with no knowledge of commodities and utter carelessness as to price.

A succession of visitors enlivens our life; Graham Wallas, the W.P. Reeveses, Herbert Samuel, C.P. Trevelyan, the Phillimores and Russells and Amoses – a stream of young radicals coming and going with easy familiarity, a sort of outer circle to the 'Bo' family.

Miss Souvestre and Alice Green each came and spent the night, the former as exuberant as ever, full of sympathy, interest and affection, looks on at the lives of her young women friends – I, alas! being

middle-aged – with warm and hearty criticism. Alice Green
withering up into a strange sort of uneasy conventionality but pathetic
in her utter loneliness and drifting intention. A multitude of tragedies
in that woman's life – always in the process of being deserted and of
deserting – and yet withal a certain faithfulness and persistency of
disposition, never daring to let go a friendship lest the friend should
turn out after all trumps. So she keeps us up, gazing on us with that
weird veiled look, uncertain whether to hold on or let go, but giving
us only her leavings. Even the clothes she comes in are always her
shabbiest! Poor Alice! She chose me as a friend and not I her, but she
was good to me in the early springtide of my good fortune and she was
one of the first to appreciate and like Sidney. For that I shall always be
grateful to her. By her friendly regard for him and her discreet praise,
she gave me self-confidence and smoothed the uncomfortable times of
our early love-making. If it had not been for Alice Green's emphatic
opinion that Sidney was essentially distinguished in character and
intelligence, who knows whether I should have had the courage to
back my own judgement against that of my own little world? For it was
reason and not love that won me, a deliberate judgement of the man's
worth and almost cold-blooded calculation of the life I could live with
him and he with me. Perhaps the final consideration that determined
me was the conviction that I should turn out better value to him than to
any other man. To a well-trained commercial mind there is charm in
making the ideal bargain, the best possible to both parties.

The Webbs had decided to take a world tour as a 'sabbatical' on completing
Industrial Democracy.

15 June. [Dorking]
Our last days here passed quickly. We have lived a luxurious life these
three months – sunshine, flowers, songs of birds, beauty of line and
colour, complete physical enjoyment. There is no existence so
delicious as the physical enjoyment enveloping two or three hours'
strenuous thought, the long hours of ease concentrating all the
strength and the intensity of the strain, giving zest to the complete
relaxation. It is the most enchanting of all contrasts. And as a
background to intellectual keenness and physical pleasure a warm and
enduring affection lighting up all thoughts, feelings and sensations
with a soft and yet brilliant glow of emotion. Shall have two-thirds of
the book in print by the time we return to London, spend a month

going over our material, then two months at The Argoed writing the last chapter and preface and finally correcting theory. Sometime in the autumn the work will be out of our hands. Already sold our German rights: will appear simultaneously in Germany and England. Then for our seven-month holiday – seeing Anglo-Saxon democracy.

Beatrice is here referring to the celebrations for Queen Victoria's Diamond Jubilee. The Golden Jubilee ten years earlier had been treated as a personal celebration: this was much more an imperial occasion.

28 June. [41 Grosvenor Road]
Back in London. Imperialism in the air, all classes drunk with sightseeing and hysterical loyalty. Our morning, hard at work proof-correcting: in the afternoon and evening friends drop in to welcome us back, Sidney absorbed in catching up arrears of L.C.C. work.

8 July. [41 Grosvenor Road]
Dined last night with Alfred Cripps and Margaret Hobhouse. Alfred full of Workmen's Accidents Bill. He is organizing opposition and scheming with the employers to get in amendments. His feelings are a queer combination of anger at the Bill and at Chamberlain, helpless in face of a government majority, backed by the united forces of the opposition and self-complacency that he, at least, perceived the danger and outrageousness of the proposal and was doing his lawyer's best to spoke the wheels of this abominable legislation. . . . He asserted that it killed 'contracting out'. . . . He admitted that it meant state compensation at no very distant date. . . . 'It is a trade union Bill – it makes all in the direction of large establishments. I know you like that. I don't. . . .' 'It is one of the triumphs of the underground force of the democracy,' said I; 'what we are now discovering is that a Conservative majority is a more effective instrument of this force than a Liberal government.' 'It is these wretched urban towns, they are the force behind Chamberlain.' How he dislikes and distrusts Chamberlain.

The Women's Jubilee Dinner and Soirée was given by one hundred distinguished women to one hundred distinguished men in the Grafton Galleries on 14 July. It was organized by Mrs Humphry Ward (1851–1920), novelist, niece of Matthew Arnold and an active opponent of women's suffrage. Flora Annie Steel (1847–1929) was a popular novelist who lived in India until 1889: her best-known book was *On the Face of the Waters*. Lady Henry Somerset (1851–1921),

President of the British Women's Temperance Association, was related to Virginia Woolf and Bertrand Russell and a friend of the Pearsall Smiths. She had insisted on a public and socially damaging legal separation from her husband on the grounds of his homosexuality. The Bishop of London was the newly appointed Dr Mandell Creighton. 'Seeing that it was difficult to discover one hundred distinguished women, some other ladies, among them myself, were called in to advise,' Beatrice wrote in *Our Partnership*. 'I remember that my contribution was the principal factory inspectors and the heads of different educational institutions. My guest was the Bishop of London. What was remarkable in this dinner was that the hundred men were extremely distinguished, including practically all the leading politicians with the exception of Lord Salisbury, and many other persons of distinction; the difficulty being that so many distinguished men were left out, who in consequence were offended.'

15 July. [41 Grosvenor Road]

A great gathering of distinguished dames entertained at dinner a corresponding number of distinguished men. It was a brilliant and polished set of people, representing a good deal of hard work. The dinner, the rooms, the flowers and the dresses were soberly luxurious and charmingly tasteful; the three speeches – Mrs Steel, Lady Henry Somerset and the Bishop of London – were eloquent and witty; the Bishop excelled himself in the polished man-of-the-world style. Strange person my friend the Bishop, a scholar, a cynic, an admirable man of business and a staunch believer in the Church, possibly also a believer in religion as a necessary element in society. But his faith is the other side of complete scepticism. His attitude towards all things is one of steady depreciation, no good in intellect, no good in sentiment, no good in science, no good in politics. Since 'good' exists there is only one place left for it – the Church! The faith that originates in cynical scepticism is not an altogether wholesome constituent towards the making of a Church.

The Cowper Commission in 1894 had proposed that a reorganized University of London should not only conduct external examinations – its role hitherto – but also admit internal students to recognized constituent colleges. A private bill to implement this reform, drafted by Webb and Haldane, was twice defeated. Balfour then backed it. The Commission under the distinguished judge Lord Davey (1833–1907) was set up under the University of London Act to draw up its constitution and statutes.

16 July. [41 Grosvenor Road]

Sidney and Haldane rushing about London trying to get all parties to agree to a Bill for London University. If it goes through, it will be due to Haldane's insistence and his friendship with Balfour, but the form of the Bill, the alterations grafted on the Cowper Commission, are largely Sidney's. He thinks he has got all he wants as regards the Technical Education Board and the London School of Economics. The Commission appointed to carry the Act out is largely favourable, or at any rate 'susceptible' to right influence.

26 July. [41 Grosvenor Road]
Spent Sunday with Alfred Cripps at Parmoor. Obviously disgusted with the ways of Parliament this session. 'Balfour has no principle,' he plaintively repeated. 'He is perpetually asking why not? to the proposals of the radical wing of the Unionist party.' 'Chamberlain has beaten us: he twirls Balfour round his little finger and Salisbury is cynically indifferent to Home affairs, except perhaps to the interests of the Church and the Land.' At other times Alfred asserted that they had succeeded in getting eighty per cent of their amendments into the Workmen's Accidents Bill, but it was quite clear that he felt the champions of liberty and property had been done in the play of the parliamentary hand. 'It is hateful fighting your own party: you are not free to use the most telling weapons: if only I could have fought Chamberlain from the opposite side of the House! But the feeling is growing against him: he will break up the Unionist party and you will have him back leading your side before this Parliament is out.'

'He is much more useful to us fighting from within the Conservative ranks, my dear Alfred, we shall do our very best to keep him there. It is only Conservatives who can make revolutions nowadays, and they are, if anything, more susceptible to democratic pressure than the Liberals.'

Alfred Cripps is, I think, beginning to discover that a government will be flattering and considerate towards an able young lawyer who is ready to advise them and defend them whenever asked; but that these amenities cease when he begins to oppose them either overtly or privately. . .

John Dillon (1851–1927) was an Irish Nationalist M.P.: his wife was Elizabeth Matthew. Edward Marjoribanks Tweedmouth (1849–1909) was a rich Liberal landowner and politician, who was a member of Rosebery's Cabinet in 1894–95. His wife Fanny was Lord Randolph Churchill's sister. George Nathaniel, Marquis Curzon of Kedleston (1859–1925) was a widely travelled politician who specialized in colonial and Asian policy. He was at this time Under-Secretary for Foreign Affairs, and in 1898 he was appointd Viceroy of India. Lady

Rothschild was the wife of Nathan Mayer Rothschild (1840–1915), the banker who made generous contributions to educational causes and was the first professing Jew to sit in the House of Lords. Ethel Grenfell (1867–1952), later Lady 'Ettie' Desborough and a notable Society hostess, was the wife of William Henry Grenfell (1855–1945). Elected as a Liberal M.P. in 1880, he resigned in 1893 and was elected as a Conservative in 1900. Beatrice inserted a seating plan in the diary note on Haldane's dinner:

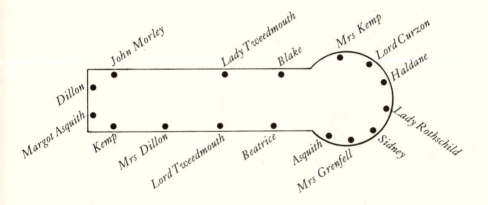

29 July. [41 Grosvenor Road]
This was a typical Haldane dinner on the night of the South African debate, typical of Haldane's weakness, his dilettante desire to be in every set; and of his strength, his diffusive friendship which enables him to bring about non-party measures.

On 26 July the House of Commons debated the report of the Parliamentary Committee set up to enquire into the Jameson Raid. When the Majority Report condemned Cecil Rhodes, but declared that neither the Colonial Secretary nor any of his officials had any advance knowledge of the venture, cynical critics spoke of the 'Lying-in-State' at Westminster. The minority wanted a more searching examination of the alleged complicity of the Colonial Office, claiming that there had been no proper investigation of this aspect of the incident. Mr Hawksley, the solicitor to the Chartered Company which employed Jameson, possessed some telegrams which he refused to produce to the Enquiry. In the debate Chamberlain was at pains to exonerate Rhodes.

30 July. [41 Grosvenor Road]
Massingham dined here last night. Greatly excited about South African debate. 'Superb rope-dancing, Chamberlain's speech.' 'Hawksley in the House ready to produce telegrams and letters unless Chamberlain repudiated condemnation of Rhodes. Harcourt

completely taken in: consented to back up government if they condemned Rhodes, and now Chamberlain declares that he accepted condemnation as a compromise and as far as he was concerned he always thought Rhodes a fine fellow. It is superb: it is a delight to watch such a man,' and Massingham bubbled over with the joy of the political dramatic critic. 'Chamberlain's career is extraordinarily interesting – every day brings its own trick.' 'The career is more interesting than the man,' added Massingham more gravely. 'He has neither the knowledge nor the convictions to make him more than a great political artist.' 'Surely', I rejoined, 'we shall look back on the last fifty years of the nineteenth century as the peculiar period of political artists: we have no statesmen – all our successful politicians, the men who lead the parties, are artists and nothing else: Gladstone, Disraeli, Randolph Churchill, Chamberlain, and the unsuccessful Rosebery, all these men have the characteristics of actors – personal charm, extraordinary pliability and quick-wittedness.'

27 August. The Argoed

The first fortnight or three weeks Sidney and I struggled painfully with rewriting the Economic Characteristics [of trade unionism], the stiffest chapter of the whole book, both of us feeling that we had 'bitten off more than we could chew' in our theory of trade unionism. At last we got into such a hopeless state of continuous argument that it was clear that we were wasting energy, so he agreed to go on by himself whilst I should begin to plan out the last chapter. So he is grappling with it alone, I think successfully. He is stronger-brained than I am, can carry more things in his mind at once. I was getting hopelessly befogged with utter weariness. We are working really too hard to enjoy it: we are bent on getting the book done with and out this autumn, and this last chapter has proved far more complicated than we thought. The weather is one continual south-west rainstorm which adds a touch of gloom to our overstrain. Bernard Shaw, too, is working continuously revising his plays, Charlotte is preoccupied with him. We are a very middle-aged party this autumn, inclined to drudge at our work. For all that, Sidney and I are peacefully happy. Now that I feel the crucial chapter is really getting on I can sit and calmly think out the last and the preface.

Julia Ravogli was an Italian singer who later became the second wife of William Cripps, married to Beatrice's sister Blanche.

10 September. [The Argoed]
The last day at The Argoed! Turned out to make room for a tenant and transplanted ourselves over the way to 'Moorcroft' for the remainder of the vacation. Spent another ten days hammering away together at the Economic Characteristics. Sidney got over the kink, but his stuff was rough-hewn and had to be polished up. Now at last we are sending the last instalment of the chapter to the printer. . . .

A Sunday spent at Standish where Blanche Cripps has a houseful of children and friends, entertaining among others the two Ravoglis, charming singers and one of them a patient of Willie's. Willie has developed into the fashionable surgeon whose patients adore him. The charming Julia Ravogli sang all day to us to show her gratitude for his skilful operation on her sister Sophia. Blanche, too, is a thoroughly happy satisfactory woman, her large income giving her full scope for her generous instincts. In spite of her mental deficiencies – absence of memory and inconsequence and extremely limited power of reasoning, her noble instincts make her into a fine woman with a good influence. To contrast her with poor little Rosy who is more *morally* deficient than intellectually wanting!

27 September. [Moorcroft]
Brain-fag and headache; for a good week enforced idleness, wandering alone over the moorland. . . These two months we have overworked for enjoyment; constantly too exhausted to care for exercise, and days when extreme exasperation from over-brainwork has made me quite incapable of enjoying the country. Also Shaw and Charlotte's relationship is disturbing. Shaw goes on untroubled, working hard at his plays and then going long rides with her on a tandem cycle. But she is always restless and sometimes unhappy, too anxious to be with him. He is sometimes bored, but he is getting to feel her a necessary part of his 'entourage' and would, I think, object to her breaking away from the relationship. He persuades himself that by keeping her occupied he is doing her good. If it were not for the fact that he is Shaw I should say that he was dishonourable. But as he has always advertised his views of marriage and philandering from the house-tops, every woman ought to be prepared for his logical carrying out of these principles.

18 October. Grosvenor Road
Worked hard since we came back, finished the last chapter. . . .

Met John Morley at a *tête-à-tête* dinner with the Courtneys. He and Sidney anxious to be pleasant to each other. A charming person for a talk on literature but a most depressing spectacle as a Liberal leader. In sympathy with no single one of the progressive ideas, he clings to his old shibboleths of non-intervention and non-expansion abroad, and Church disestablishment and a sort of theoretical Home Rule at home. When I suggested that if I had supreme power I would hesitate before I disestablished the Church he seemed aghast. And yet he dare not pronounce in favour of his old convictions; he feels instinctively the country is against him. To do nothing and to say nothing, to sit and wait for the tide to ebb from this government is the long and short of his policy. Naturally enough he is pessimistic, thinks that all things are going to the bad and that the country has lost its intellect and its character. To talk to on politics he is like a theologian who has begun to doubt his theology: in argument he always shrinks away from you, as if he suspected you of laying traps for him out of which he knew he could not struggle. A closed mind and a lack of pluck in asserting the dogmas that dominate him, give a most unpleasant impression of narrow-mindedness and nerve-less-ness. I shall send him our book: if he reads it it may antagonize him into some living thought. Leonard Courtney, one felt instinctively, was infinitely more open-minded as well as more robust in intellect, was fully prepared to consider new propositions and not in the least inclined to run away because he might have to change his mind if he stayed to look at them. John Morley is a pitiable person as a politician – all the more so because he is conscientious and upright. It makes one groan to think of that moral force absolutely useless.

Beatrice here included an extract from *The Times* of 29 October 1897 giving a report of the conference of the National Union of Women Workers at which she moved a resolution suggesting that the meeting should not start with prayers. An amendment was carried proposing 'that persons who are unwilling from conscientious scruples to be present during prayers may ask the secretaries to keep places for them'.

30 October. [41 Grosvenor Road]
So ended my official connection with the bishops' wives. I felt, rightly or wrongly, that it was necessary to clear up the situation: either the Association was distinctively Christian or not; if the former, I was gaining influence on false pretences; if the latter, the Executive had no right to impose the religious rites of a particular sect on a non-

religious body. It is difficult to know when and where it is wise to make a stand and insist on equality of treatment as a matter of principle. But I have a distrust of slipping into a sort of quagmire of latitudinarianism in which only the narrow-minded and uneducated persons are allowed to have strong convictions. And I feel one must fight against the temptation of pushing one's particular hobbies by sacrificing straightforwardness and intellectual honesty in all other issues. It is strange how a meeting is influenced by the *way of putting it*. My resolution had given great offence, and when I rose to move it I felt hostile feeling all around. But with a few frank and gentle words all the hostility vanished, and though the meeting supported the Executive I had won their sympathy and respect, which again reacted on me and I felt rather a brute to object to their prayers! The association otherwise strikes me as doing good work. Louise Creighton has distinctly a statesmanlike mind, and the group of women who now control the policy are a good sort — large-minded and pleasant-mannered. The 'screeching sisterhood' are trying to invade them but Louise's battalions of hardworking, religious and somewhat stupid women will, I think, resist the attack.

8 November. [41 Grosvenor Road]
The last pages of our revise gone back to the printer. For the last ten days 'no settled occupation': it is wearisome to get up in the morning and feel that there is no more reason for doing one thing than another. If the elections were not upon us and our journey imminent, I should begin straight away on another bit of work.

A strike called by the Amalgamated Society of Engineers in support of the Eight-Hour Day had begun in London in May and by July, when the engineering employers had discharged a quarter of their workmen to burden the union's unemployment fund, it had become a national dispute. The A.S.E. was the largest union in the country, and it held out for several months. In late November 1897 negotiations led to a compromise formula, but the union members decisively rejected its terms in a ballot. On 15 January, however, they capitulated. The separate Australian colonies were now federating into a commonwealth, and Beatrice was reading about them in preparation for her intended visit.

10 December. [41 Grosvenor Road]
A chaotic month since I last wrote! Began a course of reading on Australia and New Zealand, waded through blue-books on Federation, etc., read page after page of unreadable history, ugly facts told in an ugly manner. But this sedative occupation was soon

broken into by odd jobs, little bits of journalism that were long due, and three or four days' hard work revising the work of the scholars of the London School. Now I am beginning to think of my lecture on Methods of Sociological Enquiry, with intervals over L.C.C. campaign literature and hours devoted to turning over our travelling schemes and the outfit necessary. Also the Engineers' lock-out, Sidney constantly drafting letters and conditions, I sometimes egging him on. A wretched business! It is only those who know the rotten constitution of the A.S.E. and their guerilla policy who realize the badness of the whole business – the hold that employers have over the public opinion of all classes in the general dislike of the A.S.E.

This morning we drafted letters to the *Daily Chronicle* and the *Manchester Guardian* and wrote private letters to the leading officials of the great unions begging them to take the matter up on the ground that collective bargaining is attacked. We may be on the eve of a big convulsion – a Conservative government is always favourable to the growth of revolutionary feelings, and for the last five years working class opinion has been lying dormant. Meanwhile our portentous book [*Industrial Democracy*] is still in the press, will appear on January 4th. We must prepare ourselves for disappointment, or rather we must try not to think of success or failure, simply feel that we have done our level best and there it is – to be taken or left. Anyway, we have learnt enormously from our six years' investigation, and the life has been a happy one, full of love and interest. What more can we ask for?

Perhaps part of my chaotic frame of mind due to dabbling in society: thought it good opportunity to invite some people to dinner since it did not much matter whether I felt seedy or not the next day. My little parties are said to be successful but they don't please me. Directly you entertain for entertaining's sake, then they become hollow and unpleasant, an element of vanity enters in and you begin to wonder what impression you make, what your friends think of each other, and so on. My conclusion from this last month is that the dross in my nature is not yet eliminated! There is a good strong strain of the vain worldling left. Thank the gods, there is no trace of such feeling in Sidney. Work and love are the only gods he lives for. Oh, my boy, how I love you – past understanding!

14 December. [41 Grosvenor Road]
Asquith called here this morning and spent half an hour discussing the

Engineering dispute. He has the last few years been cold to the labour movement, and unfriendly to us, so his anxiety to be informed was an interesting sign of the times. He is a shrewd able lawyer, coarse-grained and unimaginative but sensitive like all politicians to the changes in the political atmosphere. Sidney explained the Engineers' contention and also their weakness and coached him up on the technical side of the question, gave him our chapter on the Standard Rate. We did our best, and we shall see whether it bears fruit in his speech at Stockport.

Xmas. Parmoor
Another pleasant Xmas with Alfred and his children. The house is filling up with charming bits of furniture and old china, the service becoming more luxurious than of old, and a general atmosphere of warmth and charm and comfort pervades the place. Alfred settling down with complacency to parliamentary life and a large income and thoroughly enjoying his children growing up around him. Long walks, talking chiefly of the contents of our book, of which we brought him an 'advance copy'. Rosy Williams here, a changed mortal, well in health, handsome to look at and thoroughly enjoying her life with troops of young and old men 'after her'. How long this amiable mood will last remains to be seen!

∽ 1898 ∾

11 January. [41 Grosvenor Road]
Our big book has had a brilliant reception. *The Times* gave us two columns on the day of publication, the *Standard* an abusive leader, the *Daily Chronicle* and the *Daily News* and half a dozen big provincials were all properly enthusiastic. Other papers followed suit and produced their reviews the next day – the weeklies treated us quite as handsomely. Altogether a small triumph in its way. The scientific character of the work is recognized, though of course the critics chaff us for our 'pompous phraseology'. It is a big plant on the public: a new method and a new theory!

The old Eve in me is delighted with buying a trousseau for our nine months' journey. It is a long time since I have really had a good 'go' at clothes and I am revelling in buying silks and satins, gloves, underclothing, furs and everything that a sober-minded woman of forty can want to inspire Americans and Colonials with a due respect for the refinements of attractiveness! It is a pleasure to clothe myself charmingly! For the last ten years I have not had either the time or the will to think of it. For this tour, I harmonize some extravagance with my conscience by making myself believe that I must have everything new and that I must look nice! I believe that it is a deliberate expenditure because six months ago I determined that I would do myself handsomely as part of a policy, but I daresay one or two of the specially becoming blouses are the expression of concrete vanity. My childish delight in watching these bright clothes being made is a sort of rebound from the hard drudgery of the last two years. But it is rather comical in a woman of 40! – 40 all but two weeks – forty, forty, FORTY – what an age, almost elderly! I don't feel a bit old.

Arthur Strong (1863–1904) was an orientalist and art historian. He was appointed Librarian at Chatsworth in 1895 and at the House of Lords in 1897. Eugenie Sellers, whom he married in 1897, was a well-known archaeologist.

14 January. [41 Grosvenor Road]
Poor Alice Green! For the last month or so she has become friendly to us and the other evening when I was alone with her she broke down and wept bitterly in my arms. Arthur Strong, after using her money and her influence to climb into the position of Librarian to the House of Lords, marries a brilliant and beautiful Greek scholar – Eugenie Sellers. For eighteen months the poor woman has been eaten into with bitterness; when at times I have watched her unawares she has looked like a lost soul. And a certain lack of dignity and the extreme unhappiness of her expression has alienated some of her old friends, and even Society is becoming cold to her. The world gets impatient at her restless unhappiness: at fifty years of age, with a good income, distinguished position, a woman ought to settle down contentedly. But some women never grow too old to be in love, or at least to require love. And why should they? With intellectual persons love is the passion for warm enduring affection and intimate mental companionship. Only religion can take its place. And Alice Green has no religion, no conviction, not even a cause she believes in.

Audrey (Ada) Radford (1859–1934) was the sister of Ernest Radford, poet and barrister and a friend of Marx and Engels. Aubrey Beardsley's magazine the

Yellow Book was a spokesman of *avant-garde* culture. Daniel Meinertzhagen (1875–98), the son of Georgina, died of peritonitis in Bremen.

21 January. [41 Grosvenor Road]
Sidney and I have spent much thought and time on the Engineers' dispute, but all to no purpose. . . . Meanwhile our old friend Graham Wallas has married – Ada Radford, a woman of forty or thereabouts and one of a cultivated, public-spirited, somewhat aesthetic middle-class family. She was educated at Girton, became assistant mistress of High School, then secretary to a Working Women's College, then a writer for the *Yellow Book*. A woman of a certain originality of life and with a pretty little literary gift for writing short stories. I do not take to her. She is obviously a good woman – sweet-natured (Graham says humorous) with decision and capacity. Her ideas are the old-fashioned aesthetic, secularist, equal rights sort. She is a woman who carries rigid principles into the smallest concerns of life. With Madonna-like features, good complexion and soft golden hair, she ought to be pleasant to look at: but as a matter of principle she dresses in yellow-green sloppy garments, large garden hat with bows of green silk – her hair is always coming down – and generally speaking, she looks as if she had tumbled up out of an armchair in which she had slept the night, and her movements are aggressively ugly. But as Graham sees none of this, what does it matter! They are devotedly attached: she has just enough money to make marriage – with no prospect of children – prudent if not actually desirable for Graham. I doubt whether we shall be much of friends. We are both too set in our own mould, too completely filled up with work and comrades to have time to discover the 'deeper affinities' which doubtless exist between two women who have both struggled with life and work. If we are ever thrown together we might get to like each other – for the differences are superficial and my distaste is really to her clothes. I could forgive them if they were not worn *on principle*. But principle without a deal of intelligence or some personal charm *tires* one!

16 February. Herbert Spencer's. Brighton
Second visit this year to this poor old man. 'If I believed in Induction I should be forced to believe that I was pursued by demons,' laments the poor old man; 'and who knows', he adds in strangely humble tones, 'the veil may be lifted; it may be so.' And all this arises from the fact

that one or two persons with whom he has been casually connected have misbehaved themselves with women and thus imperilled his reputation!

The last month filled up with miscellaneous work: Sidney writing signed articles. . . I spending the mornings getting out T.U. material in order for binding . . . with electioneering thrown in by the way and preparing a volume of essays to appear while we are abroad. And meanwhile a constant stream of individuals passing through our house . . . their one common feature being that they all ask questions which have to be answered.

Dan Meinertzhagen dead: Georgie's best-loved child, a terrible tragedy in our sister's life.

2 March. [41 Grosvenor Road]

A great meeting at St James's Hall – Lord Rosebery 'to the rescue'. I sat behind him and watched him narrowly. He has lost that drugged look, heavy eyes and morbid flesh, that he had as Premier. He is at once older, healthier and *better* looking. His speech had vigour, astuteness and flashes of dramatic genius. But he was woefully full of himself: his whole expression and attitude was concentrated self-consciousness and sensitiveness, not sufficient of an actor to lose himself in his part, not sufficient of a patriot to lose himself in his cause. Throughout there was an undercurrent of complaint, of personal grudge against the political world. He is not a leader. Outside foreign politics he has no creed and only a scrappy knowledge: his very egotism is ineffective egotism, an egotism that shrinks from the world's touch, not the egotism that forces itself on the world. For my part, if a man is to be full of himself I like him to have the will and the capacity to make the world full of him also!

No one knows how the L.C.C. election will turn out: both sides suffer in turn from hope and depression. The Conservative organization is straining every nerve to get the Moderates in : whilst we on our side are beating up every available progressive force wheresoever it is located. . . .

James Bryce (1838–1922), jurist and historian, became a Liberal M.P. in 1880: he was chairman of the Royal Commission on Secondary Education in 1894–95. W. M. Crook (b. 1860), a Liberal politician, was editor of the London *Echo* 1898–1900.

[?] *March*. [41 Grosvenor Road]

The L.C.C. election. We sallied forth about 8.30 a.m. (Sidney having voted first in Westminster) laden with sandwiches, teapots and oranges, to fit up the committee rooms. It was a glorious morning, the Westminster buildings rising out of the blue atmosphere and the river dancing in the brilliant morning sun. At 9.30 I had settled down at one of the six committee rooms. . . About 3.30 the 'bringers-up' trooped in – at 5 it was a crowd in the little room, each awaiting to report progress. Then came on a heavy fall of snow, but the feeling of the Progressives was so hot that they trudged on through the sleet and the slush, not one of my fifteen workers gave up working. . . . Then the hurried dinner . . . then the exciting hours of the count, then the midnight visit to the National Liberal Club all aglow with Progressive victories – and then to bed – oh! so tired – far too tired to sleep.

The Moderates are hardly 'snowed under' as in 1892, but they are soundly beaten, leaving us in a great majority for the next three years. . . . Perhaps the most striking fact of the L.C.C. election has been the complete eclipse of the Liberal leaders. The Progressive Election Committee has spurned their help, has fought the whole battle on the non-political line. And this contempt for the Liberal leaders has not sprung from the extreme left . . . but from the little knot of Progressive radicals. . . Rosebery, it is true, came forward, but expressly as a past Progressive chairman of the L.C.C. and himself disowned any official connection with the Liberals. The official London Progressives – men who six years ago would have been only too proud of the patronage of an ex-Liberal Cabinet Minister, now stand completely divorced from their allegiance to the Liberal leaders and talk of them with habitual contempt as men of no conviction and no knowledge. Even Rosebery, whom they are glad enough to use, has no influence with them. This victory will strengthen this feeling of independence, if not superiority, to the official Liberal leaders on the part of the L.C.C. Progressives. They will more and more regard themselves as able and experienced administrators, actually working out political problems, whilst they look on men like Bryce, Asquith, Harcourt, Fowler, either as mere members of a debating society or as 'London Society men' with whom they have little or nothing in common. Asquith especially has lost all his prestige in the eyes of the London Radical.

We gather, on the other hand, that there is no repentance on the part of the Front Bench Liberals – at least there was not before the L.C.C. election. Not a member of the Front Bench seems to be working at politics: they are either following their own professions or dancing attendance on London Society. Their whole attitude is certainly astounding: beyond cavilling at the government, chiefly on foreign questions, no one is ever wiser for their appearance in public. Dull banalities or flippant proposals of new issues – personalities of a well-bred sort – that is all one gets from the ex-Cabinet Ministers. I think most Progressives have ceased to read their speeches: even the I.L.P. finds it precious difficult to criticize 'a negation in opposition'.

Meanwhile the I.L.P. has collapsed in London: J.R. MacDonald, our Fabian 'lone-hander', polling a few hundred votes against the Progressives in one of the most advanced constituencies, whilst the bitter attack on Phillimore succeeded only in placing him close on the heels of Sidney at the poll – a 1,300 majority! Indeed, just as the L.C.C. election of 1895 was a defeat for us, so this election has been our victory. Fabianism, in one form or another, is again triumphant.

We therefore close this portion of our life with considerable complacency and start on our long journey with a light heart. Our book has been extraordinarily well received, our party has recovered a good working majority on the L.C.C.; the London School of Economics is growing silently though surely into a centre of collectivist-tempered research and establishing itself as *the* English School of Economics and Political Science. We can now feel assured that with the School as a teaching body, the Fabian Society as a propagandist organization, the L.C.C. Progressives as an object lesson of electoral success, our books as the only elaborate and original work in economic fact and theory, no young man or woman who is anxious to study or to work in public affairs can fail to come under our influence. We have also consolidated our position in the press. Massingham of the *Daily Chronicle* is again our friend: the *Manchester Guardian* and the *Echo* are practically our organs through Leonard Hobhouse and W.M. Crook – the provincial Liberal papers are extremely friendly. It is only the *Westminster*, the *Daily News*, the *Star* which remain somewhat cold and suspicious towards the rising of a new party. But all this does not mean that 'Our Set' is anywhere near office or nominal political power. The crust of London Society liberalism is, as yet, far too hard for us to break, and I doubt whether we are not always likely to work underground at foundations upon which a younger generation will build, perhaps not quite in the form we intended!

Our journey will be a complete break in our life. We have finished with trade unionism, we have even carted all our material round to the Library of the School. Galton leaves us finally and pushes forward in his own career as election agent and journalist; our two girls, to whom we have grown attached, leave us also and 'better themselves' by going to Maggie's larger and richer household. In most ways I shall regret them; they are attractive natures, first-rate servants and saved me much trouble. If it had not been for poor virtue's lapse last autumn into the habit of taking small doses of our whisky, a habit which I felt I had not time or inclination to root out by constant strict supervision, and Mary's slight extravagance, I should have been ready to sacrifice almost anything to keep them. It is so difficult to find servants whom you care for and who care for you! But probably it is better for them to move on to better wages and under a more careful and watchful mistress. Even our cats – two brothers who have prowled about this house for four years – are leaving us for new homes! All will have to be new and strange and perhaps difficult when we return – work, secretary, servants. We may easily, on all points, change for the worse. Meanwhile we intend to enjoy ourselves and let the future look out for itself.

I shall aim whilst I am touring at 'taking impressions' in writing of persons and scenes. The last four years I have done a good deal of hard thinking and made elaborate maps of technical facts. Now I want to sketch life as I see it casually, from day to day. . . .

PART II

Round the English-Speaking World

March 1898 – December 1898

A Summary of Volumes 17,18 and 19

'To America, Australia and New Zealand, when they might go to Russia India or China. What taste! Just what you would expect from them.' Beatrice put this remark by a Tory acquaintance at the head of the first entry she made in her diary after she and Sidney had sailed from Liverpool to New York at the end of March, beginning what she called a nine-month 'busman's holiday'. Neither she nor Sidney were much stimulated by travel or refreshed by exotic scenes. Their leisurely journey had to serve a purpose – preparation for their study of local government; and so, seeking to discover how the English municipal tradition had been transplanted overseas, they set off to visit over forty legislative and civic assemblies, from the American Congress down to tiny boroughs in New Zealand.

The record of this narrowly focused tour survives in nearly a hundred thousand words of manuscript which Beatrice roughly prepared for an omitted chapter of *Our Partnership* entitled 'Round the English-Speaking World'. 'They were there on my desk, staring at me reproachfully,' she wrote at the time, when she discussed them with Sidney and he advised against their inclusion. She hankered after publishing them, yet she recognized that they were an unsatisfactory chronicle that was out of keeping with a diary that is generally so vivid and personal. At the time she had felt inhibited about keeping a notebook which Sidney saw, and in which he wrote about a third of the entries – an effect, she admitted, which persisted for some months after she returned to London and made the diary for 1899 both patchy and stilted; and looking over the draft chapter with Sidney, some thirty years after the events it described, she saw the force of his claim that these accounts of parliaments and politicians and labour laws were too technical (and stale) for the general reader and too casual for the scholar. After her death, however, academic interest in the countries concerned was sufficient for the travelogues to be separately published

as *Beatrice Webb's American Diary* (ed. David A. Shannon, University
of Wisconsin Press, Madison, 1963); *Visit to New Zealand: Beatrice
Webb's Diary with entries by Sidney Webb* (Prince, Milburn,
Wellington, 1959); and *The Webbs' Australian Diary* (ed. A.G.
Austin, Pitman, Melbourne, 1965).

Apart from Beatrice's adolescent holiday in America, and Sidney's
three-month visit in 1888, the Webbs had never before been off the
beaten tourist tracks of Europe. They had read enough of the young
countries they were to visit to give them a sketch of the historical
background and a general idea of current problems, but they do not
seem to have taken much trouble to talk to Americans or Antipodeans
in London before they left; and though they carried many letters of
introduction, their comments about people they met often read more
like a routine of inspection than an experience they could enjoy.
Within days of landing Beatrice had struck a note of insular
condescension that was to echo through everything she wrote along the
way. She seldom made a gracious or generous comment, and as she
tired – she was ill with a fever in Chicago, suffering from neuralgia
and neurasthenia in Denver, irritably exhausted in Australia – she
lapsed increasingly into the habit of judging people by appearances
and making invidious comparisons. From the start, indeed, she
seemed able to describe but not to understand those among whom she
travelled, and though Sidney was less censorious, he showed even less
imagination than Beatrice. As the weeks passed they lapsed from novel
impressions into familiar responses. 'The longer we stay away the
more we find ourselves drifting into full investigation and spend our
whole time talking shop,' Beatrice wrote to her sister Kate from
Melbourne on 1 November. 'It is a case of "the old craving" with us:
tracking facts is like every other sport to which one has devoted the
best portion of one's life, one is restless unless one is indulging in it.'

The journey began in a holiday mood. The Webbs were travelling as
far as Washington with their friend and fellow Fabian, Sydney
Olivier (1859–1943), who was on Colonial Office business, and
young Charles Trevelyan was going all round the world with them.
Bernard Shaw, Graham Wallas and Kate Courtney were among the
group who had come to see them off at Euston, and at Liverpool Lallie
and Robert Holt were there to show off the splendid cabin which their
'capitalist connections' in the shipping trade had secured for the
Webbs on the White Star liner, the *Teutonic*. But they arrived in New

York to find America gripped by the fever of impending war with Spain. 'All the politicians to whom we have introductions are completely absorbed in Cuba,' Beatrice noted, and they were lucky to have two long talks with Theodore Roosevelt (1858–1919), then the Assistant Secretary of the Navy preparing to attack Cuba and later President of the United States – 'the most remarkable man I have yet met in America', Beatrice wrote, admiring his 'abundance of ready wit, splendid fighting courage and thorough knowledge of the world he lives in'. Yet the Webbs wanted to talk about parliamentary procedures and city government, not war, and for all the political excitement (which they found rather distasteful) they persevered with their specialist enquiries.

They formed an unfavourable view of the Congress. 'If I were an American I should feel utterly despondent about the future of the House of Representatives,' Beatrice remarked on 18 April. 'With abominable procedure . . . with no self-respect, with little intellectual leadership, with a predominantly loose moral character, it seems doomed to impotence varied by disorder.' She was equally caustic about the Senate, full of 'large-headed fine-featured men with grave and dignified manners', calling it 'a "show" body whose main function is to look dignified and impressive so as to remove from the mind of the American citizen the sense of humiliation which might have been produced by a visit to the House of Representatives'. All in all, she concluded, the congressional system was a shambles:

> There is no responsible government, no body of men who can be held accountable or whom the electors can control . . . there is always a hidden and irresponsible authority and power which shifts from group to group according to the personalities that crop up in the constituent parts of the constitution, written and unwritten.

They were in fact, rather more impressed by the Tammany organization in New York, for Sidney's years on the L.C.C. had taught them the intricacies of city government, and they could see how a political machine could weave patterns of patronage and corruption into its fabric. And in Boston, where they were much taken by Jo Quincy – the patrician mayor who was also the Democratic boss – they persuaded themselves that he was actually introducing 'Fabian collectivism' into the city.

There is a sense of disorientation in such comments, and it persists as the Webbs made the round of academic society at Cornell, Vassar, Harvard and Yale. The professors, for the most part, did not look or talk like professors. At Cornell they stayed with Jeremiah W. Jenks (1856–1929), who was becoming a foremost economist. 'From his appearance, manner and speech I should have taken him for a pushing and enterprising manager of a store in a Western city,' Beatrice said, adding that while his wife and children were 'kindly and good-natured' they had 'neither tact nor grace nor charm of any kind': the one redeeming feature of the Jenks family was their 'simple, pretty and convenient' house. She thought better of Woodrow Wilson (1856–1924), who was to be elected President a dozen years later: when they called on him at Princeton she thought him 'attractive-minded' because he had 'a peculiarly un-American insight into the actual working of institutions as distinguished from their nominal constitution'.

The particularities were tart and the generalities were sweeping, whether Beatrice was speaking for herself or reporting what others had said. Shown round the New York slums by Lillian D. Wald (1867–1940), the social worker who founded the Henry Street Settlement, she had the situation tabulated in a few sentences. 'The Jews are the best material for citizenship,' she noted, 'least open to corruption and anxious to be the good element'; the Irish 'worst because drunken and corrupt'; the Italians 'mere children – always getting into trouble at police courts and much oppressed and scared by the American methods'. She thought the 'freer and wider' culture of Catholics and 'Jewish intelligence' equally welcome deviations from the 'wearisome groove of literal language and textbook knowledge into which one usually falls in talking to any American'. And when she came to Denver, where she observed a thousand delegates attending the convention of the Federated Women's Clubs, she was quick to characterize the whole affair. '"Dressiness" was indeed the characteristic note of the gathering. . . . The meetings were never punctual, and the conduct of them was extremely amateurish . . . abounding in metaphors and grandiloquent phrases.'

This was the only occasion on which Beatrice made an extended comment on American women, and her remarks were typically ambivalent. Though she found the delegates 'pleasant and lively, full of good intentions to improve their own minds, and with a sensitive and gracious deference to other persons' opinions', she dismissed their clubs as 'simply mutual improvement societies' for women who sought 'a smattering of culture without effort'; and the best she could say of the movement as a whole was that for 'the women in the little towns and villages scattered over the vast plains of America' it 'means the yearning for a wider life and brings . . . a feeling of fellowship with other women, which may be the beginning of a desire for active citizenship'. In Colorado, as it happened, the women had opportunities which the majority of the delegates (and all Englishwomen) then lacked, for the state had enjoyed complete women's suffrage for the past four years. 'There is a universal consensus of opinion that, as far as the women's vote has had any distinctive influence at all, it has been an influence for good,' Beatrice wrote, noting that it had 'ousted certain evil livers and corrupt politicians' and had a progressive effect on education: but she added that 'it has produced absolutely no change in the woman at home.'

When she came to Utah, where she had been as a girl, she was impressed by the progress that the Mormons had made, delighted by all the evidences of social discipline and civic pride – the city hall in Salt Lake City, she said, was 'the first really *self-respecting* abode of municipal government we have come across in the United States' – and sympathetic to the case for plural marriage. Talking to a woman who had successfully run against her husband for a seat in the state senate, she agreed 'that it is a loss to the world that the experiment of polygamy was not continued by a sect exceptionally well fitted to give it a fair and full trial and to develop the experiment into other forms of "scientific breeding" if polygamy pure and simple proved unsatisfactory.' In Utah, at least, domestic circumstances were intriguingly different.

The Webbs reached San Francisco in time to ride in the July 4th procession to the sound of fireworks, pistol shots and marching bands.

Certainly our last impression of an American city will be like our first of New York. Noise, noise, nothing but noise. That is the curse both of American city life and of American travelling. In the city your senses are disturbed, your ears are deafened, your eyes are wearied by a constant rush: your nerves and muscles are shaken and rattled in the streetcars; you are never left for one minute alone on the road, whether you travel by ordinary car or Pullman; doors are opened and slammed, passengers jump up and down, boys with papers, sweets, fruits, drinks, stream in and out and insist on your looking at their wares or force you to repel them rudely; conductors open and shut windows; light and put out the gas; the engine-bell rings constantly, and now and again the steam-whistle (more like a fog-horn than a whistle) thunders out warning of the train's approach. Noise, confusion, rattle and bustle are among the disagreeable memories of American travel.

She was clearly glad to get to San Francisco, and thought the place was unique. 'It seems isolated from and unconcerned with any other part of America. It is out and away the most cosmopolitan city I have yet come across. It has no standards, no common customs; no common ideals of excellence, of intellect or manners – only one universal anarchy, each race living according to its lights, or rather according to its own impulses, seeing that all alike are free from their own racial public opinion. To the person who wishes to live unto himself without any pressure of law, custom or public opinion, San Francisco must be a veritable paradise.'

The *Coptic* sailed for Honolulu on 7 July, out of San Francisco harbour into a cold and choppy sea. 'Mrs Webb has been writing her diary, which will be the Pepys of the nineteenth century', Charles Trevelyan wrote home to his family. As the Pacific coast fell behind, Beatrice ran her conflicting impressions together in a summary she called 'Superficial Notes on American Characteristics'. 'Who would recognize as distinctly American the essentially eccentric and ugly individuals portrayed by Dickens, Trollope and Martineau?' she asked.

Of all the white races Americans have today the most agreeable manners . . . you never feel snubbed or ignored . . . you never watch ugly or weak people intentionally pained . . . you seldom or never hear an insolent word or low jest . . . there is a positive presence of kindness and humanity – an atmosphere of hospitality towards all sorts and conditions of men, a contagious desire that all alike should have a good time. . . . And these good manners do not mean effeminacy. No race excels the Americans in physical courage. If nervous will-power and sheer delight in using it, if love of risks – at any rate physical and financial risks – are the test of virility, the American has no peer.

That compliment paid, however, Beatrice went on to say that it was 'difficult to be as enthusiastic over any other American characteristic'.

She took the 'extraordinary promptness' of Americans in making decisions as an aspect of 'their gravest national defect – impatience'; and she blamed 'this inability to think things out and to persist' for 'that strangest of paradoxes of American political life, its continuous restlessness and its relative stagnation. . . . A new scheme of reform is put forward, is accepted, yields its crop of extravagant hopes and extravagant fears, and then dies down long before it has taken a practical shape.' That same impatience, she believed, led to the American delight in time-saving contrivances.

If perfectly constructed telephones, skilled stenographers, express elevators of all descriptions, could by themselves get through business, the transactions of one American city would exceed those of the world. But as far as we could make out, the very ease and rapidity with which every individual businessman can gratify his impulse to get into communication with every other businessman and insist on being attended to there and then, ends in a general dissipation of energy and such destruction of continuity of effort that fewer transactions were actually completed than would have been the case if each man had been compelled to get through his work without immediately consulting other people. All this appreciation of American contrivances seems to us a symptom of the American's disinclination to think beforehand or to do things or permit other people to do things in any methodical sequence. Each individual businessman becomes the slave of all the stray impulses and sudden improvisations of all other businessmen.

All the way across America Beatrice had been teased by her impression that the Americans seemed 'at once the most intelligent and the least intellectual of white races': it was a good example both of her tendency to take people at face value and her conviction that Americans were wearisomely uniform in their social habits and intellectual aspirations.

The most commonplace American is alert, inquisitive, sensitive to criticism, and superficially responsive to new ideas. The conductor of a car, the chambermaid at an hotel, the driver of a team, or even the ordinary office clerk, are nearly always good company; they have heard tell about most things, they are quick at answering your points, they are able to accept and put in its place any fact or argument you may give them. But if an illiterate or dullard or vulgar fellow is rare among native Americans, so are men and women of eminent distinction. This is all the more surprising since you are always meeting persons *who look distinguished;* men with shapely foreheads, finely chiselled features, keen piercing eyes and faces apparently lined with thought; women who have variety of expression and charm of gesture which would denote with us mother wit or emotional experience. But directly these attractive beings begin to talk you find yourself listening to a 'brightness' which is not wit, to sympathetic expressions which fail to be understanding, and to the same old banal assumptions and mediocre observations, repeated with uniform emphasis but without conviction – a sort of mechanical repetition of what they have been hearing all their lives. The tyranny of the stale platitude is maddening in the U.S.A.

Beatrice asked herself how such uniformity had arisen in a people so diverse in ethnic origin, settled in a land of such variety; and she attributed it to what she called two radically false and yet agreeable assumptions. The first was the notion that all men were born free and equal, 'with its derivative that one man is as good as another and equally fitted to deliver judgement on every conceivable question'. It is this belief that 'there is no such thing as the expert', she said, 'that eats away the roots of any American genius. . . . The common run of Americans object to any pretension to a higher standard of intelligence, or any assertion of an original point of view, as a direct denial of the basis of American democracy.' The second was 'the old fallacy of the classic economists that each man will best serve the interests of the whole community by pursuing his own gain.' Unlike England, where she thought the notion of public interest was generally accepted as the spring of public service, she felt that Americans

accept pecuniary self-interest as the one and only propelling motive, and are almost ashamed to admit that they are inspired by any other. . . . However diverse may be the origins and physical environment of a people, if they have but one motive there can be but one faculty. Hence the all-pervading and all-devouring 'executive capacity' of the American people. . . . No one in America seems to realize that good government rests not merely on democratic institutions but on the growth of a new motive, that of social service combined with the selection of men for the work of government according to their capacity for that work.

The Webbs arrived at Honolulu on 13 July in the ship which carried the news of the destruction of the Spanish fleet at Santiago and the annexation of Hawaii by the United States – a gala day for a small and distant territory which Sidney described as 'the Island of Skye, with Kew Gardens let loose on its beach and the temperature of a hothouse'. For once they relaxed, finding surf-riding and bathing with Princess Kaiulani (niece of the deposed Queen) far more attractive than cross-examining the Yankee oligarchs who had taken over the sugar-rich islands: it would be pleasant to stay for a year to study such an ethnically mixed community, Beatrice reflected, but in less than a week the *Almeda* sailed for Auckland.

They felt comfortable in New Zealand. The winter climate was much like home, and so were the forms of government, the manners and behaviour of the people; and the month passed most agreeably. They went to the principal towns – Wellington, Napier, Christchurch and even Dunedin, in the far south, where they addressed a local Fabian Society. They made a tour of the geysers near Rotorua, stayed with Leonard Courtney's brother-in-law (a rich sheep-farmer and member of the Legislative Council named Richard Oliver), attended a rowdy meeting of the House of Representatives (the Speaker, Beatrice noted, 'is constantly absent, incapacitated from his duties by drink'), and thought little of the unique Arbitration Court, established by their friend William Pember Reeves when he had been Minister of Labour, because its purpose had been perverted by the 'hopelessly unfit man' who was the presiding judge. Beatrice was generally critical of the men appointed by the populist Premier Richard Seddon (1845–1906), describing him as 'a gross, illiterate but forceful man' who was 'intensely vulgar' in manners – though she recognized his zeal, industry and indomitable pluck in working for 'the common people throughout the colony'. In thirteen years of office this Lancashire-born man, who had been a goldminer, a butcher and a publican, made his little country a pioneer of advanced legislation, including votes for women and some experiments in state ownership.

Before the Webbs sailed for Sydney on the *Monowai* Beatrice recorded their 'agreeable impression' of a country 'where there are no millionaires and hardly any slums', and where a people 'characterized by homely refinement' showed 'a large measure of vigorous public spirit'. Her conclusion was unusually generous.

> Judged by English standards, the New Zealanders are an easygoing race, moral but gay, lacking in puritan pugnacity, with perhaps just a suspicion of the Polynesian! Their birth-rate is among the lowest of the Anglo-Saxon world; 'bicycles and pianos are cheaper and more attractive than babies', remarked a medical man. But taken all in all if I had to bring up a family outside of Great Britain I would choose New Zealand as its home.

When the Webbs arrived in Australia the separate colonies were on the eve of Federation, but they knew too little about the issues to make the most of their meetings with the political leaders who were forming the new commonwealth, and they were also too ignorant of the history of local government in Australia to do much more than note what they were told and describe what they saw. There is a lame weariness about the diary entries (Sidney was writing a good many of them by this time) which cover their extensive tour: nothing in this vast new nation seemed to have interested or cheered them. Visiting sheep stations in the outback they admired the 'magnificent distances' but thought the 'tired colouring' made the countryside generally unattractive. They obviously did not care much for Sydney, Brisbane or Melbourne, because they said little about these cities and greeted Adelaide with a cry of pleasurable relief. They thought well of the leading politicians, for the most part, and praised the standard of the newspapers, but both the scale and the relative newness of Australian life seemed to baffle them. Even when Beatrice tried to generalize she found it hard to be more than a condescending tourist from 'back Home'. 'We are struck with the backwardness of politics here,' she wrote, overlooking the fact that in some respects Australia had been swept by the same radicalizing wave that had lifted Seddon into office in New Zealand.

> The rich people take no part and actually pride themselves on their contempt for public affairs; money-making and racing seem their only concern. . . . The working-men seem also largely non-political . . . they have no ideas of their own. . . . The most depressing feature of New South Wales is

the absence of education among the rich, and the bad manners of all classes. The well-to-do women too are uncivilized: they are dressy, snobbish and idle, and whilst they are willing to companion the men on the racecourse, they apparently think it 'unwomanly' to take an active part in public affairs.

In 1936 Beatrice added a note to this manuscript entry to say that these strictures did not apply to 'the professional women, medical and educational, of whom I met many noteworthy ones', but at the time she remarked on very few such meetings. When, indeed, she dined with the Principal at the Women's College in Sydney on 7 October she noted some of the pressures which made it difficult for Australian women to get a footing in any sphere of life outside the home. 'Like the rest of the University the Women's College is depressed', she wrote;

is, in fact, struggling into life in spite of the steady indifference, if not hostility, of Australian Society. 'Let the women keep to the kitchen,' said a wealthy man who was asked for a subscription; and he fairly represented Australian opinion. And yet the cooking is so bad! As far as one can make out, the Australian girls spend their time in making their own clothes, except when they are wearing them in the company of young men. The clothes are fresh and flashy: powder and paint ruin complexions and the women age rapidly. The women of Australia are not her finest product.

She was even more critical when the Victorian Socialists gave them a reception in an out-of-the-way, dirty and badly ventilated place, for the occasion reminded her of everything she disliked about these '"poor relations", believers in socialist shibboleths' in the labour movement at home.

The chairman was the usual S.D.F. young man, with narrow forehead, bristling hair, retreating chin and dirty coat, and the inevitable red tie. 'Comrade', 'revolution', 'trade unionism played out', 'capitalist press', 'class war', and all the rest of the socialist well-meaning cant was showered over us and we responded by a douche of cold water both as to practice and theory. In the front seats were seated a dozen or so hard-featured women, the Council of the Women's Suffrage Society, who had waived their disapproval of an economic revolution to come and hear me pronounce in favour of women's suffrage. They looked so earnest and wistful that I had not the heart to tell them that I was against the suffrage, so I slid away from the subject into an explanation of the relation between trade unionism, co-operation and socialism. Sidney in a wily address tried to explain the Fabian policy of permeation, with the result that the chairman in his concluding remarks recommended the meeting to adopt 'Mr Webb's suggestion of taking the capitalist down a back street and then knocking him on the head'!

The 'dressiness' of women always seemed to Beatrice a symbol of self-indulgence and lack of interest in social problems, and she came back to it again in her description of the Melbourne Cup meeting at Flemington racecourse (the only race-meeting she and Sidney ever seem to have attended). 'Mrs Webb is terribly contemptuous today about the dress and figure of the women at the "Cup" yesterday' Charles Trevelyan wrote on 2 November. 'But she has to admit that they are well fed if not distinguished.'

The Webbs and Trevelyan left Australia on 17 November and started on the long journey home after eight months of travel. By the time they reached Colombo, Trevelyan reported, 'Webb has already got through all the books we have brought, all those belonging to the other passengers and all in the by no means despicable library.' As the ship ran up the Red Sea Beatrice finished her diary in a deckchair. 'How can we begin about Australia?' she asked and cited Darwin's comment: 'Too great and ambitious for affection, and yet not great enough for respect.' This set the tone for her own conclusions.

Neither in its country nor in its people has it the charm of New Zealand. Plain, mountain, undulating hill and dale, all alike covered with the monotonous eucalyptus; glaring sun, everlasting winds carrying clouds of dust, dry nervous air, sickly colouring, the consciousness of the unreclaimable waste of the interior on the one hand, and of the interminable ocean on the other, gives to life in Australia a desolate combination of restlessness and ennui unknown in beautiful, fertile and wonderfully varied New Zealand. As for society in Australia, it is just a slice of Great Britain and differs only slightly from Glasgow, Manchester, Liverpool and the *suburbs* of London. Bad manners, ugly clothes, vigour and shrewdness characterize the settlements of Sydney, Melbourne, and of bush stations, exactly as they characterize the lower and upper-middle class folk of the old country. If anything the manners are worse, the dress more pretentious and glaring and lacking in taste, than with us! The well-to-do women, especially, lack culture, charm and any kind of grace; and the richer they are the more objectionable they become. On the other hand there is more enjoyment of life, a greater measure of high spirits among the young people of all classes. Australians are obviously and even blatantly a young race proud of their youth. Besides vulgarity and a rather gross materialism their worst characteristic is a lack of strenuous persistency: they are loosely built both in mind and body, inclined to self-indulgence and disinclined for regular work. . . . 'Muddling on' with a high standard of honour and a low standard of efficiency is the dominant note of Australian public life. With more careful selection in its civil service, and better-trained intelligence in its public men, the Australian government would become a striking instance of successful democratic institutions. At present it is at least a promising experiment.

PART III

Cliques of Friends and Acquaintances

January 1899 – December 1901

Introduction to Part III

THE WEBBS returned to a Britain alive with optimism and prosperity. The great trade boom of 1898–99 brought wealth beyond all precedence and the whole country was affected by it. The links of Empire were an essential part of this prosperity and the result was a growing spirit of imperialism. 'We are all Imperialists now,' said Joseph Chamberlain in a speech in Birmingham on 28 January 1899. 'We realize, but do not flinch from, the responsibilities which Imperialism brings.' The new wealth brought with it changing habits and styles of life. There was a return of eighteenth-century customs of extravagance. Weekend visits and autumn shooting-parties were rituals of entertainment; outings to restaurants became popular with the newly rich. Among all classes there was a general desire to 'have a good time'. The invention of the 'free wheel' kept up the boom in cycling. It was a symbol of freedom, especially for women, who, now unchaperoned, were beginning to make their way in careers and politics as well. The International Congress of Women in London in the summer of 1899 was one of the many signs that emancipation was in sight.

There had been so many changes in so short a time that Beatrice found it hard to settle back when she and Sidney returned to London in the new year of 1899. And in personal terms there were adjustments to make. On 12 March 1898, as the Webbs were preparing to leave England on their tour, Charlotte Payne-Townshend, upset and exasperated by her unsatisfactory relationship with Bernard Shaw, took her friend Lion Phillimore for a prolonged visit to Rome. While she was away Shaw was taken ill with an inflamed toe-joint, and, now realizing how much he missed Charlotte, encouraged her to come back to England. She returned at the beginning of May to find Shaw seriously ill and in a neglected state. It was clear to both of them that he

153

needed care and nursing. 'Charlotte was the inevitable and predestined agent, appointed by Destiny,' Shaw wrote to Beatrice. Charlotte took a house at Haslemere in Surrey where, with servants and nurses, Shaw could be restored to health. Charlotte also arranged for them to marry and the ceremony took place, with Shaw on crutches, on 1 June 1898 at the register office in Henrietta Street, London. They planned to meet the Webbs in Naples at the end of the year for a joint holiday, but Shaw was still not well enough to go. The Webbs arrived back in England at the end of December and went at once down to Haslemere to stay with the Shaws.

The main task that lay ahead for Beatrice was to begin research on the history of local government, the next project to be undertaken by the partnership. During the months she spent travelling about the country in 1899 in search of material she often had misgivings, daunted by the size of the task and the length of time it would take her to complete it. All the same she could see how well it fitted into their scheme of things. Since Sidney was so much involved in local government it was logical for them to look at forms of compulsory association, where there was public regulation of roads, prisons and pauperism, as distinct from the voluntary associations of the Co-operative and trade union movements; and this research was to pay unforeseen dividends when Beatrice was appointed to the Royal Commission on the Poor Law in 1905.

Although Sidney did his share of the work, he was more concerned with practical affairs – the reorganization of the University of London, and particularly the part that the London School of Economics was to play in it; the reform of secondary education and its effect on the London County Council; holding together the Fabian Society disrupted by the unhappy impact of the Boer War. Sidney enjoyed the continual informal discussions of policy-making and Beatrice made their home in Grosvenor Road the base for what she later called the 'extensive and peculiar' manoeuvres whereby Sidney brought his ideas to a successful conclusion. She had learned the art of *salon* politics when she was a young woman and had been her father's hostess: she knew exactly how influence could be traded across the dinner-table, for it was the milieu in which she had grown up and to which she was reverting in middle life – but with ambivalent feelings. 'This last year we have seemed to drift upward in the strata of society,' she wrote at the end of 1900, asking herself whether they would drift further 'into the stream of the big world' or into an academic backwater. 'It is a toss-up which course will best promote our plans. One cannot associate with great personages without considerable expenditure of nerves and means, and all this expenditure must come off our efforts in administration and investigation. On the other hand England is governed by cliques of friends and acquaintances. If you are inside the clique you help to rule: if you are outside you cry in the wilderness.'

For all Beatrice's misgivings she and Sidney enjoyed dinner-parties and weekend visits and were caught up in the style of the times. Beatrice was unwell and hypochondriacal for much of 1901 – 'the most unsatisfactory year of my life', she wrote at the end of it. Yet, she so responded to the seductions of success and power that by 1903 she was in 'excellent health and spirits, enjoying my work and extraordinarily happy in my love and comradeship'. She had come to like what she called 'the element of sport' in political intrigue, which called upon all her considerable skills as a hostess and her ability to puzzle out the human combinations needed, for instance, to make sure that the new arrangements for the University of London gave the L.S.E. exactly the status she and Sidney desired for it, or to find some workable educational compromise between the Nonconformist lobby and the Anglican bishops.

Feelings of guilt at hobnobbing with the great may have been one reason for Beatrice's uneasy state of mind in 1900 and 1901. The Boer War was another. After months of negotiation and protest by the 'Uitlanders' of Johannesburg about their deprivation of democratic rights by the Transvaal Government under Kruger, and a parallel yet covert intrigue by Chamberlain, Rhodes and Milner against the recalcitrant Boers, war finally broke out in October 1899. With Chamberlain's name on everyone's tongue and on the front page of every newspaper Beatrice was troubled by the revival of painful memories and feelings of sympathy for the man even when she had doubts about his policies. The long retrospective entry at the end of 1900 shows how deeply she was touched.

VOLUME 20
◢ 1899 ◣

5 February. 41 Grosvenor Road

Since we returned to England I have been disinclined to write in my diary, having nothing to relate and having lost the habit of intimate confidences, impossible in a joint diary such as we have kept together during our journey round the world. One cannot run on into self-analysis, family gossip, or indiscreet and hasty descriptions of current happenings, if someone else, however dear, is solemnly to read one's chatter then and there. I foresee the sort of kindly indulgence or tolerant boredom with which Sidney would decipher the last entry and this feeling would, in itself, make it impossible to write whatever came into my head at the time of writing without thought of his criticism.

With regard to our friends and relations, we found only two persons whose lives had been completely changed during our absence – our two friends GBS and Charlotte have married each other. Shaw has become a chronic invalid, Charlotte a devoted nurse. They live in an attractive house up at Hindhead. He still writes but his work seems to be getting unreal: he leads a hothouse life, he cannot walk or get among his equals. He is as witty and as cheery as of old. But now and again a flush of fatigue or a sign of brain irritation passes over him. Charlotte, under pressure of anxiety for the man she loves, has broadened out into a motherly woman and lost her anarchic determination to live according to her momentary desires. There are some compensations for the sadness of the sudden cutting-off of his activity.

Frederick Spencer (d. 1946) began his career as an elementary teacher, and during his six-year employment as a research assistant to the Webbs he took an L.S.E. doctorate; he went on to become a school inspector, and ended his career as chief inspector for the L.C.C. He married Amy Harrison, another secretary of the Webbs. She also moved from schoolteaching to research on industrial sociology and gained a doctorate at L.S.E.

7 March. [41 Grosvenor Road]

. . . . Sidney has been principally engaged in engineering the School of Economics into its proper place in the new University, bargaining alternatively with the Royal Commission to recognize it as a School of the

University and to create a separate Faculty of Economics and Political Science, with the Technical Education Board to endow the proposed Faculty with an income, and with Passmore Edwards to present a new building. Everything seems to be going excellently. Meanwhile we are well into our new enquiry and have elaborated a syllabus for the use of investigators. We have engaged as secretary a clever, ambitious elementary schoolteacher – F.H. Spencer – about twenty-eight years old. We tried a nice young man straight from Oxford but he was a dead failure, not realizing what constituted a day's work, and presenting us with little essays instead of research notes. . . . I am aiming at living a student's life, withdrawing from any social excitement [that is] inconsistent with regular work, regular exercise, plain food and abundance of sleep.

I.L.P. candidates were now making significant headway in local council elections, and Fabian tracts were much in demand by the newly elected councillors.

28 April. Bradford
Sidney and I left London on our first investigation tour into local government on Thursday before Easter Sunday and chose Leeds as our destination as Sidney had promised to preside over a 'Conference of Elected Persons' to be held there on Good Friday. His speech and the Conference were an unexpected success: all the papers giving full reports. . . . On Thursday of Easter week we got to work, having persuaded the Lord Mayor to place a room in the Town Hall at our disposal and to give us free use of the minutes and reports. For another week Sidney, Spencer and I were hard at work on these documents. Then we tackled the West Riding County Council, Wakefield, the Board of Guardians and School Board of Leeds. In the middle of my stay Sidney had to return to London, leaving me and our new secretary to finish up as best we might. . . .

There will clearly be no difficulty in getting our material: our hardest task will be to determine what material to select and where to stop. Between this diary and myself, I get on better at the actual investigation when Sidney is not there: he is shy in cross-examining officials, who generally begin by being unwilling witnesses and need gentle but firm handling: he hates life in provincial lodgings and seeing each day new people, and this repugnance reacts on me and I get disheartened and wonder whether I have not led him into a useless adventure. In dealing with documents he is far more efficient than I, but in the manipulation of witnesses with a view of extracting confidential information his shyness and scepticism of the use of it gives me the advantage. And I am more ruthless in the exercise of my craft when he is not there to observe and perchance disapprove of my little tricks of the trade. Moreover, whilst I give my whole thought to the enquiry, he is always preoccupied with delicate administrative problems, the present one being the establishment of the London School, with premises and an income of its own, as the Economics Faculty of London University. With infinite tact and persistency he has built up the institution, but no one outside our little group wants this new-fangled structure to stand, and there are many who would go a long way to undermine it. Hitherto our enemies are always a day late, but this constant prevision of the next attack means continuous strain. In this work I can only stand by and look on.

Beatrice was away for six weeks, doing research in Yorkshire. Andrew Carnegie (1835–1919), the Scots-born steelmaker who had made a great fortune in Pittsburgh (spelt without the 'h' at that time), had given away large sums of money, especially to found free libraries. Beatrice is probably referring to Lord Rosebery's speech to the City Liberal Club on 5 May, in which he called on his party to recognize 'the new Imperial spirit'. Herbert Gladstone (1854–1930) had held office under his father: he was currently Chief Whip of the Liberal Party, and responsible for its electoral arrangements. In this capacity he was to make the covert agreement with the emergent Labour Party whereby Labour candidates got a clear run in a sufficient number of seats to produce a significant Labour Party in Parliament in 1906.

16 May. [41 Grosvenor Road]
. . . . Whilst I am mainly occupied in this enquiry, Sidney engineers the School [of Economics] and to a lesser extent the University [of London]. He is in the background on the County Council, partly because he has been so long away, partly because he is considered a specialist in education. On educational matters he leads without dispute; the T.E.B. and the Council doing anything that he asks them to do. He no longer evokes hostility: the Moderates respect him, the leading Progressives ask his advice, but do not regard him as a rival for the position of leadership. No doubt this is due to his growing disinclination to push himself forward for any position desired by anyone else, his refusal to take any steps to start a career of political advancement. His dislike of the personal struggle for leadership becomes in fact greater and greater. He is as energetic and persistent as ever, but his energy is perpetually seeking the line of least resistance

for the cause he believes in, and the line of least resistance for his cause is the line of least advancement for himself.

Haldane dined with us last night to talk over University affairs, especially the possibility of getting Carnegie to endow London University with some of his millions. We loathe what we saw of Pittsburg and explained that we could not possibly approach 'the reptile' but thought that others could do so who knew less or thought differently. John Morley for instance? So Sidney agreed to draft some kind of description of what might be done. Haldane was down-hearted, more down-hearted than I have ever seen him about the prospects of the Liberal Party. He tried to explain away Rosebery's last speech, crying quits to Home Rule, Socialism, Temperance and other social reform, but could not do so even to his own satisfaction. The present situation – all the leaders of the party on strike – is becoming ludicrous, no one understanding what they are striking against unless they are striking against each other. Haldane brought a cordial invitation from Herbert Gladstone to Sidney to stand for Deptford or any other London constituency, all expenses to be paid by the party, a sign not of grace but of dire necessity. 'They think your standing would do them good,' said Haldane. 'But I told them,' he added in a half-bitter, half-playful tone, 'that, like Rosebery, you would neither come in nor go out.' 'Until we know who is to be the company,' I retorted, 'we shall stand in the doorway and help to block the door by standing there.'

Ten days in London has been dissipated by social duties. Three days I had to spend at Brighton with Herbert Spencer, he becoming insistent that I must visit him. Poor old friend: I verily believe that he thinks that it is a treat for me to spend so many hours in his stuffy house, subsisting on his stingy housekeeping, so stingy that sometimes I spend no little time in considering whether I can manufacture an excuse to get a good meal out. However, on this visit there was no actual lack of nourishment. Two innocuous young women are in perpetual attendance, one a pianist, the other a housekeeper; the same secretary, half-secretary, half-valet, three maidservants and a coachman – all at the call of the poor old man's money. He told me that during the last years he has been drawing from the sales of his books eight hundred a year from England and five hundred a year from America. All his savings are in the Linotype Company, in which he invested in order to break the trade union, an investment which yields high interest. So that he is more than well off considering his narrow needs. Notwithstanding all this mean living there is the stamp of heroism on his daily life. At eighty years of age he still struggles on, in pain and depression, revising his biology in the firm faith that his words are the truth.

15 June. Manchester
The third week here: Sidney stayed for a fortnight, and has now returned to his L.C.C. work. We got straight away into our enquiry and we have been working every day, Spencer at the minutes of the Town Council, and Sidney and I at interviewing officials and abstracting reports lent or given to us. Two delightful Sundays we spent in the lanes of Cheshire, one night at Tarporley where, seven years ago, he and I stayed as an engaged couple with Mrs Green as chaperone. Those Sundays were very happy days, honeymoon rambles, dodging the high roads and finding ourselves in farmyards.

At times we get discouraged at the bigness of our task; then we console each other by repeating, 'Well, if we cannot do it no one else can' – a conceited reflection. Today I am feeling somewhat lonely in the little lodging, a whole fortnight away from him.

When I am at work I do not feel otherwise than happy and fortunately I am well and can work my six hours. But after dinner when the cigarette is done I either feel depressed or my cursed habit of sentimental castle-building leads me to harp back to the past. Scenes, the vividness of which seem to make them real, dominate my mind and I lose my self-control. And then is the inevitable reaction. Oh, the mysteries of human feeling.

[*Beatrice later added this note:* 'This extract which I have typed myself, rather than give to be copied by my secretary, evokes no memory in my mind. But I assume from other entries of this and the following year that it related to my past relations with Joseph Chamberlain. This dramatizing of relationships or rather of prospective relationships has always been one of my bad habits – sometimes of quite casual and temporary relations, imaginary letters or encounters. Usually I have had some relationship 'on the stocks' – to use a vulgar expression. But these imaginary relationships have not interfered in any way with the main purpose of my life, at any rate not when I have been in normal health.']

18 June. [Manchester]
Spent Sunday with the Holts. Dear old Lallie most affectionate. Hers

is a nature which improves with the years – her character has softened, deepened and she has gained in intellectual interests. At present, in the intervals of keeping a luxuriously comfortable house for a large family with many friends she reads theology, trying to find a creed which combines rational thought with religious emotion. She has a strong mind but she has neither intellectual training nor experience of thought, and it is pathetic to watch her struggling with wrinkled brow to reach conclusions which have been reached long ago by persons of her temperament. For the metaphysic we adopt is mainly a matter of temperament. She is a thoroughgoing puritan, pious but hating authority or intellectual or emotional self-subordination. Between her and us there is a genuine regard, she admiring our persistency and strength of conviction, and we – Sidney especially – liking the orderliness and public spirit of the Holts. We go there again in September to study the Liverpool Town Council.

Clara Ryland (1861–1915) was the youngest sister of Joseph Chamberlain, and Beatrice had been on friendly terms with her during her years of association with the Chamberlain family. Clara's husband had died in April. Lina James, another sister, had been widowed rather longer. Beatrice travelled to Birmingham to visit them at their substantial home in Court Oak Road, Harborne.

25 June. Baskerville House
An act of piety. Some two months ago Clara Ryland lost her husband after a terrible illness, reaching over three years. Her letter revealing a dull despair, I offered to spend this Sunday with her. Here in a luxurious house live the two widowed sisters with no occupation except the routine of house and family, endowed with ample means, with no outside interests other than the circulating library and the talk about current politics and London Society brought them by the Great Man's family. . . . Clara, it is true, has her four little girls. But the home is empty of all but wealth; there is nothing to exhaust energy or stimulate thought – no brightness, no grace, no vigorous activity for others. There is nothing but a meaningless luxury.

This Congress was the first held by the International Council of Women. Its president, Lady Aberdeen (1857–1939), devoted herself to humanitarian causes. Mary Eliza Wright Sewall (1844–1920), a well-known educator and suffragist in America, was the vice-president.

3 July. [41 Grosvenor Road]
Back in London in time for the International Women's Congress.

The American and Continental women took it quite seriously: but the more experienced English women, whilst organizing it admirably, mocked at it in private. The press sneered at it, and the public generally ignored it – always excepting the entertainments of the duchesses and countesses who had been drawn in to patronize the Congress. It was not a failure, but hardly a success. The council meetings were stormy and unbusinesslike (I represented New Zealand owing to our recent visit to that land), resolving themselves into a duel between Mrs Creighton, backed up by the National Union of Women Workers set of English women, on the one hand, and on the other Mrs Wright Sewall (an autocratic and self-assertive American), supported by Lady Aberdeen and the American and Continental delegates. Great Britain and her faithful colonies were routed, which is what Mrs Creighton desired, as she wished the National Council [of Women] of Great Britain to withdraw from the International. It would have been better if the N.U.W.W. had refused to let itself be drawn into this adventure: it believed neither in Woman with a big 'W', nor in Internationalism with a big 'I'; it is distinctly parochial and religious – most emphatically insular. To the well-bred and conventional ladies who dominate it, the 'screeching sisterhood' demanding their rights represents all that is detestable. The public conferences were some of them informing and all of them decorous, and owing to the predominance of the N.U.W.W. clique, the discussions were practical, even technical in character. I took the chair at one of the conferences and spoke at another, and turned up at the council meetings to support Great Britain. But with Mary Playne in the house, and friends drifting in to see me, my week was wasted and my strength dissipated. Americans and Colonials turn up and claim our attention, and the completion of our enquiry seems far off and unattainable.

24 July. [41 Grosvenor Road]
This last month of hot dry weather has been spent mostly in entertaining American and Colonial friends. Some four mornings of each week have been spent at the British Museum scanning files of the *Manchester Guardian* and taking copious notes. . . . Our small circle of acquaintances is pleasant enough, easygoing, unconventional and somewhat distinguished. We are sought, we do not seek – the most agreeable way of seeing people. Not that Society pays us continuous attention: we are only casually found out by persons belonging to the

great world. We live in a pleasant backwater of our own but our social status, such as it is, is distinctly advantageous to the local government enquiry: it enables us to see any official from whom we want information. We are not going to have any trouble about getting access to facts: the task will be to select out of the mass of material submitted to us.

[Beatrice enclosed a letter from Charles Booth written on 19 August in which he congratulates the Webbs on their 'last great book' which he had recently been reading, and adding his encouragement for their project on municipal institutions.]

10 September. High Borrans
I was peculiarly glad to get this note from Charles Booth. It is on his part an unconscious testimony to the rightness of our marriage. . . It is now two years since I have seen him – we have all of us acquiesced in not meeting. But the bitterness of a broken friendship is past, and any day we might renew friendliness if not friendship.

Five weeks in Manchester in a little rented house, with our own maids to look after us and our secretary to help us – a peaceful, happy time, collecting material and, by a well-regulated life, keeping fit for persistent work. We are more interested in this enquiry than in trade unionism; the problems are multitudinous and the machinery intricate. The least invigorating part of the subject-matter are the persons engaged in the work of local government: in the present administration of English provincial local government there is a singular lack of idealism and charm, of efficiency and force. . .

The Holts had eight children. Richard (1868–1941) was the eldest, and he had married Eliza Wells in 1897. Catherine (1871–1952) also married that year to William Dampier Whetham. The other children were Robert (1872–1952), who married Alice Graves in 1899, Elizabeth (1875–1947), Philip (1876–1958), Edward (1878–1955), Mary (1880–1955) and Lawrence (1882–1961). Captain Dreyfus (1859–1935) was a French staff officer who was convicted of treason in 1894. The case was reopened when it was discovered that the evidence against him had been forged, but at a new court martial in 1899 he was again found guilty and there was world-wide indignation at the verdict. The war in the Transvaal began on 11 October after an ultimatum from President Kruger demanding the withdrawal of British troops from the frontiers of the Transvaal and the Orange Free State. Boer forces struck quickly and successfully at the ill-disposed British army. As Colonial Secretary, and the dominant imperialist in the Cabinet, Chamberlain was so plainly responsible for the breakdown of negotiations that the fighting was widely called 'Joe's War'.

10 October. [41 Grosvenor Road]

Back in London after one week in Preston and two in Liverpool, staying with sister Holt. She is a dear old thing, as ugly, voluble, and warm-hearted as a woman could well be, exuberant in her vitality and desire to make everyone happy, somewhat disillusioned with domestic life – at least with the closest relationships of the home, the relationship of wife and mother. Our brother-in-law is not improving with age: his small-mindedness and secretiveness has degenerated into a restless kind of vanity, an undignified love of social esteem. It is pathetic to see his little mind always reverting to the glory of having refused a baronetcy. Oddly enough it was his position of mayor which fostered his instinct of self-importance: one would have thought that his social position was too big for that. Dick, the eldest son, under the influence of a charming American wife, developed into a shrewd, pleasant and public-spirited man. . . Bob has made a conventional marriage with the daughter of a well-connected Liverpool man. . . Kitty is married to a Cambridge don: Betty and Molly do nothing all day but amuse themselves. Phil is conceited and airified, a selfish boy. . . Ted, a delicate refined lad, finds Liverpool cotton-broking uncongenial and is off to New Zealand: Lawrence, the youngest and most promising, is still at Winchester. The family is commonplace in outlook and mediocre in ability, hardly a credit to plutocratic environment, the only attractive element being the American woman.

Lallie, divorced in feeling and interests from her husband, finds little companionship in her children and seeks recreation in lonely theological studies. Perhaps this trend towards the immaterial and intellectual aspect of life has made her sympathetic to our work. She certainly has taken strongly to Sidney and begins to believe in his usefulness. . . .

This past summer, so far as personal life is concerned, has been full of enjoyment of work, health and love. But it has been marred by the nightmare of the Dreyfus case and the Transvaal crisis. I took a feverish interest in the Dreyfus trial, Sidney grew impatient and would not read it, but to me it had a horrible fascination, became a morbid background to my conscious activities. Equally unsavoury have been the doings of our own people in the Transvaal – an underbred business, from the Jameson Raid to the South African Committee of Enquiry, from the hushing-up of the Enquiry and the whitewashing of Rhodes to the flashy despatches of Milner and the vulgarly provocative talk of Chamberlain resulting in war with the

Transvaal republic, that remnant of seventeenth-century puritanism.

I have been mortified that I could not think well of Chamberlain, puzzled to try and resist the atmosphere of hostile criticism of his action in Sidney's and Leonard's minds. They are both for different reasons prejudiced against him. I feel the conviction growing that whatever may be the rights and wrongs of his policy in its broader issues, the methods have been vulgar and tricky, a conviction which may not be wholly impartial since I myself suffered years of pain, perhaps from the same coarse-grained indifference to other people's feelings which his critics say he has shown towards the Transvaal republic. I am a prey to an involved combination of bias and counter-bias. So I try to turn away my thoughts and refuse to pass judgement. Fortunately we are so far removed from political influence that it is not necessary for Sidney to express any opinion. We have a constant delight in our daily life of search after truth and loving companionship, far away from personal ambition, competitive struggle and notoriety. I should have hardened and coarsened if I had been subject to the strain of a big flashy social position. The sweet little person that he chose is far better suited to be his wife, a fact which may be taken to justify his action.

So far we see straight in front of us the way we shall go for the next few years. Our enquiry is stretching out before us, arduous, requiring patience and persistency, but by no means impracticable. For the rest there is the Economics Faculty to build up and our share in administration and propaganda. Our finances are sound, our health good, and there is no reason for anxiety. We must spend, if need be, our capital on our work, and we must not be disheartened by its magnitude. We are fast becoming elderly, we have not so many years left, we must make the most of our talents and leave the future to take care of itself. And it is useless to be down-hearted because of the indifference and stupidity of the world even as regards its own true interests. And it is childish to yearn after some sanction to the worthwhileness of human effort. For us who 'know not' this sanction is unattainable: we can but follow the still small voice of moral instinct which insists that we shall seek truth and love one another. Is the sanction the calm happiness in work, the peaceful delight in living?

F.J. Whelen (1867–1955) was a clerk in the Bank of England, and an active Fabian. Much interested in the theatre, he founded the Stage Society in 1898. The Shaws had just returned from a six-week Mediterranean cruise in the *Lusitania*.

30 October. [41 Grosvenor Road]

Haldane spent an hour or so with us this evening. Significant is the transformation in his attitude from a discreet upholder of Liberal solidarity to that of a rebel against the views of the majority, determined to assert himself. 'The Liberal Party is completely smashed, Mrs Webb,' and he beamed defiance. He had spent a month reading Transvaal blue-books and was convinced that Milner was right and that war was from the first inevitable. The cleavage goes right through the Liberal Party into the Fabian Society. Shaw, Wallas and Whelen being almost in favour of the war, J.R. MacDonald and Sydney Olivier desperately against it, while Sidney occupies a middle position, thinks that better management might have prevented it but that now that it has begun recrimination is useless and that we must face the fact that henceforth the Transvaal and the Orange Free State must be within the British Empire.

Sidney lecturing at Oxford: I stayed here for my usual Wednesday afternoon at home. This is rapidly becoming a series of interviews with members of my class at the School of Economics. I enjoy lecturing every Thursday. . . The weekly class brings me into close connection with the work of the School: I see some half-dozen students every week and talk over their work with them. I am glad that our life becomes every day more that of students and teachers, our intercourse with general society shrinking up to occasional meetings with casual acquaintances. . .

The Shaws have taken up their residence in Charlotte's attractive flat over the School of Economics, and Sidney and I meet there on Thursdays to dine sumptuously between our respective lectures. Charlotte and Shaw have settled down into the most devoted married couple, she gentle and refined, with happiness added thereto, and he showing no sign of breaking loose from her dominion. What the intellectual product of the marriage will be I do not feel so sure: at any rate he will not become a dilettante, the habit of work is too deeply engrained. It is interesting to watch his fitful struggles out of the social complacency natural to an environment of charm and plenty. How can atmosphere be resisted?

John Burns dined here last night. He is mellowed in temperament, he has lost his restless egotism and personal hatreds and something of his force, lost his emphatic faith and his fierce sympathies with suffering. Of course he will go on being 'progressive', and will back up anything that can be put into an Act of Parliament. But like most untrained enthusiasts, experience of affairs has unhinged his faith and dulled his enthusiasm.

Vaughan Nash (1861–1932) was a journalist, and co-author of a book on the dock strike of 1889, who became secretary to two Liberal Prime Ministers. Harold Spender (1864–1926) was a Liberal journalist who edited the *Pall Mall Gazette, Daily Chronicle, Manchester Guardian* and *Daily News:* he was the father of the poet Stephen Spender. The ousting of the pro-Boers from control of the *Chronicle* was a coup by the Liberal Imperialists.

[?] *December.* [41 Grosvenor Road]
A cloud hangs over our little group of friends. Costelloe, Sidney's old friend and colleague on the L.C.C., is dying of cancer of the brain. Willoughby Dickinson, another L.C.C. colleague, is seriously ill. Massingham, Vaughan Nash and Harold Spender have been dismissed from the *Daily Chronicle*, W.P. Reeves is out of spirits and generally Liberals of all types are depressed and uncertain of themselves. The dismissal of Massingham from the editorship, and of the others from the staff of the *Daily Chronicle* reflects the strong patriotic sentiment of its readers, any criticism of the war at present is hopelessly unpopular. The cleavage of opinion about the war separates persons hitherto united and unites those who by temperament and training have hitherto been divorced. No one knows who is friend and who is enemy. Sidney does not take either side and is therefore suspected by both. He is against the policy of thoroughness in dealing with the Boers. And who can fail to be depressed at the hatred of England on the Continent. . . Chamberlain has injured himself with the thinking men of all parties by his lack of kindliness, courtesy and discretion, but he is still the 'strong man' of politics: and the political 'pit' of men from the street likes the strong man and has no desire that he should mend his manners. Besides, he has convictions and he expresses them honestly and forcibly, qualities at present rare in the political world. I should gather from the growing irritability of his speeches that his splendid physique is giving way.

14 December. [41 Grosvenor Road]
Spencer, Mildred Sturge and I spent a week over the St Pancras Vestry minutes. We have taken on Mildred Sturge, a Newnham graduate, as a sort of paid apprentice. . . . An expedition to Norwich in bitterly cold weather to start a Miss Watson on the Norwich records

ends our autumn campaign. Next week we go to Plymouth for the Xmas recess to undertake the records there. I begin to grasp the character of local government at the beginning of this century. When we return we shall hew out of our accumulated material the first draft of our first chapter.

✑ 1900 ✑

Dissatisfaction with the government over the conduct of the war came to a head in January. There was a series of military reverses from 11 to 16 December – known as 'Black Week' – in which over two thousand men were killed. Parliament met on 30 January and the government faced charges of incompetence and mismanagement of ammunition and supplies.

31 January. Torquay

Here for three nights attending an enquiry into borough extension. . . . A month at Plymouth at work together, with Spencer to help us, at the Plymouth records. For recreation we had two days' wandering on bicycles over Dartmoor in mist and rain, one or two walks with Sidney on Mount Batten, and pacing along on the Hoe watching the setting sun after the day's work was done. Otherwise we stuck very closely to our note-taking and interviewing. I remember when we were steaming through the tropics and I was visualizing our work for the next few years I dreaded the thought that we should have to spend all our time out of London in towns. I feared that my health and my spirits would break down with sedentary office work in places like Leeds, Manchester and Liverpool, without the long holidays in the country we were accustomed to. But our life during the last year turned out not half bad. The enquiry has been unexpectedly interesting; my health excellent; and the occasional forty-eight hours' cycling in country lanes round about the towns a joy and a delight, making up in intensity of pleasure for the longer holidays in the country. Sidney has been well, interested and happy. Every day brings greater confidence in the worthwhileness of this continuous study of facts and careful reasoning from them.

But the last six months, and especially the last days at Plymouth, have been darkened by the nightmare of war. The horrible consciousness that we have, at the best, shown ourselves to be unscrupulous in methods, vulgar in manners and inefficient to the last degree, is an unpleasant background to all one's personal life – this thought is always present when one wakes in the night and returns to it every hour of the day. The Boers are, man for man, our superiors in dignity, devotion and capacity – yes, *in capacity*. That is the hardest of these admissions. It may be that conflict was inevitable. I incline to think it was. But that it should come about through muddy intrigues and capitalist pressure and that we should have shown ourselves incapable both in statesmanship and in generalship is humiliating.

I wonder whether we could take a beating and benefit by it. This would be the *real* test of the heart and brain of the English race; much more so than eventual success in a long and costly conflict. If we ultimately win, we shall forget the lessons. We shall say once again, 'We muddled through all right!' Pecuniary self-interest will be again rehabilitated as an empire-building principle, and once again we shall believe that the English gentleman's 'general capacity' is equal to the science of the foreign expert. Again our politicians and officers will bask in the smile of London Society and country house-parties, and will chatter bad metaphysics and worse economics, imagining themselves to be men of the world because they have neither the knowledge nor the industry to be skilled professional administrators and soldiers.

To us, public affairs look gloomy, government is in the hands of small cliques; the middle class is definitely materialistic, the working class stupid and in large sections selfish, with no thought but the 'latest odds'. The social enthusiasm that inspired the intellectual proletariat of ten years ago has died down and given place to scepticism about the desirability, or possibility, of any substantial change in society as we know it. There may be the beginning of intellectual curiosity, but it is still a flicker and not a flame.

And meanwhile we are rolling in wealth. Almost every class, except the miserable sweated worker, has more than they are accustomed to. Pleasure and ease, ease and pleasure, are now what is chiefly desired by men and women: science, literature and art, even social ambition and party feeling, seem to have been ousted by the desire for mental excitement and physical enjoyment. If we found ourselves face to face with real disaster, should we still have the nerve and persistency to stand upright before it? That is the question that haunts me.

Sir Henry Campbell-Bannerman (1836–1908) was a Scots businessman who became a Liberal M.P. in 1868 and an active member of Gladstone's governments. In January 1899 he was elected leader of the Liberal Party in the House of Commons and led the opposition to Chamberlain's South Africa policy. Consistently underrated and ignored by the Webbs, he became a shrewd and effective Prime Minister in 1906.

20 February. Grosvenor Road
From all accounts matters are going from bad to worse with the Liberal Party. Rosebery, Haldane says, has decided that the Liberal Party is no good as an instrument for him, and the bulk of the Liberals are angry at his aloofness and upsetting interventions. Campbell-Bannerman, nominally a 'sane' Imperialist, is at heart a 'Peace man' with all the old Liberal principles and prejudices writ large on his mind – retrenchment in public expenditure and no compulsion either at home or abroad. The little clique of Imperialists – Asquith, Grey and Haldane – have been forced to sit tight on the fence, openly condemning the methods whilst they secretly approve of the policy of the government. The small knot of thoroughgoing opponents of the war have not made themselves felt in the Liberal Party; wherever two or three Liberals are gathered together there is a wrangle which ends in a black ball or a motion for expulsion in a Liberal club. And this friction is made more distracting by the fact that the cleavage about the war runs right across the cleavage of economic affairs: the old 'Illingworth' set being again on the left of the Liberal Party whilst some of the most progressive reformers are flirting with Imperialism and even talk well of Milner. The result is that Liberal M.P.s no longer press their young friends to try to get into the House of Commons.

Meanwhile, our schemes for London University prosper. The School is recognized as the Faculty of Economics. We have secured a site and money for a building and an income of £2,500 from the T.E.B. to be spent on economics and commercial subjects. Sidney will be a member of the Faculty and represent the Faculty on the Senate. Best of all, he has persuaded the Commission to recognize economics as a science and not merely as a subject in the Arts Faculty. The preliminary studies for the economics degree will therefore be mathematics and biology. This divorce of economics from metaphysics and shoddy history is a great gain. We have always claimed that the study of the structure and function of society was as much a science as the study of any other form of life and ought to be pursued by the scientific methods used in other organic sciences.

Hypothesis ought to be used, not as the unquestioned premise from which to deduce an unquestioned conclusion, but as an 'order of thought' to be verified by observation and experiment. Such history as will be taught at the School will be the history of social institutions discovered from documents, statistics and the observation of the actual structure and working of living organizations. This attainment of our aim – the starting of the School as a department of science – is the result of a chapter of fortunate accidents. There was the windfall of the Hutchinson Trust, then the selection of Hewins as Director, the grant from the T.E.B. towards commercial education, the coming of Creighton to London and the packing of the University Commission. Again it is fortunate that in the heated controversy over denominational education Sidney inclines by conviction to the right. He has no prejudices against variety of religious belief even if the variety includes the orthodoxy of the Church of England. And we have had two very good friends helping us – Haldane and the Bishop of London, both of them trusting us completely in our own range of subjects. Of course the School is at present extremely imperfect: its reputation is better than its performance. But we have no illusions and we see clearly what we intend the School to become and we are convinced that we shall succeed.

On 20 February D.A. Thomas, later Lord Rhondda (1856–1918), a Liberal M.P., moved for a fresh enquiry into the Jameson Raid of 1895. This attack by the anti-war group revived old arguments about the whitewashing of Rhodes and crucial telegrams relating to the Raid which were not produced at the original enquiry. Chamberlain's reply was called 'a brilliant rhetorical feat'. Martinus Steyn (1857–1916) was the President of the Orange Free State 1896–1900. William Schreiner (1857–1919) was Premier of the Cape 1898–1900; his sister was the novelist Olive Schreiner.

23 February. [41 Grosvenor Road]
Beatrice Chamberlain came to lunch on Wednesday, ostensibly to tell me about poor Clara Ryland, but really to find out what we felt about the Transvaal. She was as vigorous and attractive as is her wont, a fine generous nature, reflecting the best side of her father. Her tone about the Transvaal was far more moderate and magnanimous than I expected, not nearly so partisan as some of my sisters. Against Steyn of the Free State she was distinctly venomous and she was deprecatory of Schreiner and the Cape government. 'They have been deplorably weak, they have run from one side to the other, imploring each

alternately to climb down. And though Schreiner eventually slipped down on our side he did so not out of loyalty but merely to save himself.' All this I disputed with some warmth. When her carriage was announced, I noticed a look of nervous dissatisfaction on her face and she ran upstairs to put on her veil, I following. With an effort she broke out: 'You will congratulate Papa on having smashed his detractors last night?'

'We never attached much importance to the telegram,' I answered affectionately. 'What other people say Mr Chamberlain said is not evidence,' I added. Her face brightened and she said something about misunderstandings of conversations when two persons were referring to different things, from which I gather that we are right in assuming that the telegrams are similar in character to those already published. If only Chamberlain had not whitewashed Rhodes! Though I am inclined to believe that his defence of Rhodes sprang from a defiant loyalty to a man in whose devotion to the Empire he has complete confidence, this explanation is not quite convincing.

8 March. [Brighton]
A week with Herbert Spencer at Brighton. . . The old man is better and more benign than I have seen him for years. But about the world in general and England in particular he is terribly pessimistic. . . . He still retains his personal affection for me – more out of habit, I think, for every year he becomes more suspicious of our aims and of our power of reaching these aims. His housekeeping has become quite comfortable: two bright young persons as housekeeper and pianist respectively, three maids, a houseboy, coachman and a secretary, all dancing attendance on the old man. His secretary has not had a holiday for ten years and his two young ladies are kept close at it all day and every day 'making a pleasant circle for me', he calls it. . . Poor old man, it is pathetic to see a nature so transparently sincere, warped by long-continued flattery and subordination of others to his whims and fancies into the character of a complete egotist, pedantic and narrow-minded – a true Casaubon.

Edward Henry Carson Q.C.(1854–1935) was a prominent Ulsterman and one of the leading advocates of his day. He was Solicitor-General from 1900–05 and leader of the Unionists in the House of Commons. Sir William Ramsay (1852–1916), research chemist and Nobel prizewinner, was professor of chemistry at University College, London, 1887–1913.

16 March. Grosvenor Road.

Utterly done up with a week of dissipation. The day I came back I dined with Alfred (Cripps) at the House of Commons in a private room without ventilation – a veritable hole of Calcutta. Margaret Hobhouse had to leave, finding it unbearable. I struggled on, chatting with Carson, a clever, cynical and superficial Irishman, an ultra-Tory on all questions. 'Gerald Balfour, the worst Irish Secretary we have had: he and his brother have done more to make Home Rule possible than all the preceding governments put together. When he leaves he will leave all parties united clamouring for Home Rule by making it clear that it is not worth while being loyal,' was his emphatic summing-up of the situation. It was not surprising to me that Carson thought that John Morley had been an admirable secretary. 'In all his administration he followed the advice of the Unionists.'

On Friday we had a little dinner of friends here. On Sunday we supped with Willie Cripps. On Monday I debated in the Chelsea Town Hall with an anti-regulationist, on Tuesday we had to dine with us the Creightons and Professor Ramsay to talk London University, and on Wednesday we dined with Haldane to meet a select party of Roseberyites, including the great man himself. Haldane sat me down next Lord Rosebery against the will of the latter, who tried his best to avoid me as a neighbour, but all to no purpose, Haldane insisting on his changing places. He is a strange being, self-conscious and sensitive to a more extreme degree than any mortal that I have ever come across. Notwithstanding this absurd self-consciousness he has a peculiar personal charm, the secret, I imagine, of his hold on a section of the Liberal Party and of the public. At first he avoided speaking to me. But feeling that our host would be mortified if his little scheme failed utterly, I laid myself out to be pleasant to my neighbour, though he aggravated and annoyed me by his ridiculous airs: he might be a great statesman, a royal Prince, a beautiful woman and an artistic star all rolled into one. 'Edward,' called out Lord Rosebery to Sir Edward Grey as the latter, arrayed in Court dress, hurried away to the Speaker's party, 'don't tell the world of this new intrigue of Haldane's.' And I believe Lord Rosebery winked as he glanced at me sitting by him. Which showed that he had at least a sense of humour. For the party *was* an intrigue of Haldane's, an attempt to piece together an anti-little-England combination out of the most miscellaneous morsels of political influence. 'I feel deeply honoured at the place you gave me, Mr Haldane,' I said as he saw me out of his luxurious flat, 'but if I were four and twenty hours in the same house with that man I should be rude to him.' Haldane is now amusing himself by weaving, from his gossiping imagination, a Rosebery-Webb myth.

Consequent on all this dissipation no work at the book and a feeling of disconsolate blankness when I look at our accumulating material. My brain is all wool and my thoughts, are wool-gathering.

Bill Playne was married to Manuella Meinertzhagen, a niece of Georgina's husband. Barbara Meinertzhagen (1876–1963), who married Bernard Drake in 1900, became Beatrice's favourite niece. After the early and tragic death of their son, Daniel, Georgina and Daniel Meinertzhagen gave up Mottisfont, their Hampshire mansion. See also family tree.

11 May. [41 Grosvenor Road]
A pleasant ten days at Longfords recovering tone. Arthur has become a hale agreeable elderly man with a good-natured interest in Mary's doings. The flaw in the Playnes' life is the personality of their daughter-in-law Mannie (née Manuela Meinertzhagen), a some-what unintelligent sulky-tempered young person, with plenty of money, poor physique and egotistical temperament, with whom Mary, as was inevitable, has 'got wrong'. . . . This misfit is a constant trouble to Mary Playne, but she bears up against this, and Bill's departure for the war, with her old fortitude and does her level best to be agreeable and hospitable to the unloved daughter-in-law. The Dick Holts were there with the two babies, and Barbara Meinertzhagen with her fiancé, a sterling young fellow, a friend of Dan, the lost and beloved brother. Georgie, with half a dozen children, had lodgings at Amberley, so that we were a large family party. We are on excellent terms with the Playnes and all the young people were kind to us. Sidney indeed is becoming a favourite uncle with some of them. Then a Sunday at Hadspen with all those nice young people, three days' cycling and the rest of the time investigating Gloucester and Bristol local government. Back here and a week's struggle to turn painters and electricians out of the house and settle down again to work.

20 May. [41 Grosvenor Road]
Poor Carrie Darling dying of peritonitis just as she had achieved success and pulled her school through. An heroic woman, who had

worked hard from early childhood, fearless and frank in nature with keen intellectual interests and warm affections. Before she went to the colonies she had charm and distinction. In the rough and tumble of a schoolmistress's life among rich colonial folk, she lost all her personal charm and some of her distinction but she kept intact, through tragic circumstances, her high courage and self-devotion. . . .

22 May. Marlborough
The last three months have not been satisfactory. My work has not had my best thought and feeling, foolish day-dreams based on self-consciousness and personal vanity, foolish worrying over an investment, i.e. the *Echo*, which is likely to be a dead loss and may involve us in legal complications, a certain physical reluctance to intellectual effort – have all combined to make my work half-hearted and unreal. Sidney is free from all these defects and every day I live with him the more I love and honour the single-mindedness of his public career and his single-hearted devotion to his wife. And every year I appreciate more fully the extraordinary good luck which led me to throw in my lot with him. Just as it was the worst part of my nature that led me into my passionate feeling for Chamberlain so it was the best part of my nature which led me to accept Sidney after so much doubt and delay. And certainly, just as I was well punished for the one, I have been richly rewarded for the other course of feeling and conduct. And yet, notwithstanding this conviction, I find my thoughts constantly wandering to the great man and his family, watching his career with sympathy and interest and desiring his welfare. Sometimes I think I should like to meet him again. At other times I reject the thought as a needless expenditure of feeling. But all this is sentimentalism; it has little to do with any deep emotion. I am at most times buoyantly happy in my love for my boy and in my interest in my work. My sentimentalism is a mere plaything but playthings take time and thought. . . .

23 May. [41 Grosvenor Road]
The next eight years seem likely to settle how useful we shall be to our generation. Our effort is now directed to one end – to establish on a firm basis a Science of Society. We are trying to bring this about partly by our own individual work and partly by the School of Economics. Sidney's persistent energy has attained at least a formal success for the School. We have gained university status, we have secured a building

and a site, and we have the prospect of regular income, we have attracted students and we are training teachers. But how far the new activity will prove to be genuine science and not mere culture or shallow technical instruction in the art of administration, remains to be seen. The same doubt with regard to our own work. We are lavishing time and money on the investigation, doing it in an extravagantly complete manner. Shall we have the intellectual grasp to rise superior to our material, or shall we be simply compilers and chroniclers? It is only in rare moments that I have any vision of the book as a whole; at most times I am dazed by the intricacy and technical detail of the subject. Have we bitten off more than we can chew? It may be the time is not yet come for a sound science of social organization. Anyway we have faith that the beginning will be brought nearer by our effort, even if it fails to attain for us any kind of personal success.

But if we are to think out the development of local government in all its different phases, from our chaotic notes, it is clear that I must be free from the distractions of London life. Relations, old friends, Continental and American admirers, students and persons who can help us in our investigations, all have to receive their due amount of attention. I am on excellent terms with the family — the sisters have taken to us and are beginning to wish that we should see much of them and their children. This means the giving and taking of dinners, chaperoning girls on bicycling parties, putting up public schoolboys on their trips to London. The old friends seem to look reproachful when one evades their offers to call or refuses point blank to lunch or dine with them. Then again students. Here I acknowledge a duty — one is bound to do one's little to keeping forward younger persons, less fortunately placed than oneself, to the pathway of research and investigation. Lastly there are a multitude of persons one ought to see in connection with local government. And as a penalty for possessing a social conscience, in the background of all the other, the ghostly forms of all sorts and conditions of men, who have helped me in the past to get information on the subjects I was investigating — employers, philanthropists, trade unionists, Co-operators. The only way out of the whole tangle is to get out of London. This we will do next spring.

In February 1899 Rosy married George Dobbs (1869–1946), who worked for the publishing house of Dent. After the marriage he and a colleague started their own firm to publish high quality books, but they soon went bankrupt and the

Above: Sidney and
Beatrice Webb
shortly after their
marriage

Above right: Sidney
and Beatrice Webb.
Photograph pasted
into Beatrice
Webb's diary for
1898

Right: Sidney and
Beatrice Webb
photographed by
Bernard Shaw

Left: Beatrice
Webb

Right: Cartoon of
Sidney Webb,
pasted into the front
of Beatrice Webb's
diary, volume for
1895–7

Above: Beatrice
Webb, pasted into
her diary for
1904

Right:
Mr and Mrs Joseph
Chamberlain

Right: The Cripps family. Standing left to right: Arthur, Blanche, Henry, Theresa. Seated left to right: William, Mrs H.W. Cripps, Mr H.W. Cripps, Alfred

Below: Family group at Standish c. 1893. From left to right:

Lawrencia Holt, Kate Courtney, Arthur Dyson Williams?, Leonard Courtney (seated), Beatrice Webb (seated), Lawrencina Meinertzhagen standing in front of Georgina Meinertzhagen, Rosy Williams (seated), Robert Holt?, Blanche Cripps (seated), Arthur Playne, Rachel Hobhouse (seated), Bill Playne (seated), Mary Playne, Manuella Meinertzhagen? seated in front of Polly Playne?, Margaret Hobhouse seated in front of Henry Hobhouse

Right: The Potter sisters on the same occasion. Standing left to right: Rosy, Blanche, Lawrencina. Seated left to right: Margaret, Kate, Beatrice, Mary, Georgina

Above: The Argoed

Left: 'The Platform Spellbinder'. Portrait of Bernard Shaw painted in 1893 by Bertha Newcombe

Below left: H.G. Wells with his wife Jane at Woking 1895

Below: Charlotte Payne Townshend learning to ride a bicycle c. 1896. Pasted into Beatrice Webb's diary for 1898

Right: Bertrand and Alys
Russell 1895

Above: The Pearsall Smith
family at Friday's Hill
1894. Standing: Alys and
Logan. Seated left to right:
Robert, Hannah and Mary
with her children Karin
and Ray

Right: Sir George and Lady
Trevelyan with their three
sons. Left to right: Charles,
George and Robert.
Wallington early 1890s

Right: W.A.S. Hewins 1904

Far right: Graham Wallas 1894

Above: Lord Rosebery speaking in the House of Lords

Above right: Margaret and Ramsay Macdonald 1903

Right: A.J. Balfour outside 10 Downing Street 1905

View from the drawing room window at Grosvenor Road, looking towards Vauxhall Bridge 1895

Below: 41 Grosvenor Road *Below right:* Adelphi Terrace

Beatrice Webb with Princess Kaiulani in Honolulu 1898

The Webbs crossing the Pacific

partner disappeared. The Potter sisters, who had disapproved of the marriage, offered to pay the debts provided that the couple went to live abroad. They settled in Switzerland and Dobbs worked for a travel business. But there was continuing trouble. On 20 May Beatrice wrote that Rosy was 'mad, bad or worse', and complained of the 'insane desire for flattery and for physical indulgence' that led her to 'torture' Dobbs with jealousy. Twenty years later, reading this critical note, Beatrice remarked that she was ashamed of her own 'uncharitableness and lack of reasoning sympathy' and added that Rosy had become 'one of the best and most selfless of women'. The Shaws had moved from one rented house to another and were currently staying at Blackdown Cottage, Haslemere.

12 June. Leicester

Staying at a rough boarding-house, the best in Leicester, for a fortnight's investigation . . . house dirty, meals rough and monotonous and service inefficient but willing. We pay two guineas a week each, for which we get a good bedroom, a small sitting-room and our meals with some half a dozen other boarders. . . . Sidney feels the discomfort more than I do: the greater fastidiousness of the man, I suppose. With him the need for investigation is accepted by his intelligence but it is not part of his personal life and aims. . . .

This Whitsun has been a melancholy time. The Dobbs crisis has cast a deep shadow over the whole family. . . .

Then there was the blow of Carrie Darling's death, that brave, spirited, devoted nature, thinking only of others as she lay dying; and the fact that she desired to see me, the message reaching me too late, oppressed me with a heavy melancholy. While she lay dying I was idling at Bernard Shaw's pretty little place in Surrey. A minor element in my unhappiness was the discomfort that we had more or less imposed ourselves on the Shaws and that Charlotte Shaw did not want to have us. Perhaps this was a morbid impression. But it is clear that now she is happily married we must not presume upon her impulsive hospitality and kindly acquiescence in our proposals. All this made me glad to get to work again – to enjoy the mental peace of research, unhampered by human relationship, except the one ideal relationship of marriage. . . . I need hard work and obscurity to keep me in good moral condition. The one happiness which never seems to injure me is Sidney's adoring love: that encourages me when I am despondent and holds me back when I am elated with vanity. It is purely blessed. . . .

Lord Battersea (1843–1907) was a minor office-holder who had married into the Rothschild family. George Wyndham (1863–1913) was a Conservative M.P.

and at this time Chief Secretary for Ireland. Mrs Paul was probably the wife of Herbert Paul (1853–1935), Liberal M.P. and biographer of Gladstone.

4 July. Grosvenor Road

It was on the terrace of the House of Commons that we met again – after an interval of thirteen years – one of Haldane's large dinner-parties of London Society folk. We were awaiting the last comers. Suddenly Mr Chamberlain appeared, apparently seeking some friends he expected to dine with him. We looked at each other and I stepped forward and we shook hands. 'I should like to introduce my husband to you,' I said after we had exchanged a few words. Then I left him and Sidney talking together and turned to fellow guests and tried hard to make conversation. In a few minutes he came and shook hands with me again and disappeared. The assembled company, who had watched us keenly, closed in and in five minutes we were dining in a private room, I talking vigorously to Lord Battersea and Mr Haldane.

We sat out after dinner on the terrace and just as I was explaining to George Wyndham that 'a Tory was a man without prejudices compared to a Liberal' I became aware that Mr Chamberlain had joined us. He sat by me and we talked – America, Birmingham University, economics. He looked wan and tired; he was uncertain of himself and obviously anxious to be gentle and kindly towards me. It may have been an hour that we chatted on together till I felt that this somewhat hollow talk, all the while under the close and amused observation of this little set of London Society folk, was becoming oppressive, and I rose with the words: 'I think we must be going.' 'Mrs Webb is terminating the interview,' said Mrs Paul to Sidney, as the great man grasped my hand and hurriedly departed. Then I felt conscious that all the company became exceptionally polite and I cursed the fate that brought the casual reopening of the relationship again under the eye of London Society. After I was back in my own home I had time to reflect that on the whole it is better that we have met and been friendly with one another, and that I have shown him that I have no grudge against him and that I am happy in my own life. The lines of our lives cannot bring us together. He is old, I am elderly, we are both of us absorbed in work and interests, he is in the great world currents, I in a backwater of specialism. It may be that our efforts are to some extent antagonistic. Still for all that there is a bond of sentiment between us, I for the man I loved, loved but could not follow.

One humorous incident in this melodrama. On my introducing Sidney the great man said in a tone of kindly condescension: 'I think you were in MY office, Mr Webb.' Sidney replied quickly, 'That is hardly quite correct: when I was there YOU were not.' Sidney told me afterwards that he was conscious of a gaucherie. He meant to say that he had not had the honour of serving under him. But that was not the effect.

19 July. [41 Grosvenor Road]
A month in London entertaining, shopping and seeing sisters, snatching from this waste of energy two or three mornings at the B.M. over local newspapers. Longing to get back to quiet days of absorption in our subject. Sidney struggles on, engineering the School, its site, its building, its status as a university institution. Breakfast at 8 sharp; from 9.15 to 1 o'clock we read at the B.M., then back to lunch, he off to his committees and I to anything that turns up. Nearly every day we entertain at lunch or dinner or dine out ourselves – all distractions which prevent profitable brooding over the problems of local government. For our present aims some social connections are essential; the question always is how much personal effort must be sacrificed to personal influence. In the England of today success in establishing new undertakings for public purposes depends on your influence over the various governing cliques; the more cliques you have access to the broader the foundations of your power to get things done. . . .

We have seen much of the Leonard Courtneys this spring. Leonard's determined support of the Boers' plea for independence, even more his denunciation of the war, has alienated him from both political parties. The Tories regard him as a wholly unendurable person; the vast majority of Liberals consider him to be a quixotic crank. Even the tiny group of pro-Boer Radicals think that his speeches and manifestoes are often out of season. It is only among the I.L.P. and S.D.F. working-men that he finds enthusiastic followers in his anti-government crusade. A strange turn of the wheel of political popularity. . . . What hurts him most, oddly enough, is the social boycott. Leonard has always enjoyed the leisurely society of persons of culture and position, and today he and Kate find themselves without the accustomed invitations. . . Dear Kate is an incurable sentimentalist and has no sense of humour. She gives happiness and increased self-assurance to Leonard but she aggravates his one big fault – his inveterate mental habit of thinking everyone who disagrees with him immoral or unenlightened. All the same there are few mortals for whom I have so continuous an affection and respect as I have for Leonard Courtney and his worshipful mate.

Political parties become daily more chaotic. The Tories are, as a party, complete cynics, bound together by a rampant imperialism, alternately protecting vested interests and appealing to demagogic passions they do not themselves share. But at any rate they understand the game of 'follow the leader'. The great Liberal Party – 'the engine of progress' – has lost its old faith and has no notion in which direction progress lies. The rank and file mete out contempt impartially to all their titular leaders. . . . Leonard Courtney and John Morley are acclaimed as the only honest politicians by the official Labour leaders, who have one and all gone pro-Boer. The Fabian Society, it must be admitted, is completely out of the running. The majority believe in the inevitability of the war whilst the minority accuse the majority of being the worst kind of traitors to the socialist cause.

31 July. [41 Grosvenor Road]
Spent Sunday with Alfred at Parmoor. This spring has been a bad time for him. An attack of influenza left him a hypochondriacal wreck. Following on this illness one of his boys got into trouble at school which upset him quite unnecessarily. On the top of it all came the appointment of Carson as Solicitor-General and the spiteful comments in the press of the relative advantage of being a 'bad' and a 'good' boy. Whether Alfred would have cared to give up his large income at the Bar for the Solicitor-Generalship is a question, but he would certainly have liked the refusal of it. . . Anyway he felt himself for the first time in his life unsuccessful. . . . Moreover his five children are growing up without discipline and without liking for work, and he is without a comrade and wife. Consequently in our talks together there was a note of depression and disappointment. . . .

The Webbs spent much of the summer on Tyneside, with a three-week rest at Bamburgh on the coast.

5 August. St Philip's Vicarage, Newcastle
In the intervals of reading the proceedings of the Newcastle Town Council I study the works of theologians, Protestant and Catholic, stowed away in this house. Impressed with the egotism and narrow-mindedness of Evangelical divines. . . .

Wallington was built in the reign of William III. John Ruskin later had a hand in altering this Northumberland mansion.

20 August. [Newcastle]

Spent Sunday at Wallington, the home of the Trevelyans, a moderate-sized country house with a certain stateliness, a pretension surrounded by beautiful woods and near the romantic scenery of the highlands of Northumberland. The visit was perfunctory on both sides. The Trevelyans felt compelled to ask us and we felt that it would be ungracious to refuse to go. Between the old Trevelyans and ourselves there is no sympathy and little liking. They look on us as the distinctly undesirable friends of their son, eccentric and self-complacent persons, whom they cannot exactly object to because we are respectable, hardworking and, in our own way, distinguished. But they regard us as belonging to an altogether different stratum of society – which in fact we do. Our attitude towards them is one of indifference. It is impossible to deny that Sir George Trevelyan is a public-spirited, highly cultivated man, whose tastes are refined and who has lived his life consistently according to his sense of duty and propriety. . . . Lady Trevelyan is a pleasant-tempered, con-scientious and plain-spoken woman of comely appearance who has, like her husband, acted up to her own standard of duty. What is it that makes them so unattractive to us? It is not only that they bore us with their old-fashioned views and conventional aims: it is mainly I think that they are deficient in any kind of generosity. Their whole life seems to have been one long calculation of how to get 21*s* out of 20*s.* And as they are reputed to be very rich this close-handedness is repellent. And these characteristics of the host and hostess are reflected from the top to the bottom of the household. All the arrangements and all the servants are lacking in the substance and the spirit of hospitality. I had, for instance, some difficulty in getting an early cup of tea: the housemaid enquired whether I really wanted it! . . . The guest feels that every thing is measured, from the number of fires to the number of hours that he is expected to stay. The Trevelyans have, throughout their lives, tried to do the correct thing: they have never been carried away to do the generous thing. Thus, in spite of his great wealth, Sir George has not carried weight in counsels of his party. He has been accorded high office because of his talent and his social position, but he has never won adherents or influenced situations by undertaking the burden of the day or by responding to its material needs. He has many acquaintances. I doubt whether he has any friends. Lady Trevelyan has been in this respect his faithful shadow.

As for Charles Trevelyan, our relation to him is more painfully indifferent because it ought to be friendly and intimate. Before he travelled with us I distinctly liked him. His good looks, his pleasant temper, his warm appreciation of our work and his sympathy with our views, made him agreeable as one of a group of young men who frequented our house. I was perhaps even a little flattered when he begged to go round the world with us – there was a vision of a good-looking youth dancing attendance and carrying the rugs. But though throughout our long companionship he remained good-looking, pleasant-tempered and appreciative of our opinions, we soon discovered that he, like his parents, intended to get 21s for every 20s. That Sidney had to make all the arrangements, take the tickets, pay all the bills and generally do 'courier' to the three of us was perhaps not out of order. But it was irritating to be perpetually 'done' in a small way. 'I have no change,' was the constant reply when it came to paying a cab or tipping a servant. This little meanness is a most unfortunate foible of C.T.'s and he has made himself notorious among his acquaintances for this subtle way of extracting small sums from other people's pockets. Perhaps one might have smiled at this uncomfortable habit if he had not shown in other matters an inveterate determination to get the maximum advantage for himself out of every transaction, pecuniary or otherwise. The result was that though we remained outwardly on excellent terms we became in the last months of our journey disillusioned with our companion, and no doubt, by reaction, he with us.

Since our return to England we have all of us tried hard to be deliberately friendly and his evident insistence on his people inviting us to Wallington and our acceptance of the invitation was only another example of the determination on both sides to avoid the banality of a breach of good comradeship after many months of travel together. Moreover, we respect each other, for in spite of his pecuniary meanness in shillings and pence (he was always ready to pay his fair share of any considerable outlay) and in spite of his persistent intention of getting the maximum out of all the circumstances and relations of life, Charles Trevelyan is a well-conducted fellow and good citizen. The maximum advantage does in his mind include warm family affection, faithfulness in his appreciation of friends, public work and distinct personal refinement in thought and in feeling. His brother

George has the same traits but far greater talent and great power of concentrated work. But he is a consummate prig. The middle brother, Bobbie, is the highly respectable 'wastrel' of the family; but though he is futile, he is the most human of the three. But I know of no family whom one respects so much and likes so little. It is an unlóvely attitude to be acutely conscious that one is wholly indifferent to one's host and they to one, and we were glad to get back to our ugly little vicarage from the dignified amenities of Wallington.

[Beatrice added the following note on 25 February 1920:

We saw little more of C.P. Trevelyan for the next twenty years. He secured a safe Yorkshire seat in a by-election in 1899 directly after our return to England and kept it until he was thrown out in the 1918 election as a notorious pacifist. He made no impression in the House of Commons and was ignored when the Liberals came into power in 1906, remaining on the back benches until his friend Runciman became President of the Board of Education and selected him as Under-Secretary. In this office Trevelyan remained an inconspicuous minister, neither liked nor disliked in his office or in the House, until the declaration of war in 1914, when he made the one sensation of his parliamentary life by tendering his resignation in company with John Burns, as a protest against the war. This fine gesture put him in a good position to join the Labour Party; but, unwisely, and characteristically I think, he delayed this step until after he had been defeated at the polls as an Independent candidate, with a Labour man as well as a coalition Liberal against him. The other day he came here for a talk and declared that revolution could not be long delayed and that it would be more violent and more complete than we old folk imagined. He has joined the I.L.P. and has been accepted as Labour candidate for one of the Newcastle divisions. The war has, in fact, given Trevelyan another chance of making a political career if he has learnt to spend himself and his money generously on his cause. As one of the few wealthy men in the Labour Party he has a unique opportunity. He has certainly improved: he is far less conceited and far more fervent in his convictions – whether his fervour will show itself in work and in money, as well as in words and looks, remains to be proved.]

25 September. Leeds
Staying here to start Miss Kitson on the Leeds minutes. Our vacation is at an end. Five weeks in St Philip's Vicarage, the home of a High

Church Anglican priest who is also a socialist, up on the high ground in a working-class quarter. The weather was detestable so that we had little temptation to desert our work and by the end of the time we were both of us ready for our delightful holiday at Bamburgh.

Three weeks we spent lying in a tent on the sand and watching the sea, or cycling over moorland and mountain, or wading out to rocks or islands – a quite enchanting holiday. We took with us masses of books, chiefly works on the Oxford Movement, a continuance of the theological taste we acquired at the vicarage. . . .

Sometimes Sidney and I feel that we can hardly repay by our work the happiness and joy of our life. It seems so luxurious to be able to choose what work one will do according to one's faith in its usefulness and do that work in loving comradeship. The next ten years will prove whether we are right in devoting our energies to the establishment of a science of society and whether the amount of scientific work we have mapped out for ourselves is not beyond our powers.

On our way down today we found Haldane at Newcastle and travelled with him to York. He was full of political talk. 'Not a single issue is being discussed at this election that will be remembered two years hence,' was his summing-up of the situation. For the last four months he has spent all his time, left over from his income-earning at the Bar, on building up the Liberal Imperialist party. He obstinately maintains that no frontal attack on social and industrial evils is possible for the Liberal Party: they must gain the confidence of the electors on foreign policy and any social reform must come by 'turning movements'. The Tory majority, he thinks, will be diminished, and the present government will not last more than two or three years more. Balfour is tired of it, Chamberlain is the only strong man and he is universally distrusted as supreme ruler.

The general election of October 1900, known as the 'khaki election' because the Conservatives seized the chance to capitalize on the recent victories in South Africa, resulted in an increase in the Tory majority from 130 to 134. Haldane and the other Liberal Imperialists were putting pressure on Rosebery at this time to lead the anti-Campbell-Bannerman forces within the Liberal Party. The purpose of Local Veto was to give the temperance interest local control over liquor licensing; like Home Rule and the disestablishment of the Churches of Wales and Scotland it appealed to the Celtic fringe and the Nonconformists and alienated the urban voters who had drifted away with Chamberlain and the Unionists. The newly formed Labour Representation Committee, which linked the I.L.P. and the trade unions, managed only to return Keir Hardie and one other candidate.

7 October. Grosvenor Road

Haldane's anticipation of a diminished government majority seems hardly likely to be fulfilled. The Liberal Party, divided against itself, uncertain as to its policy, is being badly routed at the polls. 'The strong man' of the government [Chamberlain] has played it down low to the man in the street: the street has answered back with emphatic approval. And in doing so the electors have shown common sense. Who would trust a party with a lay figure as ostensible leader, and as the real leaders of its sections men who hate each other and each other's ideas, more than they do the persons or the views of the enemy. And there seems little hope for the Liberals in the near future. To win back the large towns they have to give up Home Rule, Local Veto, and Disestablishment: they have to become Imperialists and develop some kind of social programme. In giving up the old politics they alienate the 'Celtic fringes' and all the provincial politicians: in Imperialism they cannot outbid the Tories: in all social questions they lack knowledge or conviction and fear to lose their remaining rich men. So they will fall back on the Rosebery plan of 'no policy', hoping that they may be accepted as the only 'alternative' to the government gone stale. That may cause the adhesion, one by one, of men (mostly of the upper and middle classes) who are personally offended with the government, or who belong to 'interests' that are threatened by the expenditure and innovation of Tory Democracy. But it will not bring back to their ranks the great mass of town workers who want some strong lead; something blatant and positive in return for their votes.

Meanwhile we go on, little concerned with the stress and storm of politics. Now and again we have a qualm lest the huge Conservative majorities in London constituencies may mean a 'Moderate' victory in the L.C.C. elections in March. Otherwise a Conservative government is as good for us as a Liberal government. . . We realize every day more strongly that we can never hope to get hold of the 'man in the street'; we are too 'damned intellectual', as a shrewd journalist remarked. All we can hope to do is to find out for ourselves the actual facts and embody them in a more or less scientific form, and to trust to other people to get this knowledge translated into popular proposals. What is more probable is the silent use of this knowledge in the unperceived transformations of law and government by men and women of goodwill. Our business is to be friendly to men of all parties, to *try* to be charitable and unassuming, and to go on with our work persistently and loyally. Sidney, in his administrative work, has considerable power to build up London secondary and university education on the lines he believes in; with the London School of Economics we have, in our own hands, the forming of the economics and political science teaching of the new University, and through the new Faculty the gradual establishment of a new science and a new art. That, with our own research work, ought to be sufficient for our faculties, indeed, it may prove to be beyond them!

19 October. [41 Grosvenor Road]
Massingham came in last Sunday week and found me alone. Of course we talked politics, he still bent on destroying Rosebery, upholding the old Liberal doctrine of non-intervention except in favour of small races! He led the conversation on to Chamberlain. 'I hear he has trouble at home: his wife has left him; at least,' he said slowly, 'she took no part in the elections and is travelling on the Continent.' I was so taken aback that I was silent for a few seconds and I felt Massingham looking at me. 'How very terrible,' escaped from me. 'I thought they were so fond of each other.' And then I began to talk of other matters.

Since then I have been struggling with a terrible depression. It may be that I am not physically well. But the thought of the misery of the man I loved haunts and disables me. I find myself wondering in a useless sort of way why there has been a breach in what from all reports was the most fortunate marriage for him, whether she has repudiated him on account of the 'contract scandal' in which his name has figured. Anyway, if it is true, it is horribly cruel, equal misery to each of them, for what can one of them do without the other? Then I console myself: the whole story may be a libel, invented by hostile journalists. I am allowing myself to be a victim to a foolish and exaggerated sentiment. For after all, what have I to do with it? I have my own life, and my own love, and my own work and I am fully absolved by the past from any responsibility for his happiness. But oh! the pity of it!

Leonard Courtney did not stand as a parliamentary candidate in the election of 1900. His views on the Boer War had put him out of favour with both the Unionists and the Liberals.

16 November. [41 Grosvenor Road]
A month of miserable suspense, watching the newspapers to see if Chamberlain was travelling with his wife, a horrible suspicion that he may be acting brutally to her, and yet suffering himself and laying up for both a store of pain in the future. Oh, my cursed imagination. And

then a morbid consciousness that owing to that most unfortunate meeting on the terrace in the summer there are some persons who are going about attributing to me the separation, I who have never met her and I who have only seen him once in thirteen years. Of course at the base of this morbid feeling there is a strain of self-conscious remorse. If I had not felt assured that these two were absolutely devoted to each other, that they had as an ideal relation to one another as I and Sidney, I would not have remained friends with Clara Ryland and Beatrice. But I desired to be friends with him and his wife and was anxious to intimate that I bore no grudge to either of them. However all this is morbid and exaggerated. I must turn my thoughts away. All I want to feel certain of, in my own conduct, is that if ever I meet him again my whole influence, if I have any, shall be devoted towards their reconciliation.

And to think that I am over forty, and he is over sixty! What an absurdity!

One sad result of this election is the exclusion of Leonard Courtney from Parliament. He and Kate have fought splendidly for the cause they believe in, and though they accept the fact that the country is dead against them they have accepted it with a quite magnificent cheerfulness. And yet to Leonard it means probably the end of his career, the loss of an occupation which gave him public influence, agreeable society, and which minimized the results of his loss of sight. . . .

Fabianism and the Empire, written by Shaw, was in part a justification of imperial expansion at the expense of small backward states, in part a restatement of municipal socialism. It seems to have been directed as much at the 'Limps' as at the Fabians.

9 December. [41 Grosvenor Road]
A delightful Sunday with the Bertrand Russells and Haldane – talking philosophy, University organization and politics. Haldane still devotedly attached to Rosebery; trying hard to make friends for him even among such humble folk as ourselves and the Russells. And we used our opportunity to press for the adoption of this policy of a 'national minimum' of Health, Education and Efficiency, leaving free play to the competition between private enterprise and public administration *above* that minimum. 'Rosebery has his back to the

wall and will not be forced into a premature declaration of policy: all
he is pledged to, is that there shall be no tampering with the Empire.
Apparently the great man is an admirer of *Fabianism and the Empire*
and has sent various gracious messages to the Shaws!

The Tuesday following I lectured at the Birmingham University
on 'How to study Social Questions'. The three Chamberlain sisters
watched me from the Front Benches. . . An evening spent with Clara
Ryland who has three of four children down with drain poisoning.
Gather that there has been trouble in the family of one sort or another –
bitterness at false accusations, financial embarrassment and some past
discord in the family, though this last seems happily settled, for which
the Lord be praised.

Charles Booth called one afternoon last week. I was pleased though
surprised until I discovered that he had come to canvass Sidney with
regard to the post of L.C.C. statistician on behalf of one of his
research secretaries. . . .

My relationship to the Booths seems now permanently broken.
Last winter there was a flicker of friendliness but when I offered to
cycle over with Sidney to Gracedieu from Leicester, last Whitsun, I
was peremptorily put off, I think with some incivility, for they knew
we were in lodgings for over a fortnight in broiling hot weather a few
miles from their gates and they did not ask us even to lunch! That I
think was a conclusive intimation that all relations were at an end and
Charlie's formal call to canvass Sidney for a good situation for one of
his cast-off workers was hardly a tactful act, or likely to accomplish its
end, even if the end has been a legitimate one. I often wonder what has
caused this breach, and why Mary at any rate has never been willing to
bridge it over. I still hate the thought of it, but as each effort of mine is
a repulse and fresh pain, there seems no other way than to look on those
two friends – for I care for them still – as to me dead. But it hurts one to
see their ghosts.

Our autumn has been dissipated with odds and ends. Sidney has
been absorbed in his administrative work. London University proves
to be the most formidable addition to the L.C.C. and the Technical
Education Board. . . And I have been wasting my time as far as our
work is concerned, in rather bad health, nursing Alfred, lecturing at
the School – and dreaming. I often wonder how much I lose by my
persistent habit of 'romancing' – perhaps, after all, it fills up time
when energy is at a low ebb. But it is not wholesome and leaves a bad
frame of mind. We need an authoritative mental hygiene.

Lord Reay (1839–1921), Under-Secretary of State for India 1894–95, was the first president of the British Academy 1902–07.

15 December. [41 Grosvenor Road]
Met Campbell-Bannerman at Lord Reay's last night. A quite stupid person, for a leader, well suited to a position of a wealthy squire or a sleeping partner in an inherited business. Vain.

ᔓ 1901 ᔐ

See Volume I for a full account of the experience Beatrice here recalls.

New Year's Day. [?41 Grosvenor Road]
Every newspaper is national stocktaking, reviewing the new year and forecasting the future in jerky epigrams. Back from ten days' holiday I feel vigorous and active-minded and inclined to give way to prevailing epidemic of reviewing the past.

Slack and emotional has been my life this year, not worthy of my better self. A certain amount of mechanical research work, a few fresh thoughts on methods of investigation (brought out in preparing my lecture at Birmingham), a development of our theory of competition (result of six lectures at the School), some reading and pondering on the religious life of the century, Alfred Cripps pulled through a troublesome illness, tender companionship with Sidney and helping his schemes by entertaining and otherwise – these have been the credit side of my account with my conscience. On the loss side I have been dreaming away energy in imaginary relationships, I have allowed myself to be the prey of exaggerated sentiment, I have dethroned my reason and intellect for whole hours each day and allowed emotion to play the devil with my imagination. Outwardly this has not affected my life; it has not altered the way in which I have passed each day, each month, and the whole year has been spent according to our plan of work. But it has starved my work of inspiration. The obedience of my faculties to my reasoned plan of life has been mechanical not vital.

And looking back on my life as a whole how does it read? Difficult to express in its complications. Three strands of consciousness, intertwined with each other and yet distinct – the body, the emotions and the intellect. Chronic bad health and constant physical pain made me, as a child and a girl, detestably aware of my body – spells of over-

189

exertion and overeating were followed by exhaustion and under-nourishment. Such mental life as I enjoyed was almost exclusively intellectual. My emotions were not roused. One or two pale friendships, arising from common intellectual interests, some religious feeling and aspiration curbed by intellectual doubts, cynicism and distrust in social intercourse, no philanthropic feeling or public spirit. Such was my soul's existence until Mother's death in 1882.

Then came the spring of my nature into health and vigour and a rich seed-time of intellectual life. My life became inspired with the spirit of modern science, search after truth and social reconstruction based on the ascertainment of facts. Believing that I could alter the conditions of human life for the better I began to love humanity. This phase of my life was connected with my relations with Herbert Spencer, unmeasured admiration for his intellect on my side, and affection for my personality on his part. At home, free performance of my duties as head of a large household and an affectionate though limited companionship with Father gave restfulness to my life.

Then came the catastrophe of my life. At a London dinner-party I met Joseph Chamberlain. At once, and I think on both sides, there arose the question of marriage. He was seeking a wife, attractive, docile and capable. I was ripe for love, revelling in newly acquired health and freedom, my intelligence wide awake, my heart unclaimed. I was ambitious, more ambitious than perhaps I knew, to play a part in the world. He had energy and personal magnetism, in a word masculine force to an almost superlative degree. Instantaneously he dominated my emotional nature and aroused my latent passion. But my intellect not only remained free but positively hostile to his influence. In our talks together I found no common intellectual ground. He had no faith in science, no understanding of its methods, he had no interest in philosophy or metaphysics, no care for music or poetic prose, no inkling of religion. I did not even recognize in him the finer strains of public spirit. Bound up in the pedantry of dogmatic individualism I was then incapable of appreciating Chamberlain's intense desire to remedy the grosser forms of social misery. And so it came to pass that in spite of great personal attraction on both sides we did not marry one another and that after four years' storm and stress I was left bleeding and wounded while he departed to seek more attractive metal. What happened to him throughout this long adventure I do not know. Probably the whole episode was comparatively unimportant. Undoubtedly his pride was wounded in the early stages; he felt that he had been snubbed by my family and possibly by myself; afterwards his taste was unsatisfied. That last visit in 1887 he saw a woman, no longer young, living without the surroundings of wealth and social position, badly dressed and without any apparent distinction. And in spite of knowing that I loved him desperately, he turned away and left me. At the time I was ready to condemn him. But that condemnation has long passed away. A riper experience of life has taught me that the one mortal sin towards another is to enter into the intimacy of married life (with or without the marriage ceremony) without love, without faith in your enduring love. So after a period of fourteen years there remains only a tenderness for the man I loved, taking the form of an almost exaggerated desire for his success and happiness.

Meanwhile between 1883 and 1887 my intellect had been leading a quite separate life, almost uninfluenced by the life of the emotions. The physical and mental misery of unsatisfied passion interrupted my intellectual work by spells of disabling pain, but strangely enough it did not alter it. I never yielded one inch of ground to Chamberlain; my faith in the scientific method as the basis for political action remained intact. Indeed my pain and humiliation seemed to intensify my desire to push forward on my own lines. Rent collection in Whitechapel, visits to the homes of cotton operatives in Lancashire, my investigations with Charles Booth, hard reading and still harder thinking in the early hours of the morning at home, were all different ways of pursuing my one aim – the discovery of the laws which underlie social action. In all this business of life I remained hard-headed and cold, using whatever feminine charm I possessed to further my intellectual ends. Sentimental relationships I had, but the sentiment was always on the other side.

Possibly I owe a debt to Chamberlain. He absorbed the whole of my sexual feeling, but I saw him at rare intervals and loved him through the imagination, in his absence more than in his presence. This emotional preoccupation made my companionship with other men free from personal preferences and deliberately controlled with a view to ends. And my home life though gloomy was admirably suited to my intellectual training. Dutifulness to Father kept me occupied for a certain number of hours every day in a mechanical way. There was even an object for motherly tenderness in poor dear old Father. . . But there was no call to any kind of exertion and there was absolute physical comfort. All this left free the whole nerve force for intellectual development.

So these six years of Father's illness rolled on. Passion burnt itself out and ended in the winter of 1888–89 in an almost religious resignation of the woman's life. Intellectual interest grew year by year. From the publication of a letter in the *Pall Mall*[*Gazette*] in 1886 this intellectual life was stimulated by the consciousness of somewhat unusual success. The very month of my deepest humiliation as a woman, August 1887, was the very month that my first article was accepted by Knowles of the *Nineteenth Century;* the time of my greatest pain, November 1888, when Chamberlain was getting married to the charming American, I was 'starring' it at Oxford, acclaimed as a new light in a new science. Intellectual production had always seemed to my reason the ideal state of being and the most complete satisfaction to my ego. In spite of the intense but intermittent pain the balance of these years was, I think, satisfaction.

Passion conquered, the woman's pride trampled underfoot, Father mentally dead, the field was open for the advent of the perfect comrade. Warm friendship I had enjoyed, of friendly acquaintances I had many. But I had to look forward to complete loneliness because whole hours of the day I could not work and I needed help in work, lack of training making the mechanical side of authorship extremely arduous. And then the mother's instinct, to some extent satisfied by my care of Father, cried for satisfaction.

In this state of mind I met Sidney one day early in January 1890; from the first meeting I realized that he would fall in love with me. His energy, his ingenuity, his faith in intellectual principles, his desire for reform and capacity for absorbing knowledge, made him at once my comrade. His lack of social position, even his lack of personal attractiveness gave him in his relation to me, the odd charm of being in every respect the exact contrary to Chamberlain and my ill-fated emotion for that great personage. In the new relationship I had, at any rate, complete intellectual sympathy and an identity of moral aim which had been wholly lacking in the other. The fact that neither my physical passion nor my social ambition were stimulated by the relationship seemed in itself an element of restfulness and stability. Then again my pity was appealed to. I felt his love for me was so overpowering that his life and work might be wrecked if I withdrew myself. Added to all these thoughts and feelings there was a curious strain of altruistic utilitarianism. I had a competence, more than enough to sustain one intellectual worker. I had social position of a kind, I had knowledge of men and affairs; all these Sidney lacked to be successful. Why not invest my different kind of capital where it would yield the best results from the standpoint of the community? And so we pledged our words at the Co-operative Congress May 1891.

Nearly nine years of married life leads me to bless the institution and my good fortune in entering it with such a partner. We are still in our honeymoon and every year makes our relationship more tender and complete. Rightly or wrongly we decided against having children; I was no longer young, he had been overworking from childhood, we were both of us unusually energetic. Our means, though ample for ourselves and our work, would not have allowed a family and continued expenditure on investigation and public life. But perhaps the finally conclusive reason was that I had laboriously and with many sacrifices transformed my intellect into an instrument for research. Child-bearing would destroy it, at any rate for a time, probably altogether. Sometimes I wonder whether I have been dutiful to the community in shirking motherhood, whether in point of fact I have not lost at once a safety valve for feeling and a valuable experience. But on the whole I do not regret the decision, still less does Sidney.

And our work, how has it prospered? For the first six years of our married life we struggled with our big undertaking, the history and analysis of trade unionism. We lived little in the world: long vacations from the L.C.C. were spent at The Argoed and elsewhere, with Shaw and Wallas as companions. The expectation with which I married that in future my life would be spent in a humble sphere, friends and acquaintances drawn from the intellectual proletariat, was to a large extent fulfilled. This last year we have seemed to drift upward in the strata of society: I say drifted because we have not sought it, we have simply been carried there by the currents of our work. The establishment of the London School of Economics, its inclusion in London University, our friendship with the Bishop of London, with Mr Haldane, with a set of well-placed young disciples, have all forced us into the outer circles of London Society. Sidney has lost his shyness and his aggressiveness while retaining his independence and dogged persistency in our aims. It may be that the circumstances of our work will drift us more into the stream of the big world; it may be that we shall remain pretty well where we are today.

It is a toss-up which course will best promote our plans. One cannot associate with great personages without considerable expenditure of nerves and means, and all this expenditure must come off our efforts in administration and investigation. On the other hand England is governed by cliques of friends and acquaintances. If you are inside the clique you help to rule: if you are outside you cry in the wilderness. This is of course only true of immediate results. The ultimate course of society is decided by the thought of the time and your effectiveness will be determined by your contribution to this thought. But even if this be accepted a true decision is not easy. In actual reasoning you may do better work by isolating yourself; but in the collection of the material required as a basis for this thought social prestige opens up opportunities otherwise closed. So I am inclined to drift on, not seeking society, not evading it. We must live our own life and take what comes on our own terms. Too much is not likely to be tendered!

I close this book of reminiscence until next year. Shall I be able to justify the next year's life better than I can today? I have to curb and control my imagination, to keep before me steadfastly the rule of conduct that I would have others adopt. 'Do unto all men as you would have them do towards the world,' is the new version of the Christian maxim.

Maggie Hobhouse also recorded the visit to Hadspen. On 1 January 1901 she wrote to her daughter Rachel: 'The Sidney Webbs are here, very clever, very conceited, very full of energy and life. Altogether a good spurring cold-water shower-bath, leaving me with a sense of being rather flabby and inferior and requiring a good rubbing-up!' Margaret Harkness was a cousin with whom Beatrice had been friendly before her marriage. A journalist and novelist, much involved in the socialist movement until 1890, she became a convert to the recently founded Salvation Army and soon after left for Australia. Beatrice criticized her as boastful and personally disloyal. Samuel Augustus Barnett (1844–1913) and his wife Henrietta (1851–1926) had been close friends when Beatrice had worked in the East End of London. He was Warden of Toynbee Hall, the Whitechapel settlement house, from 1884 to 1906. Benjamin Jones (1847–1941) was the London manager of the Co-operative Wholesale Society and had helped Beatrice with her book on Co-operation. Bella Fisher had been secretary to the eminent geologist Sir Charles Lyell (1797–1875), whose work had played a vital part in evolutionary science. She had encouraged Beatrice in her social research. Edward Talbot (1844–1934), a brilliant High Churchman, became Bishop of Rochester in 1895. Sir Alfred Lyall (1835–1911) was an author who had been a senior official in the Indian civil service. William James (1842–1910), philosopher and brother to the novelist Henry James, published his *Will to Believe* in 1897 and *Principles of Psychology* in 1890.

2 January. [41 Grosvenor Road]

Back in London after a few days with the Playnes and Hobhouses. The sisters do not grow apart as years roll on: indeed the last few years have seemed to bring us all nearer together. Blood relationship is a very tenacious tie. It outlasts many relationships of choice, wears better than any other relationship (except marriage), though it is seldom so close or satisfying as the special intimacy of the moment. For as one gets middle-aged intimate friendships seem to fade away and one is too much occupied and, in a sense, too utilitarian, to make new friends. One sees persons who are for the time one's fellow workers and these individuals are not necessarily sympathetic.

Old friends die, or marry, or become estranged or indifferent. Of my early friendships few remain: the Booths and Margaret Harkness estranged, Carrie Brown dead, the Barnetts, Ben Jones, Ella Pycroft, Alice Green, Bella Fisher and Miss Souvestre all extremely friendly when we meet but we meet perhaps once a year; in the case of these latter perhaps two or three times a year. There are, it is true, Herbert Spencer and Clara Ryland, both of whom I occasionally visit, in each case out of piety to an old sentiment. Then the two dear comrades and friends who for some half-dozen years regularly spent their holidays with us – Wallas and Shaw – are both of them married, and though when we meet, we meet as old friends, we seldom see each other. With Audrey Wallas I find it difficult to be sympathetic because she is so extremely unattractive; still, my respect for her increases year by year. Charlotte Shaw does not specially like me, and while meaning to be most friendly, arranges her existence so as to exclude most of Shaw's old friends. And possibly they would all of them say that we were too much absorbed in each other to care for others and that our friendliness was more an overflow from our happiness than any special love for them. In fact a sort of universal benevolence to all comers seems to take the place of special affection for chosen friends. It is only the persistent yet slack tie of sisterhood that seems to survive these inroads of indifference.

The man we see most of nowadays is Hewins: every Tuesday he lunches with us to discuss the affairs of the School. He is original-minded and full of energy and faith. Shaw always declares he is a fanatic. So he is. But he is also a born manipulator. We never know whether he is telling us his real opinion or his real intention. We feel that we are being 'handled' just as we watch him handling others. He ought to have been an ecclesiastic, and would have entered the Church if it had not been for the 39 Articles to be swallowed, just at a time when physical science and historical criticism made these tenets seem intellectually contemptible. In thought he would be a reactionary if the present trend of Liberal opinion did not happen to be a reaction from the doctrine of 'individual freedom'. He hates disorder, he detests 'Protestantism' or following the 'inner light', or any other rebellion against the reasonable will of the community. He is a great admirer of Chamberlain, dislikes all the Liberal leaders equally, votes Progressive, and is a member of the National Liberal Club. He is a churchman and ardent believer in the scientific method in economics and politics. He is disinterested with regard to money, he is ambitious of power – altogether he is one big paradox. But the most characteristic paradox of his nature is the union of the fanatic and the manipulator. With such a character it is difficult to be intimate, however much it may excite one's admiration, liking and interest.

Naturally enough we have a large circle of friendly acquaintances, some of whom might be considered friends. Haldane, the Reeveses, the Bishop of London and Louise Creighton, the women factory inspectors, Lion Phillimore, the Bertrand Russells, the staff of the London School of Economics, the Senators of the new University, the Bishop of Rochester and his wife, Sir Alfred Lyall, the Richard Stracheys, and other more or less interesting folk – come and go. A still larger circle leave cards and force me, by so doing, to all the quarters of residential London. But, for the most part, we are left to ourselves and allowed to spend our energies on our own special work.

At present I am writing the opening chapters to a small book on 'Factory Legislation: its Theory and Practice' or rather adapting portions of our Part III of *Industrial Democracy* to a more popular audience. . . It is to be a counter-blast to the persistent opposition to factory legislation on the part of the Women's Rights Movement reinforced by the employers' wives. This opposition has for the last ten years blocked all progress in the effective application of the Factory Acts to other industries. It is led by a few blatant agitators who would not count for much if they were not backed up by many Society women who belong to the governing clique and by a solid opposition to further reform from vested interests. What we have to do is to detach the great employer, whose profits are too large to feel the immediate pressure of regulation and who stands to gain by the increased efficiency of the factors of production, from the ruck of small employers or stupid ones. What seems clear is that we shall get no further instalments of reform unless we gain the consent of an influential minority of the threatened interest.

I feel sometimes in despair about 'the Book'. Beyond a little mechanical research, my mind has been entirely off the subject of local government, either preparing lectures in 'Industrial Competition' or on 'Methods of Research' or brooding over the 'Religious Question' and the provision of a metaphysic and a mental hygiene. I have been reading at large on these questions: theology, saints' lives, James's *Will to Believe* and his *Psychology*, various works on Scientific Method and so on. The one subject my mind revolts at is local government. But we shall have to set to and do it directly the L.C.C. election is over. I am making elaborate arrangements for a good five months in the country and hope to accomplish at least the first part (prior to 1835). We have masses of material but all the thinking has to be done.

15 January. [41 Grosvenor Road]
Mandell Creighton, Bishop of London – dead. One of our best friends.

When we returned to London this autumn we found him invalided. He had broken down on his holiday and was by the doctor's orders confined to the house. Three or four times I went down to Fulham to see him either with Sidney or alone. He was singularly gentle and sympathetic, eager to talk, the same delightful combination of banter and deep philosophy, the same enigmatical view of all things, whether of God or Man. The very last time, in fact just before Xmas, I had a long talk with him whilst the other guests were at tea. I told him our plan for reforming the Church, our idea of religion as 'mental hygiene' and the way in which we thought the High Church doctrine more consistent with it, than the Evangelical. To all of which he listened, and half seriously and half playfully agreed. Then I sent him James's *Will to Believe* . . .

I first knew the Creightons in August 1887. I remember so well that visit to Worcester: my interest in the versatile and pleasant ecclesiastic and don, my attraction to the handsome and direct-minded Louise, so different from each other, and yet so completely complementary. From that time forward I remained a friend and until they came to London used constantly to visit them. Those visits to Cambridge and Worcester were among the happiest days of my life during the long and trying time of Father's illness: the friendship, coming just at a time when I was suffering intensely, seemed a new opening into the world of distinguished men and women. And from the first they liked and trusted me, liked me for my best side. When I engaged myself to Sidney, they accepted him as their friend without hesitation, saw him through my eyes, and trusted him as they had trusted me.

Meanwhile Dr Creighton had changed the life of a professor and author for that of a bishop. There are many of his friends who regretted the step. The freedom of view, the brilliant dialectic, the subtle paradox, which often covered a daring hypothesis – all these were in place in a Cambridge don; they became impossible, or at any rate most baffling, in a bishop. Agnostic friends, sensitive to the proprieties of life, no longer dared to join in this intellectual adventure, with one who ought to feel himself to be a successor of the Apostles. And owing to a strange contrariness and rebellious audacity, a reaction possibly from the daily routine of a bishop's life, the change of position seemed for a time to accentuate the frivolous side of his intercourse with the outer world. . . . [Beatrice continues her assessment of Creighton for two or three pages.]

Our intimacy with Dr Creighton and to a lesser extent with Dr Talbot has brought constantly before us the Church, its present difficulties and its future. Any outside demand for disestablishment and disendowment is dead at the present moment. A few political dissenters and Radical political workers in the smaller provincial towns still hold to the old doctrine of the iniquity of a union between Church and state. But as far as the bulk of the people are concerned this doctrine is obsolete. The town workman is now neither a Nonconformist nor a secularist. He is simply indifferent to the whole question of religion or metaphysic. On the other hand he is inclined to think the hardworking curate, who runs his club, looks after his children on Sundays and holidays, stirs up the sanitary inspector and is sympathetic because acquainted with the struggle for better conditions of employment, a good fellow. He sees the dissenting parson moving out to the suburbs, the rich congregation preferring a new and fine building there than the old meeting-place down town. But the priest of the Established Church remains in the old city parish and is constantly abroad in the slums. The workman sees no distinction between the appropriation of the Church income by the clergy and the appropriation of mining royalties or ground values by the landlords, except in the expenditure of the income, a comparison immensely in favour of the clergyman. 'The majority of them do a day's work for us, and it is precious poor pay they get for doing it,' is a frequently heard remark. 'If we take to disendowing and disestablishing we will deal with the landlords first,' is the half-conscious thought of the revolutionary workman. The educated classes who are not Church members are also losing their objections. 'Nature abhors a vacuum.' 'All metaphysic is equally untenable if you require scientific proof.' 'The Christian metaphysic no more than the Hegelian. Why not leave the people with the old traditional faith?' are the dictates of the enlightened. 'If the people wanted three state churches, I see no reason why they should not have them,' remarked Lord Rosebery. Moreover, state endowment, state control, state ownership are all the order of the day.

Hence there is no fear of destruction from without. But within there are disruptive tendencies. No man of culture can nowadays be a Protestant Churchman of the old type – the dogma and doctrine, the written word of revelations is too ugly and impossible taken in its crudity. . . . 'More room,' cries the young churchman, 'freedom from the limitations of the Elizabethan compromise. Let us push forward where thought and feeling lead us.' 'Impossible,' says the lawyer, 'here are the 39 Articles and I am charged as the representative of the state to interpret them, and eventually enforce them. . . .'

We do not want a lawyer's interpretation of the 39 Articles in the Prayer Book; we want a sympathetic interpretation by persons whose whole duty and life is to consider the national needs in the matter of religion. The secular state gets its control over the Church by the Prime Minister's nomination of the bishops and by parliamentary power to legislate. That is sufficient. Give such a Church, deriving its authority directly or indirectly from the people, freedom to develop along its own lines.

Of course, our object is to enable the Church to grow out of its present superstitious doctrine and obsolete forms. We have faith that the development would be along the right lines. No doubt at first the direction would be sacerdotal and ritualistic. Personally I do not altogether object to this. The more ritual, the more mystery, the more indefiniteness of thought, the greater the play for emotional purposes. . . . And though there are aspects of the priest which are distasteful, yet I desire to see the minister of religion practising the art of mental hygiene. I do not believe that the ordinary man is capable of prescribing for the diseases of the soul any more than they are for the diseases of the body. We need the expert here as elsewhere. Religion, to my mind, should consist in the highest metaphysic, music and ritual and mental hygiene.

And I desire that the national life should have its *consciously* religious side. If, as a state, we are purely rationalist and selfish in our motives and aims, we shall degrade the life of the individuals who compose the state. I should desire the Church to become the home of national communal aspirations as well as of the endeavour of the individual towards a better personal life. Meanwhile I prefer the present Church with all its faults to blank materialism or competitive sectarianism.

Queen Victoria died on 22 January but Beatrice does not mention it. Sir Leslie Stephen (1832–1904), father of Virginia Woolf and Vanessa Bell, was the founder of the *Dictionary of National Biography* and published the three-volume *The English Utilitarians* in 1900.

25 January. [41 Grosvenor Road]
Reading Leslie Stephen's *Utilitarians*. Always interesting to compare one's own point of view with that of one's parents! For Bentham was certainly Sidney's intellectual godfather and, though I never read a word of him, his teaching was transmitted through Herbert Spencer's very utilitarian system of ethics and his method through Spencer's deductive reasoning from certain primary assumptions. How has the position of the disciples shifted from that of their past teachers?

First we agree that human action must be judged by its results in bringing about certain defined ends. . . . We altogether reject 'the happiness of the greatest number' as a definition of our own end, though other persons are perfectly at liberty to adopt it as theirs. I reject it because I have no clear vision of what I mean by 'happiness' or what other people mean by it. If happiness means physical enjoyment, it is an end which does not recommend itself to me, certainly not as the sole end. I prefer to define my end as the increase in the community of certain faculties and desires which I happen to like – love, truth, beauty and humour. . . . But we differ with the Benthamites in thinking that it is necessary that we should all agree as to ends, or that these can be determined by any science. We believe that ends, ideals, are all what may be called in a large way 'questions of taste' and we like a society in which there is a considerable variety in these tastes.

Science and the scientific method can be applied, not to the discovery of a right end, but to a discovery of a right way of getting to any particular end. And here it seems to me the Benthamites fall lamentably short in their understanding of the scientific method. They ignore the whole process of verification. They deduced their ways of arriving at their own particular end – human happiness – from certain elementary observations of human nature, but they never sought to test this 'order of thought' by the 'order of things'. They never asked – is it so?. . . Hence they omitted from their calculation some of the most powerful impulses of human nature: reverence for mystery, admiration for moral beauty, longing for the satisfaction of an established expectation, custom and habit, tradition, sense of humour, sense of honour, passionate longing for truth, loyalty, besides a host of mean vanities and impulses none of which produce happiness or aim at producing it, but are just blind impulses.

John Massie (1842–1925), professor of theology at Oxford, was chairman of the Congregational Union, Treasurer of the National Liberal Federation, and an expert educationalist. He became a Liberal M.P. in 1906.

9 February. [41 Grosvenor Road]
Met Lord Rosebery at Haldane's again. Asquith, W.P. Reeves, Professor Hewins, Professor Massie and ourselves made up the party. I sat next to the great man, who was gracious and less self-conscious than last time. But the entertainment was a futile business. We talked and laughed, 'showed off': we never got anywhere near a useful discussion on questions in which we were interested. Professor Hewins, Sidney and I had hoped to talk about the School with Lord Rosebery who is probably to be president [of the L.S.E. board], but we got nowhere near it. He is a strange capricious creature, always posing to himself and others, anxious only to attain right *expression*. I was angry with myself afterwards, and was strangely enough, a bit vexed at being the only lady! That would not have mattered had we talked seriously, but in mere light banter 'the eternal feminine' will intrude and in that case one likes companionship.

But undoubtedly our excursions into Society advance the interests of the School. We are to have a meeting at the Mansion House with the Lord Mayor in the chair; Lord Rosebery to make a great pronouncement in favour of commercial education in the abstract and the School in the concrete, Lord Rothschild to act as Treasurer and other great persons to play up, the whole intended to raise a Building and Endowment fund for the School. All this is Haldane's doing, partly out of friendship for us, partly because he wants to interest his chief in *uncompromising* advance movements. Also he delights in 'intrigue' and he is amusing himself with putting into one company most unlikely co-workers. An institution which has united as its supporters ourselves, Rosebery, Rothschild, the Bishop of London and the Fabian Society is just the sort of mixed party which Haldane revels in. 'My dear Hewins,' says Haldane, 'you ignore the personal factor in politics.' For Hewins, though he willingly accepts the result, does not wholly like this 'Society' development.

And, in truth, it has its unpleasant side. It is much wholesomer to win by hard work than by these capricious gusts of fancy in great folk. I feel that I am skating on rotten ice which might suddenly give way under me. I am not afraid of losing the support of the 'Personages' because one does not count on its continuance and takes gratefully all one can get, knowing that it will come to an end. What I do fear is weakness in my own nature, incapacity to keep my intellect and heart set on our own work, undistracted by personal vanity or love of admiration. Fortunately Sidney is absolutely single-minded. But like Hewins he does not *quite* like it.

8 March. [41 Grosvenor Road]
Brilliant victory at the L.C.C. election. For the last three or four months (indeed since October) Sidney has been organizing the election: writing the election literature, insinuating articles in the press, gathering up the Progressive forces all through London, as well as engineering the Deptford fight. We fully expected to lose seats in London and a portion of our own Deptford majority. But the Water Companies, at the last moment, won our battle for us by their proposed water regulations. Directly these appeared we knew the tide was in our favour; the only problem was to make it flow as quickly as possible. Hence the articles contributed to all the halfpenny press, so that by the election day, every 'halfpenny' was on our side and even the *Daily Telegraph* came out in our support! Still, the sweeping majority for the Progressives means that the London elector has confidence in the 'old gang' which has now ruled London for twelve years, and that, in spite of the fact that the old gang are exclusively Radicals whilst the vast majority of electors are Tories. It is a striking testimony to the industry and capacity of a small body of administrators. The Moderates, on the other hand, are mediocrities, the larger number of them will not work. As a party they suffer from the same fatal defect as

the Liberal Party in national politics; the majority of them have unpopular convictions and run away from them. To have unpopular convictions is bad enough; to run away from them is fatal.

And now that the election is over we can at last turn back to the Book. I have already begun to sort both the material and my ideas for our country sojourn. I am not satisfied with myself but hope to be more so after country air and exercise and concentration on our subject. London life, with its constant clash of personalities, its attractions and repulsions, its manipulations and wire-pulling, is distracting and somewhat unwholesome. And this last year I seem to have passed into an emotional and imaginative phase, which, while it gives me a certain magnetic effect on others, knocks me to pieces myself. Indeed, I feel [that I am] becoming mediumistic. Country life and intellectual concentration will, I trust, bring back a saner frame of mind. Brainwork is a wonderful specific against the manifold forms of hysteria.

Lord Rothschild succeeded Dr Creighton as president of L.S.E. Alfred Harvey (1840–1905) was a banker much interested in promoting education in economics.

22 March. [41 Grosvenor Road]
Our long-planned meeting at the Mansion House came off yesterday. As far as we were concerned there was no hitch in the arrangement. But from Lord Rosebery's black looks when he came on the platform something had evidently gone wrong, and afterwards we gathered that he had intended making the meeting an occasion to answer the somewhat futile remarks of Lord Salisbury on commercial education, but the Lord Mayor had intimated that such a course would be undesirable and that Lord Rosebery had therefore found himself cut off from the most effective part of his speech. It was not an able pronouncement but it sufficed, and has been a great advertisement for the School. Haldane spoke with real enthusiasm and Harvey (of Glyn Mills) with knowledge of the subject. Lord Rothschild was unable to come but heads the contributions with £5,000. The whole affair is an audacious advertisement and appeal. It will be a marvel if it does not provoke an attack on the management and teaching of the School. We are sufficiently firmly seated in the saddle to risk it. I feel now that we have done our utmost to give the School an independent life; that it is time that it toddled out of our nursery and to some extent took its own line. Sidney is now turning his mind to the University and has drafted

a scheme for the complete reorganization of the University as a great centre of applied science.

And now we can (or at any rate I can) turn my thoughts wholly to the Book. Fortunately my mind has become clear of the romancings which perturbed it a few weeks ago. One of those strange and mysterious alterations which go on seemingly uncaused in our mental life – a sudden regaining of complete control over thought and feeling and a positive *desire* to concentrate all my mental energy on intellectual work. It is as if a hidden influence had been withdrawn and my mind was again moving freely. But the mere physical exhaustion of London life prevents me from doing good and sustained work, and I am longing for our three months in the country.

Meanwhile my boy is exceptionally well and happy. He is full of active thought and work, his health is excellent, he is conscious of success, and each day he seems more supremely happy in his love of me. All asperity and harshness has left him. He is always eager but has lost the note of 'exasperation' which used to characterize him. There is no slackening in his effort: he is perpetually working. He has as much if not more faith, though possibly faith in science has increased and faith in any particular economic doctrine has decreased. He is less of a doctrinaire than of old, more of an investigator. He is not a leader of men, but he is an initiator of policies. His influence is not concentrated in his own personality; it ramifies through many organizations and persons, the outcome of multitudinous anonymous activities. And I think the 'setting' I have given him of simple fare and distinguished friends suits him, both in reputation and taste. It satisfies his sense of consistency to adhere to a democratic standard of expenditure, and yet he reaps many of the advantages, in the scope and variety of social intercourse, of belonging to the inner circle of the political and scientific world. For all practical purposes we can associate with anyone we choose and on our own terms. Of course that would cease to be so if our social intercourse were not regulated by a 'practical purpose'. It is as co-operators in work, not as associates in pleasure, that we have free access to those who sit in high places.

Beatrice, still feeling unwell, spent Easter with Sidney at Lulworth Cove in Dorset, and for much of the summer she stayed with the Russells at Friday's Hill, the country home of the Pearsall Smiths. In the extract from Walt Whitman's 'Thou Mother with Thy Equal Brood' on p. 208, the italics are Beatrice's.

2 April. [Friday's Hill]

Delighted to get away from London and to look forward to a long spell of work on the Book. . . It will be a long pull and a strong pull to get through the work. If I were to remain in anything like my state of the last six months I should not succeed. But I am already a different being and with courage and prayer I shall pull through.

Hewins came as usual to lunch today: he was in thoroughly bad humour. No money to speak of has come in as the result of the Mansion House meeting, and he declares that the Mansion House meeting was a big failure. The plain truth is that in the first place he expected far too much from the meeting; in the second place he managed with less skill than usual. He seems to have got on Rosebery's nerves; he failed to impress the Lord Mayor, and he delayed sending out the appeal until five or six days after the meeting, we having understood that it went out on the very night of the meeting. Now he puts down the ill success to the connection of the School with Lord Rosebery and the Fabian Society! We tried to calm and cheer him, suggested that Lord Rothschild's £5,000 was more than we had originally thought of raising, and that at least the meeting had advertised the School. But he was not to be comforted. Hewins has three weak points: he suffers from attacks of quite unreasonable impatience and depression; he is a slack organizer of his staff; he seldom takes his 'chiefs' into his confidence as to what he really intends to do. This destroys any complete reliance on him. But he has magnificent energy and persistence, loyalty to his own ideas (which are in the main the same as our own) and personal disinterestedness.

24 April. Churchfield, West Lulworth, Dorset

A large thatched cottage with low straggling rooms, plain, clean but not too comfortably furnished, has been our living place for the last three weeks. The village is in a hollow of the chalk downs, without trees and cut off from the sight of the sea. From our sitting-room window we look on to the road, then a hedge, then an orchard, beyond – other thatched cottages. But once on the downs, there are glorious stretches of well-shaped hill and abrupt chalk cliff, expanses of sea and sky, and on the other side the most beautiful plain of heath and moor and wooded promontory with bright little rivers running in all directions except seaward. The colouring these last days has been exquisite, the sea – sapphire, amethyst, emerald, moonstone – the white chalk cliff rising out of it in mysterious lines of white, pink, grey. Brilliant yellow gorse in the foreground and on the other side the dark russet of the yet unfolded beech buds, the dull green-black of the fir and the rich tones of heather and scrub covering the plain and creeping up the little valleys of the bare neutral-tinted chalk downs.

The first fortnight was wet and cold and, beyond our regulation two hours' walk in the afternoon, we stayed in and worked at 'the Book'. We had brought with us ten pamphlet boxes of material, MSS, minutes of vestries etc. The first three days I spent struggling with the first draft of our first chapter rearranging each section and, when I had rearranged it, submitting it to Sidney. Then he would begin (I sitting by his side) to rewrite it, both of us breaking off to discuss or to consult our material. Indeed this constant consultation of our 'specimens' is the leading feature of our work. We are always handling our material. One of us will object 'that is not so' or 'that is not always the case' and then forthwith it becomes a question of evidence, and how far the facts we have under our hands are representative of the whole. The last three or four days we have gone systematically through all the facts and accounted for all the similarities and divergencies between our 'specimen' vestries. At last our chapter on the parish is complete and I sent it off to be typewritten this afternoon.

Sidney has spent many hours reading. In the three weeks we have had two batches of London Library books – twenty-six in all – and he has devoured every one of them. I have glanced through one or two, but when I am 'composing' I find all other brainwork out of the question, and content myself with the daily papers. The last week has been glorious summer weather and we have taken lovely rides inland or long walks along the cliffs on either side. Other times I have blissfully brooded and prayed for guidance and strength. A great peace has come over me. I am again completely absorbed in my subject and completely satisfied with the companionship of nature and the comradeship of my partner, lover, husband. The beauty and charm of the country, the isolation and regularity of the life, the spells of hard brainwork, varied with spells of physical exercise and physical and mental rest, is exactly the life that suits me in body and mind.

Sidney away and I play. He has journeyed up to London to University and T.E.B. business. The day is gloriously hot and I find myself cradled on the rocks with my feet (well above my head) toasting in the sun, the rest of my body enjoying the cool shade of a pillar-like rock which guards a tiny cove right away from the village. Sensations are delicious, and thoughts and feelings, memories and dreams drift past the Recorder and mingle with the sensations. Heat and coolness, motion and rest, sun and water, tide and rock – is it the contrasts that are so enchanting? The long undulating smooth-surfaced hill of neutral tint, abruptly terminated by the jagged white cliff standing out against the brilliant blue of the sea; the slow-flapping white gull, the fussy black rocks, the melancholy cry of the one, the cheerful chattering of the others. The music of that slow withdrawing of the ocean swell from the pebbled beach, a sound of infinite sweetness and sadness, like the inevitable withdrawal of a lover from a mistress he still loves; the bubbling and gurgling of the tide in the caves of the rocks beneath me, the spirit of children not yet born to life. On the horizon the stern outline of Portland and visions of convicts working under the midday sun on the [prison] quarries, squalid lives behind them – mean streets, hot, crowded, one-roomed homes, lack of nourishment, drink, intolerable vacant-mindedness, gambling, monotonous labour, adventurous crime, darkness and dirt, glaring lights and debauch – contrasted evils! I watch the sun's rays dancing on the sea and my thoughts wander back to the days we spent on the tropical ocean. . . . And then I drift on to the personal question. Are the books we have written together worth (to the community) the babies we might have had? Then again, I dream over the problem of whether one would marry the same man, in order to have babies, that one would select as joint author? The old, old question, always being put afresh to our civilization. Ought a man or a woman to have many relations with the other sex or only one? I think of the peace and happiness of these last weeks – the strenuous thought, the long hours of joyful enjoyment of light, colour, form, the physical relief of exercise and the equal relief of rest. I see my boy's blue eyes resting on me with love as he grasps my bicycle to push it up a hard bit of hill, I hear his voice praising me for some rearrangement of our chapter, I see him writing page after page, hour after hour, while I am mooning over a fire or wandering up and down a lane, 'cried off' because I am tired! I think what a fraud I am apart from him, how little I really contribute to the joint work, merely a 'fly-wheel' to get him over 'dead points'.

I decide that the answer is: one lover, not only in the letter but in the spirit. And this is all noonday dreaming, another contrast, a purely fanciful contrast, with no bearing on my personal life.

The sun is high in the heavens, the heat creeps from foot to hand, from hand to head. I move and lie full length on the beach and watch the marvellously tinted wave break on the pink pebbles and then withdraw itself with sweet low moan, weeping white spray, a surface grief only, meant to be repeated endlessly. I remember I am well over forty, growing grey and somewhat wrinkled. I get up, shake myself, mentally from sunshine dreams. Tomorrow I must plan out the chapter on the 'Select Vestry' otherwise it won't be ready for him to write on Thursday, our first day at the Russells.

Brain of the New World, what a task is thine,
To formulate the Modern – out of the peerless grandeur of the
    modern,
Out of thyself, comprising science, to recast poems, churches, art,
(Recast maybe discard them, end them – maybe their work
    is done who knows?)
By vision, hand, conception, on the background of the mighty past the
    dead,
To limn with absolute faith the mighty living present.

Walt Whitman

At this time Russell was collaborating with the Cambridge philospher Alfred North Whitehead (1861–1947) on the second volume of *Principia Mathematica*, and it was Whitehead's wife Evelyn who was ill in Cambridge. She had suffered a heart attack when the Russells were staying with them in February. Leopold von Ranke (1795–1886), the great German historian and one of the most influential figures in his profession, published his six-volume *History of England* in 1875.

1 July. Friday's Hill
A pleasant, comfortable house – with no special distinction, surrounded by tall spreading trees, a terraced lawn, with meadows sloping in curved lines towards the Fernhurst Valley behind wooded hills; beyond them again, the bare South Downs streaked with chalk quarries and roads. Behind the house, shaded lanes lead up some two miles to Blackdown with its wonderful view over the Weald. In another direction grass paths stray through tangled underwood to find their outlet on the heath of the Marley Common.

The Russells are the most attractive married couple I know. Young and virtuous, they combine in the pair personal charm, unique intelligence, the woman having the one, the man the other, in the superlative degree. Romantically attached to each other, they have divine interests; Alys concerns herself with social reform, Bertrand with the higher mathematics. The scheme of their joint life is deliberately conceived to attain ends they both believe in, and persistently yet modestly carried out. The routine of their daily existence is as carefully planned and exactly executed as our own. They breakfast together in their study at 9 o'clock (we breakfast at 8!), then Bertrand works at mathematics until 12.30, then three-quarters of an hour reading together (Ranke's *History of England* since we have been here), a quarter-hour stroll in the garden together. Lunch with us 1.30, chat in our sitting-room or out-of-doors over cigarettes and coffee: then Bertrand plays croquet with Logan [Pearsall] Smith (Alys's brother who lives near here) until tea at 4.30. After that mathematics until 6 o'clock: reading with Alys until 7.30, dine at 8 o'clock, chat and smoke with us until 9.30: another hour's reading aloud with Alys until 10.30. They sleep and dress in the same room, and they have no children.

As individuals they are remarkable. Alys comes of an American Quaker family. She is charming to look at – tall, graceful, with regular features, clear skin, bright blue eyes and soft curly nut-brown hair, always smiling, often laughing, warm-hearted and sympathetically intelligent. She has not the gift of intimacy except with her husband. Her manner is the same to everyone, at least as far as I have seen. She has no art of flirtation, if anything she prefers women to men, and I think really likes the womanly woman better than the professional. She has no moods or they are controlled. She seems always happy and grateful for happiness and yet perpetually thinking how to make others happier. Since we have been here she has spent days away nursing a friend at Cambridge, with no consciousness of virtue, responding to a call of friendship as readily as most women respond to a call of pleasure. If she has a defect it is a certain colourlessness of intellect and a certain lack of 'temperament'. But in a woman are these defects?

Bertrand is a slight, dark-haired man, with prominent forehead, bright eyes, strong features except for a retreating chin, nervous hands and alert quick movements. In manner and dress and outward bearing he is most carefully trimmed, conventionally correct and punctiliously polite, and in speech he has an almost affectedly clear enunciation of words and preciseness of expression. In morals he is a puritan; in personal habits almost an ascetic, except that he lives for efficiency and therefore expects to be kept in the best physical condition. But intellectually he is audacious – an iconoclast, detesting religions or social convention, suspecting sentiment, believing only in the 'order of thought' and the order of things, in logic and in science. He indulges in the wildest paradox and in the broadest jokes, the latter always too abstrusely intellectual in their form to be vulgarly coarse. He is a delightful talker, especially in general conversation, when the intervention of other minds prevents him from tearing his subject to pieces with fine chopping logic. He is always fruitful, especially in clearing up definitions and distinctions or in following out logical conclusions. He is fastidious with regard to friends and acquaintances. He dislikes bores and hates any kind of self-seeking selfishness or coarse-grainedness. He looks at the world from a pinnacle of detachment, dissects persons and demolishes causes. And yet he recognizes that as a citizen you must be a member of a party, therefore he has joined the Fabian Society! And more or less accepts Sidney as his 'representative' man. But the kernel of his life is research into the processes of reasoning. Of this new and highly abstract form of logic, more abstract than mathematics, I have no vision. All that one can say is that the effect on his own mind of these processes of pure reasoning is to make him singularly helpful in clearing up more concrete issues, even when he starts with no specialized knowledge of facts. To sum up, he is an expert in the art of reasoning, quite independently of the subject-matter.

A vigorous intelligence, at once subtle and honest, with the best kind of pride, the determination not to swerve from his own standards of right and wrong, truth or falsehood, are perhaps his finest characteristics. What he lacks is sympathy and tolerance for other people's emotions, and, if you regard it as a virtue, Christian humility. The outline of both his intellect and his feelings are sharp, hard and permanent. He is a good hater.

I observe in Bertrand a curious parallel between his intellectual and his moral nature. He is intolerant of blemishes and faults in himself and others, he dreams of Perfection in man. He almost loathes lapses from men's own standards. So in his thought he is almost violently impatient of bad reasoning. A right conclusion come to by bad arguments is offensive to him. It is the *perfection of the reasoning* that he seeks after, not truth of the conclusions. Now it seems to me that there is the same sort of connection between an intellectual concentration on applied science, and a tolerant, if not lax judgement of men. Just as I am always striving to adjust my order of thought to the order of things – exactly as I am always looking to results as the test of right reasoning (power of prevision, for instance, by the result of shockingly bad reasoning?) so I am perpetually excusing myself and others for any lapses in morality. I analyse and describe my own and other's faults. But these faults seldom offend me in themselves, but only because they result in what is unpleasant and ugly. I have no 'sense of sin' and no desire to see it punished. Bertrand, on the other hand, is almost cruel in his desire to see cruelty revenged.

So much for our hosts. Besides these two, Logan Smith, a refined and gentle-natured bachelor, with a pretty talent for turning out sentences and a taste for collecting bric-à-brac, is a daily visitor and chats with us over afternoon tea. He, like his sister, is tall, delicately featured, always smiling. But behind this smile there is a deep-seated melancholy, due to a long record of self-conscious failure to become an artist of words. The world has proved too complex for him to grasp: he is perpetually breaking off before he has mastered even the smallest portion of it. He was meant, like Alys, to be a complementary being: as a man he cannot find a career or even a wife to suit him.

J.W. Sauer (d. 1913) was a South African lawyer and politician who had served in the Cape Colony government under Rhodes. John Xavier Merriman (1841–1926) was a South African politician who was a member of the committee set up to enquire into the Jameson Raid and had written the report which censured Rhodes but cleared Chamberlain. These two men were on a mission to England to try to secure a settlement in South Africa but they failed to influence Chamberlain. David Lloyd George (1863–1945), brilliant Radical leader and foremost opponent of the Boer War, was to become the president of the Board of Trade and then the controversial Chancellor of the Exchequer in the post-1906 Liberal government and Prime Minister in 1916. Alfred Milner had returned to England on leave on 24 May.

The Boer War had reached a stage of guerrilla war in which the British army was trying to complete its victories in the field by burning farms and driving the civilian population into concentration camps. At a dinner of the National Reform Union on 14 June Campbell-Bannerman condemned this policy as 'the methods of barbarism'. Many of his supporters thought he had gone too far and in a House of Commons vote some fifty Liberals showed their disapproval by abstaining in a vote against the government.

Asquith led the attack on the Liberal leader and the Liberal Imperialists arranged a dinner in honour of Asquith on 19 July. Meanwhile Rosebery confused his colleagues by writing a letter to *The Times* saying he did not wish to return to party politics; he refused an invitation to preside at the Asquith dinner and declined an invitation to speak at the annual meeting of the City Liberal Club on the same day, accompanying his refusal with a statement attacking Campbell-Bannerman. He then turned up unexpectedly at the City Liberal luncheon and made a provocative speech which stole Asquith's thunder. 'I must plough my furrow alone,' he said. 'That is my fate, agreeable or the reverse.' There were so many political dinners and counter-dinners that it was said there was 'war to the knife and fork' among the Liberals.

Shaw was urging Sidney to support Rosebery as the politician most susceptible to permeation, and as the potential leader of a new political group which might lead to a government of national efficiency. Sidney drafted a forceful article, polished with Shaw's characteristic brilliance in polemic, which was published as 'Lord Rosebery's Escape from Houndsditch' in the September issue of the *Nineteenth Century*. The leaders of the Liberal Party, Sidney wrote, were simply a set of political tailors (Houndsditch being the centre of that trade) who were 'piecing together the Gladstonian rags and remnants' to make 'patched-up suits'. Lord Rosebery was the only person who had 'turned his back on Houndsditch and called for a completely new outfit'. Sidney then set out the Fabian repertoire of social reforms which he thought would regenerate English society and help 'the rearing of an imperial race'.

9 July. Grosvenor Road

Haldane spent yesterday at Friday's Hill, brought us news of the Liberal split, and enlisted Sidney on Asquith's side.

We had been watching with half indifference, half annoyance, the retreat of the Liberal Party within the old lines of 'Gladstonianism', under the leadership of Campbell-Bannerman nominally but of the pro-Boers actually. The whole of the spring, the vacuum left by lack of any clear thinking among those who can think has been filled with pro-Boer sentiment of an extravagant kind and the old sort of individualist radicalism. Morley and Harcourt, supported by the *Daily News*, were showing signs of returning to political life: Campbell-Bannerman, a weak and vain man who all along has been in his heart pro-Boer, had been entertaining Sauer and Merriman. The Liberal Federation meeting at Bradford had been strongly pro-Boer in sentiment, though passing lukewarm resolutions of the official type. Meanwhile, the Imperialist section – Haldane, Asquith, Grey – had been working at the Bar, enjoying themselves in London Society and letting things slide. Suddenly, they woke up to find the Liberal Party in the House of Commons, under the leadership of Lloyd George, declaring itself definitely against the war, accusing Milner and the army of gross inhumanity and asserting the right of the Boers to some kind of independence. Campbell-Bannerman had been captured.

Under the influence of his old friend Lord Milner (now in London) Asquith came down heavily, declared that the war was inevitable, that there had been no wilful cruelty and that independence, in any sense the Boers would understand it, was impossible. He followed up his speech by voting against Campbell-Bannerman and the Irish and Welsh contingent and led out of the House some thirty M.P. Liberals (the bulk of the English Liberals seem to have abstained either by accident or with intent). Then to emphasize this protest the more enthusiastic M.P. Liberals insisted on giving a dinner to Asquith – to fête him for his defiance of C.B. Hence the uproar: the uncomfortable spectacle of Asquith, Grey, Haldane, supported by the Tory press, in flat rebellion against C.B., the chosen leader of the Liberal Party, supported by Morley, Harcourt and the whole force of pro-Boers.

'We are fighting for our lives,' said Haldane to me: 'both Asquith and I would attach much importance to Sidney being present at the dinner: we do not like to press it, because the whole movement may be a failure.' A dilemma: Sidney is pro-Boer in sentiment; he agrees with Asquith and Haldane by reason, but he has not thought out the question, has paid little or no attention to it. It suits him infinitely better to keep out of the whole affair: he has already made his position among the Radicals 'suspect' owing to his attitude with regard to School Boards. Moreover, in many details, such as the retention of Lord Milner as administrator, he is not convinced and he would be prepared to risk complete colonial self-government in the Orange Free State and the Transvaal. On the other hand, Haldane has always trusted him in matters he cared about, has been the most loyal friend in all his educational projects. 'I attach little importance to the dinner,' Sidney said to me when I told him of Haldane's desires, 'and no importance to my being there. If Haldane wants me to go I certainly will. I would rather, of course, have kept out of the whole affair but one must be ready occasionally to step forward for one's friends if one has no conviction to the contrary. As between the two sections of Liberals, my sympathies are with them. I think very little will come of either party, but Haldane and Asquith are at least not hostile to our views: the others are. I will go. But you need not imagine it of any importance, one way or the other.'

And now that he has agreed to go I am worrying about it. First and foremost I know he loathes the war, thinks that the whole episode of the Rand and the Joseph Chamberlain negotiations a disgrace to this country (though he attributes the inevitability of the war to the granting of the Charter to the South Africa Company and the discovery of gold on the Rand); he distrusts Milner; above all he feels uncertain as to his own opinions, having carefully avoided reading anything on the subject. 'It is not my show,' he has often said when I have suggested he should read blue-books. From a more selfish point of view it suits him better not to be on either side so as to get what he can from both for his projects. Then I don't believe in the genuineness of the Liberal M.P.s on Home questions: they live in the wrong atmosphere and are incurably lazy. They are desperately in awe of the 'City', consider the opinion of *The Times* and have their eye on the goodwill of manufacturers, even on that of the brewers. Intellectually they are more with us than the more radical section but they have no pluck and no faith. All these considerations rushed through my mind as I half deprecated Sidney accepting, but my instinctive wish was that he should accept in order to please Haldane who has been so good to us. But no doubt, as Sidney says, his going or not going is of no importance.

The 'young American' was Sally Fairchild, from a Boston family who had entertained the Webbs on their American visit.

26 July. [41 Grosvenor Road]
On the night Rosebery issued his famous letter to the City Liberal Club and to the press Sidney was pacing the terrace of the House of Commons with Haldane and Grey, explaining to them the attitude they ought to adopt on Home affairs, having been called in to consult with them. At the time when the journalists in the Lobby were humming with excitement about the letter, Rosebery's devoted lieutenants were absolutely unaware of its existence! 'We are not in communication with Rosebery,' Haldane had said sadly to Sidney. Again on the Friday afternoon, just before the Asquith dinner, I met Haldane in the House (whither I had gone to escort a young American lady) looking terribly grave, almost agitated. 'He has made a great speech to the City Liberal Club, has repudiated the Liberal Party, has announced his intention of "ploughing his own furrow" – all within a few hours of Asquith's speech tonight without a word of consultation. He is a Puck in politics,' added Haldane with almost a note of exasperation.

The dinner, however, went off all right. It was a scratch assembly and Sidney was among the most distinguished of the guests. Margaret Hobhouse and I viewed it from the gallery. Asquith's speech was manly and sensible, finely phrased and spoken with considerable fervour. But read in cold blood the next morning it suffered in comparison with Rosebery's artistically sensational utterances. We did not take the tragic view of Rosebery's intervention taken by the little set of his immediate followers. If Lord Rosebery really means business, really intends to come forward with a strong policy, then he has done his lieutenants a good service by stepping boldly out of the ranks of an obsolete Liberalism. Asquith, Grey and Haldane can only proclaim their freedom within the Liberal Party; they cannot denounce the other sections of it for the simple reason that it is not business for them to step away from the Front Bench. To the Front Bench they must stick so long as they can stick also to their own principles. But Rosebery is bound by no ties and can do the necessary work of the iconoclast of the Gladstonian ideals. Rosebery's business is to destroy Gladstonianism. Whether or not he is to become a real leader depends on whether he has anything to put in the place of a defunct Liberalism. Mere Imperialism will not do: that the other side have. Now supposing he fails, as I think he will fail, to be constructive, then he leaves the field open to Asquith, Grey and Haldane with a good deal of the rubbish cleared away.

Whether this sort of reasoning glimmered into Haldane's brain I know not. But when he came in on Monday evening he was in high spirits. Asquith and he had made it up with Rosebery (they are forgiving mortals!). It was agreed, he said, that Rosebery and Asquith were to plough parallel furrows. Meanwhile GBS writes urging us to plunge in with Rosebery as the best chance of moulding Home 'policy'. We have succumbed to his flattery and now Sidney, with occasional suggestions from me, is engaged on an article entitled 'Lord Rosebery's Escape from Houndsditch'.

A.C.F. Rabagliati (b. 1843) believed in diet and muscular training as the basis of good health. A notable food reformer, he wrote *Air, Food and Exercise* in 1897.

1 October. Grosvenor Road

A most unsatisfactory vacation. Four weeks spent high up in a Yorkshire dale with mountain pasture and moorland stretching upwards some 1500 feet above us, and one bad road up and down the vale. For a long-distance walker [Sunniside?] would be a delightful spot, but for Sidney and I who depend on bicycles and can only walk some six or seven miles, it was monotonous and tiring. We never seemed to get out of sight of the village. Then our quarters at the inn were noisy – children, clogged, playing on stone sets, herds of cows coming home to be milked and the whole village turning out to talk, laugh and smoke in the summer evenings. Our hostess was always in a slatternly condition, and her kitchen combined the cooking of food with a village bar. There was a miserable little boy about the place – a pauper nephew who lounged through his days being persistently scolded and sworn at without being put to work. Perhaps it was because I was not well that 'Tommy' got on my nerves – the thought of this little, unhappy wretch, underfed, untrained, picking up vices and virtues, kept on there because it was less expensive than apprenticing him to a trade, became intolerable. And my personal sensations throughout the time were the reverse of pleasant: a constant feeling of fatigue and nausea, a total incapacity to concentrate my thoughts or control my feelings. Sometimes I felt that I despaired of myself, that I had drifted into a morass of ill health, idleness and unwholesomeness of thought. For a whole week I gave up the struggle to work and lay out on the heather praying for strength of mind and rightness of feeling. Then in a half-hearted way I rallied to Sidney's side and actually wrote the summing up of the chapter on the Justices [of the Peace] and rearranged the substance of it. But my work had lost its spring. My mind was a prey to idle chatterings of personal vanity, to childish castles in the air which left me with mental indigestion of an acute kind.

Then we moved to Saltburn. Here my mental health improved, but physically I remained ill-at-ease and constantly fatigued. But the sight of the sea, watching of the waves breaking on the sand, stretches of sky and water, all helped to soothe my nerves and strengthen my will. . . Then the morbidness took another turn. I was overtaken with a presentiment of disease and death: I had some mortal complaint, the heart, the kidneys, were probably diseased. I cried myself to sleep and woke up in the morning bemoaning poor Sidney's future loneliness, romanced copiously. . . . and generally played the sentimental fool. But I had settled in the back of my mind that when I got home I would at once go to a good London doctor and be thoroughly overhauled.

But I was to get my advice without a professional fee. We stopped on our way south at the Byles at Bradford. There at dinner we met a certain Dr Rabagliati, author of various books on the subject of diet. By chance the conversation drifted on to public health. Suddenly the little man fired up and gave us a discourse on the one cause of diseases –

216

eating too much and at too frequent intervals. He was an enthusiast and described in convincing detail how cancer, influenza, pneumonia and almost all modern diseases arose from the one incontrovertible tendency to eat more than was necessary! Even the working class and the slum-dwellers were going to perdition by overfeeding! Bad air, drink, dissipation were as nothing to this terrible and accursed habit of the human animal. But apart from rhetoric he gave so many instances of recovery from chronic complaints by systematic abstemiousness that I was persuaded. 'How much ought a woman to eat who is over forty years of age, weighs 8 stone 11 lbs, height 5ft 6ins, and who is a brainworker?' 'Three-quarters of a pound or at most one pound in the twenty-four hours: but taken twice a day, but at most three times a day. If she is over forty, best food containing starch once a day only.' 'Thanks for the prescription,' I laughingly replied. 'I have had bad health for some months, and I will give the treatment a trial. No wonder the medical men hate you: for if the experiment succeeds with me, you will have done a London doctor out of at least two guineas, probably four.'

Now I have begun the experiment which I propose to note carefully. I limit myself to one pound of food daily, four ounces at 8 o'clock breakfast, six at 1.30 lunch, and six at 7.30 dinner. I have one small cup of tea without milk or sugar at 7 o'clock in the morning, another at 4.30 in the afternoon and a cup of black coffee after dinner. I take very little water with my meals, having a breakfast cup of hot water at noon and another at night. I take no starchy food after breakfast, taking out my quantity in meat, green vegetables and fruit, sometimes a little cheese and butter.

The first days I have felt queer though on the whole better. All flatulence and indigestion has disappeared, my brain seems stronger, I feel much more inclined to read, but my heart is somewhat uncomfortable and I have uneasy feelings in my stomach! Moreover I slept badly for the first two nights. The most troublesome complaint from which I suffer – acute eczema of the ears and all over the body is neither better nor worse. But this, the fourth day, is still early to see results of the treatment. Meanwhile my spirits have risen with the greater control which I seem to have over my thought and feelings and the prospect of better working health. If only I can have a steadfast mind in a healthy body my life will approach the ideal. Abstinence and prayer may prove to be the narrow way to salvation in this world – at least for such as me.

Sidney's article in the *Nineteenth Century* has been a brilliant success. No doubt there are some who found the self-assertiveness and contempt of others somewhat intolerable, but everyone has read it and found it new and full of substance (GBS corrected the proof and inserted some of the brilliance). The Asquith, Haldane, Grey lot are delighted with it: Rosebery evidently pleased. The newspapers have taken it seriously and it has improved his standing I think and made people feel that he is to be reckoned with. Now I am urging him to publish the positive side in a Fabian tract and I intend to give the substance of it in a lecture at Oxford.

Meanwhile we have no illusions about the Liberal Imperialists. We think that neither Rosebery nor Asquith mean to declare themselves in favour of our measure of collectivism. But they hold no views that are inconsistent with it, have nothing to offer but a refusal to take up the distinctive side of the old Liberalism. The time will come when, if they are to be a political force, they will have to 'fill up' the political worker with some positive convictions. Then we think for the needful minimum of nourishment they will fall back on us and not on the other section.

But national affairs are not invigorating at present. The wretched war drags on, the newspapers nag and scold and the government seems helpless and the opposition are more and more divided. The pro-Boers are very naturally rubbing their hands and saying 'I told you so.' Personally if there is no danger of [foreign] intervention, I do not think the South African situation so intolerable as other persons do, and the longer and more determined the resistance the more complete and thoroughgoing will be the collapse of the Boer nationality. And with a race with so much patriotism, stubbornness and superstition, one wonders whether any more easy settling down would be permanent.

13 October. [41 Grosvenor Road]
It is over a fortnight since I began the treatment. I weighed myself Monday 6th at Charing Cross: 8 stone 10½ lbs; today I weigh 8 stone 10¼ lbs, practically no change. All flatulence and indigestion has disappeared, and my 'monthly period' was passed over with great comfort. On the other hand the eczema is no better: water clear, bowels absolutely regular. I do not sleep well. Somewhat depressed too by feeling muddle-headed and weary: work still wretched in quality and quantity. But perhaps a thirty-mile ride on Saturday was

rather a strain to put on my powers. I was less tired after it than I was three weeks ago after twenty miles. On the whole I am better, but not yet 'fit'.

Started Miss Harrison [research assistant] on Leeds newspapers, discovering for us the internal history of the Leeds Council from 1855 onward. An excellent clear-headed worker. Every Monday she comes to tea and we discuss her notes.

Sidney and Hewins in first-rate spirits about the School: building nearly complete and paid for, equipment provided from the hung-up grant of the Technical Education Board, a small but certain income from the same source and plenty of students. Hewins, who now sees before him a fine position and £600 secured, is somewhat elated and would, I think, tend to have a swelled head if it were not for the amount of skill and self-subordination required to engineer the business over the shoals of the University organization. Again one realizes how, in a large and complicated society like the London education world, the whole power of moulding events falls into the hands of the little clique who happen to be in the centre of things. Ten years ago Sidney could no more have influenced the teaching of economics and political science in London than he could have directed the policy of the Cabinet. But now no one can resist him: he wields the L.C.C. power of making grants, he is head of the one live institution [as chairman of the Administrative Committee of the L.S.E.], he is, on his own subjects, supreme on the University Senate (because he is thought to have the L.C.C. behind him) and he knows every rope and has quick and immediate access to every person of influence. Somehow I doubt whether such a state of things is quite wholesome. Of course one believes that in this case the hidden hand is beneficent and efficient! But the converse – the feeling of absolute helplessness against the doings of less efficient cliques! is not so pleasant. One wonders whether it would be possible to conduct a country's government with efficiency and yet with 'free access' and 'no favour' to all concerned.

21 October. [41 Grosvenor Road]
Weighing machine at Charing Cross station (which I patronize every Monday morning) registers 8.8 – a drop which we will hope is due to a readjustment of the machine. That possible loss of weight and the continued presence of eczema are the only unsatisfactory symptoms. Otherwise I feel extraordinarily better. My brain is now working

well and I feel free from discomfort. And I have complete control over my thoughts and feelings, a delightful change from the last nine months' mental indigestion.

Treatment slightly altered: hot water instead of tea at 7 o'clock, no hot water in the evening. (Note: changed back again as I find it indigestible.) Breakfast of toast and butter, without egg. And the last two days an arsenical mixture to help to clear away the eczema.

It is as difficult to clear one's mind of all 'waste' matters as to clear one's blood! And the simple plan of starvation does not answer. Quite the contrary; in no place does nature so abhor a vacuum as in the realm of thought and feeling. Since I have taken to my 'diet' I can read much more and so fill up my spare time. . . .

1 November. [41 Grosvenor Road]
I am prospering though somewhat erratically. Mercury ointment effectually killed the eczema, leaving me with oh! such a sore mouth. This is yielding to treatment but I am an emaciated white creature, unfit for play or work. So off I go to Freshwater with the Playnes to see whether little food and perfect air will re-establish me. But I mean to persevere and see the experiment out, short of ceasing to exist. The hypothesis is too interesting to be left untested: it promises to solve so many problems.

Mr Asquith and Haldane dined here alone on Monday, the latter proposing to bring the former for a quiet chat. The talk did not come to much. They are, I think, somewhat depressed. Rosebery had 'carted them' so Haldane said, and was going to take his own line quite aloof from anything they might think or write. Asquith was preparing set speeches on social questions. But Haldane was still keen on winning the 'centre', a term which he always uses as synonymous with the 'non-political voter' in whose ultimate power we believe. In reality these two sections (the centre and the non-political voter) are entirely different and to my mind very unequal in importance. What Haldane sees is the moderate politician, the capitalist or professional man who desires little social change and the Empire maintained. But the class we wish them to appeal to is the great lower-middle class and working class, who want change, but don't know in what direction. Any party that knew its own mind as well as the facts and had will to apply the one to the other, would succeed in the long run in getting hold of the class from its policy of reform.

Rosebery is really on the same line as Haldane though playing a different tune. Altogether the position seems somewhat hopeless. Asquith impressed me with his manliness and unselfconsciousness, also with his shrewd open-mindedness, but he is a coarse-grained instrument and will never [stir?] the imagination of any large section of men.

Beatrice was away for most of November, first in the Isle of Wight and then at Longfords. Bill Playne was serving with the Gloucestershire Regiment in South Africa. Beatrice quotes Byron's journal for 16 January 1814: 'I have simplified my politics into an utter detestation of all existing governments. . . . The fact is, riches are power, and poverty is slavery all over the earth, and one sort of establishment is no better, nor worse, for a *people* than another.'

10 November. [Freshwater]
Ten days at Freshwater. The eczema has practically disappeared, mouth is now cured. But I am overcome with apathy, mental and physical and the urine is muddy which means there are still waste products, I suppose. Clearly I shall not be able to do any work for some time. No trouble with thoughts now: I have none. My mind is a blank!

Interesting passage from Lord Byron's *Journal* showing his appreciation of the non-relevance of political constitution to the problem of rich and poor. . . . Byron was the shrewdest of critics of contemporary social organization. He had neither the faith, the patience nor, I think, the capacity to *construct*. Neither had he any realization of Science. Action was what he admired and was his antithesis to sentiment and literary thought.

14 November. [41 Grosvenor Road]
Dashed to find my weight had gone down in the fortnight three pounds in spite of absolute rest at Freshwater. Began to eat a trifle more but produced attacks of flatulence. . . . Cure is evidently going to be a somewhat long business and will need patience and persistence. But life in London is not favourable: had visitors all Wednesday afternoon, Passmore Edwards and pro-Boer party to dine in evening. Friday lectured to Anglican young ladies, Saturday gathering of students here in the evening with all the consequent arrangements. Tomorrow go to Longfords for a week or ten days rest. If I am not stronger when I return I shall begin to despair of my cure by this treatment. It is disappointing to find my digestion impaired by abstinence.

221

Lost 2 lbs during the six days in London. Now weigh 8 stone ¼ lb.

28 November. [Longfords]
Twelve days at Longfords, keeping to diet and living ideally restful and healthy life. Result: gain of ½lb in weight, eczema entirely disappeared, no aches or pains. Digestion, bowels and kidneys in good order, monthly period somewhat delayed (usually it is the other way with me), weak in body and mind, and suffering from lack of sleep. The amount of sleep I get varies from three to six hours in the twenty-four hours.

My visit to the Playnes at Longfords a distinct success. The comfort of Longfords, Mary's cheery good sense, the very impossibility of settling to anything for more than half an hour without interruption, exactly suited my state of body and mind. And it was interesting to get a vision of the Playnes at home now that they have both become distinctly elderly. One change is remarkable: there is no bad temper in the house. When I think of Arthur's detestable temper in early life and his very infirm one in middle life, this change excites wonderment. Now he is a light-hearted hale elderly man, hunting and shooting two or three times a week, spending two days on 'county business' and the remainder of his time poking about his estate. He always seems in good spirits and enjoying himself, eats and drinks with scrupulous moderateness and does not worry himself even when a loss of £3,000 is reported from the mill. Certainly he is a 'functionless' being for I do not think that the 'country business' comes to much more than a journey to Gloucester and a gossip with fellow magistrates at the County Hall or the lunatic asylum. He resolutely refuses to concern himself about the mill, though it is just at the bottom of his garden, and is managed by two young men eager for help and advice.

Mary, on the other hand, is always full of plans and though she works only casually yet she achieves a good deal owing to her excellent abilities. Helping her is a pleasant and capable little woman, half-secretary, half-companion, who assumes the position of a daughter in the house.

The two preoccupations of the Playnes are the war and their unfortunate relation with their daughter-in-law. Ever since I have known the Playnes there has always been someone nearly connected with their home and life with whom they are on the worst of terms, first his old father, then our mother, then the Pollocks, and now

Mannie, their daughter-in-law. They got wrong with me when I lived at Box, though owing to my resolute refusal to be a party to the quarrel it never came to open estrangement. This time, I believe, they are more sinned against than sinning, but they have aggravated it by their inveterate habit of talking themselves into an exaggerated frame of mind. The war is the other occasion for thought, talk and feeling and here they can only discuss with persons who hold more or less their opinions. Hence the *rapprochement* between us and them — all the more so as Mary's special 'chums' in the family happen to be pro-Boer. With Kate and Lallie she feels that she must abstain from intercourse and even with the milder Georgie Meinertzhagen she is under constraint. Perhaps if one's only child were continuously fighting one would feel equal bitterness.

P.W.L. Ashley (1876–1945), lecturer in history at L.S.E. until 1906, became a civil servant in the Board of Trade. In the course of the autumn Rosebery made a characteristically equivocal bid for leadership. In a speech at Chesterfield, Derbyshire on 16 December – a much anticipated occasion for which special trains were run from London – he came out for a negotiated peace in South Africa and repudiated the traditional Liberal domestic policies, particularly Home Rule for Ireland: he called, he said, for 'a clean slate', and a new policy based on 'efficiency'.

7 December. [41 Grosvenor Road]
Slightly modified my diet: take a good 6 oz at supper in addition to 8 oz at lunch, total about 18 oz excluding fruit. Feel very much stronger in body and mind, weight remains stationary. Hope to get to work again about the beginning of the new year.

Haldane called in twice the last week to discuss affairs and ask us to recommend him an able young man to act as political 'devil' in priming up matters for speeches. We recommended Percy Ashley, whom he has taken on. Haldane distinctly 'down on the luck' of the Liberal Imperialists. 'We are in communication with Rosebery but he has not consulted us about his speech: we are all going down to the meeting.' It is clear that Rosebery whipped them to heel and has reversed the position of a year ago when he was, more or less, their appendage. He is now master of the 'Limps', but he is not yet master of the Liberal Party. The pro-Boers scored at the Derby Caucus meeting, so much so that it may now be taken that 'annexation' of the Boer republics is an open question with the Liberals. Sidney thinks that the events of next session, especially the government Education

Bill, will play into the hands of the pro-Boers unless there be a collapse of the Boers in the war.

Dr William Garnett (1850–1932) was a physicist and educationalist who became Secretary to the Technical Education Board in 1893. He had decisively undermined the claim of the London School Board to provide secondary and adult education when he encouraged two ratepayers to challenge its expenditure for these two purposes. On 20 December 1900, in a case loosely known as the 'Cockerton Judgement', Mr Justice Wills ruled that such payments were *ultra vires*, and he was upheld by the House of Lords in April 1901. Garnett's tactics (in which Sidney Webb may have played a covert part) made the need for a fresh start in secondary education more urgent.

Beatrice had revised parts of *Industrial Democracy* into a small book called *The Case for the Factory Acts*, which was published in 1901.

9 December. [41 Grosvenor Road]

There are now but a few days to the end of the year and a few pages to the end of this book, which will then be sealed up with the other diaries. . . .

This year has been the most unsatisfactory year of my life since I married. How far I must apportion the blame between a bad state of physical health and a rotten state of mind, I cannot tell. But for, egotism, self-conscious vanity, and for total incapacity for a really good day's work I have excelled all previous record. No one has been aware of this but myself. I have kept a brave face, have seemed to be fully occupied by other thoughts, and my relations to other persons have even been softened and improved by my own intense humiliation at the condition of my mind. I have become infinitely more charitable to Rosy Dobbs for instance (who, by the way, has recovered herself almost miraculously) on the score of character, far more appreciative of other people's small abilities. This is, indeed, the only asset against the deterioration of my own effort. And all this weakness and foolishness has not interfered with my tenderness for my own darling boy. It has intensified my feeling of his superiority to myself alike in moral and intellectual qualities. The bad result has been confined, in fact, to a much smaller and worse intellectual output and with possibly a weakening of the fibre of character and intelligence. And to what has this state of things been due? Doubtless the 'waste products' accumulated by wrong feeding have had largely to do with it, stimulating activity in some organs and clouding the brain. Until I took to the rigid diet, the sensual side of my nature seemed to be growing at the expense of the intellectual. . . . This year has found me far more emotional than I have ever been. I longed for music, was inclined to be religious, and allowed my mind to dwell on all sorts of sentimental relations. This was the subjective state. Acting on this state was a real or imaginary (I really don't know which) increased personal attractiveness, typified by the admiration – which I thought I had, or actually had – excited in the minds of some prominent personages. . . And owing to a very natural desire to hide away my vanity, I spoke to no one, not even to Sidney, about this ridiculous business. Fortunately besides a sense of conduct I have also a sense of humour and the wholesome fact of 'grizzled, wrinkled and over forty' was constantly intervening to check morbid growth.

But, thank the Lord, I am now recovering . . . three weeks at Margate and slightly increased food, well assimilated and the careful resumption of intellectual work, will, I believe, complete the *physical* cure. As to the mental ailments, all I can do is to grip on to work, to set my will hard on finishing the first volume of local government by the end of the year. And to do this I shall need all my thought and imagination. . . .

At present it looks as if our future life will still continue to be the present dual work of local administration and scientific investigation, but a change of circumstances might make it wise for him to step into the political arena. If so it would be well to add to his name the designation of 'great authority on local government' to the 'great authority on labour questions'.

And what about the little set we live in? The Bernard Shaws are still our true friends, Charlotte subscribing to the School, helping forward the Fabian Society, always sweet and helpful to Sidney in his various enterprises. GBS stimulating and extraordinarily good-natured in spending days in correcting the more topical of our productions. Hence the lucidity which characterizes the opening chapter of *The Case for the Factory Acts* and the brilliance of Sidney's article in the *Nineteenth Century* are both due to the careful touching-up of our literary 'ghost'.

The sort of partnership that exists between GBS and ourselves, based on a common faith and real good fellowship, is of the utmost advantage to both, we supplying him with some ideas and he, on crucial occasions, enormously improving our form.

With our old friend Graham Wallas relations are somewhat strained through the antagonism between School Board and Technical Education Board and also by the growing distrust of democracy which

Graham is developing combined with a distrust of the expedients which Sidney is ready to invent and adopt for making the democratic form more practicable and efficient.

With Hewins, Garnett and the leaders of the Progressive Party on the L.C.C. Sidney remains on admirable terms. His position in the University and on the L.C.C. has been improved by the work of the last year. He is also acquiring a non-partisan influence in education being consulted by men of all parties.

This year marks our definite though loose adherence to the Liberal Imperialist group of politicians. If Sidney has a political future it will be as a colleague of these men.

VOLUME 22

H.G. Wells (1866–1946) had already made his reputation as a writer of scientific romances, beginning with *The Time Machine* in 1895. By the turn of the century he was beginning to write naturalistic novels and utopian predictions. In November 1901 he published *Anticipations,* which had an immediate success and much impressed the Webbs by its application of scientific ideas to social development. They welcomed him as an ally with great propagandist skills, and he was chosen to be one of the Twelve Wise Men, all of them prominent in public life, who in September 1902 were invited by the Webbs to form a dining club called The Co-Efficients: it was to discuss 'the aims, policy and methods of imperial efficiency at home and abroad'. He was also the only newcomer to the Fabian Society who rose to equality with the Webbs and Shaw – a position of considerable influence he was soon to squander in a series of factional and personal quarrels.

[?] *December*. [41 Grosvenor Road]
Wells's *Anticipations.* The most remarkable book of the year: a powerful imagination furnished with the data and methods of physical science working on social problems. The weak part of Wells's outfit is his lack of any detailed knowledge of social organizations, and this, I think, vitiates his capacity for foreseeing the future machinery of government and the relation of the classes. But his work is full of luminous hypotheses and worth careful study by those who are trying to look forward. Clever phrases abound, and by-the-way proposals on all sorts of questions – from the future direction of religious thought to the exact curve of the skirting round the wall of middle-class abodes.

PART IV

A Slump in Webbs

January 1902 – October 1905

Introduction to Part IV

'ONE WONDERS WHETHER all this manipulating activity is worth while,' Beatrice wrote in July 1902, 'whether one would not do just as much by cutting the whole business of human intercourse and devoting oneself to thinking and writing out one's thoughts.' For all her doubts, however, she felt her life of *salon* politics combined with research was increasingly 'happy and fruitful' as she became reconciled to the 'tiresome fact' that wire-pulling was necessary 'to get things done in what one considers the best way'. For the next four years she and Sidney were in their prime – physically healthy, seemingly tireless in pursuit of their ends, able to cope with all the stresses of living on the fringe of smart political society and to make the most of their regular retreats to write in the country; and the diary entries clearly reflect Beatrice's pleasure at ths varied and stimulating existence. They are, of course, mainly concerned with the Conservative Education Acts of 1902 and 1903, which were difficult to draft and even more troublesome to implement, and they show how well Beatrice complemented Sidney's tactical ingenuity.

The difficulties over these measures were due in part to the government's own divisions and uncertainties, in part to the religious issues that they raised, and in part to the reluctance of many local councillors to accept changes which appeared to favour the Anglican and Catholic churches. Lord Salisbury, who was in the last months of his premiership, wanted to strengthen the role of the churches, not least because he felt a political debt to the Anglicans for support in the 1901 election. But the Duke of Devonshire, the Minister responsible for education, was better known for his interest in sport than his knowledge of pedagogy, and in any case he was a Liberal Unionist who was unwilling to use public funds to support church schools. Chamberlain, still the most powerful figure in the Cabinet, shared the

Nonconformist objection to denominational teaching. And Sir George Kekewich, the senior civil servant concerned, favoured the school board system and thought it should be allowed to develop its own secondary and technical schools.

Reform was badly needed, both to extend the school systems and improve them – church schools had long been noted for the poor standard of their teachers and equipment, and many of the voluntary secondary schools left much to be desired; and there were, moreover, great variations in coverage and quality between one part of the country and another. Sidney Webb was so aware of the need for modernization that he was prepared to compromise with the bishops on points that his Nonconformist colleagues considered matters of principle, and he was equally prepared to risk his reputation in a long-drawn-out campaign to get these critics of the Bills to accept and work them.

In this muddled situation Robert Morant was instructed to prepare a Bill on which the divided Cabinet could agree; and while the able Morant consulted and drafted (with much help from Sidney), the Webbs were busy trying to rally support for the measure. The first version was not acceptable: there were sharp arguments within the government and vociferous opposition in Parliament and the country, but a modified proposal was passed on 20 December 1902. It abandoned the locally elected school boards and made the counties and county boroughs into comprehensive education authorities, permitted payments from their rate revenues to voluntary schools, and put the oversight of religious instructions into the hands of managers appointed to each school – it being understood that the 1870 Act's exclusion of any denominational teaching in public schools remained in force.

The Act was bitterly opposed by Nonconformists and secular educational reformers who saw it as a capitulation to clericalism and reaction. Some objectors refused to pay their local taxes because the government had 'put Rome on the rates', and in a few Nonconformist strongholds the councils declined to apply the changes for several years. But Sidney considered the Act the best measure that could be expected – better, indeed, than anything a Liberal government might have been able to cobble together under pressure from its powerful Nonconformist faction. What he wanted, above all and most urgently, was a modernized system of education which made the best use of all the available resources and offered the best available schooling to all children, irrespective of religion or class. The Act was no harbinger of an educational utopia, he knew: all the same, it was a beginning, and its main features remained unchanged for another forty years.

The resistance to the Act cast a shadow over its successor, which dealt with the particular and even more difficult situation in London. Here the religious dispute was compounded by the Conservative dislike of the L.C.C., controlled by its opponents in the guise of Progressives, and tainted by municipal socialist notions. For some years the government had blocked an attempt by the L.C.C. to take over the private water companies which served London: the Conservative solution was to set up an independent board with strong representation from London's borough councils (the local bodies subordinate to the L.C.C.), and many Conservatives favoured a similar *ad hoc* body to control public education in the capital – what Beatrice called the 'Water Board' model. Sidney was strongly opposed to such an authority. As chairman of the Technical Education Board he had shown what the L.C.C. could do for the education of Londoners, and he wanted to broaden not abolish that responsibility. He also thought the Conservatives were foolish as well as spiteful in slighting the L.C.C., pointing out that such an *ad hoc* body might actually give the Radical Nonconformists more power over the schools than they could exert through an Education Committee which would have to reflect the balance of parties and interests in the Council as a whole. He was thus in a most tricky situation. On the one hand he had to persuade the Conservative government to make the L.C.C. the education authority for London. On the other hand, harassed by London School Board partisans and Nonconformist critics in his own party, he had to induce the Progressive majority to accept the unpopular Act and work it.

It was a tribute to Sidney's clever pertinacity that by the early months of 1903 he had found a compromise formula. He had still to ensure that his own party did not repudiate it, and in their anxiety the Webbs carried intrigue to the point of disloyalty. With L.C.C. elections due in March 1904, they did their best to lop off 'the rotten part of the Progressive Party' and to bring in Moderates who could be counted on to vote the right way. The intrigue failed, for the Progressives did well at the election; and it proved to have been superfluous, for they accepted and worked the Act. But deviousness for good causes had damaged the reputation of the Webbs and limited

Sidney's influence: he was never to recover the eminent position he had occupied before they left for America and the Antipodes, and the defeat of the Conservatives in 1906 finally cut off the lines to Westminster and Whitehall on which he had depended in this struggle for educational reform. In that struggle, moreover, the Webbs had acquired a taste and a skill for intrigue which became a bad habit, to which Beatrice was especially prone; it was to bring short-run results when she sat on the Royal Commission on the Poor Law, but it was also to bring the long-run disadvantages of suspect motives, unpopularity and political isolation.

∽ 1902 ∾

30 January. [41 Grosvenor Road.]
I have been so hard at work on the book that I have had no energy left over for diary-writing.

We spent Christmas with Alfred [Cripps] and the Courtneys. Our host was in splendid form: well in health and full of public affairs. He had been in close communication with Balfour and Chamberlain trying to arrange some sort of compromise between them with regard to the Education Bill. Joseph Chamberlain was against state aid, fearing the recrudescence of the 'Church Rate' crusade. Balfour felt the force of the Church's cry 'now or never'. He and Sidney discussed the question: as usual the 'little Jewel of an Advocate' had not thought out the position and, though he and Sidney agreed on main points, Cripps was inclined to leave all knotty points to be settled by the House, a counsel of despair when the knots are so complicated. Dear old Leonard kept out of all this confidential talk, he and Kate spending their time with the young people, while Alfred, Sidney and I sat over the library fire. I fancy that Alfred feels his feet again in politics, and sees office near at hand should the opportunity for a new man arise. We laughingly decided that, if the three brothers-in-law were in leading positions in the House, it would end in Sidney and Alfred arranging compromises between the two Front Benches with Leonard always in opposition! The Courtneys were as self-righteously pro-Boer as ever, but more subdued. 'We are passing through some smoke,' (effect of Lord Rosebery's speech) said Leonard, 'but it will clear off.'

Then we went to Margate into lodgings taking the devoted Emily [the maid] with us, which made the lodgings quite homely. We worked well together and almost ended the difficult chapter on 'Municipal Corporations'. The number of times Sidney and I have laboured through these four volumes of Royal Commission reports of 1835 is tiresome even to think about, arranging and re-arranging the evidence and arranging our facts in endless ways so as to find coincidences and perhaps causes. . . .

The regime of restricted diet is beginning to tell most satisfactorily on my health. I have ceased to lose weight and am working better than I have done for many months. The quality of effort remains good and it looks like a satisfactory year. I am devoting my whole energies, poor at the best, to getting on with the work, trying to put in a good four hours, three in the morning with Sidney, and one or two in the afternoon alone. But I cannot manage this every day. The best effect is, however, on the *content* of my thought: the chatterings of personal vanity have ceased to trouble me. I have become cool and sensible and absorbed in getting the best out of myself. Physically the cure is not complete. I am far too thin (only 8 stone), the eczema lingers on, and every now and again it flares up in the ears or on the back.

The regime now is breakfast, 2 oz of toast, egg, butter, cup of cocoa (mostly milk); dinner, meat 3 oz, green vegetables and fruit; supper, glass of hot milk and 5 or 6 oz of milk pudding or two poached eggs and 2 oz of toast. Beyond the eczema I have no ailments except occasional flatulence and a certain lack of robustness.

15 February. [41 Grosvenor Road]
Met Clara Ryland at Margate and asked her and her little girl to stay here. A strange explanation by which I believe I 'builded better than I knew' for the happiness of others. It was late in the evening (Sidney was out lecturing) and Clara and I had grown somewhat sentimental, sitting close to each other, she with her arm round my waist, talking over her great sorrow and my happiness. 'You deserve your happiness, Beatrice. I always believed that with your strength and devotedness you would end by being happy and it is a joy to me to feel that my thought has come true.'

'*Luck*, my dear Clara,' I retorted, '*extraordinary luck*! If I had married when I was young I might have been swept by passion into a life that would not have suited me.' Clara started and coloured and I saw at once that I had seemed to her to refer to my relations with her brother. 'You would have suited another life perfectly,' she replied warmly. 'No, I shouldn't,' I urged with growing emphasis, 'or rather, the life would not have suited me. I was made for a working comradeship with a man who was no more than my equal in age, capacity and position; only work and work *on equal terms* would have called out my strongest qualities. I needed to be leader in some respects and servant in others to be perfectly happy in marriage: for an ornamental position I am not suited. To put it bluntly, I am not sufficient of a lady. I should have hardened and coarsened in a Society life and as the wife of some great personage,' I added defiantly.

Clara rose from her seat with an expression of half offence and half amusement. 'I don't agree with you at all,' she said calmly after a moment's silence. 'However, it is sufficient for me that you are happy. And now I must go to bed and leave you to wait up for Mr Webb.'

I have done that little woman in Prince's Gardens [Chamberlain's London home] a good turn and gratified my frankness and my pride—all in a few words.

Harold John Tennant (1865–1935), a Liberal M.P., was Asquith's private secretary and brother-in-law; he was married to Mary Abraham, the first woman factory inspector. J.R. MacDonald continued his feud with Webb (supposedly inspired by the denial of a teaching post at L.S.E.) to the point of covert complaints that the School was merely propagandist—charges Sidney felt obliged to answer in a long and convincing letter to the Vice-Chancellor of London University on 3 January 1903. In July 1902, in a letter to Beatrice, he described the sources of the School's income in the past seven years—a total of £44,000, of which a quarter had come from the T.E.B., £11,000 from Passmore Edwards, £5,000 from Rothschild, sums of £3,500 from Charlotte Shaw and the Hutchinson bequest, and the remainder in smaller gifts from Fabians and other supporters. 'I am putting these figures about,' he told Beatrice, as he knew 'that J.R.M. will attack the finances on Monday week.'

When Wells was still a youth his parents separated, his mother Sarah going to work as a housekeeper at Uppark, a mansion near Chichester where she had been a lady's maid and her husband-to-be had been a gardener. After their marriage they ran an unsuccessful china shop at Bromley, Kent, and Joseph Wells eked out his income with fees earned as a professional cricketer. Wells had made a series of false starts in life. After the apprenticeship to a draper, described in *Kipps*, he trained as a science teacher (the basis of his novel *Love and Mr Lewisham*), and worked for a time in a tutorial college before becoming a full-time writer. His first marriage to a cousin broke down in divorce: he then married Catherine Robbins, always known as 'Jane', who had been one of his students. At this time he was living at Spade House, Sandgate, near Folkestone, which had been built for him by the advanced architect C.F.A. Voysey (1857–1941).

28 February. [41 Grosvenor Road]

We are at present very thick with the 'Limps'. Asquith, Haldane, Grey, Munro-Ferguson, the Tennants, form a little family group into which they have temporarily attracted Sidney by asking him to their little dinners and informal meetings. Close acquaintance with them does not make one more hopeful. Asquith is wooden, he lacks every kind of enthusiasm and his hard-headed cold capacity seems to be given, not to politics, but to his legal cases. His brother-in-law, Jack Tennant, and Haldane both assure us that he could retire tomorrow from the Bar if he chose and that he only stays at it 'for an occupation'. Strange lack of imagination not to see that there is an over-abundance of hard persistent work ready to his hand in politics, alike in thinking out reforms and in preaching them, and organizing a party to push them. That lack of imagination and sensitiveness to needs lies at the root of Asquith's failure as a leader of men. For the rest, he has no charm or personal magnetism. He has to gain his position by sheer hard work and that work he is not inclined to do in politics.

Grey is a 'slight' person. He has charm of appearance, of manner and even of character, but he is, I fear, essentially a 'stick' to be used by someone else! 'Politics have completely changed,' he said plaintively to me when he was last dining here. 'Formerly you had your cause made for you; all the politician had to do was to preach it. Now you have to *make your cause.*' Beyond foreign and colonial policy (whatever that may mean) Grey has no original ideas and finds it hard even to appreciate the ideas of others. And he has no notion of work as the main occupation of life. Politics is merely, with him, an episode in his daily life, like his enjoyment of nature, books, society, sport (mostly nature and sport be it said).

Neither Asquith nor Grey are, as politicians, well served by their respective wives. Margot is, I believe, a kindly soul, but, though she has intelligence and wit, she has neither intellect nor wisdom. She is incurably reactionary in her prejudices. Her two delights are hunting and other outdoor exercises, and fashionable society. She is said to be ambitious for her husband; but if so, her method of carrying out her ambition lacks intelligence as well as intellect.

Lady Grey is a fastidious aristocrat, intensely critical of anyone to whom work is the principal part of life. She is clever enough to see that work alone counts and yet knows in her heart of hearts that neither she nor her husband are capable of it.

As for Haldane, to whom we are both really attached, he is a large and generous-hearted man, affectionate to his friends and genuinely enthusiastic about the advancement of knowledge. But his ideal has no connection with the ugly rough and tumble workaday world of the average sensual man, who is compelled to earn his livelihood by routine work and bring up a family of children on narrow means. Unmarried, living a luxurious physical but a strenuous mental life, Haldane's vital energies are divided between highly skilled legal work and the processes of digestion – for he is a Herculean eater. He finds his relaxation in bad metaphysics and in political intrigue – that is, in trying to manipulate influential persons into becoming followers of Rosebery, and members of the 'clique'. Be it said to his credit, that he has to some extent manipulated us into this position.

Munro-Ferguson is merely a pleasant young aristocrat. Perhaps the most keen of the lot are the Jack Tennants. Mrs Jack, formerly an inspectress of factories, is a fine-natured woman, with real knowledge and enthusiasm. She has inspired her husband with the same helpful attitude towards social questions. But 'Jack' is a *little* man, physically and mentally, and the notion of his being a 'force' approaches the ridiculous.

There remains the mysterious Rosebery. At present he is an enigma. Whether on account of his social position, or of his brilliancy, or because of his streaks of wit and original thought, he can make all the world listen. He has imagination and sensitiveness, and he is a born actor. He is first rate at 'appearances'. Moreover he seems to be developing persistency and courage. But, as yet, he shows no sign of capacity for co-operation or even for the leadership of a group of subordinates. All he has yet done is to *strike attitudes* that have brought down the House at the time, and left a feeling of blankness a few days later. To be a great leader, a man must either understand problems himself or be able to handle men who do understand them. Rosebery sees many persons, but only in order to extract from them the essence of public opinion so as to appear before the world in a 'popular attitude'. He never asks how actually to work the machinery of government so as to get the best results. Has he any clear and definite view of the character of the results he wants to get? I fear not.

And why are we in this galley? Partly because we have drifted into it. These men have helped us with our undertakings, they have been appreciative of our ideas, and socially pleasant to us. They have no prejudice against our views of social reform, whilst their general attitude towards the Empire as a powerful and self-conscious force is one with which we are in agreement. Moreover, the leaders of the other school of Liberalism are extremely distasteful to us. We disagree with them on almost every point of home and foreign policy. Before we can get the new ideas and new frame of mind accepted, we must beat out the old. That is why we are not against the policy of the 'clean slate'. We want to be rid of all the old ideals and enthusiasms. We want to stamp out the notion that the world can be bettered by abolition of some of the existing institutions. We want, on the contrary, to set people to work to build up new tissue which may in time take the place of the old.

237

In Ireland, for instance, we don't want to abolish the union with England, but so to reconstruct the internal government that it will make the bond of union of secondary importance. We do not want to abolish or remodel the House of Lords, but to build up precedents for their non-intervention with national expenditure, all collectivism coming under this head. We do not want to disestablish the Church, but to endow science and secular ethics and any other form of intellectual activity that may seem desirable. We don't want to abolish or restrain the development of private enterprise, but, by creating dykes and bulwarks, to control its mischievous effect on the character of the race. We do not want to unfetter the individual from the obligation of citizenship. We want, on the contrary, to stimulate and constrain him, by the unfelt pressure of a better social environment, to become a healthier, nobler and more efficient being.

To these ideals the old Liberalism of Leonard Courtney, Morley, Campbell-Bannerman, and the bulk of the Celtic members of Parliament [M.P.s from the Liberal strongholds in Wales and Scotland] are not only unsympathetic but really hostile. Asquith, Haldane, Grey and, I think, Rosebery, are sympathetic though timorous. They will not themselves push these ideals (Rosebery is as likely as any to do it) but they will follow any one who does, *if there seems to be the least response from public opinion*. And, if Sidney is inside the clique, he will have a better chance of permeating its activities than by standing aloof as a 'superior' person and scolding at them. So I am inclined to advise him to throw in his lot with them in the days of their adversity and trial, when an addition to their ranks from the democratic side is of great value to them. Half the art of effective living consists of giving yourself to those who need you most *and at the time of their most pressing want*. And, seeing that politics is a mere by-product of our life, our own special work today being administration or investigation, there seem few reasons against this course of action. If we came to throw our main stream of energy into political life we should have to choose our comrades more carefully.

The Technical Education Board is a source of worry and anxiety to Sidney. The hostility of the Conservative government to the School Board, and the threat to abolish it, has reacted on the Radical L.C.C. and made them inclined to refuse to compete with the Radical School Board for the administration of education.

J.R. MacDonald, Sidney's old enemy in the Fabian Society, slipped into the Council at an uncontested by-election and apparently spends his time in working up the feeling against the Technical Education Board and Sidney's administration of it. He is anxious to get on to it, and Sidney is doing his best to get him in, believing that an enemy is always safer inside than outside a democratic body. But it means friction and a good deal of bickering. MacDonald does not hesitate to accuse Sidney of taking advantage of his position to favour the School of Economics, an accusation which is perfectly true, though we think absolutely harmless. In administration you must advance the cause which you think right and are therefore 'interested' in. The unpleasant sound of the accusation is conveyed by the double meaning of the word 'interested' which in most men's mouths means *pecuniarily* interested. We believe in a school of administrative, political and economic science as a way of increasing national efficiency, but we have kept the London School honestly non-partisan in its theories. Otherwise 'interested' we are not, unless the expenditure of our own energy and money on an institution be termed 'interested'. And Sidney's energies have by no means been exclusively devoted to the subjects he is intellectually interested in. He has, I think, been quite exceptionally catholic in his organization of secondary, technical and university education in London, alike in the class of students to be provided for and the range of subjects taught. Heaven knows there are arrears to be made up in politics, economics and the science of administration.

The Progressives are not very happy among themselves. The most eminent of them having served as chairman or refused to do so, there comes the question whether [one of] the hardworking little 'cads' of the party shall succeed to the chair, or whether some well-bred nonentity shall be promoted. Sidney, though willing to back up the majority of the party in any course they think fit (he does not attach much importance to the whole business), is inclined to advise a frank recognition of the plebeian character of the L.C.C., and to take an excellent and devoted member who drops his 'h's' rather than an insignificant lord. The matter has been compromised by the choice of a plebeian as chairman and a lord as vice-chairman. But it has left heart-burnings and ill feeling within the party committee, Sidney acting as peace-maker. By his colleagues he is considered a 'non-competitor': he has made education his province and rules over it undisturbed. He has no desire to be chairman or vice-chairman or leader of the party in the Council itself.

We have seen something lately of H.G. Wells and his wife. Wells is an interesting, though somewhat unattractive personality except for his agreeable disposition and intellectual vivacity. His mother was the housekeeper to a great establishment of forty servants, his father the professional cricketer attached to the place. The early associations with the menial side of the great man's establishment has left Wells with a hatred of that class and of its attitude towards the 'lower orders'. His apprenticeship to a draper, his subsequent career as an assistant master at a private venture school, as a 'government student' at South Kensington living on £1 a week, as an 'army' crammer, as a journalist and, in these last years, as a most successful writer of fiction, has given him a great knowledge of the lower- middle class and their habits and thoughts, and an immense respect for science and its methods. But he is totally ignorant of the manual worker, on the one hand, and of the big administrator and aristocrat on the other. This ignorance is betrayed in certain crudities of criticism in his *Anticipations*. He ignores the necessity for maintaining the standard of life of the manual working population; he does not appreciate the need for a wide experience of men and affairs in administration. A world run by the physical-science-man straight from his laboratory is his ideal; he does not see that specialized faculty and knowledge are needed for administration exactly as they are needed for the manipulation of machinery or [natural] forces. But he is extraordinarily quick in his apprehensions, and took in all the points we gave him in our forty-eight hours' talk with him, first at his own house and then here. He is a good instrument for popularizing ideas, and he gives as many ideas as he receives. His notion of modern society as 'the grey' — not because it is made of uniform atoms of that shade, but because of the very variety of its colours, all mixed together and in formless mass; his forecast of the segregation of like to like, until the community will become extraordinarily variegated and diverse in its component parts, seems to us a brilliant and true conception. Again, democracy as a method of dealing with men in a wholesale way, every man treated in the bulk and not in detail, the probability that we shall become more *detailed* and less *wholesale* in our provision for men's needs, that again is a clever illumination. Altogether, it is refreshing to talk to a man who has shaken himself loose from so many of the current assumptions, and is looking at life as an explorer of a new world. He has no great faith in government by the 'man in the street', and, I think, has hardly realized the function of the representative as a 'foolometer' for the expert.

His wife is a pretty little person with a strong will, mediocre intelligence and somewhat small nature. She has carefully moulded herself in dress, manners and even accent to take her place in any society her husband's talents may lead them into. But it is all rather artificial, from the sweetness of her smile to her interest in public affairs. However, she provides him with a charming well-ordered home, though I should imagine her constant companionship was somewhat stifling. They are both of them well-bred in their pleasant tempers, careful consideration of the feelings of others, quick apprehension of new conventions and requirements, but they both of them lack ease and repose, and she has an ugly absence of spontaneity of thought and feeling.

The dissension within the Liberal Party grew more acute during the winter. After a series of meetings at the house of Lord Rosebery, the Liberal Imperialists set up the Liberal League to promote its ideas but it lacked the resolution to present a serious challenge to the party leadership. Rosebery was its president and Sidney was a member. Sir Robert Perks (1849–1934), known as 'Imperial Perks', was the organizer of the group. He was a Wesleyan, a temperance reformer, a successful railway engineer and a Liberal M.P. since 1892. His tactlessness and lack of grace made him a social liability. Jabez Spencer Balfour (1843–1916) was a Radical M.P. for Tamworth before he was sent to prison in 1895 for fourteen years for an insurance fraud that ruined many investors. At the end of this entry Beatrice copied some extracts from a controversial book of lectures by Adolf van Harnack (1851–1936): *What is Christianity?* she said, "expresses exactly our religious feeling."

19 March. [41 Grosvenor Road]
Met 'Imperial Perks' at Mr Haldane's – a repulsive being. Hard, pushing, commonplace, with no enthusiasms except a desire to have his 'knife into the Church', a blank materialist although a pious Protestant, who recognizes no principle beyond self-interest. I confess the thought that Perks was a pillar of the new Liberal League staggered me. How could we work with such a loathsome person! A combination of Gradgrind, Pecksniff and Jabez Balfour. And the choice of this man as their first lieutenant throws an ugly light on Lord Rosebery. Anyway, we and Perks are 'incompatible' in views, in tastes, and in all our fundamental assumptions as to ends and methods. . . . The situation is made worse by the fact that Perks is the only man in the group who is in deadly earnest and therefore *if the group succeeds* likely to come out top. To think of Perks as an English Cabinet Minister: ugh! The very notion of it degrades political life.

Two months 'sampling' of the Liberal Imperialists has not

heightened our estimate of them. Asquith is deplorably 'slack'. Grey is a mere dilettante, Haldane plays at political intrigue and has no democratic principles, Perks is an 'unclean beast' and, as for Rosebery, he remains an enigma. He, at any rate, has personal distinction, originality and charm, but he seeks only 'appearances', has no care for or knowledge of economic and social evils, lives and moves and has his being in the plutocratic atmosphere, shares to the full the fears and prejudices of his class. Moreover, he is a bad colleague and suffers from lack of nerve and persistent purpose. As for the rank and file, they are a most heterogeneous lot, bound together by their *dislikes*, and not by their positive convictions. They have no kind of faith in any of their leaders, and are in constant fear as to their 'political future' and 'personal careers'. And rising up against them is a force which will become apparent at the next election – labour candidates officially run by the great trade unions, backed up by pro-Boer capitalists. That combination will have no constructive power – for here, again, the two elements are bound together, not by a common faith, but by a common hatred. But it will be able, in many places, to smash the Liberal Imperialist. Thus the Liberal Party seems cleaved into two equally unpromising sections – Rosebery appealing to the grey mass of convictionless voters on the broad and shallow ground of Empire and Efficiency, Campbell-Bannerman relying on every description of 'separatist' interest – on all the 'anti's'; anti-war, anti-United Kingdom, anti-Church, anti-Capitalist, anti-Empire. Both combinations seem to me equally temporary and equally lacking in healthy and vigorous root principles.

Having done our little best to stimulate the 'Limps' into some kind of conviction, and having most assuredly failed, we now return to our own work. Three months' peaceful and strenuous effort in the country seems a delightful prospect. And between me and this diary, I think the 'Limps' will be glad to be rid of us! Our contempt for their 'Limpness' and our distrust for their reactionary views are too apparent.

Annie Besant (1847–1933), brought up a strict evangelical, had separated from her clerical husband and fought fiercely for custody of her child. She then turned to Secularist agitation, birth-control propaganda, Fabianism, trade unionism, feminism, theosophy and Indian nationalism.

26 March. [41 Grosvenor Road]
The eve of our departure for the country. This year has opened with

greater promise of good work. Thanks to a simple diet I am in better health of body and mind. But I have leeway to make up alike in physical strength and in purity of feeling and concentration of thought. I think I know what physical regime suits me if I have the physical self-control to keep it. I also know that I have to be equally watchful of the contents of my mind. For this I can only rely on some spiritual help arising from prayer. Every morning therefore I will concentrate my desire on physical self-control, intellectual concentration and moral purity. Health, truth and love of God. Amen.

Annie Besant's little book on *Thought Power, its Control and Culture,* though mixed with a good deal of oriental quackery, is a useful textbook of mental hygiene. . . .

Lawrence and Standish Cripps were the two eldest sons of Blanche and Willie Cripps. Lawrence was born in 1878 and Standish in 1881. Alfred Beit (1853–1906) was a South African financier and diamond merchant, a partner in the firm of Wernher, Beit and Co. He was one of the rich men from whom Beatrice hoped to get funds for the School of Economics, and other projects. Sidney's 'stocktaking' article, which set out a coherent plan for all levels of education in London, was published in the *Nineteenth Century* in October 1903.

25 April. Crowborough Beacon, Sussex
A pleasant four weeks, camping out in the large rooms of a girls' school on Crowborough Beacon. For the first ten days the Bobby Phillimores were here. Poor dears. I have rarely seen two mortals incapable of guiding their own lives into health and successful endeavour, largely due to a most consummate conceit of their own abilities, not offensive because Lion is brilliant and sympathetic and Bobby is admirably well-bred, but pitiful in its results. They both suffer physically from the eating craze, Lion having been ordered to 'stuff' and Bobby having a quite morbid appetite. They have too large a fortune to become poor through Bobby's foolish desire to play at business; but they seem not unlikely to eat themselves into disease. Meanwhile, they take up one question after another, fully persuaded that they are going to solve it; local government, housing, the army, the Irish question. However, they seem genuinely attached to one another in spite of a certain disparity in age and training.

Another Sunday we had Lawrence and Standish Cripps – melancholy lads, living in dreary lodgings, one a young medical man, the other articled to a solicitor. Lawrence, who is an honest, good-hearted youth, has caught his father's cheap cynicism, and the cheaper philosophy of the 'survival of the fittest' school; but he lacks the capacity and force which makes both these intellectual garments decent covering for an able man. Harrison Cripps's philosophy of life, as it has developed in these latter years, has certainly not been justified by its results on the home life. Poor Blanche is thoroughly unhappy, the children are cynical and discontented and often ill. For Willie himself, it is *perhaps* a success. He seems to thoroughly enjoy the consciousness of his power whether exercised as a superlatively good 'operator', a successful businessman, or in entertaining house-parties at Abbotsford [Sir Walter Scott's former home] made up of the smartest of his patients. 'I hate and disapprove the life,' said poor Blanche to me tragically. 'The place is no good to the children and the people who come and stay don't interest me or respect me. I could not have believed that I should have to live this sort of life.' Of course her husband has his view of the matter. In spite of her nobility of character, Blanche has been an inefficient wife, quite as unable to sympathize with the higher side of his nature – his love of science and professional zeal – as with his scheme of wealth-getting and social advancement. From the time she ceased to satisfy his emotional and physical nature she has been a simple 'negative', perhaps even an irritating negative, causing a reaction into positive antagonism. The marriage has been for the last five or six years an unhappy one, bad for both of them and worse than useless for the children. I have drifted completely out of my old camaraderie with Willie, partly because he took a dislike to Sidney and partly because his whole attitude towards private and public matters is abhorrent to me.

We have had a happy and successful time here: writing the chapter on the Commissioners of Sewers, sorting the material from structure into function. I have been thinking out the 'assumptions' underlying the working out of local government prior to 1834. . . . The book is getting into the interesting and philosophical stage, and I am looking forward with hopefulness and happiness to the ten weeks with the Russells.

Poor Sidney is somewhat distracted with anxiety with regard to the future of the School, the development of opposition to the Technical Education Board and the L.C.C. His principal concern is the exact constitution of the educational authority for London to be proposed next year. It so happens that he can use the fear of the borough councils as the authority to frighten the opponents of the T.E.B. on the

Council. It is an open secret that a strong section of the Cabinet is in favour of a joint committee of the borough councils, which would be a disaster of the first magnitude to the whole of higher education in London. To avert this disaster we are moving all the forces we have any control over – our friends in the Church, university education-alists, permanent officials and anyone having influence over ministers, against the proposal of an education authority elected by and from the borough councils.

It is perhaps fortunate that Sidney is known to approve the lines of the present Bill applying to the country outside London. Indeed our Radical School Board friends scoff about 'Webbs' Bill', which of course is an absurdity. They will scoff the more if next year we are hoist by our own petard! Meanwhile he is writing an article for the *Nineteenth Century* for June on the London University in the hope of catching a millionaire! Beit is biting!

A few days absolutely alone in the country pass happily now that I have my health. A long morning's work, then the lounge before tea, two or three hours' walk or ride, revelling in the beauty and joy of the spring; a peaceful evening's reading or brooding over my work, and the night spent with window wide open with neither curtains nor blind to keep the moon or sunlight from streaming in upon me. This life is luxurious to me, if luxury consist of mental and physical joy of life. . . I am no longer plagued by foolish fancies and absurd day-dreams. At times my imagination strays to the lives of greater ones; but it is only to wish them well and the desire that some day, when both the struggle and the fame of life has past, I might be of some service. That is hardly possible.

The reading in which I find most relaxation is religion. It seems to rest my brain and refresh my spirit. And I am constantly pondering over the legitimacy of prayer – one's quite unaccountable faith in it, resting as it does on the good one gains from the practice of it. I enjoy the 'religious life' and it seems to enhance and not to weaken my capacity for secular work. And yet I cannot bring my faith and my practice into line with the Christian religion. I cannot acquiesce in the claims of Christianity. I should love to worship with others and to feel the support and the charm of a regular and definite ritual. But directly I hear the words in which Christians clothe their religious aspirations my intellectual sincerity takes alarm. I do not believe in their doctrine. I am not even attracted by their God, whether in the Jewish or in the Christian version. My faith is more in spiritual influence – at present being exercised by good men and good thoughts, in the communion of saints here on earth, and the relation of the good men and good thoughts to the mysterious spiritual universe which I believe surrounds us.

Robert Morant (1862–1920) was a civil servant who was the chief author of the Education Act passed in 1902: the Webbs, who worked closely with him, considered him the ideal type of public servant for the collectivist age. Sidney's article stressing the need for the University of London to provide scientific and technical training was published in the *Nineteenth Century* in June 1902.

4 May. Friday's Hill

Settled again for our nine weeks' sojourn with the Russells. Hard at work on Poor Law Report of 1834. I had to break into this work to help Sidney through with his University of London article. Can concentrate my brain completely and work good hours, but still troubled with indigestion whenever I exceed by the smallest amount the regulated diet, thus alternating between hunger and flatulence! Interesting to see whether this phase wears off as I become more and more rigidly abstemious. Not completely rid of eczema though this much better, and not inclined for much physical exercise. I am in fact on a lower level of physical strength and a higher level of mental effort than last year.

Alys Russell is away undergoing a 'rest cure'. Bertrand is working as usual – well and hard in health, eager to find someone with whom to talk philosophy but despairing of companionship in his higher mathematics. He and I see much of each other, as Sidney is away for a day or two each week. Usually we drift into talking of the 'conduct of life' in its widest sense with every now and again excursions into our respective 'shop'. Sidney is somewhat distracted with his undertakings and feels himself at times unequal to them. 'I am not a big man,' he says plaintively to me. 'I could not manage any larger undertakings.' But as I tell him it is exactly this consciousness of imperfection, whilst others find him competent, that shows that he is more than equal to his task. We only feel completely complacent with our effort when we have ceased to grasp the *possibilities* of the situation.

Enjoyed my week's work on the University article, a relief from the grind of facts, a chance for 'scheming', an intellectual occupation I dearly love.

Sidney had Morant to stay here. Morant is the principal person at the Education Department. He has occupied the most anomalous position the last six months. Taken into the office as a nondescript in a humble capacity some years ago, Gorst picked him out for his private secretary. In that way he became acquainted with the politicians – Cabinet Ministers and Conservative private members who were concerned with education bills and educational policy. Presently these folk, specially the Cabinet Ministers, found him a useful substitute for Kekewich (Permanent Head) who was deadly opposed to their policy, and to Gorst with whom they were hardly on speaking terms, the situation being complicated by the fact that Gorst and Kekewich were complete 'incompatibles' having no communication with each other! So Morant has been exclusively engaged by the Cabinet Committee to draft this present bill, attending its meetings and consulting with individual members over clauses, trying to get some sort of bill through the Cabinet. Both Kekewich and Gorst have been absolutely ignored, neither the one or the other having seen the bill before it was printed. Just before its introduction in the House, Morant wrote to Gorst saying he assumed he 'might put his name at the back'. Gorst answered: 'I have sold my name to the government, put it where they instruct you to put it.'! Morant gives strange glimpses into the working of one department of English government. The Duke of Devonshire, the nominal Education Minister, failing through inertia and stupidity to grasp any complicated detail half an hour after he has listened to the clearest exposition of it, preoccupied with Newmarket [horse-racing] and in bed till 12 o'clock; Kekewich trying to outstay this government and quite superannuated in authority; Gorst cynical and careless, having given up even the semblance of any interest in the office, the Cabinet absorbed in other affairs and impatient and bored with the whole question of education. 'Impossible to find out after a Cabinet meeting', Morant tells us, 'what has actually been the decision. Salisbury does not seem to know or care and the various Ministers, who do care, give me contradictory versions. So I gather that Cabinet meetings have become more than informal – they are chaotic, breaking up into little groups, talking to each other without any one to formulate or register the collective opinion. Chamberlain would run the whole thing if he were not so overworked by his own department.'

Sidney and he discussed for many hours the best way of so influencing the Cabinet and its advisers that we get a good authority for London. Decided to send out the T.E.B. Report widely with

personal letters and to set on foot quiet 'agitations' among the Church
folk and other Conservative circles. Among others, Sidney has
written a short note to Chamberlain drawing his attention to the policy
of 'delegation' by the T.E.B., leaving it to be understood that he
would be prepared to delegate management of the elementary schools
(properly safeguarded) to borough council committees. Also to
Balfour; in fact I think he has written to every prominent personage,
to each according to his views and degree of influence.

A peace treaty was signed with the Boers at Vereeniging on Saturday, 31 May.
Dr J.G. Robertson (1867–1933) was professor of German at King's College,
London. Professor A.W. Rücker (1848–1915) was a scientist who became
Principal of the University of London in 1902. At this time Sidney had joined
Haldane in a campaign to provide London with a first-class institution for science
and technology. Much affected by the attention paid to these subjects in Germany
and especially by the flow of qualified manpower from the Charlottenburg Institute
in Berlin, they were seeking support and endowments for a comparable college in
London. What was called in their shorthand 'the Charlottenburg scheme' was to
merge the Royal College of Science and the School of Mines at South Kensington
with the City and Guilds Institute, thus forming what eventually became the
Imperial College of Science and Technology. Meanwhile the L.S.E. had
completed the building paid for by the benefaction from Passmore Edwards.

30 May. [41 Grosvenor Road]
Yesterday the formal opening of the new building of the School of
Economics, a day of satisfaction for Sidney, Hewins and myself. Our
child, born only seven years ago in two back rooms in John Street,
with a few hundred a year, from the Hutchinson Trust, despised by
the learned folk as a 'young man's' fad, is now fully grown and ready to
start in the world on its own account. There is the building and
equipment, all admirably planned to suit the sort of work and life we
have built up; there are the staff of teachers modestly but permanently
endowed; there are the formidable list of 'governors' over which
Sidney presides; and last but not least the School has attained
university status with its own curriculum, its own degrees, and with
even a prospect of its own 'gown'. Meanwhile Sidney's personal work
has broadened out into the administration of University affairs as a
whole; his position on the Senate is strong and seems destined to
become stronger, since he is always mentally on the spot long before
the others have arrived there. He and Hewins too are a strong
combination among the warring atoms and are reinforced by Dr
Robertson of King's and such outside members as W.P. Reeves and

Davey, whilst Sidney is one of Dr Rücker's (the new Principal) more confidential advisers. Should he become one of the trustees of the fund that Haldane is trying to raise, still more should he persuade the L.C.C. to 'go' a $\frac{1}{4}d$ or $\frac{1}{2}d$ rate, his influence with the Senate will become alarmingly strong and no doubt create anger and envy in various quarters. He will then have to walk 'warily' and not abuse his predominance. Fortunately for his work he never suffers from inflation; he is too completely absorbed in getting things done and too sincerely modest to lose his head. All his aggressiveness has disappeared with his good fortune, that is, his personal aggressiveness; he remains a good fighter when he has his back to the wall. In his opinion, fighting should always be the last resource before being beaten on some main issue of real importance. . . . Bertrand away for three weeks with his friends, the Whiteheads, Alys still undergoing the 'rest cure'. We are getting anxious about her.

Peace with the Transvaal; political burial of the pro-Boers. Immediate increase in popularity of government: rise of Rosebery 'futures'. He is playing the game of leading the Liberal Party on his own terms with consummate deftness.

Arthur Penryn Stanley (1815–1881) was Dean of Westminster from 1864 to his death, and the outstanding advocate of ecumenicalism in the Broad Church movement.

5 June. Friday's Hill

Graham Wallas spent the afternoon and evening here without Audrey. He is more in his old form than I have seen him for years. The approaching abolition of the School Board, in which he acquiesces (on general grounds of objection to *ad hoc* bodies and I think on the particular experience of the L.S.B.) has detached his mind from the minute details of School management and left it freer to turn back to the student's life. He and I had a long discussion – walking on Marley Common – as to our respective position with regard to denominational religion. He recognizes, but deplores, the growing tolerance of, if not sympathy with, religious teaching, on the part of professed agnostics. He distinguished with some subtlety between the old broad church party, who wished to broaden the creed of the Church to one which they emphatically could accept, and those 'religious-minded' agnostics who accept Church teaching, not because they believe its assertions to be true, but lest worse befall the child's mind in the form of a crude materialistic philosophy. 'I cannot

249

see the spirit of genuine reform, if there is no portion of the Church's teaching which you object to more than any other; if you cease to discriminate between what you accept and what you reject, denying all and accepting all, with the same breath — denying the dogmas as statements of fact, accepting them as interpreting a spirit which pleases you. Dean Stanley and the Broad Churchmen were in quite a different position: they denied the Athanasian Creed and wished it ousted, they believed the Apostles' Creed and fervently and sincerely desired it to be taught.' I admitted there was much in his contention. I could only shelter myself by the argument that the reform of the Church was not the work I had undertaken to do or which I was trained to consider. The practical alternatives before us constituted a very simple issue, whether we were to throw our weight against the continuance of the present form of religious teaching and help to establish pure materialism as the national metaphysic or whether we would accept, provisionally, as part of the teaching in the schools, the dogmas and ritual of the Christian Church of today.

For my own children, and for those of other people, I deliberately believed the lie of materialism to be far more pernicious and more utterly false than the untruths which seem to me to constitute the Christian formula of religion. Moreover, we are face to face with the fact that the vast majority of the English people are, as far as they think at all, convinced Christians. By insisting on secular education I should be not only helping to spread what seems to me a bad kind of falsehood but I should be denying to others the right to have their children taught the creed they hold to be positively true. I see no way out of the dilemma but the largest variety possible of denominational schools, so that there may be the utmost possible choice for parents and children, and, let me add, the widest range of experiments as to the results of particular kinds of teaching on the character of the child and its conduct of life.

Jane Harrison (1850–1928) was a classical scholar and archaeologist. Sir Arthur Bowley (1869–1957) was an economist and statistician. Sir Halford J. Mackinder (1861–1947) was reader in geography at Oxford and later professor at the Univeristy of London. He became the Director of the London School of Economics in 1903. In the autumn of 1901 the Russells moved to Cambridge to live with the Whiteheads at Mill House, Grantchester. At the beginning of 1902, Russell wrote later, 'I went out bicycling one afternoon and suddenly, as I was riding along a country road, I realized that I no longer loved Alys.' When he bluntly told her how he felt she became depressed to the point of breakdown (though the marriage continued, formally and uneasily, until 1911), and Beatrice proposed to take her on a Swiss holiday as a reviving distraction. Alys was at first resistant to the proposal. She found Beatrice's letters 'very nice, so kind and sensible', she wrote to Russell on 20 May but thought she would 'hate' the proposed vacation. 'I should dislike being much with Mrs Webb alone because she likes to talk all the time, and has no pursuits when she is resting,' she added on 1 June; and the next day she made a similar objection: 'I do not feel as if I could discuss food and Wells's novels with her for three weeks.' But on the following day she had made up her mind to accept the invitation, conceding that 'my feelings about people when I am down are no good at all.' Russell had done his best to persuade her to a more favourable view of Beatrice. 'I am getting to like Beatrice,' he wrote on 19 May: 'she has many very good sides, and seems to me to improve from year to year' – though, on 24 June, he confessed that 'her prompt energetic executive ways got on my nerves.' After eight years of difficulty over the licensing of Shaw's *Mrs Warren's Profession* it was finally performed at the New Lyric Club on 5 January 1902.

7 June. Friday's Hill

The last days of our stay – Sidney in London and I packing up our MSS. and blue-books preparatory to the advent of a large party of Berensons etc.

I have worked well but with small result in actual stuff written. . . . But what I have done is to get the whole Poor Law section planned out and about half written as well as the general scheme of Part II of the book conceived, so that now the work will go straight forward. Sidney has only been able to write out (he always elucidates and completes my rough draft) what I have done, spending only one or two days a week down here. It has been a broken time for him, absorbed in University and T.E.B. Committees, consultations, redrafting of Garnett's and Hewins's reports, writing memoranda for Haldane on University matters, for Conservative M.P.s and bishops on 'The New Education Authority for London' and keeping an eye on the Fabian Society and the Liberal League, altogether a somewhat distracted life. But he is very happy in his activity, feels ways opening out before him of getting at least some things done in the direction he believes right. Sometimes he is weary and longs to retire to 'a cottage' with me and 'write books' but more often he is happily active, unconscious of anything but his desire to transact the business in hand successfully. He has a delightful unselfconscious nature. He has (thank the Lord!) no 'subconscious self'. When not at work, or asleep, or talking, he reads, reads, reads – always ready for a kiss or a loving word, given or taken. 'I am frightened at my own happiness,' he often says.

251

Alys being away we have had few visitors. Miss Jane Harrison of Newnham spent Whitsun here – a bracing personality and workmanlike scholar, not attractive either mentally or physically, a somewhat narrow mind, caring only for archaeology or 'masterpieces' of literature, detesting politics, careless of history, and ignoring philosophy, ignorant of science. . . . Then she has poisoned herself with tea and tobacco, drinks the most poisonous brew frequently and smokes some thirty cigarettes a day. And she has the weakness of desiring to appear young.

Hewins, Bowley, Garnett and Wallas have been down to talk business. This last Sunday we have had Mackinder and Beatrice Chamberlain. Mackinder is an able lecturer on commercial geography, energetic traveller and organizer. He has political ambitions and is by way of attaching himself to the Rosebery group. He is a coarse-grained individual (Bertrand says brutal) but with a certain capacity for oratory, and strong picturesque statement. If he got his foot on the ladder he might go far towards the top, especially as there is an absence of able young men. Signs in him of negroid blood?

For about three weeks out of the eight Bertrand Russell has been away staying with his friends the Whiteheads, and poor Alys has been too unwell to be here. A consciousness that something is wrong between them has to some extent spoilt our sojourn here, both Sidney and I being completely mystified. We became so concerned about the situation that I suggested that I should take Alys off to Switzerland to complete her cure, and Sidney acquiesced out of affection for her and genuine admiration for Bertrand. It would be a sin and a shame if these two should become separated, and altogether wanton misery for both. Our impression is that they have both erred in sacrificing themselves and each other to an altogether mistaken sense of obligation to other people. It is quite clear to me that Bertrand is going through some kind of tragedy of feeling; what is happening to her, I suppose I shall discover in the next three or four weeks. It is the wantonness of this unhappiness which appals me, saddens and irritates both of us.

Bertrand Russell's nature is pathetic in its subtle absoluteness: faith in an absolute logic, absolute ethic, absolute beauty, and all of the most refined and rarefied type. His abstract and revolutionary methods of thought and the uncompromising way in which he applies these frightens me for his future and the future of those who love him or whom he loves. Compromise, mitigation, mixed motive, phases of health of body and mind, qualified statements, uncertain feelings, all seem unknown to him. A proposition must be true or false; a character good or bad, a person loving or unloving, truth speaking or lying. And this last year he has grown up quite suddenly from an intellectual boy into a masterful man struggling painfully with his own nature and rival notions of duty and obligation. His hatred of giving pain and his self-centred will, I think, will save him from the disaster of doing what he would feel afterwards to have been wrong. But it is always painful to stand by and watch a struggle one cannot help. The background of life here has, therefore, not been happy, especially for me, as I have had time and opportunity to observe and brood over it. Sidney, though most anxious and willing to give a helping hand (even to the extent of letting me leave him for three weeks!) is somewhat impatient with this quite unnecessary pain. However, the problems of human relationship have a way of unravelling themselves when those concerned are intelligent, warm-hearted and healthy in body and mind.

The first thing to be done is to get Alys well. I am myself looking forward to the complete change and rest. My cure is not complete; still suffer from eczema in one of my ears, due, I believe, to my greedy persistence in drinking coffee which I believe is rank poison to me. Also my recent attempts to companionize Bertrand so as to keep him here (which I believe to be Alys's desire) have meant more mental exertion than is consistent with regular work. And I have not always been quite faithful to the regimen: now and again a naughty greedy feeling overtakes me at a meal and I exceed! But I am improving in that respect; keep always before me the scale and the weights. I wanted, having spent yesterday in packing, to get back to the book, but I cannot stand the knocking and cleaning going on in the house – so off I go into the woods with *Mrs Warren's Profession*, just sent me by GBS.

VOLUME 23

21 July. Sils, Engadine
Three weeks in Switzerland – one week at Monte Generosa and the rest of the time here. Complete rest of body and mind, the only occupation being to act as a good companion and to Alys Russell and to tide her over a bad time. She has turned out a most restful and pleasant

companion and I feel that it is I who have been enjoying the rest cure, with her as a bright and sympathetic attendant. All the same, I believe I have done her good. I have given her back a sane perspective of her own and Bertrand's life. She is a warm-hearted, intelligent and attractive woman, and deserves to be happy and useful. The days and nights have been one long dream of pleasant sights, sounds and scents, varied by memories of past events, broodings over present problems and a certain background of sadness at the mysteries of the futility and pain of the great bulk of life, even judged by our low human standards, a melancholy brought about by absence from my dearest comrade and friend. How terribly lonely life would be without his ·worshipful love and that joyful combination of helpfulness and dependence.

The coronation of Edward VII took place on 9 August after being postponed because of the King's operation in June. Beatrice makes no reference to it. Lady Elcho (d. 1937) was the wife of the Earl of Wemyss, a friend of Arthur Balfour and one of the Society hostesses who belonged to 'The Souls'. The Webbs were staying at Hulland House, Chipping Campden, in the Cotswolds near the Elcho house at Stanway. The Gifford lectures on theological and ethical subjects, given at Scottish universities, were founded by Lord Gifford (1820–87). William James (1842–1910) gave a series of Gifford lectures in Edinburgh 1901–02 on the psychology of religion and published them in 1902 under the title *The Varieties of Religious Experience*. Haldane gave the Gifford lectures at St Andrew's 1902–04 and they were published in 1903 as *The Pathway to Reality*, one of four substantial works on philosophy. Lord Hugh Cecil (1869–1956) was the youngest son of Lord Salisbury and Conservative M.P. 1895–1906. He was a close friend of Balfour, who had become Prime Minister after Salisbury's resignation on 10 July. Asquith, Home Secretary in 1893, was long held responsible for the death of three miners, shot by troops suppressing a riot at Featherstone in the South Yorkshire coalfield during the strike of that year.

[? September] *41 Grosvenor Road*
Four fruitful weeks at Campden whither we return for another three tomorrow. We have done good work completing our chapter on Poor Law. . . . Our work on local government will be a big indictment, not only of the eighteenth century, but also of the present-day local government.

Meanwhile we are having a most happy holiday. The countryside is beautiful, a subtle charm to me, as the Evesham Vale resembles in general effect, and in all its little details, the Severn Vale, and brings up the sentiment for the old home as background to present content and happiness.

We have had pleasant companionship with Hewins, Mackinder and the Russells, and latterly we have seen something of Lady Elcho, a fascinating and kindly woman married to a card-playing and cynical aristocrat, living in the most delightful old house – Stanway.

Read William James's book (Gifford lectures) written in a fascinating style and full of suggestiveness; Bertrand Russell would say sceptical reasoning. . . . The book interested me because of the stress it lays on prayer – faith in the practice of prayer as a means of personal salvation from the promptings of the lower self grows on me every year. I find myself quite simply and naturally 'going to Church' on Sundays and sometimes even on weekdays, feeling kinship with other mortals in this communion. Sidney does not sympathize with my faith in prayer, and perhaps, in his heart of hearts, regards it as 'neurotic' but intellectually he accepts as tenable James's position in the 'will to believe'. But to him personally James's thesis is irrelevant as he has never experienced the prayerful or religious attitude.

Mr Haldane came to lunch with us yesterday. He has been immersed in writing his Gifford lectures and was absorbed by his peculiar and personal vision of the Absolute. He is still keen on the University and full of energy and hopefulness. But much depressed about politics, does not evidently trust Rosebery. Thinks the Conservatives are going to pieces, that the leaders would even like to be defeated and retire for a year or two; that Campbell-Bannerman would grasp at office on any terms and that it would end in the fresh discredit of Liberalism with the 'Limps' forced into the position of Liberal Unionists. If asked, Rosebery might accept a coalition with the younger Tories and leave his lieutenants in the lurch and the Liberals in a discredited opposition. For the present he is chiefly concerned to prevent the defeat of the Education Bill and came to consult Sidney about it. Sidney advised a demonstration in the *Nineteenth Century* of educationalists in favour of the Bill to strengthen Balfour's hand and again to urge the inclusion of London. Sidney has to write a memorandum on the London situation to go through Hugh Cecil to Balfour.

Odd letter from Rosebery. I sent him a card for my trade union teas, more to let him know what we were doing than expecting him to come. Foolish of him not to have responded to the request from the trade unionists for an entertainment at his house. He needs strengthening on the democratic side and it would have cost him so little! The half-heartedness of these leaders to their work of leadership annoys us. If it is worth our while at great inconvenience and expense to us – we who have nothing to gain politically – how much more is it their game. Asquith, too, with a house at St Albans within one hour of London, cannot bestir himself to come up for one day for the Congress, let alone entertain the delegates in his empty house in Cavendish Square. He, too, with the memory of Featherstone to wipe out! Why play the game at all if you mean to play so carelessly and with so little enjoyment of the process or concern for the result.

Attended one or two meetings of the Trades Union Congress and had delegates to tea for three days. Dominant note of the Congress is determination to run Labour candidates on a large scale and faith in the efficiency of this device for gaining all they require. The notion is to have Labour men in the field in a number of constituencies before the Liberal candidate is selected. There is no leadership in the Congress; little respect of one man more than another; but a certain unanimity of opinion among the delegates; less cleavage between trade and trade, or between old and new unionists than in any congress I have before attended. Practically the Congress has been captured (as far as its formal expression of opinion is concerned) by the I.L.P. We find ourselves quite out of harmony with it collectively, though on cordial and confidential terms with many of the delegates.

Charles Richard John Spencer-Churchill (1871–1934) was the ninth Duke of Marlborough and his wife Consuelo Vanderbilt of New York: the Duke was the cousin of Sir Winston Churchill.

29 September. [41 Grosvenor Road]
We came back to London in good spirits and excellent working form. Two days' [bicycle] ride to Parmoor from Campden, sleeping at night at Woodstock in order to interview the Town Clerk and see Blenheim [Palace]. Mr Haldane had arranged for our reception at the Palace and we found the private secretary (the Duke was away meeting the Duchess just returned from America) awaiting us. A good soul but garrulous, affording us great entertainment by his 'by-the-way' descriptions of the wayward weakness of his aristocratic little master – as a man with no training, no taste, no capacity, no public interests, but just like a child playing with a great property and a great position. The Duchess, a pretty American without strong character or intelligence, drifting about among great personages, the two drifting

away from each other. An ill-regulated family of Churchills of various generations descending on Blenheim with their children, nurses and governesses and 'upsetting' (as the secretary said) the Duke's mind by resenting the Vanderbilt furniture and the Vanderbilt regime in this old home. Not a pleasant picture – vacuum as regards intellectual and public life, quarrelsome in domestic matters, great luxury in daily life, and above all, incapacity to turn to good account the splendid opportunities for right social leadership. Poor little American! She is said to sometimes sigh that she did not marry an American of her own set, free from the responsibilities and stately routine of the ducal establishment and the strange requirements of public interest and public work from an English *grande dame*.

Alfred [Cripps] we found in good health and happy with his children. But he is evidently out of gear with Balfour and is turning towards Chamberlain, but is generally defiant in his attitude towards the party. If they pass him over in the forthcoming legal appointments he will be yet more of a rebel. He suffers alike personally and politically from living in an intellectually low-standard atmosphere. He never uses his brains except for his money-making law business. He thinks that all problems can be solved by a clever compromise improvised on the spot, between antagonistic interests and proposals, reads few books and those he does read are stale and commonplace works. He sees no one but his legal friends and his relations and children. It is characteristic that in ordering some hundred new books to fill new bookcases he sent for two rather badly devised 'series' on 'towns' and 'countries', and a few old stagers in the way of standard histories. It does not seem to occur to him to wish to study thoroughly any particular question, or period, or country, or even to read the new controversial books which bring knowledge and thought up to date in various departments. . . . Alas, for the loss of Theresa! It is exactly in the employment of a hardworking professional man's leisure that the companionship of a charming wife is of untold use. Still, he has the satisfaction of professional success and the happiness of a close and devoted relationship with his five children. . . . In all probability, too, he will get the prize he is looking for – the solicitor-generalship. It would be bad business for Balfour to pass him over for a personal friend like Alfred Lyttelton, who is manifestly his inferior at the Bar. And perhaps, if he attains the nominal position, he will not perceive that he has had no real influence in shaping the course of events.

257

14 October. [41 Grosvenor Road]

All our Radical friends bitter or sullen with us over Sidney's support of the Education Bill. Certainly if he had political ambitions it would have been a suicidal policy on his part. Fortunately we enjoy the incomparable luxury of freedom from all care for ourselves. We are secure in our love for one another and we are absolutely content with our present daily life as far as our own interest and happiness is concerned. Well we may be! I have a constant wonder whether we are earning our excellent maintenance. Sidney certainly does, assuming that his work is in the right direction, for he is at it from 9 o'clock in the morning continuously until 7.30 and once or twice a week lectures in the evening as well. For myself I peg along every morning at the book for three or four hours, sometimes putting in half an hour in the afternoon. But generally I find it pays better to do nothing in the afternoons except take exercise, specially as almost every day we have someone to lunch or to dine to talk shop. We have had the whole professoriat of the School (twenty-five) to dinner in detachments, and a selection of the students in afterwards. As president of the Union, I am trying to develop the social side of the School and have arranged to be 'At Home' to students on alternate Wednesdays next term.

10 November. [41 Grosvenor Road]

The School has opened with éclat. There are now actually at work five hundred students and the staff is hard put to it to meet the new strains. The Railway Companies have at last come into it with a determination to make use of the lecturing both as an educational training and as a test of capacity of their staff of clerks. For the last three years the Great Western Railway has sent some thirty or forty and paid their fees, but the attendances have been perfunctory and usually tailed off towards the end of the term. . . . The Great Northern General Manager, at the instigation of Lord Rosebery (who is said to talk of 'our School' at the meetings of the Directors) has had a long talk with Hewins and arranged to send a contingent to the classes and to require them to pass examinations before being promoted. If this precedent be followed by other business undertakings and by public bodies, we shall have done a good deal to promote efficiency in administration.

Hewins of course is a little bit over-confident and elated, but that is his temperament. He inspires confidence in men of affairs and has, in fact, more the business than the academic mind; though sufficiently intellectual to state concrete facts in terms of general principles. His weak point is lack of accuracy and rapidity in the despatch of business. He is slovenly in such matters as proof-correcting and dilatory in getting certain things done. But there is usually method in his carelessness and things left undone or mistaken are usually matters about which his judgement has been overruled or to which his aims are slightly different from those of the Governors. . . .

But he and Sidney, and to a lesser extent, I myself, make a good working trio. The whole internal organization of the School is left to him with suggestions from Sidney. The whole financial side is in Sidney's hands, whilst my domain has been roping in influential supporters from among old friends and connections. Every Tuesday Hewins lunches here and we discuss the affairs of the School in all its aspects. He consults Sidney about the curriculum, Sidney tells him the requirements for securing L.C.C. Technical Education Board and University support. I submit to both my little schemes for entertaining various persons likely to be useful.

Almost every week since early in October we have had dinners of eight to ten – of lecturers and governors, likely friends and supporters; and students to lunch. The rest of our social life, which is both lively and interesting, is deliberately designed to help forward the University, the Progressive party on the L.C.C. and to a slight extent to give Haldane and his friends a friendly lift whenever an opportunity comes that way. The Liberal League, notably Haldane and Rosebery, have been good friends to us, and we feel bound to return in kind.

Haldane and Sidney are constantly co-operating in educational matters. Haldane has taken a bold line in supporting the government Bill and breaking from his political friends. His position as a party politician was so damaged before that I doubt whether it has been much worsened. Undoubtedly if Rosebery goes under and the Campbell-Bannerman lot romp in, Haldane is pretty well done for, unless they should be desperately short of men. On the other hand, he has improved his status as a leader of opinion, has shown that he knows and is keen about the higher branches of education. And the higher branches of education is one of the coming questions. It seems likely that the beginning of the twentieth century will be noted as the starting point of the new form of university training and university research – the application of the scientific method to the facts of daily life, politics and business. In this 'movement' Haldane will have played one of the principal though unseen parts. His career is interesting as combining that of a considerable lawyer, an education reformer and an intriguing politician (though the intrigues are always to promote a cause, never to push himself). It is a paradox that a mind that is essentially metaphysical, laying stress on the non-material side of human thought and feeling, should have been as a matter of fact chiefly engaged in promoting applied physical science.

Rosebery is not making way in the country and is, I imagine, having a bad time with himself. He has no grip of anything except 'appearances'. He is so intent on trying to find out which course will *appear right* to the ordinary man of affairs that he forgets altogether to think out which course will work out best in social results. He seems positively frightened at the thought of any such enquiry. Publicly and privately Sidney has pressed on the Liberal League the necessity of its directors making up their minds as to what they would do if they had the power. Rosebery and Haldane hang back – they do not want to be committed. 'Quite so,' says Sidney. 'Don't publish anything or decide on any course, but let us at least have the facts at our command and know all the alternative courses.' He is, however, a voice in the wilderness.

Meanwhile we are hammering out our conclusions and throwing them at the head of the public in the form of massive historical analysis. It is a time, we think, for big artillery in the way of books. But hard thinking takes time. For a whole month I played about with propositions and arguments, submitting them, one after another, to Sidney, before we jointly discovered our own principles of Poor Law administration. And each of the services will have to be taken up in the same exhaustive manner! How could we do it, if working together were not, in itself, delightful. It is a curious process, this joint thinking; we throw the ball of thought on to the other, each one of us resting, judging, inventing in turn. And we are not satisfied until the conclusion satisfies completely and finally both minds. It is interesting too, to note that we never discover our principles until after we have gone through the whole labour, not only of collecting, classifying and marshalling our facts, but of sifting down in front of them until we discover some series of hypotheses which accounts for all the facts. This final process seems to me to be not at all unlike testing in a laboratory, or manipulating figures in the working-out of a mathematical problem. It is experimentation, and constantly testing the correspondence between the idea and the fact. I do most of the experimentation and Sidney watches and judges the results, accepting some, rejecting others. It is he who finds the formula that expresses our conclusions.

Lady Horner (1860–1940), was Frances Graham, daughter of a wealthy Liberal M.P. A great beauty, she was a friend of Haldane and a member of 'The Souls'. She was married to the barrister Sir John Horner and had two daughters, Cicely, and Katherine, who married Asquith's son Raymond in 1907. Sir Owen Roberts (1835–1915) was Master of the Worshipful Company of Cloth Founders and later High Sheriff of Caernarvonshire. Sir John Dickson Poynder (1866–1936) was a Tory landowner, M.P. and a Moderate member of the L.C.C. Sir Frederic Lacy Robinson (1840–1911) was an Inland Revenue official who was also an L.C.C. Moderate. Sir Herbert Wilberforce (1864–1941) was a London magistrate and an L.C.C. Progressive. Thomas Wiles (1861–1951) was a City merchant, a member of the L.C.C. 1899–1907, Whip for the Progressive Party, and a Liberal M.P. after 1906. Henry Devenish Harben (1874–1967) inherited a substantial shareholding in the Prudential Insurance Company. He stood for Parliament as a Tory candidate in 1900 and as a Labour representative in 1906. He supported many radical causes; he was a prominent Fabian for many years, a friend to the Webbs, and one of the backers of the *New Statesman* in its early years. Isaac Mitchell (1867–1952) was a leading official of the Boilermakers' Society. Sir Edwin Perry (1856–1938) was a distinguished physician at Guy's Hospital. He later became vice-chancellor of the University of London.

28 November. [41 Grosvenor Road]
I took the Prime Minister in to dinner! I say 'took' because he was so obviously delivered over into my hands by my kindly hostess, who wished me to make as much use as possible of the one-and-a-quarter hours he had free from the House. It was a little party of eight at the house of the charming Mrs Horner – high priestess of 'The Souls' in their palmy days, now somewhat elderly and faded but gracious to those she accepts as 'distinguished'. The other guests were Lady Elcho and Haldane, Mr Horner and a handsome daughter.

Balfour has the charm of genuine modesty and unself-consciousness, and that evening he seemed in earnest about education. He is delightfully responsive intellectually, a man with ever-open mind, too open perhaps, seeing that on no question has it been sufficiently closed by study and thought to have developed principles. There comes a time in life when surely the mind should be 'made up' conclusively as to the particular questions with which it is mainly concerned; man's work in life is action and not enquiry. Balfour's intellect has not the organic quality; there is no determinate result from the combination of his reason with his knowledge of facts. His opinions shift uneasily from side to side, the one permanent bias being in favour of personal refinement of thought and feeling. But I doubt whether he has any clear notion of how he would attempt to bring about this refinement in other people, except by personal example and influence. On the other hand he has no bias in favour of *laissez-faire*. Action or inaction are open questions, and it is a chapter of accidents on which side he throws himself. But he intends to work on the side which at the moment he *thinks right*, not merely on the side that will appear right to other people, which I fear is Lord Rosebery's predicament. All this elaborate analysis based on one hour.

I set myself to amuse and interest him, but seized every opportunity to insinuate sound doctrine and information as to the position of London education. Sidney says I managed skilfully, but then he is a partial judge! We found ourselves in accord on most questions. Perhaps that is only another way of saying that Arthur Balfour is a sympathetic and attractive person who easily tunes his conversation to other minds. I can understand how colleagues in the House of Commons forgive his incapacity for transacting business. The flavour of his personality is delightful.

At last the section on Poor Law is finished, at least as far as I am concerned. . . . Now we have turned our minds to police and regulation generally. . . Meanwhile Sidney is working full speed at University, T.E.B. and School administration and has, moreover, a brief for Liverpool University to which he gives scraps of his attention. It is his first and I should think his last brief: he appears before a Privy Council committee with C.A. Cripps against him! I am entertaining extensively – a Conservative dinner and evening party on the 20th and a 'Limp' dinner and reception on the 27th. Fortunately my two-meal system (no breakfast and a light supper) suits me exactly. I have never been so fit before – perhaps if I had the self-denial to cut off the coffee and tobacco I might be fitter still. But it is hard to break at once with all self-indulgence. . . . I have not the physical courage to cut myself off from luxuries, luxuries which do not seem to affect me but which in all probability diminish my capacity for work. The medical profession have made the downward way of self-indulgence easy, and the upward way of asceticism difficult by their lack of courage and knowledge.

Three dinners and two evening parties at one's house in eight days is severe! But it seemed desirable to give a Conservative L.C.C. dinner and London University reception; and also a 'Limp' dinner and 'Limp' reception. Then there was a dinner to Lady Elcho to acknowledge her kindness to us in Gloucestershire and her introduction to Balfour, an introduction which may have good results. So I asked her to meet John Burns, the Shaws, H.G. Wells and Asquith. John Burns took the palm: his unselfconscious exuberance, dramatic faculty and warmth of feeling amounted to brilliancy. He gave us vivid pictures of prison and other episodes, views on the army, Eton and the aristocracy, on working-class and middle-class life, all fresh and interesting with a certain romantic sentiment for what was ancient and distinguished. Shaw and Wells were not at their ease – GBS was jerkily egotistical and paradoxical though he behaved well in encouraging Burns to take the stage. Wells was rather silent; when he spoke he tried too hard to be clever, he never let himself go. Asquith was simply dull. He is disheartened with politics, has no feeling of independent initiative and is baffled by Rosebery, snubs and is snubbed by Campbell-Bannerman. He has worked himself into an unreal opposition to the Education Bill. He is not really convinced of the iniquity or unwisdom of the bill he is denouncing. He eats and drinks too much and lives in a too enervating social atmosphere to have either strenuousness or spontaneity. Clearly he is looking to the money-making Bar for his occupation in life. As a lawyer he is essentially common quality, [with] no interest in, or understanding of, legal principles, no ingenuity or originality in making new influences or adapting old rules to new conditions. However, he is under no delusion about himself. He has resigned himself to missing leadership.

The dinner was successful and 'thrilling' – Lady Elcho on the new sensation of meeting such strange forms of distinction as Burns, Wells, Shaws 'at the house of the Sidney Webbs'.

The educational and 'Moderate' dinner consisted of Sir Alfred Lyall and wife, Sir Owen Roberts (Clerk to the Clothworkers and an excellent friend of ours) and wife, Sir John Dickson Poynder (Moderate L.C.C. and Conservative M.P., a simple-hearted public-spirited country gentleman of attractive mien), Sir Lacy Robinson (L.C.C. Moderate, former civil servant and new Governor of the School), Mrs J.R. Green and Beatrice Chamberlain and Charles Booth (whom I happened to meet in the street the day before). After dinner we had some thirty or forty of the educationalists and university menfolk – Sir John Gorst and some eight Moderate L.C.C. They all knew each other, or wanted to know each other, so that talk was incessant.

Finally we had one 'Limp' dinner yesterday – Sir Edward Grey, Haldane, B. Russell, Wilberforce and Wiles (two Progressive L.C.C. men) Harben, (a promising young Liberal Leaguer), Isaac Mitchell (one of the ablest of the younger trade union officials) and Perry (the most influential of the University 'medicals' and a Liberal Progressive). Lion Phillimore the only lady to keep me company. In the evening some sixty men came in – trade union officials, Progressive L.C.C., journalists and 'Limp' M.P.s. I introduced vigorously and they all chatted and chattered – sometimes in confidential tête-à-têtes, sometimes in groups. Haldane, who had dined with us, chaffed me about the 'resurrection' of 'The Souls' in Grosvenor Road. Mrs Horner came to see what was up, and was glad to make the acquaintance of H.J. Mackinder who is, to a small circle of knowing ones, beginning to loom as a coming man.

The interest of the evening to me was a long talk during dinner with Sir Edward Grey. Like Balfour he is a man of exquisite 'flavour'. He is high-minded, simple, kindly and *wise* without being able or clever, an ideal *element* in a Cabinet containing some strong master mind. But he is not the master mind. I doubt whether it would be physically or mentally possible for him to work eight hours a day for, say, ten months of the year. He has neither the knowledge, the depth of feeling or the personal grip on life to have a strong will or deeply rooted convictions. His temperament is an exquisite poise, far above human passions and human prejudices, in an atmosphere rarefied by public spirit, fastidious honour and widely diffused human fellowship – essentially a passive and receptive nature revelling in the beauties of nature, the interest of books and the charm of one or two intimate friendships with men and women of like character in simple and refined surroundings.

Sir William Anson (1843–1914), a distinguished jurist, was Parliamentary Secretary to the Board of Education from 1902–05. Walter Long (1854–1924) was a Tory M.P. who was president of the Local Government Board 1900–05 and he set up the Metropolitan Water Board in the face of bitter opposition. The Marquis of Londonderry (1852–1915) was president of the first Board of Education under the new Education Act. Nonconformist opposition to the Act was breaking out into a campaign of passive resistance and non-compliance.

[?] *December*. [41 Grosvenor Road]
Morant dined here last night alone to talk over chances of London Education Bill – wearied out with the autumn campaign and the

prospect of having to superintend the working out of the new Education Act with a rotten staff and a hostile minority in each district determined to wreck the Act. He says that Balfour is furious with the Church and the Church disconsolate with its bargain, Londonderry a bull in a china shop and Anson too academically clever to be a comfortable fifth wheel in the coach. He had drafted a bill for London of two clauses applying the Act – 'quite satisfactorily to you', but alas! Walter Long, elated with his triumph over the consitution of the Water Board, says he will be damned before he sees the L.C.C. the education authority. Morant doubts whether anyone wants any particular change sufficiently to get discordant views into line – the Church hesitates as to the worthwhileness, the Unionist members are terrified at the N.U.T. on the one hand, and the Tory political worker on the other. No member of the Cabinet is keen to enhance the dignity of the L.C.C. though all except Long realize that the borough councils would be impossible. But Long is a loud-voiced persistent creature who talks his colleagues down at Cabinet and committee meetings and is in touch with the commoner kind of obscurant Tory. So matters look dark and the present unsatisfactory situation is likely to persist, at least for the forthcoming year.

A little breeze with Hewins. He wanted to jump Sidney into increasing his salary from £600 (it was raised from £400 only six months ago) to £800. Sidney agreed to an extra £100 to cover unusual expenses, but refused to make even this permanent. So long as nearly the whole income comes from the L.C.C. (either through the University, £2,400, or through the T.E.B. £1,200) he feels that it would risk all to double the salary of the Director, a personal friend, in twelve months. It is, of course, a delicate position. The School has had an extraordinary amount of support from the L.C.C. owing to Sidney's influence. But most councillors regard it as his 'fad' (it is called the 'Webberies') and have acquiesced not on the ground of their own faith in the institution but on account of their confidence in him. It has, indeed, been a sort of 'confidence trick' – we believe fully justified – but still there are limits to this sort of influence, both ethical and practical! Hewins, who has a swelled head over the increase of students and visions of the whole City coming to be educated under his direction (and who, I suspect, has spent £300 more this year on the basis of the extra £200), was quite improperly insistent and had to be gently but firmly reminded of the actual dependence of the School on Sidney's influence in the L.C.C. However, he seems to have taken

Sidney's long and decidedly paternal letter in good part. He has one great defect – perhaps only one important defect – he lacks *veracity*. He is always deceiving himself and trying to manipulate others through an *ex parte* statement of facts, which he generally manages to believe, at least for a time. His conceit is only the defect of his great quality – hardworking optimism – and does little harm except that it backs up his lack of veracity. I am convinced that Hewins is habitually 'castle-building', always forgetting the collapse of one castle because he is so busy constructing another. As GBS says, 'Hewins is mad!' One of the delights of living with Sidney is his absolute sanity – a sanity and sense of perspective which keeps him free from all elation at his little successes. He errs on the other side. He is perpetually apprehensive. This does not prevent his undertaking ventures but makes him wary and tactful in carrying them out. That is why he finds my audacity and pluck and my familiarity with the risks and chances of big enterprises – the result of being brought up in the midst of capitalist speculation – so comforting and helpful. Father taught me the habit of mind of starting many things and being satisfied if one in ten succeeded, of being 'detached', though persistent in 'trying all things'.

This autumn has been thoroughly satisfactory, though today I feel worn out and nostalgic. I have done my morning's work swiftly and without interruption with very few days off, and have kept up the social side of our work besides. Now we are off with our trunk of books and MSS. material for Overstrand for a month's quiet work in perfectly healthy surroundings, our ideal recreation.

ᔆ 1903 ᔆ

The Webbs were staying on the estate of Lord and Lady Battersea at Overstrand, near Cromer. Raymond Asquith was visiting his friend, Lord Battersea (Cyril Flower) and had tea with the Webbs. 'Webb is like a pawn-broker,' he wrote, and his wife 'a woman of great beauty (though forty-four) and charm: she has a most lustrous eye, most graceful figure, and any quantity of intelligence. She never says silly things about the lower classes as most Socialists do . . . ' None of Shaw's plays had yet had a good run. He called *Man and Superman* 'one of the most colossal efforts of the human mind'.

16 January. Overstrand
The last afternoon here. . . . A happy time; spent the first ten days

sorting and pondering over the material on Vagrancy and classifying the subject under 'devices', Sidney meanwhile clearing up odds and ends of work. . . . This would take up our mornings – four hours. In the afternoons there would be a walk on the beach or more rarely a ride, and then a quiet read at eighteenth-century literature. Sidney must have devoured some fifty or sixty books. I only accomplished two or three, together with a few novels borrowed from Lady Battersea. Half a dozen times we went in for a chat with our neighbours in their resplendent villa, or Lady Battersea came in to us. She is a good and true-natured woman and quite intelligent, though like all these 'Society Dames' quite incapable of anything but chit-chat, flying from point to point. He is distinctly objectionable, a man without either intellect or character, and I should imagine with many bad habits of body and mind – a middle-class Croesus, ex-Adonis, ennobled for party purposes, a most unpleasant type of functionless wealth. They live in a gorgeous villa filled to overflowing with objects of virtue and art, with no individuality or taste. There are no children. He has no public spirit. They are both overfed. If it were not for her genuine kind-heartedness and good intention the household would be positively repulsive. . . .

But we did not depend on the Batterseas for companionship. For the first time for many years the three old friends – Sidney, Bernard Shaw and Graham Wallas – spent a week together with their wives as chorus, the Shaws at the big hotel near by and the Wallases with us. Three delightful evenings we spent listening to GBS reading his new work – the *Superman*. To me it seems a great work, quite the biggest thing he has done. He has found his *form*, a play which is not a play but only a combination of essay treaties, interlude, lyric – all the different forms illustrating the same central idea, like a sonata manifests a scheme of melody and harmony. I was all the more delighted with it, as I had not been impressed with the bits I had heard before and Sidney had reported unfavourably of the play itself. Possibly the unexpectedness of the success had made me over-value it, a reaction from a current in my mind of depreciation of GBS. Then I am so genuinely delighted at his choice of subject. We cannot touch the subject of human breeding – it is not ripe for the mere industry of induction, and yet I realize that it is the most important of all questions, this breeding of the right sort of man. GBS's audacious genius can reach out to it.

Graham was somewhat depressed, physically and mentally, and

though affectionate and pleasant to us he has a deeply-rooted suspicion that Sidney is playing false with regard to religious education. He wants all religious teaching abolished. As Sidney is not himself a 'religionist' Graham thinks that he too should wish it swept away. Politically this seems to Sidney impossible, whilst I do not desire it even if it were possible. So between us we are prepared for a working agreement with the mammon of ecclesiasticism. Poor dear Wallas consequently sees this working agreement writ large in every act of the T.E.B., however irrelevant it may be to the religious issue (an issue which appears to Sidney to affect only a minute part of public education). Whether the T.E.B. takes action or omits to take action on any question there is always in Graham's eyes the priest behind the policy. This suspicion makes frank co-operation between Sidney and our old friend impossible, and though personal relations remain affectionate and appreciative, I fear there must be some official friction if not actually hostility. As Sidney's side is bound to win, though possibly Sidney himself will be sacrificed, it is to be hoped that Graham will retire from educational administration. He tried to talk GBS round to his view but failed. GBS is too rootedly sceptical about all alternative philosophies to be inclined to oust Christianity by *force majeure*.

This year has been both happy and fruitful. We have got on well with the book, though the task grows bigger and more complicated as we toil to complete it. We find ourselves really writing the internal history of the eighteenth century, and for this purpose I am reading eighteenth-century literature, trying to discover what were the good features of the time. . . . But what a lot of the eighteenth century survives in the twentieth! Progress seems to have been made chiefly by the lower-middle class and upper artisans. . . .

Alfred Harmsworth (1865–1922), later Lord Northcliffe, founded the *Daily Mail* in 1896 and the *Daily Mirror* in 1903. He was the creator of modern journalism and at the peak of his success in the first decade of the century. George Earl Buckle (1854–1935) was Editor of *The Times* 1884–1912. H.L.W. Lawson (1862–1933), later Viscount Burnham, was the owner of the *Daily Telegraph*, Liberal M.P. and member of the L.C.C. Henry Spenser Wilkinson (1853–1937) was professor of military history at Oxford and a writer on the *Morning Post*.

1 February. [41 Grosvenor Road]
Sidney hard at work making public opinion as to the Educational Authority. He interviewed Harmsworth and his 'boy' editor

268

[William Kennedy] and the former handed over the direction of the campaign in the *Daily Mail* to Sidney. He has seen Buckle of *The Times* and Lawson of the *Telegraph* and Spencer Wilkinson of the *Morning Post*, and he is stimulating the Church and educationalists generally to put pressure on Balfour. Haldane reports that it is still undecided, Walter Long holding out for a borough Educational Authority, or at any rate a majority of borough councillors on the L.C.C. Committee. Progressives of L.C.C. sulky, some jealous of Sidney, others conscientiously opposed to any compromise with regard to church schools. If L.C.C. finds itself as the Authority it will be, I believe, entirely due to Sidney, to the excellent reputation of the T.E.B. under his guidance and to his persistent efforts to stir up public opinion in favour of the L.C.C. But all this means Sidney's distraction from the book. And as it also entails a good deal of entertaining, it is a serious drain on my energy. However, the aim is worth the labour. From the standpoint of the book the worst is that if we succeed it will result in a big, difficult and continuous task for Sidney. All the more reason for me to keep in the highest degree of efficiency. Abstemiousness of body and calmness of mind the one way.

Beatrice quotes the last stanza of Emily Brontë's poem beginning 'No coward soul is mine', written in 1846. Charlotte Brontë noted that some of the amended words were 'the last lines my sister Emily ever wrote'.

2 February. [41 Grosvenor Road]
Journeyed down to Brighton to see the poor old philosopher, or rather on the chance of seeing him, for he thought himself too ill to risk asking me to come down. Found him lying on the sofa, wretched and depressed, much aged and unhealthy looking . . . . Poor old man: the last ten or even twenty years he has been the prey to demons of egotism and self-deception, demons bred by an utterly false and inadequate conception of human conduct. The last quarter of his life has been a tragic parody of a Theory of Personal Rights.

Read through Haldane's *Pathway to Reality* on the journey to and fro – out of friendship for the author. To me his metaphysic seems an attempt to 'intellectualize' the emotional assertion of a Beyond which is bound to fail. What is called 'verification' is impossible; there is no conceivable external test of the truth of your thought, and therefore no way of convincing those who do not think the same thought as you. . . . Emily Brontë's 'last lines' are to me a more convincing *Pathway to Reality:*

There is not room for Death,
    Nor atom that his might could render void
Thou — Thou art Being and Breath
    And what THOU art may never be destroyed

Cosmo Gordon Lang (1864-1945) was Bishop of Stepney until 1908, when he became Archbishop of York: he later was Archbishop of Canterbury. The notion that borough councils would be dominated by members of the National Union of Teachers (N.U.T.), sympathetic to Liberal and Nonconformist interests, was one of the propaganda squibs used by the Webbs to circumvent such Tories as Walter Long, who wanted these councils rather than the Progressive L.C.C. to run London's schools.

25 February. [41 Grosvenor Road]
A succession of dinners re. Education Bill, mostly Conservative and Church. Among our guests the Bishop of Stepney, a remarkable man who will go far. He is Creighton without either his defects or his finest qualities but, for that very reason, far more effective as an ecclesiastical statesman. The new kind of ecclesiastic with his eye on the *new social classes,* intent on winning for the Church democratic support. An Erastian in doctrine, anxious to see the 39 Articles and all other inconveniently obsolete documents regarded simply as formulae of historical interest but not binding on the conscience. The Dean of Westminster [Joseph Robinson], a scholar and mystic, is more attractive to me, but not nearly so efficient.

Met Sir William Anson at Alfred Cripps's (our brother-in-law has come out as an L.C.C. man); a pleasant subtle-minded don, a perfect head to a college but singularly out of place in an administrative position. Far more interested in discussing the relation of the Privy Council to the local authorities of the seventeenth and eighteenth centuries than the proper authority for dealing today with London's education. Indeed one felt he knew so little of the elements of the latter subject that it was barely worth while talking to him. Still, it is desirable to have him not 'agin us' and he must be asked to dinner. The interests of the School and the University and the smooth working of the L.C.C. have all to be considered in our little entertainments. Meanwhile we try to get a morning's work, however perfunctory, at the book.

We often long for that cottage in the country and the peaceful existence of a student life. We sometimes wonder whether such an existence would not be, in the long run, more useful. But then someone must do the rough-and-tumble work of government. It is a tiresome fact that, to get things done in what one considers the best way, entails so much – to speak plainly – of intrigue. There is no such thing as spontaneous public opinion; it all has to be manufactured from a Centre of Conviction and Energy radiating through persons, sometimes losing itself in an unsympathetic medium, at other times gaining additional force in such an agent as the Bishop of Stepney or the *Daily Mail*. Of course there is always the element of 'sport' in this life of agitation, watching the ideas one starts, like, for instance, 'the dominance of the N.U.T. over borough councils', wending their ways through all sorts of sources to all sorts of places and turning up quite unexpectedly as allies in overthrowing counter interests and arguments. It is fortunate when one happens to believe in one's own arguments: one always does in a fashion, the most one does is to suppress the qualification. Is that 'debasing the currency' or is it permissible to accept the position of an advocate to tell the truth but not the whole truth? As a matter of fact, with regard to administrative work, we plunge without hesitation on to the position of an advocate pledged only to display the arguments which tell in favour of the cause we believe in. In our scientific work, however, we honestly seek to tell the truth, the whole truth and nothing but the truth, a distinction in standards that puzzles and perplexes me.

2 March. [41 Grosvenor Road]
I took the chair for H.G. Wells's lecture on 'Areas of Administration' at the Students' Union. Like ourselves he is impressed with the need for some scientific adjustment of units of administration to functions or services, the obvious absurdity of Newcastle and Jarrow, for instance, being separate units of tramway administration instead of the whole of Tyneside. He suggested some ideal area for all purposes based on the function of locomotion. In summing up the debate I threw out, on the spur of the moment, the suggestion of sweeping away all fixed areas, of instituting one unit of representation: e.g. one representative for every ten thousand persons for all purposes whatsoever and of combining these units with each other according to function, in many different groups of governing bodies. Thus the five representatives of Deptford would sit together for street cleansing and lighting purposes, would sit with the other London representatives for Education, Main Drainage, and with these and those of the home counties for Water, etc. etc. The grouping would be done by Order in

Council according to the service and according to fixed or changing conditions with regard to population, industry, climate etc. The local government, through the country, would thus be fluid, indefinitely elastic, the same units grouped in any number of ways. Each constituency would fix its eyes on the one man and take precious good care to get a good representative. This would involve a great development of statutory committees with co-opted members, as some of the groups would be too large in membership to admit of direct administration by the whole body. Also it might be necessary in rural districts to provide for the election or nomination of purely subordinate administrative bodies who would manage the local affairs under the supervision of the large body. GBS was delighted with the suggestion. There may be some grain of usefulness in it.

Walter Leaf (1852–1925) was a banker and classical scholar who was a Progressive on the L.C.C.

14 March. [41 Grosvenor Road]
The L.C.C. Progressives or some of them are playing the fool about the London Education Authority. So determined are they to 'spite the government' and so anxious for a good battle-cry that they are steering straight into a 'Water Board' authority for Education. A little clique headed by J.R. MacDonald are fighting all they know how Sidney's influence on the T.E.B., and some of the weaker of the rank and file, somewhat jealous of Sidney, are playing into their hands. Sidney thought it better to offer himself to the Progressive cause as chairman of the T.E.B. this year in order to facilitate negotiations with the government, but has given it to be understood that he does not wish to be chairman except with the full consent of the Progressive members on the Board.

J.R. MacDonald has set to work to detach them from him and has succeeded with the Labour men (who are secularist, *ad hoc*, and anti-Higher Education) and one or two other middle-class members who are ambitious to be chairman themselves. It remains to be seen whether he carries the caucus tomorrow. Sidney has refrained from canvassing and stood on his dignity – we both thought that if the L.C.C. Progressives deserted him it would be better to play for a 'reaction' in his favour by having an inferior man elected chairman under whom the Board would chafe. Of course the dissension will injure the chances of the Bill being on the right lines, as it will be open to the Moderates to say to the government that the one good man ready to carry out the Act has been rejected by his own party. It is strange that these personal enemies don't see that Sidney's position will be immensely stronger on a mixed Board of borough councillors, L.C.C. and outsiders, than in a genuine L.C.C. committee and that if he were playing for his own dominance he would go straight for that. Meanwhile it will be a big misfortune for democratic government, even of the kind they believe most in, if the L.C.C. is put on one side as unfit to be the Education Authority.

I have been pondering over the question whether I could have done anything to stop the 'slump in Webbs' on the Progressive side. Of course our attention has been absorbed in getting hold of forces in the enemies' camp and our frequent coming and going has excited suspicion on our own. They have not the wit to see that if a government is in power with an overwhelming majority it is no use fighting it, at least not unless the other way has proved unavailing. Whether or not he is elected chairman tomorrow I shall turn my attention seriously to the Progressive member of the T.E.B. when we come back from Longfords and see what can be done to counteract J.R. MacDonald's machinations. I have suggested that whatever happens Sidney adopts an attitude of beneficent helpfulness. In only one eventuality would he fight the Progressive caucus – that is if J.R. MacDonald got himself nominated for chairman. In that case Sidney would propose Dr Leaf, or failing him stand himself. But J.R. MacDonald is too shrewd to try that little game.

The complaint against Sidney resolves itself into this: 1) He is 'in' with the government; 2) He might sacrifice the interests of primary to secondary and university education; 3) He ignores the 'religious' difficulty and is willing to be impartial between Anglican and 'undenominational' Christianity. Number 1 and number 3 are true in essence; number 2 is not true, at least in our most impartial moments we believe not. We don't believe you can raise the standard of elementary education and save it from mere mechanical efficiency unless you have the university in organic connection with it, unless you have mobility between all classes of teachers from the assistant master of the present elementary school to the research professor. The same with the students. The university must be open to them in fact as well as in theory. It lacks imagination to think that elementary education can be stimulating and progressive except as the broad base to the higher learning. Those who feel themselves specifically the representatives of Labour fail through lack of ambition for their own clients and, be it added, through self-complacency with themselves as ideal reformers of society.

A.J. Shepheard and A.L. Leon were Progressive members of the L.C.C. William Crooks (1852–1921), mayor of Poplar in 1901, won a notable by-election as the Labour candidate for Woolwich in 1903.

15 March. [41 Grosvenor Road]
The 'slump' in Webbs proves to be serious. Sidney was defeated only four to three in a little caucus of Progressives on the T.E.B. but then the others had not troubled to turn up or had stayed away purposely – which means indifference if not hostility. The Board after a little spluttering acquiesced in the election of Shepheard and Leon, both *ad hoc* anti-voluntary-school men, but not personally hostile to Sidney. There are indications too that this feeling of antagonism is not confined to this little group – the rank and file of the Progressives do not want the L.C.C. to be the authority and they think that Sidney with his press and backstairs influence is bringing it about. The Crooks election [at Woolwich] has swelled the Progressives' heads and they feel inclined to fight for an *ad hoc* body and unsectarian education. The position has been worsened by an indiscretion of Dr Garnett (which would not have occurred if Sidney had been chairman) in circulating a memorandum in favour of a definite scheme of L.C.C. administration. Everyone believes Sidney to have had a hand in it.

But there is [such] a very real cleavage between our views and those of the rank-and-file Radicals that I do not see my way honestly to bridge it. We are not in favour of the cruder form of democracy. And we *do* believe in expenditure on services which will benefit other classes besides the working class and which will open the way to working-men to become fit to govern, not simply to represent their own class; and we are in favour of economy as well as expenditure. But then what is the good of having means of one's own and some intelligence unless one is prepared to advocate what is unpopular!

N.W. Hubbard was a Progressive member of the L.C.C. T. McKinnon Wood (1855–1927) was leader of the Progressives on the L.C.C. and in 1906 became a Liberal M.P. John S. Sandars (1869–1934) was private secretary to Arthur Balfour from 1892–1905. Dr John Clifford (1836–1923) was a Baptist minister and the most powerful figure in the Nonconformist churches. T.J. Macnamara

(1861–1931), a strong Nonconformist Liberal M.P., was the editor of the *Schoolmaster*.

27 March. [41 Grosvenor Road]

Matters not much mended. Hubbard, an honest Nonconformist rank-and-file member of the L.C.C., had put down a resolution in favour of an *ad hoc* authority some weeks ago. McKinnon Wood and Collins, both in their hearts anxious for the L.C.C. authority as unifying London government, called a party meeting to try and get a decision against bringing the question up before the government produced their Bill. With great skill Collins succeeded in getting the party to vote thirty to twenty on a non-committal resolution in favour of a directly elected body (understood to mean the L.C.C.) but blaming the government for attacking School Boards and subsidizing voluntary schools and, by an overwhelming majority, for adjourning Hubbard's resolution. Meanwhile the government, scared by Woolwich and Rye [by-elections], took fright. Morant wrote begging Sidney to let him know the result of the meeting; Londonderry's private secretary came down to ask permission to attend with a shorthand writer, the L.C.C. debate so that the Cabinet might have a correct and complete version of the L.C.C. views. Last Tuesday the Council as a whole prevented the taking of Hubbard's resolution by talking at length on other matters. Sidney went at Haldane's request to see Sandars and the Conservative Whip and to encourage them to introduce the L.C.C. Bill. But today we learn in confidence that the Cabinet yesterday decided that it would not introduce their Bill giving L.C.C. the whole of Education and complete control of its committee unless they could, by this means, secure the support of the L.C.C. Progressives. Failing this it is to be the *status quo* and the settlement of London education left over to some future government. Now it remains to be seen whether the official leaders of the Progressives are willing and able to get Hubbard's resolution negatived. Sidney does not believe that they can carry the rank and file with them even if they plank themselves down on the policy of L.C.C. authority.

Haldane tells us that 'the rot' has set in severely within the Cabinet. They are panic-stricken – all except 'Joe', who holds himself somewhat detached from the rest and lets them stew in their juice of muddle and mistake. They have been so shaken by Woolwich and Rye and the rising tide of Nonconformist N.U.T. agitation in London that they were actually considering the making of an *ad hoc* authority for London – a complete capitulation. However, they were shaken out of that by Sidney's assertion that not only would Clifford and Macnamara dominate such an authority but it would light up the flame throughout the country against the Act by all sorts and conditions of malcontents. So they were prepared to throw themselves into the arms of the L.C.C., if they had been asked, by so doing to get a rest from virulent opposition. The L.C.C. has not been able to rise to the emergency! Possibly it has proved that it would not be equal to running the concern. The success of the T.E.B. is largely owing to the fact that Sidney removed it from the first out of the practical control of the L.C.C. But he lost 'consent' in gaining 'efficiency'.

Gave my presidential address to the Students' Union which cost a good four days to prepare, on the relative function of the Investigator, the Man of Affairs and the Idealist. . . .

3 April. [41 Grosvenor Road]
The Progressives in a better frame of mind. The 'Limps' acted foolishly in defying the party meeting and moving the adjournment of the standing orders to discuss Hubbard's motion for an *ad hoc* body. They were voted down by 67 to 20, a vote which had all the appearance of a rejection of the *ad hoc* authority. Meanwhile we believe that the Cabinet has decided to trust the L.C.C. in a thoroughgoing fashion, since Anson sent for Sidney to consult him as to the day the Act had better come into force. What exactly the Progressives will do if they find themselves 'willy-nilly' the Education Authority in the government Bill to be introduced next Tuesday, we do not know. A bare dozen of the party are in favour of it, and half those dare not vote for it. General feeling among them that it will be a troublesome job and may upset Progressive politics. Also the leading Progressives have got a bit tired of local administration and are looking to Parliament as their proper sphere of action. It will be interesting to see whether there is any great competition for the post of chairman of the new Authority and whether in spite of virulent malcontents there will not be a general disposition in the party to fall back on Sidney. I tell him to be coy of accepting it.

[? April] *Longfords, Minchinhampton*
Listened from the Speaker's Gallery to Anson introducing the London Education Bill. Met with cold reception. Opposition jeering

and supporters gloomily silent. An inept speech. As it stands the Bill is a bad one, though rather than the *status quo* or an *ad hoc* authority *we* would accept it as it stands. But it is clear to us that the borough council representatives on the central committee have been stuck in to be knocked out and that the control of the L.C.C. over the local administration of elementary education will be indefinitely strengthened in Committee of the House. If our prophecy be proved correct the Bill is much what Sidney would have himself drafted except that he would have defined in the Bill the outside element to be co-opted by the L.C.C. Committee and not left it to the free will of the L.C.C. But this may be unduly distrustful of his Progressive colleagues. But of course the Bill as it stands has been received by every section of Progressives with contemptuous disapproval, almost delight, because it is considered so bad that it will not pass. Hewins and Pease have however been so indoctrinated by Sidney that they are almost enthusiastic about the present draft. Sidney goes up today to a Parliamentary Committee to reconnoitre the position and see how far he can modify the outburst of L.C.C. disapproval.

A compromise had given the new boroughs some say in the governance of local schools that would in all other respects be run by the new L.C.C. Education Committee. Mary Playne, the adopted daughter of Beatrice's sister Mary, had an unhappy marriage to the lawyer Erskine Pollock, and poisoned herself in April 1910.

29 April. [41 Grosvenor Road]
L.C.C. Progressives rapidly coming round to notion of L.C.C. being the authority – the natural desire of a public body to increase its dignity and power overcoming the party feeling in favour of an *ad hoc* authority. Clear also that government intend to give way if pressed. All the Conservative Party organs on our side as to strengthening of the L.C.C. position, though they differ about borough representation on the central committee and the powers of the borough local committee. Looks as if Sidney would get his way all along the line even with regard to the constitution of the Education Committee.

Happy time at Longfords with dear sister Mary Playne, clouded over by the separation between her and Bill through the determined hostility of his wife [Manuella Meinertzhagen]. This young woman is a bad example of the self-indulgent, self-willed and self-complacent middle-class woman, who has never been taught to work or think or feel for others – to me she is simply repulsive physically and mentally. But she has a certain animal attractiveness and an obstinate strong will, ready to go any lengths to get her own way. She has succeeded in poisoning Bill's mind and he behaves with a strange combination of indifference and insolence to his parents, tempered by anger at their not giving him a larger share of their worldly possessions. He has no profession, unless a little cadging of orders for the mill be a profession, and [spends] a few days with the Yeomanry every month or so. He has neither intellectual curiosity nor public spirit nor any kind of philanthropy. He has lost his *joie de vivre*, which gave him as a boy a certain charm. Altogether he is not a good product and Mary who has spent the better part of her life planning and scheming for him, is bitterly and finally disappointed. Whether there was good stuff to work on in his nature I somewhat doubt – the shape of his head is not encouraging. But she feels that she has brought him up without any kind of creed and with little sense of duty. She has made him into a healthy man with, at present, physical self-control and dislike of vice or morbid desires and a certain willingness to take risks. . . . I am inclined to think that his conceit is responsible for his mediocrity – he never learns. . . .

Otherwise her life now is fortunate in circumstances. Mary Pollock has become a true daughter to her – a sensible warm-hearted woman, and Erskine is a quite passable relative, the two boys well conducted and agreeable. If Bill remains childless Mary's children will be quite agreeable heirs. Arthur, though no more capable or responsible, has become a pleasant-tempered, affectionate and interested person, and they are both immersed in county work which brings them in contact with men and affairs. The nurse-companion, Miss Ross, is devoted to Mary, a bright, capable and true-hearted nature, also interested in public work. Longfords is a most delightful home and is more the centre of the Richard Potter family than any other house. But all this does not make up to poor Mary for the virtual loss of the affection of her one and only child, a loss which is heightened by the conviction that his life has been made barren by the violent temper and idle ways of his mate, [barren] of public spirit, intellect, interest or even joy. Whether one day he will break loose and what he will do if he does is a problem of the future.

Mary Playne's views have undergone a complete change. She has ceased to be cynical, has a turning towards religion and public work as two elements of home life without which it is apt to degrade, even from the level of a finely developed and sane animal. 'I see now,' she says bitterly, 'that I made a mistake not to teach Bill to be unselfish, not to bring him up with some sense of obligation towards the world. If he had some such feeling he would not have allowed Manuella to wreck his life – he would have had a reason for resisting her.'

Meanwhile our eldest sister [Lawrencina Holt] has been going through a tragedy of discord. For some time the family life has been one constant wrangle between the two unmarried daughters and the two unmarried sons, the three married pairs and the father – now one combination, now another. . . .

A melancholy reflection on their upbringing. Here again there is the note of utter selfishness. Lallie has slaved to make her home one of perfect comfort – every arrangement has been exactly fitted to produce the maximum satisfaction to the 'average sensual man'. And Lallie herself has redeemed all this materialism by most unbounded devotion to the material needs of her family, her friends and even her servants. But the children have been flattered and allowed to behave badly to others and to live a life of pleasure. Now they have turned against her and each other.

Poor silly Robert lost his head over the social position which Lallie, by her energy, created for him, and is now consumed by a sort of mixture of jealousy, irritation, and a certain weakly distaste for Lallie's bad manners and unattractive person. Sidney and I went there for a Sunday and tried to be pleasant all round. But it is a gloomy business and does not seem capable of amendment.

Observing the results of the luxurious bringing-up of children does not make me *less* anxious to redistribute wealth. There must be a long tradition of social service behind property to prevent it from being deteriorating to the ordinary nature, and perhaps the tradition without the property would do just as well and be less likely to be lost. To think that the Holt ménage is the outcome of Robert's maxim of 'levelling up', i.e. *improving your own position*. It is a ghastly joke. *Sordid* is the right word for the result; not even respectable!

To us the outlook for the upper-middle class is not encouraging. Without discipline and without technical training with a mere sham of 'culture' the young men and women of these households seem an almost worthless product. Possibly the 'opportunities' open to those who *are* self-controlled and finely tempered give this tiny minority a larger basis to their life than if they came of narrower circumstances – but, for any nature, it is a terrible moral handicap to be able to refuse the work persistently and strenuously. Even with the best of them it seems to entail a lower standard of effort. As to which I would rather my children were brought up in narrow circumstances than in the midst of luxurious expenditure. What people call 'style' seems fatal. Beautiful surroundings with scanty housekeeping seem the ideal, so long as there is enough for *mobility* and varied intercourse. Scanty fare, a tiny dress allowance with free travelling, free education, and free lodging in a beautiful home: animal *contempt* for voluntary idleness or ill health, the sort of contempt that is now given for deformity of body or mind or, by some of the baser of mankind, for poverty.

Here ends another volume of my diary. It leaves me in excellent health and spirits enjoying my work and extraordinarily happy in my love and perfect comradeship. I have become a vegetarian and keep rigidly to the two meals a day — and those light ones. I hanker after giving up tea, coffee and tobacco — all poisons — but the appetite overcomes my better will. I intend, however, to reduce them.

VOLUME 24

The Webbs spent much of the summer of 1903 at Newlands Farm, Aston Magna, a few miles from Moreton-in-the-Marsh. While the Webbs were engaged in 'little schemes' with the Moderates and the Progressives to achieve their educational ends, there was a significant shift in the focus of national politics. After Chamberlain returned from a visit to South Africa he delivered a sensational speech to Unionists in Birmingham on 15 May in which he came out strongly for a system of fiscal preferences as a means to Imperial unity. This 'bombshell' split his own party for many Liberal Unionists were passionate free-traders; and it so divided the Cabinet that Balfour had to declare tariff reform 'an open question' for his government. Chamberlain's declaration also put an end to any possibility of a new party emerging from a rapprochement between the Liberal Imperialists and the Liberal Unionists — a 'national efficiency' grouping of the kind the Webbs favoured.

Before the Webbs left for the country Sidney had been appointed to a Royal Commission on Trade Union Law. Beatrice hoped that this would restore their lost contact with the trade union leadership but the Trades Union Congress decided to boycott the proceedings and the Commission procrastinated ineffectively. The Webbs had drifted so far into the shadow of the Balfour government that Sidney's agreement to serve on the Commission diminished rather than improved his standing with the trade unions. The talk of a new 'Education' party, like the founding of the Co-Efficients dining club in September, was a measure of the Webbs' alienation from mainstream politics and of their feeling that they must start enterprises of their own to express their own policies.

15 June. Aston Magna, Gloucestershire

We left London seventeen days ago tired out but with the restful consciousness that our plans had come off. The School gets its grant of £1,100 from the T.E.B. renewed without opposition, J.R. MacDonald not being there. The Education Bill passed through committee the day before we left in almost exactly the same shape Sidney would have given to it: the L.C.C. absolutely supreme, the borough councils relegated to the quite subordinate part of selecting the majority of the local managers, but these latter having no more power than the L.C.C. chooses to give them. In fact the Bill endows the L.C.C. with rather more freedom of action than Sidney would have suggested as the ideal arrangement. He would have preferred a statutory constitution for the Education Committee, instead of leaving it open to the L.C.C. to decline having any representation of the voluntary schools of other outside interests. It was easy to get the L.C.C. ten years ago to appoint a reasonably broad committee for Technical Education when none of the Council were interested in the matter. It is another thing to persuade the Progressives, with their enormous majority and strong Nonconformist element, to be fair and sane about the outside interests. Hence our anxiety is now passed from Parliament to the L.C.C. itself. So long as we can get the present Council to consent to frame a scheme under the Act and so long as the scheme is not outrageously one-sided, that is as much as we can do. The working of the Act will be a matter for the 1904 Council. We are concerned now to see to it that this Council has the right complexion.

The whole controversy between the Progressives and Moderates is stale and has lost its significance. The Progressives, beyond sticking to some old shibboleths, have lost all impetus to further action. The Works Department, the old symbol of collectivism, is a mere device for keeping the contractors in order. The taking over of the tramways has been accomplished in principle, if not in fact, but Water is lost to the L.C.C., at any rate for the next decade or two; and with regard to Asylums, to Housing, to Sanitary and Building By-laws committees, the work of the Council has become mere routine. In fact it is asserted by some that the 'old gang' who run the administrative departments have become cautious and economical to the last degree. On the other hand, while the Council has lost the impetus to do constructive work, it has secreted a good deal of destructive radicalism of the old type. Some thirty members of the Progressive Party are standing for Parliament and owing to the latter-day developments, they are, many of them, likely to get in. This will increase the disinclination of the Progressive leaders to a vigorous municipal policy, and identify them more completely than ever with parliamentary Liberalism. And all these general considerations have been enormously heightened by the raging controversy over the Education Bill. In this the old nihilistic spirit of the 1843–70 Nonconformist (who deliberately preferred *no education* to the teaching of a rival dogma) is rampant. A powerful rump of L.C.C. Progressives imagine themselves to be in favour of Education with a big E but at best it is only primary education of the most mechanical and uniform type that they want to promote. Behind them, and working with them, are two other more sinister forces, the Labour men who want no money spent on secondary or university education, and the N.U.T., who want all appointments, secondary as well as university, to fall into the hands of the superior elementary teachers.

Meanwhile the Moderate party has become even more stale than the Progressives. Beaten down and divided by their last crushing defeat, they no longer have any heart for their work of opposition. Moreover, there is nothing for the most moderate of the Moderates to oppose in the thoroughly business-like, cautious and economical ways of the Progressive administrators. Just as the Progressives have permeated the Moderates with all that was immediately practicable in their schemes, so the Moderates have permeated the Progressives and forced them to adopt economical and business-like methods. This mutual permeation is exactly what is accomplished by the English system of committees in which party cleavages are lost sight of and the actual outcome being always a compromise – in a good body, the 'better reason' of both parties. All this, from the point of view of efficiency, is very encouraging. But when both sides feel that they have got a good deal of what they wanted and have persuaded themselves to give up the remainder, the spirit both of reform and of criticism is apt 'to go dead'.

Now it is a question which Sidney and I have been mooting between ourselves, whether out of these elements we can produce a new party, formally or informally held together by a broad catholic and progressive educational policy. The planks would be: 1) Fairness to the voluntary schools, complete freedom for them to teach their religious doctrine in their own way; 2) Unsectarianism in the board schools, these latter constituting, broadly speaking, the supply for the Nonconformist and secularist children – and as regards all kinds of elementary teaching *through efficiency* in staff and structure; 3)Development of secondary and technical education on the present lines of independent governing bodies aided and inspected by L.C.C. and kept up to the mark on their educational side, but completely free to be as denominational or anti-denominational as the governing body choose. And last but not least, a great London university – independent of L.C.C. but subsidized and influenced by it – not only a leading university organized on a democratic basis, but a great centre of the highest and most 'useful' science, scholarship and metaphysics.

The better part of the Moderate party would be in favour of this – so would the Church, so would the Catholics, so would some of the best of the Progressives. But the rank and file of the Progressives and even a majority of the present L.C.C. would be indifferent, and would be largely got hold of by the fanatical 'Noncon' Labour man. Can we silently and quietly prepare the ground to alter the composition of the Council next March so as to have a majority pledged or sympathetically inclined to this new policy? That is the problem before us. To put it bluntly, we want a *small* Progressive majority, the rump of the Progressives superseded by good Conservative educationalists.

It is a delicate task for us to bring this about, and we may go under in attempting it. Though the Progressives have thrown Sidney over as regards the T.E.B., yet he is still elected as one of the party committee and retains much of his influence with the leading men. He has openly told them that if they refuse to act as the Education Authority or if they announce their intention of refusing help to voluntary schools he will organize the press in London against them. But that is easier said than done, and prevention is better than cure. I have therefore strongly advised him to quietly and discreetly begin to work at once organizing electoral influence for the L.C.C. election, just as we began to organize the parliamentary press last year in view of the Bill of this year. . . . We hope to remain throughout on the Progressive side, but, if circumstances compelled, Sidney would come out in the open as the avowed organizer of a new party. This, however, would detract from his real power which will consist in drafting a compromise between the new Progressive party and the new Moderate party.

Meanwhile our little schemes have been submerged, even in our own minds, by the new ferment introduced by Chamberlain into Imperial politics. Protection versus Free Trade is going to supersede all other political issues for many years to come. From the public point of view we do not regret the advent of the 'new ferment'. Here again controversies between parties had got stale. This issue at least will force people to think, will force them to consider new facts and to apply new assumptions. The absurd notion that the 'natural' channels of trade are necessarily the best will be quickly given up; the notion that 'cheapness' is the only aim in a nation's commerce will also be demolished. The need for investigation and the desirability of deliberate collective regulation will be enormously advertised. All this is to the good and makes towards economic science and we think collectivism of the best sort.

To Joe's specific proposals – a tax on food and eventually 'protection all round' we are, as at present advised, opposed as politically impracticable, unnecessarily costly to the consumer and likely to lead to international friction and internal uncertainty. We do not agree, however, with the extreme hostility to these proposals. Our trade depends on quite other considerations than tariffs or no tariffs. But we think Chamberlain's aim, the Empire as a unit, could be better and more cheaply and conveniently attained by other devices. Sidney, at present, inclines towards bounties and colonial imports as a likely compromise between the British consumer, the British manufacturer and the colonial producer.

Viewed from the standpoint of our own little projects the diversion of public interest from the educational controversy to the tariff [issue] is wholly to the good. It will require, however, careful steering to prevent the School of Economics from being indiscreetly identified with either side. Hewins, somewhat impetuously, has decided to throw in his weight with Chamberlain; that will mean that Sidney must be, as he fortunately is, against the new proposals. All he will do is to get the Fabian Society to work to prepare the ground for some intermediate plan combining imperialism with sound national economy.

Just before leaving London Sidney was appointed on the small expert Royal Commission to enquire into trade union law. This was our friend Haldane's doing, made easy by Mr Balfour's kindly view of us. The job is eminently one for him to do and will have the incidental advantage of bringing us again into communication with the trade union world. Sidney's relations with the Labour men of the L.C.C. having been strained by J. R. MacDonald's ill service, it is all the more necessary to be on good terms with other sections. The Parliamentary Committee of the Trades Union Congress has never forgiven us our scathing description of them and their doings in *Industrial Democracy*. With John Burns we are very friendly, but this is only because he is jealous of Macnamara and Crooks and has an old grudge against MacDonald. Next spring we shall resume our intercourse with the Co-operators in preparation for an official history of the Movement.

Meanwhile our big work on local government grows slowly and surely; but still there is a good deal of ground to cover. . . . Four hours every morning have we worked either together or separately. . . We have worked all the harder because we have been absolutely undisturbed and the weather has been bad, so that Sidney has worked on in the afternoon and I have brooded over the chapters trudging in the rain along the dripping lanes. Some delightful rides we have had together in the few fine days, happy hours of light-hearted companionship, arguing about our book or plotting our little plans. . .

A pathetic three days at Brighton just before we left London. A note from Herbert Spencer's secretary one morning saying that the old man was very ill, made me take the train to Brighton. I did not like the thought that he should be nearing death without any old friend by his side. . . . The poor old man looked as if he were leaving this world, and what pained me was his look of weary discomfort and depression. I kissed him on the forehead and took his hand in mine. He seemed so glad of this mark of affection. . . . Thinking that he could only last a few days I came back the next day and established myself at an hotel near by. I saw him once or twice again and both times he talked about the future of society. . . As he grew stronger his desire to live, which had given way in his extreme weakness, returned and again he became chary of seeing anyone who excited him. Now he seems to be gaining strength and it looks as if he might live for many a day. . . .

3 July. [41 Grosvenor Road]
Melancholy letter from Herbert Spencer. Ran down to see him. . . Was extremely sensitive as to his reputation and influence, felt that he had dropped out and was no longer of much consideration.

'What you have thought and taught has become part of our mental atmosphere, Mr Spencer,' I said soothingly. 'And like the atmosphere we are not aware of it. When you cease to be our atmosphere, then we shall again become aware of you as a personality.' 'That is a pleasant way of putting it,' and he smiled.

I tried to suggest that he should give up the struggle against ill fate and accept the rest of his existence. 'Why should I be resigned?' he retorted almost angrily. 'I have nothing to hope for in return for resignation. I look forward merely to extinction, that is a mere negative. No,' he added with intense depression, 'I have simply to vegetate between this and death, to suffer as little as I need, and, for that reason, I must not talk to you any more: it prevents me sleeping and upsets my digestion. Goodbye – come and see me again.'

It is tragic to look at the whole of man's life as a bargain in which man gets perpetually the worst of it. But the notion of contract – a *quid pro quo* – is so ingrained in the poor old man that even illness and death seem a nasty fraud perpetuated by nature.

'We have been living in a veritable whirl – we had twenty-five persons to dinner or lunch last week, having others to see us in the afternoon,' Beatrice wrote to Mary Playne on 9 July, telling her that the 'Charlottenburg' scheme to set up a new science college in Kensington had been successfully launched and that they were actively seeking financial support from 'the City Magnates'. Describing a fierce dinner-table argument about free trade she added: 'Sidney and I kept the balance in the centre – a position in which we seem determined to find ourselves on every issue that turns up.' Sidney thought that Hewins might embarrass the L.S.E. by his fervent support for tariff reform, and was much relieved when he resigned from the School to work for Chamberlain's campaign. Halford J. Mackinder then took his place as Director.

8 July. [41 Grosvenor Road]
Fagged with combination of work and entertaining. Before the 'Charlottenburg' scheme was launched we spent our selves, money and energy in tuning the press and trying to keep the Progressives straight. But of course they unconsciously resent having a situation 'prepared' out of which there is only one way, i.e. ours. But there is so little statesmanship in the party that it is only by an elaborate preparation of the ground that they can be induced to take up the right position. Latterly I have been sampling the Progressive members – they are not much to be proud of – a good deal of rotten stuff, the rest upright and reasonable but coarse-grained in intellect and character. Even the best of them are a good deal below the standard of our

intimate associates such as Hewins, Mackinder, Haldane, Russell, etc., and the ordinary Progressive member is either a bounder, a narrow-minded fanatic or a mere piece of putty upon which any strong mind can make an impression, to be effaced by the next influence – or rather the texture is more like gutta-percha, because it bounds back to the old shapeless mass of prejudice directly you take your will away. It is very tiring for poor Sidney and he comes back from an L.C.C. or [Technical Education] Board meeting exhausted though usually victorious, always so when he has had time to prepare the ground – when he does this the enemy usually don't turn up or collapse immediately and his trouble seems thrown away.

Hewins has complicated matters of the L.C.C. and the School by his vehement adhesion to Chamberlainism; not only letting out his authorship of *The Times* articles but resigning sensationally from the National Liberal Club. Fortunately the articles have been ineffective, but the fact of his partisanship makes our position more difficult and has necessitated Sidney flying the free-trade flag. He would have preferred to keep quiet and not to take part but that is impossible in view of Hewins's and GBS's indiscretions (see GBS's letter to the *Daily Mail* some days ago). Meanwhile we struggle on in a lame way every morning. For three days I have been off with strained eyes, strained not with work but with dissipation of strength at four dinners last week. My diet saves me from worse ills than mere fatigue. Unfortunately I don't always stick to my regimen, specially when I am bored.

Winston Spencer Churchill (1874–1965), who had been a soldier and war correspondent, entered Parliament in 1900 as a Tory but broke away on the question of tariff reform and became a member of the Liberal government in 1906. His father was Lord Randolph Churchill.

8 July. [41 Grosvenor Road]
Went in to dinner with Winston Churchill [at the Hobhouses']. First impression: restless, almost intolerably so, without capacity for sustained and unexcited labour, egotistical, bumptious, shallow-minded and reactionary, but with a certain personal magnetism, great pluck and some originality, not of intellect but of character. More of the American speculator than the English aristocrat. Talked exclusively about himself and his electioneering plans, wanted me to tell him of someone who would get statistics for him. 'I never do any

brainwork that anyone else can do for me,' – an axiom which shows organizing but not thinking capacity. Replete with dodges for winning Oldham against the Labour and Liberal candidates. But I dare say he has a better side, which the ordinary cheap cynicism of his position and career covers up to a casual dinner acquaintance.

Bound to be unpopular, too unpleasant a flavour with his restless self-regarding personality and lack of moral or intellectual refinement. His political tack is Economy, the sort of essence of a 'Moderate'; he is, at heart, a Little Englander. Looks to the *haute finance* to keep the peace – for that reason objects to a self-contained Empire as he thinks it would destroy this cosmopolitan capitalism, the cosmopolitan financier being the professional peacemaker of the modern world, and to his mind the acme of civilization. His bugbears are – Labour, N.U.T. and expenditure in elementary education or the services. Defines the Higher Education as the opportunity for the 'brainy man' to come to the top. No notion of scientific research, philosophy, literature or art, still less of religion. But his pluck, courage, resourcefulness and great tradition may carry him far, unless he knocks himself to pieces like his father.

Sir J. Wolfe-Barry (1836–1918) was a consultant engineer whose work included the London underground railway, the docks and Tower Bridge. He also served on a number of Royal Commissions. Balfour dined at the Webbs on 21 July. Beatrice implies that Balfour mistook Charles Booth for William Booth, the founder of the Salvation Army. Mary Playne sent up 'roses, carnations, sweet peas and grapes' from the country for this dinner.

23 July. [41 Grosvenor Road]
Our season ended with a brilliant little dinner here to meet Mr Balfour. Naturally enough I talked almost exclusively at dinner to the guest of the evening. A man of extraordinary 'grace' of mind and body, delighting in all that is beautiful and distinguished – music, literature, philosophy, religious feeling and moral disinterestedness, aloof from all the greed and grind of common human nature. But a strange paradox as Prime Minister of a great empire. I doubt whether even foreign affairs interest him. For all economic and social questions, I gather, he has an utter loathing, whilst the machinery of administration would seem to him a disagreeable irrelevance. Not a strong intellect and deficient in knowledge, but I imagine ambitious in the sense that he feels that being Prime Minister completes the picture of the really charming man, gives tone to the last touch of

colour, piquancy to his indifference as to whether he is in or out of office.

I placed Charles Booth next him – I doubt from his manner whether he knew who Charles Booth was – wondered perhaps that a 'Salvationist' should be so agreeably unsettled in his opinions. Bright talk with paradoxes and subtleties, sentiments and allusions, with the personal note emphasized, is what Mr Balfour likes, and is what I tried to give him! From nineteenth-century schools of philosophy to eighteenth-century street life, from University to Tariff, from Meredith to GBS, we flashed assertions and rejoinders; and 'Bernard Shaw, the finest man of letters of today' was one of his dicta. But he had not read *Mrs Warren's Profession:* 'it is one of the unpleasant plays. I never read unpleasant things,' he added apologetically, and looked confirmed in his intention when I asserted that it was GBS's most 'serious work'. 'I am reading Haldane's *Pathway to Reality* and should like to answer it, but somehow or other I don't get any time for philosophy,' he added with a note of graceful surprise. 'I had hoped that the tariffs issue would turn us out, but I am beginning to doubt it.' Then I explained to him with much benignity the powerful forces of the cotton trade and the Co-operative Union which would, I thought, bring about his release from office. Haldane and he returned to the House soon after 10 and I had a pleasant chat with Sir J. Wolfe-Barry, the engineer.

Sidney got through the £20,000 grant [L.C.C.] to the 'Charlottenburg', having drafted a careful report. Of the leading Progressives some really approved, others dare not refuse Rosebery – only eight of the rump actually went into the lobby against it. J.R. MacDonald made a long and virulent attack on Sidney. 'Mr Haldane and Mr Sidney Webb had presented a pistol at the head of the Council.' He was supported by the Labour men. The farce of Sidney not being chairman of T.E.B. when every agenda or report is obviously drafted by him is becoming glaring and will make J.R.M. more angry than ever. Massingham and Macnamara too are trying to work up opposition to him in London. But Macnamara, in laying down authoritatively the issues upon which the L.C.C. election next March is to be fought, has overshot himself and disinclined the Progressive leaders to follow him. The I.L.P. is making the Liberals very angry, and in that direction J.R.M. will not increase his influence. Meanwhile the Moderates show some signs of working to capture Sidney for their side, and the moderate Progressives are beginning to fear they may lose him and are inclined to be more on-coming. It looks as if the Rump would try to turn him out of the party, the Moderates would try to claim him, and the centre Progressives make some sacrifice to keep him. So long as he keeps his temper and head and goes on quietly asserting his own education policy his position is a strong one. But it is clear that the next election will be a scrimmage and we may go under. What would suit us least well (assuming that Sidney keeps his seat) would be a large Noncon. majority; what would suit us best would be either a small Moderate or small Progressive majority, perhaps the former best of all. At this juncture the Progressive forces are really against a constructive policy or a large expenditure on education, more particularly in that direction in which it is most needed – higher education. Class, sectarian and professional jealousy leads them to a desire to stint education. Labour, Nonconformity, and N.U.T. dislike the advent of the university professor as part of publicly maintained instruction.

Our general social policy is to construct a base to society in the form of a legally enforced minimum standard of life, and to develop all forms of 'shooting upwards', whether of individuals or of discoveries and refinements. Doubtful which party in the state will help us most; protection is all to the bad, so is Nonconformist fanaticism – that is to say the positive policy of both Chamberlain and Campbell-Bannerman is bad and retrograde, and they are equally indifferent if not hostile to our programme. We have in fact no party ties. It is open to us to use either or both parties.

24 July. [41 Grosvenor Road]
One wonders whether all this manipulating activity is worth while, whether one would not do just as much by cutting the whole business of human intercourse and devoting oneself to thinking and writing out one's thoughts. It would certainly be a far pleasanter because a far less complicated life, with fewer liabilities for contraventions against personal dignity, veracity and kindliness. It is so easy to maintain these qualities in a vacuum! In rubbing up against others, one's vanity, one's self-will and any strain of spite gets uncovered and revealed in all their ugliness to oneself, one's friends and one's opponents. But someone has to do this practical work, and possibly it is just as well that it should be done by those who have 'the other life' to withdraw into so as to keep up their standard of thought and feeling. That disgust with oneself which always follows on a time of turmoil,

the consciousness that one has lamentably fallen short in dignity, gentleness, consideration for other people's lives and feelings, and in transparent truthfulness, is a wholesome reminder of one's own radical shortcomings. If one frankly realizes one's own moral incapacity during spells of activity, it makes one more careful not to admit unworthy desires and thoughts in the time of withdrawal from the world, and the whole level of one's mental life is raised and supported by the wholesome fear of the Eternal Fall of the man of action.

From an intellectual standpoint it is good too, because one is constantly testing one's hypotheses by the course of events, proving whether a given social process does, as a matter of fact, bring about a given social result. Nevertheless it is with a sigh of relief that we look forward to some months of restful intellectual work before the hubbub of next spring. And if Sidney *is* turned out of the London administration, the lot will bring its compensations. It would be a mental luxury to give the whole of our joint strength to the completion of our big task, especially if we felt that we had fought hard and were in no way responsible, by carelessness, for affairs taking the wrong turn – that we had not resigned the heavier and more disagreeable work but had been dismissed as 'not wanted' by the people of London.

Josiah Royce (1855-1916) was an American idealist philosopher who taught that man's ethical obligation was to the whole community. *The Times* was running a quiz competition which Sidney hoped to win.

4 August. Aston Magna
Settled in an attractive old farmhouse. With pleasant farmer, wife, son and daughter in a little hamlet inhabited by farm labourers and brick-makers – no public house, only 'Anne Sabin: licensed to sell tobacco', a place of discreet and orderly resort and probably of an 'occasional glass' taken with the tobacco. Only drawback, certain amount of noise from the holidays of the youngsters. But we have a tent out on a piece of unkempt land, where absolute quiet reigns except for the wind in the large silver poplars which overtop the apple trees and brambles, and the trains which pass up the valley, some rushing at express speed, others crawling heavily laden, every half-hour or so.

The first four days I spent mastering Royce's *Outlines of Psychology*, a useful little book to a complete ignoramus like me, and suggestive for our analysis of the experiments on the volition of the individual man, which to our mind constitutes so large a part in the art of governing. To construct good habits and yet not to interfere with the development of mental initiative is the problem set to the art of social regulation. But psychology as set forth by Royce seems to be in a rudimentary state, having organized and classified only the more obvious data known to any careful observer of human nature. There is, however, value in getting the old empirical axioms stated as carefully analysed processes.

Whether it was the three mornings of hard thinking involved in this careful study and abstract of Royce, or the after-effect of our busy London life, I have today collapsed with inertia and nervelessness, quiescent and not unpleasant collapse except for my over-sensitiveness to noise. I still maintain my regimen of two meals, but today took some meat for the first time for many weeks. I watch myself with interest, not only to secure the greatest efficiency but also to discover whether sustained health is possible on so cheap and easy a fare. If two meals a day, of cereals and milk with small quantity of green vegetable or fruit, is really all that most of us require for efficiency, the economic problem as distinguished from the human problem is comparatively an easy one to solve. The experiment is somewhat vitiated, for general application, by the fact that I am at a time of life when restriction of food may be specially desirable. I may also have to slack off work, but so far I have done more persistent brainwork this year than ever before, though perhaps I have taken less physical exercise. Certainly the mental efforts of a restricted diet and work while fasting, both in use of intellect and control of conduct, are all to the good.

My regimen now consists of an early cup of tea 7 o'clock, lunch 1 o'clock, of macaroni or semolina (or occasionally a poached egg and toast), green vegetables with some kind of fruit tart or pudding, a minute bit of cheese, biscuits and a little butter. Afternoon cup of tea. Supper at 7.30 of cereal pudding – grape-nut is my favourite and a little marmalade or sultanas, minute bit of cheese and biscuit and butter, half a small cup of black coffee. I don't think I consume more than about 1½ oz of dry cereal at each meal. I have resumed my monthly periods (rather too frequent I fear) which stopped for six months last summer. I suffer from no headache or constipation or colds, very little indigestion and very slight eczema. I sleep well and enjoy a placid and unworried state of mind. Today I have a feeling of drag and subconscious headache which disinclines me to exercise –

some congestion I should imagine – to be looked for at forty-six years of age. I am lying up to prevent a premature period, and I am stopping off my book.

While I spend four whole mornings in mastering the contents of one little book and rest the whole afternoon and evening in order to work again the next day, Sidney will get through some eight or ten volumes bearing on local government or likely to contain out-of-the-way references to it, besides spending the whole morning finishing up his *Times* questions. One would have thought that his administrative work and our big tasks were occupation enough! But he succumbed to the delights of being again an examinee, the 'old craving returned'.

The continuous activity of his brain is marvellous. Unless he is downright ill he is never without a book or a pen in his hand. He says that he cannot think without reading or writing, and that he cannot brood, for if he has nothing before him more absorbing he finds himself counting the lines or spots on some object. That is why when he is in a street or a bus he sees and reads and often remembers the advertisements. If I would let him he would read through mealtimes. A woman who wanted a husband to spend hours talking to her or listening to her chit-chat would find him a trying husband. As it is we exactly suit each other's habits. Long hours of solitary brooding is what I am accustomed to and without which I doubt whether I could be productive. It is restful for me to wander off in moor, in lanes and fields, or even to sit silently by his side in our tent or by the fire. I have my thoughts and he has his book, and both alike go to complete and fulfil our joint task. . . . Sometimes I am a bit irritated because at some off-time he will not listen to what seems to me a brilliant suggestion – dismisses it with 'that is not new' or with a slight disparaging 'hmm'. But I generally smile at my own irritation and take back any idea to clear up or elaborate or correct with other thoughts, or to reject as worthless. Sometimes I flare up and scold, then he is all penitence and we kiss away the misunderstanding. Our love gives an atmosphere of quiescent happiness (to use Royce's classification) and our work gives us periods of restless or energetic happiness. And when we are alone in the country together there is no other thought or feeling to intrude on this peaceful activity. We have no incompatible desires, either together or apart. Our daily existence and our ideal are one and the same. We sail straight to our port over a sunlit sea. But the point we make for seems sometimes an unconscionable way off!

293

Eustace Miles, who published *Muscle, Brain and Diet* in 1901, was a prolific author on food reform topics.

10 August. [Aston Magna]

A week without work owing to nerveless and disturbed state but, with increased rigidity of diet, am pulling round. Read E. Miles, *Brain and Diet*, which confirmed me in my faith and from which I get more useful hints as to regimen. Last two days reading William James's delightful *Talks with Teachers*, supplementary to Royce and unlike Royce with an open window on the spiritual side of human nature. . . .

Beatrice worked with Sidney on an article on 'London Education' for the *Nineteenth Century:* it was both a stocktaking and a prospectus of education in the national capital. The 'clever doctor' was Sir Michael Foster (1836–1907), professor of physiology at Cambridge and Liberal Unionist M.P. for the University of London 1900–06. Lord Salisbury died on 23 August and the loss of his influence left Chamberlain in a position of greater power. In the autumn Chamberlain made a series of speeches round the country in which he came out openly for a tariff reform programme. Algernon Freeman-Mitford, Lord Redesdale (1837–1916) was a diplomat and author, an M.P. 1892–95, who lived at Batsford Park in Gloucestershire. His elder daughters were Frances (b.1875) and Iris (b.1878). Charles Gore (1853–1932) was a High Church leader and Christian Socialist who founded the monastic Community of the Resurrection at Mirfield. At this time he was Bishop of Worcester. C.R. Ashbee (1863–1942) was an architect who founded and directed the Guild of Handicrafts, whose workshops were established at Chipping Campden. Mrs Patrick Campbell (1865–1940) was one of the leading figures on the London stage at the turn of the century.

26 August. [Aston Magna]

Sidney sent off the article to be typed prior to submitting it to various critics.

Meanwhile we have been entertaining and being entertained. We cycled over to the Elchos' and spent a couple of hours chatting with them and Mr Balfour and a clever Cambridge doctor, the P.M charming as usual but absorbed in the state of the weather and the chance of getting his golf, also waiting sadly for the death of his great-uncle. Then the Playnes came for two days and we took them to see the Ashbees at Campden and to a formal lunch at our neighbour's, Lord Redesdale, afterwards spending a tiring afternoon standing about in his pretty garden of bamboos. A melancholy household – this handsome, vain and autocratic elderly gentleman absorbed in his hobbies and somewhat hazardous enterprises, his wife mad at intervals and usually away, and a family of nine young people. The two elder girls, simple, attractive, but living an isolated and useless life shut up in their grand house and park, kept too short of money to see life as aristocrats and too dignified to see it as ordinary folk. When we asked them to tea at the home of their own tenant within half a mile of their gate they thought it necessary to drive here – a carriage and pair with footmen – keeping it for two hours awaiting them. And yet clearly not able to go up to London for more than a week in the year!

On Monday Sidney and I went to dine and sleep at 'Bishop's House', Worcester. Dr Gore is a delightful-natured pious ecclesiastic, without guile, with extraordinary fervour and earnestness, a mystic, a reformer, a preacher, but with no natural turn for administration or Church politics. He is not a wholly satisfactory bishop in the ordinary English sense. Refuses utterly to take up his position as a social magnate. He has given up his palace and settled in a large plain villa on the outskirts of Worcester where he lives with three other priests, a life of austere work and fervent worship. We found him deeply depressed, hating the administrative drudgery of the bishop's position, not caring for its dignity and feeling how hard it was to be a simple missionary when clothed in bishop's purple. Into this monk's abode Sidney and I broke for one long evening's talk about the Education Bill and the position of the Church generally. It was a strange proceeding – we non-Christians talking intimately with these 'true men of God' as to possible co-operation between them and us in any reform of society. When we woke in the morning we heard mass being said in the room beneath us and when we came down to breakfast three out of the four were robed sacerdotally. But they were eating a hearty breakfast, whereas I was fasting, and I amused myself by upsetting their consciences on the 'simple food' question and the desirability of living on six ounces a day. So in spite of my heterodoxy I left in an odour of 'personal abstemiousness' akin to an odour of sanctity!

On our way home we picked up Beatrice Chamberlain whom we had asked to come to discuss the question of London school management. In the afternoon a party assembled itself in our little parlour for tea –Lady Elcho bringing Mrs Pat Campbell (the actress), the Freeman Mitford girls, the Ashbees – a gay and talkative affair developing an antagonism between the actress and the economists. This morning Beatrice and I wandered over Lord Redesdale's garden and during the walk she formally proposed that I

should make the acquaintance of her stepmother – she would bring
her to call etc. Of course, I insisted that I should come some Thursday
when she returned to London, which appeared to relieve the mind of
my old friend of a difficult negotiation. The next day Lord Redesdale
drove us over to see the Ashbee [handicraft] works, and in the
afternoon she left.

The Russells were staying at Beaumont-le-Roger in Normandy. Frédéric
Bastiat (1801–50) was an economic individualist and proponent of *laissez-faire*
theory.

5 October. Grosvenor Road

A refreshing holiday in Normandy amd Brittany lasting the best part
of three weeks, first a week with the Russells and then two weeks alone
together. The Russells we found settled in uncomfortable lodgings in
a little Normandy village, riding and reading together but not
serenely happy, a tragic austerity and effort in their relations. They
are both so good in the best and most complete sense; Alys has so much
charm and Bertrand so much intellect that it is strange they cannot
enjoy light-hearted happiness in each other's love and comradeship,
but there is something that interferes, and friends can only look on
with respect and admiration and silent concern. Perhaps they will
grow into more joyful union; certainly they have the big essential
condition – a common faith so far as personal conduct is concerned.

We two thoroughly enjoyed our time. Cycling abroad is a new
discovery to us. Sightseeing completes each day and alternating with
lively exercise, rests instead of tiring one. And here we are, back in
London and thoroughly fit for an autumn's work.

We spent last Sunday with Alfred Cripps. He is in exuberant
spirits, coining money at the Bar and spending it freely in extensive
enlargements of Parmoor and in providing lavishly for his children's
pleasure. He has developed in the last six months into an ardent
follower of Mr Chamberlain's. He is angry and contemptuous of
Balfour and longs to depose him from the position of leadership. He
gives us to understand that that is the general desire among
Conservative M.P.s and still more so among Conservative wire-
pullers. With 'Joe' he seems to be on the most friendly terms and I
should imagine looks forward to being one of his Law
Officers. . . . He has, I think, made up his mind to become one of
Chamberlain's henchmen during the next months. And certainly he
will find himself much more sympathetic to J.C.'s signboard painting

and vigorous philistine creed than to the slack ways and fastidious culture of Arthur Balfour. . . . Alfred with his close professional connection with capitalist corporations and his intimate official relation to the Church would be exactly the man for a nominally Conservative but reforming and Nonconformist Premier to have as one of his instruments.

I had a confidential chat with him about the situation with regard to London education. He is to advise the Church to bestir itself and the Conservatives to drop their 'Moderates' and run go-ahead educationalists against the administrative nihilists of the Progressive party.

As to the fiscal controversy, both sets of economic arguments seem to me extraordinarily irrelevant. The notion that a protective tariff can *ipso facto* increase employment by keeping out foreign products is a stupid fallacy and can be tritely answered by the Theory of International Exchange. But the automatic effect of an unfavourable rate of exchange in reducing the price of home products and thus stimulating exports, rests on the assumption that the quantity and quality of productive energy remains constant, or at any rate unaffected by the competitive process. But this is exactly the point in dispute. The free-trader will assert that competition will stimulate the energies of the brainworker and capitalist, and that in spite of finding his market closed he will go on producing. This is no doubt true; there is more overtime in bad times than in good and concerns go on turning out goods long after the demand has begun to slacken. By the time this slackness of demand has affected prices sufficiently to close the concerns, the automatic effect of the rate of exchange in favouring exports from indebted countries has generally begun and is indeed in full swing. All that may be granted, exactly as we grant that the underpaid worker will work longer hours than the well-paid worker, may for a short time turn out more product.

But that does not answer our objection to Sweating, i.e. that the quality of the effort deteriorates and ultimately the worker degrades as an instrument of production. Now it may be likewise with the brainworking side of an industry. Unless the entrepreneur is secure of a good price in the home market he may not care to investigate and try experiments in processes. He may refuse to take on the proverbial 'sixty experts' bent on discovering new processes – at work in the German establishment. It may be more profitable for him to economize in standing charges and chop and change his product according to the whims of the foreign customers. Again the effect on a man's energies of feeling his market captured by a flood of 'foreign' imports which he believes to be subsidized and to be the outcome of processes he does not understand, may be quite different from being undersold by a neighbour producing under similar conditions or whose processes he is able to adapt. All this is mere conjecture, but I do not see that any one so far has adequately dealt with these psychological reactions.

The actual result of a protective tariff on the quantity and quality of technical skill and inventiveness [must depend] on the measure of patient thought and expensive experiment put into . . . manufacture. Whether these human factors will be increased or decreased by protection seems to me to be at the root of the question. I suggested this to Sidney but he dismissed it as tiresome. As it suits him to be a free-trader at present, and it obviously irritates him to raise the question of the possible expediency of 'vulgar protection', I won't trouble myself further about it. I daresay I don't understand all the complications of the Theory of International Exchange in its mechanically automatic adjustments which seem to me like Bastiat's Economic Harmonies – 'too good to be true'.

But personally I do not believe that driving trade into this and that channel is of such intrinsic importance as both parties think – and the uncertainty as to whether the consciousness of being secure or the stimulus of competition will be the best way of increasing the quantity and quality of productive energy, makes the game hardly worth the candle. The urgent question nowadays is not maximum production or even equality of distribution but the *character of consumption*, the vital problem of whether the use of a particular commodity or service does or does not increase efficiency? Probably we could, with advantage, cut away half the private expenditure of the nation and absolutely increase its happiness and capacity if we were permitted to select which part to cut off. At present we leave this vital problem of character of consumption to be solved by the appetites of each individual, even to the extent of permitting them to poison themselves and their children. It will not be so very long before a whole system of sumptuary laws – at any rate as regards non-adults, will come into force. That was a brilliant suggestion of H.G. Wells that we should divide the world into adults and non-adults. For some purposes we would raise 'the age of consent' to say, fifty!

Exactly a month today we returned to London. . . All our little enterprises prosper. The School term has opened successfully, just a slight increase of students and fees on the boom of last year. The Progressive Party is shaping well for the administration of the Act and the agitation against it, as far as London is concerned, is dying down out of fear of a Moderate majority. Towards Sidney the Progressives are on their good behaviour. They fear, I think, his power to bring about the Moderate majority at which he discreetly hints when they talk aggressively. . . . He is extraordinarily skilful in producing the impression on all parties that 'he is doing his best' to promote their *real* aims, and he seems to give this impression without in the least concealing his own views as to the next step to be taken or hiding his intention of taking it!

Victor Bulwer-Lytton, second Earl of Lytton (1876–1947) was strongly in favour of free trade and women's suffrage: his sister Constance became a notable suffragette, and his sister Betty married Gerald Balfour. He was made Viceroy of India in 1925.

1 November. [41 Grosvenor Road]
Have been working well on the whole, especially as I have had to lecture every week. But have been unnecessarily 'dicky' for two days owing to three dinners at which I have indulged. If we are to get through this local government book before the millennium I must keep at my maximum fitness.

Haldane dined with us alone. I gather that events are pointing (in that circle) to Asquith as Prime Minister with Rosebery serving under him as Foreign Secretary. Our friend was very vague as to politics. Not very definite as to Charlottenburg scheme, which Professor [Sir William] Ramsay is crabbing in all directions and the low state of South African finance making more difficult of attainment. Had secured young Lord Lytton to run about for him and wanted us to come and meet him, but that proved impossible.

Augustine Birrell (1850–1933) was a Liberal politician, lawyer and writer who became president of the Board of Education in 1905. John Morley's *Life of Gladstone* was published that autumn.

3 November. [41 Grosvenor Road]
Dined at the Asquiths'. Lord Hugh Cecil, the Lyttons, Sir Alfred Lyall and the Birrells. Our host and hostess most gracious, Lord Hugh disappointing, a bigot even on fiscal questions dominated entirely by a sort of deductive philosophy from *laissez-faire* principles

held as theological dogma. The Lyttons a charming young couple with the delightful gracious deference of the well-bred aristocrat. Sir Alfred gloomy, the Birrells somewhat hack 'diners-out', but on the whole a pleasant party gratifying to one's social vanity. Margot certainly has vitality and was full of fervour for the free-trade cause and scepticism of all other aspects of the Progressive programme, told us plentiful gossip about 'Arthur' [Balfour] and called all the élite of High Political Society by their Christian or pet names. It is a strange little clique, in which the bond of union is certainly not common conviction or desire for any kind of reform. (I fancy we are admitted to it, strange to say, not as reformers and experts but as persons with a special kind of chic.) I suggested that why Chamberlain would make headway, in spite of his bad arguments, was because he had a vision, desired to bring about a new state of affairs and was working day and night for a cause, that no one else wished anything but a quiet life and the *status quo*. Whereupon Lord Hugh and Margot [Asquith] exclaimed, 'Why change the present state of things – all is well.' Whereupon I burst out: 'That's all right for you, Lord Hugh, a convinced ultra-Tory, but is that a possible attitude for the leader of the Liberal Party who, one would think was, or ought to be, "professionally" aware of the mass of misery, vice and distorted human nature of our present state of society?' But conscious of the absurdity of indignation whilst eating and drinking at the Asquith table I calmed down and tried to make up for my useless and somewhat self-righteous indignation. I suppose it is well to be on good terms with these people, but I come back from their society to our shabby little home and regular hard work with a deep sigh of gratitude that I am an 'outsider' and have not the time or the energy to become one of them even if they opened wide the doors. Probably the door is kept open because we do not try 'to enter in'.

Becoming obsessed with my scheme of transforming English local government by sweeping away all areas, paying skilled men as representatives and adding, by co-option, residents and expert nucleus for different purposes. Such a body, say six hundred representatives for England, would make a Grand Council for all England's internal affairs, a similar Grand Council for Wales, Scotland and Ireland, breaking up into smaller units of local government according to function. Salaries of £1,000 a year out of national funds. . . .

Alfred [Cripps] called in splendid form. Very discontented with

Archbishop's attitude towards Education Act. Gave him the names of the bitterest opponents to the Act on L.C.C., the rotten part of the Progressive Party which would be best lopped off. Took care not to compromise Sidney.

Reading Gladstone's *Life*. Interesting to note that when after ten years' political experience he became convinced that the state had to be an infidel state and could not be used to promote religious truth, he turned straight away into a *laissez-faire* democrat holding persistently to the policy of diminishing the function of government and doing nothing but what every individual consented to, in advance. Hence his doctrine of nationalities and in the end Irish Home Rule. Add to this genuine alteration of intellectual creed, the heady emotion of feeling himself in accord with crude democracy and, owing to his superlative talent as a revivalist preacher, leading it, and you have the Gladstone of 1869–80. After 1880 he was out of sympathy with the collectivist trend of the newer democracy of town workmen and became a reactionary, appealing pathetically to the Nonconformist middle class in terror of the new creed and hating the new apostles. His soul was wrapped up in his own principles, religious and economic, each set in a watertight compartment; he never realized the new order of ideas. Moreover he was socially an aristocrat and disliked the parvenu in riches and political power, such as Chamberlain.

Progressives gained considerably (as I predicted) at borough council elections, which will perhaps wake up the Catholics and Church to action and possibly lull the Progressives into confidence for L.C.C. election: we shall lie low and say nothing and look after our own constituency.

MacDonald had been on a visit to South Africa, had been absent when the electoral register was compiled, and was thus ineligible for re-election.

18 November. [41 Grosvenor Road]
Hewins sends in his resignation of the Directorship of the School of Economics, having taken service under Chamberlain to work out the details of his tariff proposals. So ends our close relationship with this remarkable man, remarkable for audacity, enterprise, zeal and skill in presenting facts and manipulating persons, most remarkable for confidence in his own powers, more than confidence – an overestimation of them. These qualities have served us well in

building up, from nothing, the reputation of the School, in steering its fortunes through the indifference and hostility of the London academic and business world, in obtaining and keeping the co-operation of men of diverse views and conflicting interests. These same qualities are exactly those which will fit him to manipulate the tariff or the promise of a tariff so constructed as to bring wealth to all. . . He is an ideal henchman for Joe – fanatical, well-informed, unveracious and devoted to his cause. The only weak point is his overdone duplicity – he loves a mystery and duplex behaviour even when both are unnecessary, and that quality in him engenders a certain suspicion and dislike among his fellow workers. . . .

Meanwhile to us falls the task of finding a successor and reorganizing the staff of the London School. Hewins has published his resignation without consultation with Sidney as to time and terms, has given us a certain impression of snapping his fingers at us, which has half amused and half irritated us. But I tell Sidney we must see him safely off the premises, he taking our hearty good wishes and we, I hope, keeping his good word and good will, inwardly as well as outwardly, the best of friendly partings. . . .

A strange piece of luck! J.R. MacDonald knocked off the Register and disabled from standing for the L.C.C. at the next election, an iniquitous flaw in the law, but not for us, an 'ill wind'.

J.P. Altgeld (1847–1902) was the reforming Democratic governor of Illinois 1892–96. The Webbs had met him in Chicago in 1898. Rosebery's political position was steadily declining owing to his reluctance to assert any clear leadership and the growing strength of Liberal unity as tariff reform divided their opponents.

26 November. [41 Grosvenor Road]
Bryan, the late Democratic candidate for the U.S. Presidency, dined with us last night. A most attractive personality, a large-bodied and large-brained man with great simplicity and directness of nature, a delightful temper and kindly attitude towards life. Knew nothing of administration and was, in all the range of political and social questions, dominated by abstractions – by words and not by things as they actually are. A Jeffersonian Democrat like Altgeld. But shrewd in his estimate of men and women and with a strong unselfconscious and vivid faculty of speech.

Took him to Rosebery's meeting. Sidney and I sat and listened with consternation to 'our leader' declaiming against public expenditure *per se* and suggesting as an excellent reason for objecting to a

Protectionist tariff that it would lead to the regulation of the sweated industries at home. Playing straight into Joe's hands, verifying his assertion that free trade in commodities is inseparable from free trade in labour! Suicidal for a leader of the Progressive party. After a sleepless night I sent off an angry little note to Haldane. . . . I daresay Rosebery did not mean all he said but that is no comfort to us. It is the outward effect of his words not their internal origin that interests us. If Joe were to take up the 'national minimum' he would quite romp in after a few years propaganda.

28 November. [41 Grosvenor Road]
Kept my pledge against coffee and alcohol for the month – treated myself to a cup after lunch today, and retake the pledge for two months from this evening. I am better without either, and, though coffee is a temptation, I have practically got over the worst part of giving it up and might as well stick to it. Have taken cream inadvertently two or three times in the month, but shall avoid it in future, without insisting on total abstinence. Should like to get into the habit of never taking a mouthful more after I feel that my hunger is satisfied. I have reduced myself as a rule to three cigarettes a day. Health better than ever before.

All through Sidney's courtship he had sought to persuade Beatrice that their combined abilities of $1 + 1$ made 11 not 2.

1 December. [41 Grosvenor Road]
Sidney somewhat disappointed at not getting a prize in *The Times* competition. He had almost persuaded himself that he would win the £1,000 because his number was 4124 which added together makes 11, *our* mystical symbol of partnership. Dear boy, I love him for his simplicity and his entire lack of 'side' and 'pretension'. It never occured to him that he was too busy and important to spend spare hours and risk defeat in competing with 16,000 others in answering catch questions. Moreover he made the competition a subject of conversation whenever he was gravelled for lack of matter with relatives and dinner-parties. As Graham Wallas once said when he watched him running to catch a train: 'What I like about you, Webb, is that there is no damned nonsense about style.'

Mr Arthur Acland has been in once or twice lately to talk over education with Sidney and to arrange for interviewing Austen

Chamberlain and Morant. We got on to Rosebery – Acland not cordial to his leadership, intimated that he had been intolerable as head of the Cabinet 1894–95, shy, huffy and giving himself the airs of a little German king towards his Ministers. Had neither the quality of public-school Englishmen nor the courteous and punctilious formality of the well-trained *grand seigneur*, which is the best substitute for it. 'He complained that his colleagues never came to see him, but when we did go he had hurried off to the Durdans or to Dalmeny. Then after a Cabinet he might ask one of us to come to lunch – but of course we had, as busy Ministers, already mapped out our day with deputations and parliamentary work. If we pleaded a previous engagement, he would seem offended.' Then he gave us a vision of the strange weird ways which Rosebery indulged in at home – delighting in surrounding himself with some low fellows and being *camarades* with them – then suddenly requesting one of his free-thinking colleagues to go to church with him, or insisting that some elderly conventional guest should drive out at ten o'clock at night for a couple of hours in an open victoria, with a postilion galloping at high speed through the night air. 'Always posing,' was Acland's summary, 'imagining himself to be an extraordinary being with special privileges towards the world.' It is odd how that impression exactly corresponds to my memory of him on board the *Russia* thirty years ago [on Beatrice's visit to America in 1873] and with my estimate of his attitude towards us during the last four years. For instance – a very considerable amount of pose – fictitious sentiment obviously a source of enjoyment to himself. He is certainly unique – whether for good or for evil – an asset or an incubus to the Progressive Party is a question.

Saw Hewins at the School today and had a chat with him. Suffering from a reaction of regret in giving up the School and dread of the difficulties of his task. Already at work interviewing manufacturers. Warned me to keep a tight hand on Mackinder and to maintain the concrete side of the School. We have work cut out for us as usual.

Sir Edwin Cornwall (1863–1953), later a Liberal M.P., was currently the Whip of the Progressive Party in the L.C.C.

6 December. [41 Grosvenor Road]
Haldane looked in this afternoon to consult on [London] University business. Reproached him half seriously and half in chaff with Rosebery's attitude. 'If Joe were to take up the notion of a national

minimum of wages, health and education and run it alongside of preferential duty or a protective tariff you would be done, Mr Haldane.' 'But Joe won't do that,' he retorted with a self-complacent emphasis. 'He would break up his party if he did.' Obviously the Liberal leaders do not seriously want social reform and would only take it up in a practical manner if they were forced to do so by competition. They are in fact relying on the stupid conservatism which they profess to despise and to fight. And I fear our friends the 'Limps' are in this respect the worst sinners. The others have some sort of hazy notion that after pulling down the existing structure they would build up something in its stead on the basis of more equal distribution of wealth. We cannot join with them because we don't want to pull down the existing structure; all we want is to slowly and quietly transform and add to it. So that we remain isolated from all political parties as far as party cries are concerned, though willing and eager to work with any party who are consciously or unconsciously engaged in constructive work. But it is unpleasant, this perpetual transit from camp to camp, however bitterly hostile these camps feel to one another. It is perilously near becoming both a spy and a traitor, or rather being considered such by the camp to which we officially belong. No wonder the Progressives are beginning to feel uncomfortably disposed towards Sidney!

Up to last week he had brought the Progressives along nicely in accepting the Education Act and agreeing to work under it. But without consulting him the other members of the party committee decided to bring forward a 'scheme' leaving out all outside members from the Education Committee beyond five women and five members of the existing School Board. He protested but they were obdurate. 'They say that you have hitherto led us by the nose, Webb,' remarked Cornwall pleasantly. 'Now it is your turn to follow.' He won't succeed in getting them over the stile and I am not sure that I wish him to. Of course it is his duty to give them his best advice, but there are some good reasons why it is better they should 'harden their hearts' and demonstrate to the Church and the Catholics that they mean business. 'Withdraw yourself somewhat from their counsels and be silent and serious, quietly prophesy Moderate victories as the result of this action. They will not listen to your warnings, but if the event prove you right, they will remember – if wrong they will be too flushed with triumph to think of you. Moreover,' I add, 'victories the Moderates are *certain* to have; it is only a question of the number.'

8 December. [41 Grosvenor Road]

My old friend [Herbert Spencer] passed away peacefully this morning. Since I have been back in London this autumn I have been down to Brighton most weeks – last week I was there on Monday, Friday and Saturday, trying to soften these days of physical discomfort and mental depression by affectionate sympathy. 'My oldest and dearest friend,' he has called me these last visits. 'Let us break bread together,' he said on Monday and insisted on a plate of grapes being set on the bed and both of us eating them. 'You and I have had the same ends,' he repeated again. 'It is only in methods we have differed.'

On Saturday he was quite conscious and bade me an affectionate farewell, but he clearly wanted to be let alone to die and not trouble with further mental effort. Certainly these last months, while he has been looking for death immediately – even longing for it – he has been benigner and less inclined to be querulous about his own miseries. But what with his dogmatic perversity in persisting in pernicious ways of living, his fretfulness towards and suspicion of his household, his pessimism about the world, it has been a sad ending. Indeed, the last twenty years have been sad, poisoned by morphia and self-absorption and contented with that strangely crude vision of all human life as a series of hard bargains. . . . Still, if we strip Herbert Spencer's life of its irritation and superficial egotism – brought about, I believe, by poisonous food and drugs – and of its narrow philosophy of conduct, there remains the single-hearted persistent seeker after truth, the absolute faith that a measure of truth was attainable and would, if sought for earnestly, bring about consolation and reformation to mankind – the implicit assumption that he must live for the future of the human race, not for his own comfort, pleasure or success. If he had only not dogmatically denied that which he could not perceive or understand; if he had, with sincerity, admitted his own deficiencies of knowledge and perception – perhaps even of reasoning power – if he had had a ray of true humility – what a great and inspiring personality he might have been. As it was, he was a light to others in the *common places* of existence, but one that failed in the greater crises of life and was quenched by sorrow or by temptation. Did the light that was in him survive even for himself? To me he seemed in these last years to be stumbling in total darkness, hurting himself and then crying aloud in his lonely distress, clinging to his dogmas but without confident faith, with an almost despairing and defiant pride of intellect. Again I assert that all these strange shortcomings and defects were like an ugly and distorted setting to a small but brilliant stone. This setting may drop from him at death and the everlasting brilliant of truth-seeking remain. He will be among the elect.

9 December. [41 Grosvenor Road]
As I sat this morning arranging the papers for our next chapter my thoughts were perpetually drifting to the dear old man, trying to recall the details of my long debt of gratitude for his friendship. As a little child he was perhaps the only person who persistently cared for me – or rather who singled me out as one who was worthy of being trained and looked after. Intellectually he had no dominant influence until after the age of twenty, when I first began to study his work systematically. But though I had not until then grasped his philosophy, merely talking to him and listening to his long and pleasant discussions with Mother stimulated both my curiosity as to the facts and my desire to discover the principles or laws underlying these facts. He taught me to look on all social institutions exactly as if they were plants or animals, things that could be observed, classified and explained and the action of which could to some extent be foretold if one knew enough about them.

It was after Mother's death, in the first years of mental vigour, that I read the *First Principles* and followed his generalization through biology, psychology and sociology. This generalization illuminated my mind but the impression it created was only temporary – the [several] parts of it became incorporated in all my future work. The importance of functional adaptation was at the basis of a good deal of the faith in collective regulation I afterwards developed. And during those years it was mainly his intellectual influence that forced me, against my feelings and my interests, to withstand the imperious demand for the submission of my intellect to another powerful personality. In that way the philosopher beat the politician. With this episode Herbert Spencer's direct influence over me was exhausted.

Once engaged in the application of the scientific method to the facts of social organization, in my observations of East End life, of Co-operation, of Factory Acts, of trade unionism, I shook myself completely free from *laissez-faire* bias – in fact I suffered from a somewhat violent reaction from it. And in later years even the attitude towards religion and towards supernaturalism which I had accepted from him as the last word of enlightenment have become replaced by another attitude, no less agnostic but with an inclination to doubt materialism more than I doubt spiritualism, to listen for voices in the great Unknown to open my consciousness to the non-material world – in prayer. If I had to live my life over again according to my present attitude I should, I think, remain a conforming member of the National Church. My case, I think, is typical of the rise and fall of Herbert Spencer's influence over the men and women of my own generation.

It is more difficult to unravel the effect of his *Example* in the conduct of life. The amazing loyalty to a disinterested aim, the patience, endurance, the noble faith manifested in his daily life sustained me through those dark years of discouragement, before success made continuous effort easy and loving comradeship made it delightful. Contrariwise, the fitfulness, suspicion, petty irritations and antagonisms which have disfigured the later years have, perhaps unjustly, increased my distaste for all varieties of utilitarian ethics, all attempts to apply the scientific method to the *purposes* as distinguished from the *processes* of existence. His failure to attain to the higher levels of conduct and feeling has sealed my conviction in the bankruptcy of science when it attempts to realize the cause or the aim of human existence.

14 December. [41 Grosvenor Road]
The last words, honest and noble words, were said by Leonard Courtney to a few friends, and one or two disciples and admirers gathered together in the little brick hall of the Crematorium on the outskirts of London. The ceremony was simple and dignified – with an absence of rite or ostentation – every detail executed according to his instructions, with puritanic spareness, decorum and precision, but with perfect 'consideration towards those who wished to attend'. And here ends a long-drawn-out tie of friendship, extending from my earliest childhood to past middle life – a tie unbroken by growing discordance of opinion, by marriage, or by extreme old age and disease.

The swing against the government at the Dulwich and Lewisham by-elections had been less than anticipated.

17 December. [41 Grosvenor Road]
Sidney went to lunch with Bishop of Stepney ten days ago to consult about L.C.C. elections. The Bishop asked him definitely whether the

Church should throw its whole weight in the Moderate side or should attempt to discriminate. I gather that Sidney intimated that he could not honestly say that the Progressives, if in a majority, would administer the Act fairly to the Church or well from the point of view of education. In short he has made up his mind in favour of a Moderate majority in spite of all the disadvantages. I think the Progressives clearly understand that he and they have come to the parting of the ways, at least for the coming election. Before Dulwich and Lewisham they were inclined to defy him; whether they won't presently get into a funk remains to be seen. But it will be too late — they and we must abide by our respective policies and one or other of us has to be defeated on March 5th. From the standpoint of efficient administration of the law as it stands the Progressives are too thoroughly infected with the Nonconformist microbe to be of any service. For the next three or six years they must be kept under water to rid them of that little parasite. But very naturally they think it better that 'one man' should suffer and doubtless feel confident of their strength to bring him to justice. The issue lies in the hands of the mass of non-political voters. Sidney awaits the decision with equanimity. He does not expect to lose his seat because in the last extremity he could appeal to the official Conservatives to support him and he will have the enthusiastic support of Catholics and Church. But if there is to be an overwhelming Noncon. majority he thinks it better that they should have the whole responsibility of deciding on a policy without any obstruction from him, and hence it might be better for him to be out of the Council, for a time at least.

Ilya Metchnikoff (1845–1916) was a Russian biologist whose work concerned the prevention of intestinal putrefaction. He became assistant director of the Pasteur Institute in Paris. J.M.E. McTaggart (1866–1925) was a Fellow of Trinity College, Cambridge and Hegelian philosopher. Ferdinand Canning Scott Schiller (1864–1937) was a German-born British philosopher.

18 December. [41 Grosvenor Road]
Bertrand Russell published a short article — 'The Free Man's Worship' — in the *Independent Review* which throws an illuminating light on his character and conduct. In it he adopts, as a starting-point, the pessimistic hypothesis of the universe, that it is 'blind, mechanical, cruel', lower than man, that man alone has, by accident, attained to morality and intelligence (much the same hypothesis as that in Metchnikoff's *Nature of Man*). Upon this hypothesis he bases, by a

process of reasoning which it is not easy to follow, a fine morality, tender towards others, stoical towards self – a morality devised to sustain us in this tragedy of life. The interest of the article does not lie in the fine passages on conduct but in his betrayal of the purely agnostic attitude, and his deliberate acceptance of a hypothesis which cannot be proved to be true by the scientific method. This course he has always declared to be immoral in cases in which the choice has fallen on the religious hypothesis – hence his indignation at William James's *Varieties of Religious Experience* or at such Hegelians as McTaggart, Haldane, Schiller. I thought he held that, as pure reason and scientific verification could not be applied to anything but phenomena, it was a betrayal of the integrity of the intellect to accept *any explanation* of the universe as a whole. But it is clear that his personal bias towards the tragic in life has made him select and dogmatically affirm the most tragic of all the hypotheses of the nature of the great 'unknown' – the one in which man poses as the supreme martyr of life, condemned to suffer until extinguished as an individual or a race. Realizing this bias towards the tragic explanation of the universe, one feels less perturbed at what he conceives to be the concrete tragedy of his present life. Tragedy is a pose with him, and both the facts of the universe and the facts of matrimony must live up to it. As a matter of fact, his marriage is an amazingly fortunate one – but if the facts are not such as make up a tragedy so much the worse for the facts! Fortunately his splendid morality outweighs his tragic propensities and I doubt whether Alys realizes that he thinks his married life an heroically lived tragedy.

The Nature of Man by Metchnikoff, a book just now causing some sensation, is based on the same pessimistic hypothesis. But it is more practical in its deductions, which are to find out 'the secret of physical health', 'longevity' and 'the desire for death, when death becomes inevitable'. And towards the solution he throws out a brilliant scientific hypothesis – that, owing to a bad regimen, we never attain physiological old age but always die a violent death, eaten up prematurely by our own phagocytes; and therefore, we object to and resist the process – exactly as a healthy-minded man usually does object to violent death. His moral is a simple life – above all things simple food and little of it. As description of processes I believe both in his account of what does happen and his suggestion of what would happen if we lived the wisest kind of life. But he seems to me to transcend the sphere of the scientific method when he asserts that science alone will discover 'the goal of human existence'. The book of

310

course is rank materialism of the crudest sort and Metchnikoff would have as little patience with Russell's 'The Free Man's Worship' as he would have of Catholic Christianity. Indeed, he hints that the teaching of any *unverified knowledge* should be prohibited like the consumption of poisons. How far his own book with its daring excursions into the land of conjecture would survive the application of this principle is doubtful.

Lord Stanley of Alderly (1839–1925) was a Liberal M.P. until 1885 and vice-chairman of the London School Board until 1904. He was an educational pioneer who resisted proposals to strengthen the influence of voluntary or denominational bodies in public education.

20 December. [41 Grosvenor Road]
The effect created by the accession of Charles Booth to the protectionist ranks proves what power, nowadays, is wielded by a non-party expert who is free to throw himself on one side or the other, and who is widely known to be personally disinterested, if not, indeed, philanthropic in his ends. Intrinsically I do not attach much importance to C.B.'s opinion on the fiscal question – he has no special knowledge, a great deal of prejudice, and by no means any marked capacity for intricate reasoning. But for the world at large his credentials are seventeen volumes, a public life of thirty years' service, and a great expenditure of private means for public objects. A platform which even a more powerful politician might well envy. Such a position is the sort of thing I aim at for Sidney.

Lewisham and Dulwich have sobered the Progressives, and nothing could be better in substance and form than McKinnon Wood's explanation of the Progressive policy. But sad to say we have no confidence that it means a change of spirit – it is only a 'lying low' until after the election. If they come back in a majority, or at least a large majority, they intend to make Lord Stanley chairman and carry on the old School Board tradition both in procedure and policy. 'If we have to aid the voluntary schools,' Stanley said a few years ago, 'there won't be one left in six years.' And what is worse from our standpoint, the advent of the School Board Progressives to power means the squeezing out of the secondary as against the higher elementary schools and the starvation of university education. It is an intensely disgreeable situation, Sidney and the Progressive leaders in an armed truce, watching each other with dire suspicion. . . . The election will be the last of three duels which Sidney has fought within a year –

the first with Macnamara to get the L.C.C. made the Education Authority, the second with Dr Clifford to make the Progressives take action under the Act, and the third with the Progressive leaders – to return an L.C.C. which will carry out his adminstrative policy. He has won hands down in the first two, which for ultimate purposes are by far the most important. In the last he may well be beaten, which will mean a temporary retirement from administrative work. If we are beaten we must take it good-temperedly. It is clear to me there is no way out of the fight – the policies are incompatible. But I want the fight well in the open.

∽ 1904 ∾

6 January. [41 Grosvenor Road]
C.P. Trevelyan married to the handsome daughter of my old acquaintance Hugh Bell, a man Sidney and I thoroughly like and respect, intellectually and morally. Mrs Bell is an elegant and pleasant woman; the daughter is a fine-looking good-tempered somewhat hard young person with little public spirit and few intellectual interests. As her husband says, she is a good bargain – splendid health, capable, well off, well connected, well conducted and a good comrade. But when they lunched here the other day I felt that neither life would be wasted owing to the hardness of the other nature. They would be prosperous and uninteresting. Whether their affection for each other will survive the first years of passion except as an alliance to extract as much as possible from the world I doubt, but there will be no tragedy. Perhaps I am a wee bit sorry for the woman, for Charles Trevelyan has an arid character and a narrow intelligence, and possibly Molly Bell is better than her looks – less superficial in thought and feeling than circumstances have made her to the outward eye. Heaven preserve the woman who ceased to be a good bargain, or who discovered that she had a 'soul'.

The reception was an agreeable meeting of friends of the political and literary worlds, interesting because the casual chat revealed the strange cleavages which the fiscal and educational issues have brought about. It is now impossible to say on what side you may find any friend. Such enlightened folk as the Fred Pollocks and Hugh Bell are hot free-traders, Mrs Humphry Ward a hot anti-Education Act, so that we find ourselves far more sympathetic with the present government than those who ten years ago would have considered us rank rebels. Whether this recruiting of reactionary enlightenment will strengthen the Liberal Party is, to my mind, doubtful. It makes it still more difficult to agree on any constructive policy and without this constructive policy one would think that it was impossible for the Liberal leaders to cure the rebellious section within the 'anti-conservative' party. Meanwhile all who wish actual reform carried out without reference to other considerations cast their eye on this or that Conservative leader.

[Beatrice here gives a resumé of progress on their book on local government.]

17 January. [41 Grosvenor Road]

[Sidney] has been absorbed most mornings in preparing for the L.C.C. election both at Deptford and in London. Seven letters he wrote yesterday to editors enclosing his book and turning their minds to an anti-Nonconformist movement, to end in a considerable reduction of the Progressive majority, if not in a moderate victory. If he brings off his plan and becomes responsible for the administration of the Act I shall get still less of his time and thought for the book. Fortunately I keep splendidly fit and can work steadily every day but I am deplorably slow in getting over the ground and have to be constantly stopping to call for clearer and more copious evidence.

Except for four dinners of the staff of the School of Economics, with gatherings of the students afterwards, which I have arranged for February and March, I am keeping myself free from social engagements. It is not the time, but the energy I lack, unless I deliberately abstract it from my work. In the afternoons I take exercise, ponder and read – about twice a week I walk along the Embankment to St Paul's and listen to the anthem and join in the beautiful liturgy of the evening prayer. Sidney's news, letters and newspapers, an occasional friend or student to lunch, now and again a few friends to dinner or a 'dinner out' are sufficient from the standpoint of the greatest output. How any sane mortal with resources of their own and a few intelligent friends can exert themselves to get into 'Society' passes my comprehension. And yet I have just expended 21 guineas on an evening dress! I hasten to add that it is four years since I paid the same amount for my present evening garment. Still, I might have done without it, if I had been quite single-minded in my indifference to social glamour. The cold-drawn truth is that though I am honestly indifferent as to whether or not I see the great world, when I do enter in I like to do credit to my reputation – an unworthy desire, I own, unworthy of an ascetic student and a collectivist reformer!

In December 1903 Sidney published a book, *London Education*, which was an expanded version of his October article in the *Nineteenth Century*.

25 January. [41 Grosvenor Road]
Everything looks promising for Deptford election. The Church and the Catholics are at present enthusiastic for Sidney, the Labour party solid and even the Nonconformists after Sidney's meeting with them on the 22nd January have veered round and promised to support him and Phillimore. . . . The last week or so there has been a closing-up of Progressive forces and a great disposition to be conciliatory to Sidney in spite of the issue of his *London Education* which to all intents and purposes is an anti-Nonconformist manifesto and is so treated by the Conservative papers. But the Liberal newspapers insist on claiming it as the utterance of an enthusiastic Progressive with cranky views on elementary education. As regards the general contest we have become passive – in fact, it will be impossible for Sidney not to support some Progressives. However, we have given the Moderates a good push forward, if they cannot now run by themselves they are not worth much! Candidates seem to be the difficulty – a man who is at once public-spirited and a Moderate seems a rare animal, sensible and pleasant creatures when you do light on them.

The Conservatives were no more linked, officially, with the Moderates than the Liberals were formally associated with the Progressives, though in both cases there was a close political tie. War between Japan and Russia broke out in February 1904. In England there was considerable support for Japan and the Webbs were among those who admired Japanese efficiency, which seemed to contrast with the British weaknesses revealed by the Boer War.

13 February. [41 Grosvenor Road]
Conservative opposition at Deptford collapsed – in other constituencies too, worse luck. Conservative associations refuse to back the Moderates, not wishing to be beaten so soon before the parliamentary election, Progressives promising the Church to be 'good boys'. 'Interests' feel that they have nothing more to fear from a

Progressive L.C.C. – ratepayers (if such a party exists) cease to be interested in the maintenance of voluntary schools now that they are to come on the rates. Altogether an astonishing apathy in the forces of *reaction*. Most inconsiderate to us who are going to go on working with the old Progressive Party, purged we hope of some of its more obstreperous members. We are inclined to be philosophical about it, feeling ourselves powerless to control the situation.

Looking beyond parochial affairs one notes a distinct retrogression in the Chamberlain movement. The tariff commission is already spent as a rallying force and the Great Man's recent appearance on the platform and in the House have not been a success. How far an undercurrent of demand for protection is growing among manufacturers it is difficult to estimate, but the surface waters accumulating from all sections of the enlightened are running straight towards free trade. The troubles of the new coalition will begin when the Liberals come into office – then will be Joe's chance if he seizes it.

Meanwhile, enter little Japan into world politics, a rising star of human self-control and enlightenment.

Bernard Shaw had been adopted as Progressive candidate for South St Pancras.

27 February. [41 Grosvenor Road]
Sidney and Phillimore returned unopposed for Deptford, a somewhat striking comment on the threats of last summer that 'he shall lose his seat.' He is now turning his attention to getting GBS in for St Pancras. What effect GBS's brilliant slashing to the right and the left among his own nominal supporters will have, remains to be seen; the party organizers have long ago given up the seat as lost. Sidney has written to every clergyman in St Pancras (about twenty-one) sending them a copy of his book and imploring them to go hard for Shaw. He has even got the Bishop of Stepney's blessing sent to the Rural Dean. He has now taken charge of two-thirds of the constituency, installed the Spencers [Webb research assistants] in a committee room and called up the whole of the Fabian Society on Shaw's behalf. Whether this effort will win what would be a forlorn hope to any other Progressive candidate, and will counteract the enemies GBS makes in our current ranks we cannot tell. The Shaws have been good friends to us and we would not like them to have a humiliating defeat. What that erratic genius will do, if he gets on the L.C.C., heaven will know some day, but I am inclined to think that in

315

the main he will back up Sidney. And he will become the *enfant terrible* of the Progressive party and make Sidney look wisely conventional. In the Fabian Society they have certainly managed to supplement each other in a curiously effective way – let us hope it will be the same on the L.C.C. But he is not likely to get in!

Meanwhile our old friend Graham Wallas is left in the cold, with even a cross against his name so far as our influence with the Church is concerned. It is an uncomfortable fact that we are convinced that on the Council he will obstruct our side of things without promoting his own. One has, in this ruthless world, to accept uncomfortable facts and act on them. We try to persuade ourselves that it will be better for him if he drops out for the next three years, or at any rate has the minor position of a co-opted member. However the party say that Hoxton was a safe win and St Pancras a certain loss and our wish may well be father to our thought.

It is strange how impossible it is for the keenest observer to foretell the result of an election when three years have elapsed from the last. We want a small Moderate majority. . . . The best we can hope for is a largely decreased Progressive majority, and between that and a small Moderate majority there is not much to choose. If the Progressives come romping back, which they certainly would have done if Sidney had not bestirred the Church and the Catholics, it will be bad for education.

R.T. Reid, later Lord Loreburn (1846–1923), was a lawyer and Liberal politician who became Lord Chancellor in 1905. The 'Chinese labour' issue arose when the mine-owners of the annexed Transvaal imported indentured Chinese workers for the Rand goldmines: the outcry of religious, labour and reformist opinion against the Balfour government was fierce and electorally damaging to the Conservatives.

1 March. [41 Grosvenor Road]
Dined with the Munro-Fergusons one day, Haldane the next: little parties of 'Limps'. There is depression in those ranks. Within the Liberal Party the Campbell-Bannerman, Spencer, Morley crew, followed by Reid, Lloyd George, Macnamara, etc., are in the ascendant and are asserting their right to make the future Cabinet and include as much or as little of the Roseberyites as they choose. Especially against Haldane is there a set. Rosebery is also at a discount – a heavier discount than he has been since he came back to speech-making politics. Partly due to growing discredit of the results of the

war (Chinese labour!) and dislike for expenditure on the Forces, partly to Rosebery's disclaimer of social reform, and to the quite opposite reason, the rehabilitation of *laissez-faire* by the free-trade propaganda. Little Englandism, crude democracy, economy, secularism, are all again to the front in the official Liberal Party, are in fact the only actively militant forces with a policy to push. The vacuum over which the 'Limps' have zealously watched cannot be kept intact, and the old creed and the new cries are rushing in, in default of better stuff.

The success of Sidney in wheeling the Progressives round to promise the energetic and prompt administration of the Act has been enormously helped by the publication of his little book with its extensive and detailed constructive programme. It has made it quite impossible for anyone to fight him as an obstructive or reactionary as the Campbell-Bannerman Liberals are fighting Rosebery and Haldane. . . . Our poor 'Limp' friends are indeed a pitiful spectacle. With the other sections of the Liberal Party we are completely out of touch and are held to be of no account. This matters less to us since we don't believe they can accomplish anything of importance if they *do* come in, and if they are able to do so some one or other of them will sooner or later find his way to Sidney to pick his brains. A man who has brains and is willing to lend them freely to anyone who can use them will sooner or later have his share of real power. The trouble is that the C.B. set which are coming into office are not likely to achieve the position in the country which would enable them to make use of suggestions – it will be the stalemate of progress. Rosebery sneering at everything, and Chamberlain rampaging through the Empire for the rotten device of import duties. If Joe could only grasp the whole policy of a *national minimum* I would willingly throw in the import duties as a silly and expensive ornament to attract the employing class to the policy of state regulation.

Sir George Lawrence Gomme (1853–1916) was Clerk to the L.C.C. from 1900–15. Robert Harcourt (1878–1962) was a radical Liberal M.P. and journalist. His brother was Lewis Harcourt (1863–1922) who became Liberal M.P. in 1904. They were both sons of Sir William Harcourt (1827–1904).

3 March. [41 Grosvenor Road]
As I sat at home this morning working at the Book, Sidney having gone up to GBS's committee room, three typical interruptions occurred. Gomme, the Clerk of the L.C.C., came down in haste to

consult Sidney on new information before the committee met this afternoon as to exact wording of the reference to the Education Committee by the new L.C.C.; a messenger came with a note from the Editor of the *Daily Mail* urgently begging Sidney to write the leader telling the citizens of London How to Vote on Saturday; and Robert Harcourt broke in to beg Sidney's advice and help to stave off a Labour candidate against his brother in Rossendale, the latter an altogether mistaken estimate of our influence with Labour leaders! But the discreet guidance of important officials and hidden influence in the press are both characteristic of Sidney's peculiar gift for 'getting his own way' without anyone quite realizing how.

7 March. [41 Grosvenor Road]
GBS beaten badly, elsewhere the Progressives romping back with practically undiminished members. As to the first event, we are not wholly grieved. GBS with a small majority might have been useful, with an overwhelming one [he] would simply have been compromising. He certainly showed himself hopelessly intractable during the election, refused to adopt any orthodox devices as to address and polling cards, inventing brilliant ones of his own, all quite unsuited to any constituency but Fabians or Souls. Insisted that he was an Atheist, that though a teetotaller he would force every citizen to imbibe a quartern of rum to cure any tendency to intoxication, laughed at the Nonconformist conscience and chaffed the Catholics about Transubstantiation, abused the Liberals and contemptuously patronized the Conservatives – until nearly every section was equally disgruntled. His bad side is very prominent at an election – vanity and lack of reverence for knowledge or respect for other people's prejudices; even his good qualities – quixotic chivalry to his opponents and cold-drawn truth ruthlessly administered to possible supporters – are magnificent but not war. Anyway, we did our best for him, Sidney even puffing him outrageously in the *Daily Mail,* and he and Charlotte are duly grateful. He will never be selected again by any constituency that any wire-puller thinks can be won.

As for the general result – it is perturbing. The Church and the Catholics have apparently exercised no kind of influence, those sent to Coventry by the ecclesiastics being apparently no whit the worse. The Moderates in many constituencies, deserted by the official Conservatives, have had to bear the full brunt of the government's unpopularity – they come back as they went out, virtually powerless. . . .

11 March. [41 Grosvenor Road]
To our delighted surprise the Progressives, so far as the leaders are concerned, have returned to Spring Gardens [the L.C.C. offices] in admirable temper; they seem literally *chastened* by their prosperity. At the lengthy party committees that have been held prior to the party meeting today they have welcomed Sidney back into their counsels with great cordiality, quite disposed (now that they see that the party is safe and sound) to listen to his advice on education matters. They have even gone the length of suggesting that he should be chairman of the Education Committee, though they realize the difficulties, but he has decidedly negatived that notion, if anyone else can be found who will take the job on and let him work under them. . . . Altogether matters look far more promising than we could have hoped, with a thumping Progressive majority. It really seems as if Sidney had converted his own party by his book, at the infinitesimal cost of not being chairman for the first year, or perhaps not at all, in many and important ways a positive advantage. I am going to open an 'educationist' address book of persons likely to be useful in that sphere. I must *organize* our contact with them; we must learn the facts ourselves and spread our own ideas. . . .

15 April. [41 Grosvenor Road]
Ten days at Felixstowe and only one lazy one, Good Friday. For the first three we worked hard finishing the chapters on 'Nuisances', the last five or six we spent on county, town and vestry records with the Spencers at Ipswich and Woodbridge, a happy and really restful time because it turned the current of Sidney's thoughts away from the little intrigues and jealousies of the L.C.C. and its Education Committee on to the bigger currents of past developments in local government. We have quite settled to devote the next year and possibly three years to the Book. Sidney to slack off the L.C.C. I intend to take him off the scene early in July. . . . I am considering Scotland and the possibility of a really long sojourn there with our material and the Spencers looking up things for us in London. . .

19 April. [41 Grosvenor Road]
We have had a couple of days with H.G. Wells and his wife at

Sandgate, and they are returning the visit here. We like him much –
he is absolutely genuine and full of inventiveness, a 'speculator' in
ideas, somewhat of a gambler but perfectly aware that his hypotheses
are not verified. In one sense he is a romancer spoilt by romancing, but
in the present stage of sociology he is useful to gradgrinds like
ourselves in supplying us with loose generalizations which we can use
as instruments of research. And we are useful to him in supplying an
endless array of carefully sifted facts and broad administrative
experience.

I asked him to tell me frankly why Wallas and some others were so
intensely suspicious of us, and seemed bent on obstructing every
proposal of Sidney's. He threw out two suggestions – first that Sidney
(and no doubt I) was too fond of 'displaying' his capacity for 'tactics';
that he gave a 'foxy' impression; that he had better fall back on being an
enthusiast; secondly that we were always regarded as a 'combination'
working into each other's hands but not impelled by *quite* the same
motives, or inspired by quite the same purpose; that I was regarded as
a 'reactionary' with an anti-radical creed and it was suspected that
Sidney would eventually veer round to my side. Of course we have got
to be ourselves, whatever may be the drawbacks, but his criticism
increases my inclination for a somewhat severe abstinence from trying
'to run the show', for a quiet and unselfconscious withdrawal into
other work for the next three years. Directly the grant for the School is
safe we will go into retreat with our papers and books until the
October session.

Frederic Thesiger (1868–1933), afterwards Viscount Chelmsford, was a
Moderate member of the L.C.C.

20 April. [41 Grosvenor Road]
For the Wells's we had a little dinner – carefully selected – Mr
Balfour, the Bishop of Stepney, the Bernard Shaws, Mrs Reeves and a
Mr Thesiger, a new L.C.C. Moderate. The P.M. finding himself in
a little party of intimates (Thesiger was the only stranger) belonging
to a strange world completely detached from party politics, let himself
go and, I think, thoroughly enjoyed the mixture of chaff and dialectic
which flew from GBS to Wells and round the table to Sidney, the
Bishop and myself. There is always method in our social adventures
and at my instigation Sidney, after we had left, backed up by the
Bishop and Wells and Shaw, gave an elaborate argument in favour of
our half-time scheme for boys. As I had told Mr Balfour that the

grand distinction between him and the Liberal leaders was that his attitude towards proposals of social reform could be expressed by Why not? and theirs by a grudging Why?, he felt bound to be sympathetic and was I think somewhat taken with the notion. He is honestly concerned about the alleged degeneracy of the race, and inclines to, at any rate, 'flirt' with new proposals. And in these days, when the mind of every Liberal leader is as closed as a live oyster, one must be grateful for small mercies.

2 May. [41 Grosvenor Road]
Ever since we came back I have been hard at work on 'Roads'. I am extremely fit, compared to old days, and barely take my Sabbath of one in seven days off. Have finally given up not only alcohol but coffee and tobacco. Tea remains my one concession to self-indulgence, with occasional overeating of my 'simple food'. In the course of the year I hope that will go too.

The mystical doctrine of theosophy, which claims that human beings may know God through absorption in the infinite, had a long tradition in western philosophy, and it was reinforced by borrowings from Vedic, Buddhist and Brahmanical literature. *The Secret Doctrine* (1888) was the best known of the books by Madame Helena Blavatsky, who founded the Theosophical Society in 1875: Annie Besant succeeded her in the leadership of this troubled and schismatic organization. The Kemp-Welch sisters were minor water-colourists. Joseph Fels (1854–1914) was an American soap manufacturer and a keen follower of the reformist author Henry George, who advocated a 'single tax' on land as a means for correcting social inequality. Fels came to England, made friends with many radicals, and bought land in Essex for the resettlement of the unemployed. He gave generously to many social and political causes, including a loan to Lenin when he was in exile in London. C.F.G. Masterman (1874–1927) was a journalist who became a Liberal M.P. in 1906 and made something of a reputation with his book *The Condition of England* (1909). J.H. Morgan was a lawyer and journalist who wrote for the *Daily Chronicle* and the *Manchester Guardian*. R.C.K. Ensor (1877–1958) was a journalist and historian, active in the Fabian Society, who was a leader writer for the *Daily News* and the *Daily Chronicle*. He later wrote a standard history, *England 1870–1914*. Reginald Bray (b. 1879) was a Fabian on the London School Board and a Progressive on the L.C.C. 1904–07, and Warden of Toynbee Hall 1906–11. A.F. Basil Williams was Clerk in the House of Commons 1892–1901 and a Fabian: he later became professor of history at Edinburgh. Sir Hubert Parry (1848–1918) was a composer whose wife was an enthusiast for good causes. Thomas Spring-Rice, second Baron Monteagle (1849–1926), had literary and political interests and was brother-in-law to the historian Sir George Prothero, who was co-editor of the *Cambridge Modern History*. Lord Stamford (1850–1910) and his wife Elizabeth were active in many charitable and religious organizations.

321

The sneer at Joseph Fels in this entry, like similar comments on Progressives, I.L.P. enthusiasts and others to whom Beatrice took an élitist dislike, was characteristic of the condescending snobbery of her class and time, a snobbery which often persisted even among persons of otherwise advanced opinions. She and Sidney, moreover, were influenced by current talk of selective breeding to eliminate the unfit and to produce a superior race capable of fulfilling its imperial destiny – the doctrine, in its most respectable form, known as 'eugenics'; it was developed by Sir Francis Galton (1822–1911), whose studies in heredity made a considerable contribution to statistical science, and by his disciple Karl Pearson (1857–1936). Bron Herbert (1876–1916) was the son of Beatrice's old friend Auberon Herbert and a close friend of Raymond Asquith. Wounded in the Boer War, he survived to become a Cabinet Minister. He became Lord Lucas in 1905, joined the Royal Flying Corps in 1915 and was reported missing in 1916.

[Whitsun?]. *Bramdean*

A fortnight in quiet pleasant rooms in a pretty little Hampshire village by the Meinertzhagens' new place – Brockwood. We left London tired out with the routine work, mingled with entertaining and being entertained, and Sidney's endless committees. . . . Before I left London I had been reading theosophy, lent some half-dozen books by Annie Besant by my old friend Mary Kemp-Welch, who is an ardent believer. As a working hypothesis for the conduct of life the whole theosophical conception of the Universe and Man's destiny has many points in its favour – if it were true and held to be true the world would gain in goodness, capacity and charm. But for Mrs Besant's wonderful fairy-tale there is at present no verification, and some of it is obviously invented to fit the occasion. It is a daring piece of intellectual gambling – 'the Ancient Wisdom' twisted with amazing logical skill to fit all modern problems of life.

But I am inclined to think that the theosophic ethic combining the search after objective truth with personal holiness and love is, at any rate, justified by its beneficent results. I am inclined to believe in some of the extreme positions – in the complete subordination of *Desire*, the rooting out of its hold on thought, feeling and action. The ideal to be aimed at in public education, as in personal culture, is a religious purpose concerned with scientific processes together with the perfect control by the Will of all the faculties of man, the will making use of scientific methods in attaining the end aspired to by religious feeling. . . .

In the life of a little village one notes how far happier and more dignified is the existence of the hardworking daughter of the middle-class farmer or shopkeeper than that of the rich young woman who drifts through life in the big upper-middle-class houses dotted about the country. There are seven Miss Legges in the big house next door, there are five Meinertzhagens at Brockwood, there are countless other young ladies all 'awaiting' with more or less self-possession the lot of the marriage market or a useless old maidenhood. Compare these listless young persons to pretty energetic Dolly Hawkins who 'runs' our little lodgings, helps her father, the postmaster, and thoroughly enjoys her casual flirtations, restricted to her few spare hours or afternoons. The cottager lives at too low a level of health and intelligence – the men are brutalized, the women prematurely old, but the respectable and successful lower-middle-class country-bred person now combines physical comfort, personal freedom and a considerable education, and stimulus to activity, a rising standard of ease and comfort, but not too high for efficiency. The Brockwood household, on the other hand, is extraordinarily stagnant, dulled by overfeeding and lack of exercise of body and mind.

In the middle of our stay we ran up to London to take the Fels to the University reception to the foreign academics, for once breaking our rigid rule of refusing to appear at evening parties. One reason for so doing was the desire to be polite to the Fels. Dowdy little Americans to look at – he a decidedly vulgar little Jew with much push, little else on the surface – she a really refined and intellectual and public-spirited little body who, by mere force of character, has dragged her husband and his partner into the Fabian Society and other advanced movements. The partner, Coates, who lives with them, is a mild-mannered and dowdy Yorkshireman, a refined and gentle-spirited young clerk who has been made by Fels a partner in his concern – the concern being Fels Naphtha Soap. Perhaps, after all, it was to the Soap that we gave the dinner? Certainly, if it could have been demonstrated to us that the Soap was a lie that would be found out, that dinner would not have been given. But a subscription of £100 to the Fabian Society and the report of Golden Soapsuds, set us thinking of the Fels as possible 'Founders' yet uncaptured; while the lunch made us take a genuine fancy for her, while not finding him repulsive, so we 'speculated' an evening on them – more than that, a journey up to London!

At the reception Rosebery was resplendent in Chancellor' coat – later in the evening he discovered us and began a jerky and perturbed conversation with me as to the alarming growth of London University! But the man was clearly not at his ease and I was equally constrained and glad to escape, on the introduction to him of some distinguished foreigner. He seems worried by a hankering after us yet is not willing to be friends or even friendly acquaintances. And politically I think he is past praying for. Sidney is abstaining from all Liberal League gatherings – public or private – as a modest protest against Rosebery's Surrey Theatre speech in the autumn. For all that I am sorry for the man: he suffers and is not ennobled by his suffering. And he has a charm, a power of original thought and vigorous expression beneath the eternal Rose. Has he written himself down a failure? I suspect so. Whenever I look on that distracted and distempered face I think of that magnificently self-complacent young man who swelled it on the *Russia* thirty years ago ('swelled it' *is* the appropriate expression, however vulgar it may sound) with health, power, intellect, charm. And now? 'I have added wealth,' might be his reply!

I note a certain change in our surroundings. Some of our old comrades of ten or even eight years ago have become indifferent or even hostile to our ideas – Graham Wallas, Llewellyn Smith, Hewins, Leonard Hobhouse, C.P. Trevelyan and Herbert Samuel and Bobby Phillimore are no longer, for one reason or another, *habitués* of Grosvenor Road. Massingham, Vaughan Nash, the Spenders have become distinctly hostile. Edward Pease, Macrosty and some humbler Fabians are still faithful supporters of Sidney's, and the Bernard Shaws, though much more attached to the Independent Theatre cause, are still warm friends. Haldane remains staunch, so do the Barnetts; W.P. Reeves and his wife are always at hand – the same in opinion, but he has grown stale in English politics and is settling down to a certain plaintive dullness of spirit and aim. The Bertrand Russells, still affectionate and personally interested, have cooled in comradeship, he becoming every day more decidedly Whig and abstract in his political thought, impatient with our criticism of the Liberal opposition and our constant reiteration of the need for concrete knowledge.

On the other hand, there is a new group of friendly young men disposed to take our views seriously – Masterman, Morgan, Ensor, Bray, Isaac Mitchell, T.E. Harvey, Basil Williams, Bron Herbert, and with a certain reservation, George Trevelyan, are all anxious to see more of us. What is perhaps a less wholesome sign is the accession of Society folk – Hubert Parrys, Batterseas, Elchos, Lyttons, Fergusons, Monteagles, Alfred Lytteltons, Asquiths, Thesigers,

Stamfords, Sydney Buxtons, Bryces and Gorst have been added to those who ask and are asked to dinner, but all of these have a certain usefulness. Some new *friends* we have made within the same period – H.G. Wells the foremost and the George Protheros; H.J Mackinder is a new colleague. And then there are the other circle of [University] senators, L.C.C., School lecturers and educational administrators, and bishops and distinguished foreigners. On the whole it is an extraordinarily varied and stimulating society. The dominant note in our intercourse with these people is *Social Reconstruction* – in all the little dinners at Grosvenor Road and the tête-à-tête talk at other people's dinners, it is always round some project that the conversation ranges. What is utterly lacking is art, literature for its own sake, and music, whilst physical science only creeps up as analogous and illustrative matter; history appears in much the same aspect. The relation of man's mind to the universe is constantly present as a background in my own thought and with some of our more intimate acquaintances – with Harvey, Masterman, Haldane and Russell I have long talks, but the subject bores Sidney as leading nowhere and as not capable of what he considers valid discussion – exactly as he dislikes discussing what train you will go by before he has got hold of the Bradshaw [timetable]. He prefers reading a statistical abstract or L.C.C. agenda. His relation to the universe – in the spiritual sense, he mockingly suggests – consists in his relation to me!

Originally the Webbs had called for a 'national minimum' of welfare and education as a matter of social justice: they were now arguing for it more as a basis of a more efficient society.

8 June. [41 Grosvenor Road]
Turned from 'Roads' to help Sidney to write an article on 'The Policy of a National Minimum'. Before we left London we had a little series of young Progressives to discuss the possibility of pushing the policy of creating an artificial bottom to society by collective regulation and collective expenditure – 'canalizing' the forces of competition so that all the individuals in the community should be pressed upwards, not cast downwards. The upshot of this was that we had an urgent request for an article to embody our doctrine. Five thousand words, necessarily topical, are a poor medium. We were tired and disinclined to turn from our own proper business, but we felt obliged to accept. I thought it better for Sidney to sign the article singly, the double signature overloads so slight a thing and it is too political, in its tone, to

warrant the intervention of the female partner. I believe in mere 'wife's politics': only in research do I claim equality of recognition!

This was Beatrice's first meeting with Chamberlain's third wife, Mary Endicott, whom he married in 1888. Sir William Hill Irvine (1858–1944) was a British-born Australian politician, Attorney-General and later Governor of Victoria. Sir Michael Hicks Beach (1837–1916) had been a Conservative M.P. since 1864 and had a long record as a prominent figure in the House of Commons. He was Chancellor of the Exchequer 1895–1902 and a strong opponent of tariff reform.

10 June. [41 Grosvenor Road]
In response to a repeated request from Beatrice I called on Mrs Chamberlain on her 'at home' day. A charming little lady, exactly as she is always described – bright, conventional and kindly with a flow of intelligent talk. She looks true and warm-hearted within the limits of her somewhat narrow nature, in spite of her Society equipment. We talked of colonial premiers and I suggested that Mr Chamberlain might like to meet Mr Irvine, ex-Premier of Victoria, a Conservative free-trader who is in favour of the preferential tariff and who is longing to meet the great man. It appears that the ex-Colonial Secretary is keen to do some propaganda in that direction.

In the evening we had the Herbert Gladstones, Winston Churchill and Lloyd George, the George Trevelyans, C.F.G. Masterman to dine and a motley score of Labour men and Progressives to meet them in the evening. Herbert Gladstone is a heavy but pleasant 'diner-out' with a sort of common sense which comes from years of experience of party wire-pulling, but he is a mere party hack, absolutely unconcerned for any mortal thing, beyond his own comfort, but his party's success. He has some inkling of our ideas, but dislikes them. The deciding fact is, as he frankly asserted, 'People with advanced opinions do not pay,' and he looked at me as much as to say, 'How much have you ever subscribed to party funds, I should like to know?' His look was so unmistakable that I found myself explaining that most of us were poor – 'Moreover', I added, 'as far as I am concerned I have never been a Liberal and my husband is not in politics but only in local administration.'

On my other side sat Winston Churchill. The impression he makes is an unpleasant one: he drinks too much, talks too much, and does no thinking worthy of the name. Such ideas as he has are a quaint jumble of old-fashioned Radicalism and mere Toryism; at present, wishing to be advanced, the old-fashioned Radicalism is in the ascendant. He is completely ignorant of all social questions and does not know it. He is chock full of prejudices and catchwords, and constantly strives for new and effective ways of stating these. He has no sympathy with suffering, no intellectual curiosity, he is neither scientific nor benevolent. I tried the 'national minimum' on him but he was evidently unaware of the most elementary objections to unrestricted competition and was still in the stage of 'infant-school economics'. He was more interested when I boldly tackled the personal question. 'I have watched politics and politicians for thirty years, Mr Churchill, and I feel warranted in giving you a word of warning. Unless you can persuade yourself that the newest doctrine in Liberalism is right, stick to the Tory Party. There is more office in it, anyhow, and the future of the old-fashioned believers in retrenchment and personal freedom on the Liberal side of politics will be rapid and ignominious extinction. In the Tory Party these doctrines will always seem distinguished because sufficiently rare, and the role of economist will be really popular because it represents the substantial class interest of the mass of the Conservatives.' 'I am interested in your advice,' he quickly responded, 'because it is exactly what Beach wrote me: "a Liberal with Conservative opinions, or a Conservative with progressive opinions, will always be out of the running".' 'Beach is right,' joined in Herbert Gladstone, 'about the Liberal-Conservative opinions . About the other combination I am not so sure.'

Lloyd George is altogether superior both in character and in intellect to Winston Churchill or Herbert Gladstone. He is a worthy little person with intense personal ambition, but with assiduous industry and honest convictions and brilliant parliamentary talents. But he, also, has no notion of national administration or the problems that it involves. McKinnon Wood, Cornwall and some other L.C.C. [members] came in afterwards. They compared favourably with the parliamentarians in the reality of their grip of actual affairs.

Andrew Bonar Law (1858–1923) was a Tory Unionist M.P. who supported Chamberlain's scheme of colonial preference and tariff reform. At this time he was parliamentary secretary to the Board of Trade. He became Prime Minister in 1922. Sir Ernest Bickham Sweet-Escott (1857–1942) was a colonial administrator, and Governor of British Honduras 1904–06.

17 June. [41 Grosvenor Road]
We lunched yesterday with the Chamberlains – to introduce the Irvines – others there were the Bonar Laws and a certain Sweet-

Escott, Governor of Honduras. I sat on one side of my old friend and we talked without constraint. He is obsessed with the fiscal question – has lost his judgement over it – refuses to think or talk of anything else. He looks desperately unhealthy, rather than old, a restless look in the eyes, bad colour, and general aspect of 'falling in'. But I should imagine that there is plenty of force in the man yet, an almost mechanically savage persistence in steaming ahead. I tried to suggest the 'national minimum' as a complementary policy to import duties. 'I have no prejudice against it,' he answered, 'but it would not do for me to suggest it – it would be said that I was trying to bribe the working class. But there is no reason why it should not be added on by some one else.' Then we drifted on to the Education Acts 1902 and 1903 which he quite clearly does *not* favour, afraid of the advent of the bureaucrat. The trail of the profit-maker in industry is in everything that Chamberlain proposes or opposes; he detests the salaried expert, and like many others who share this dislike, he tries to ignore the necessity for the official government of society instead of devising safeguards from the evils of it. 'If I had been Prime Minister you would not have had the Education Act.' 'The one and only reason for my not regretting that you were *not* Prime Minister,' I answered pleasantly and we passed on to other things.

Sidney says that after the ladies had left Chamberlain urged almost *passionately* on Mr Irvine the need for preferential tariffs (Sidney devoting himself to Escott as it was clear that Chamberlain wanted to talk more or less confidentially with Irvine. Bonar Law had left). Upstairs we four ladies had agreeable conversation, drifting from gossip about Rosebery and the future Liberal Cabinet into a serious discussion as to the relative merits of Protestantism and Catholicism. I take to Mrs Chamberlain; there is a look of sincerity and simple feeling in her face, a somewhat pathetic expression of life being too much for her, though she obviously enjoys, to its full, the social side of the position, and I should imagine worships her great man. But there must be times when the great personage, with his irritability, one-idea-dness, physical unhealthiness, egotism and vulgarity is rather a heavy handful for that refined and charming little lady!

As I walked back through the Brompton churchyard I blessed my luck in life and thought with a glow of happiness of the true comradeship with my beloved workmate in my attractively simple little home. Bless him! And I wondered what were Joe's meditations over this second meeting in seventeen years?

Lady Wimborne (1880–1948), the daughter of the Duke of Marlborough, was a prominent hostess. Millicent, Duchess of Sutherland (1867–1955), a distinguished figure in Edwardian Society, was such an enthusiast for social charities that she was nicknamed 'Meddlesome Millie'. She was the model for Arnold Bennett's do-gooding Countess of Chells in the Five Towns novels. Sir Gilbert Parker (1862–1932) was a Conservative M.P. and author, noted for his social ambitions.

[?] *June.* [41 Grosvenor Road]
Sidney's influence on the joint life is wholesome in curbing my 'lower desires'. There have been three separate entertainments that I should like to have gone to – Lady Wimborne's, Mr Balfour's, and the Duchess of Sutherland's evening parties. Feeling secure in the possession of an attractive garment I should like to have paraded myself. But Sidney was obdurate. 'You won't be able to work the next morning. And I don't think it is desirable that we should be seen in the houses of great folk – know them privately if you like, but don't go to their miscellaneous gatherings. If we do, it will be said of us as it is of Sir Gilbert Parker – in the dead silence of the night you hear a distant but monotonous sound – Sir Gilbert Parker, climbing, climbing, climbing.' And I recognized the better voice and tore up the cards.

All goes well with the L.C.C. and the Education Committee. First-rate officials are being selected, the routine administration is being digested and the plain man is learning his lesson. Sidney finds himself on agreeable terms with all parties, the School Board women being apparently the only persons who bear him a grudge. I have been somewhat assiduous in my cultivation of the Progressives – successfully so I think, and by leaving London the end of June we have at least convinced them that Sidney does not want to run the show. Antagonisms are being developed between some of the members, but Sidney has kept well outside them. He has been re-elected on the party committee, the grant to the University and the School went through without a word, and some of the leading Progressives have signified that they think he has acted 'nobly' in subordinating his claims to the chairmanship of the Education committee. . . So we go off to Scotland with our books and our papers for our three months with a good conscience and good hope.

The last weeks Sidney's days have been over-filled with committees and the work arising from them Yesterday, for instance, 8.45–11 a.m. drafting a report for a chairman of one of the sub-committees of the

E.C. of the L.C.C.; 11'oclock Royal Commission on Trade Disputes; 12.30 sub-committee at School Board offices; 1.30 p.m. took train to South Kensington, lunching in the train, for 2 o'clock Departmental committee on Royal College of Science; 4.30 took the chair at the London School of Economics at meeting of railway magnates to decide on Railway Department (secured £1,000 a year to start Department); 6 o'clock arrived late at Higher Education Committee at School Board office and transacted, as chairman, remainder of business; 8 o'clock dinner here – Bernard Shaws, Jack Tennants, John Burns, Munro-Fergusons and Stephen Hobhouse; after dinner group of young Progressives to be introduced to John Burns and GBS; to bed 12 o'clock; began work again at book at 8.45 a.m. Very naturally there is not much brain left for the book, and until we get right away from London we shall only muddle on. . . .

The Webbs went to stay at Fyrish, the estate of their friend, Munro-Ferguson, on the Cromarty Firth.

16 October. Grosvenor Road

The three months in Scotland were so completely a joint existence that there was neither the desire nor the opportunity to record it in this book. When Sidney is with me I cannot talk to the 'Other Self' with whom I commune when I am alone – 'it' ceases to be present and only reappears when he becomes absent. Then the Old Self, who knew me and whom I have known for that long period before Sidney entered into my life, who seems to be that which is permanent in me, sits again in the judgement seat and listens to the tale of the hours and days, acts, thoughts and feelings which the Earthly One has experienced.

Beautiful and peaceful have been the scenes of our long working holiday, especially enchanting the hillside of Fyrish, with heather and fir-clad mountains rising up behind us, and Cromarty Firth and the North Sea rolled out beneath us; the 'Golden Gate' as we called the North and South Suters, will remain in my memory as one of the most beautiful expanses of water, land and sky . . . . Except for four days' cycling on the West Coast and the two days broken by our change of quarters at the end of July (from Nethy Bridge near Grantown to Fyrish, near Evanton) we worked steadily six days out of seven at the book, for the four morning hours, spending the afternoons in reading and exercise. Once a week we would take a sabbath and go some thirty miles to see friends or explore the mountains of the Black Isle.

Excellent health and greater bodily and mental vigour than I have ever known before, made me feel as if I were still in the very prime of life, and Sidney too seemed unreservedly happy. We saw a good deal of neighbours, made friends with the elementary teachers and ministers in both places and at Fyrish had, as agreeable acquaintances, the mother and daughter of the Laird of Novar – Munro-Ferguson.

We made some superficial and scattered observations on Scottish education and social life, but I doubt whether they are worth recording. I brooded, in lonely walks, over the book, or over the new philosophy which is gradually taking shape in my mind, or praised the unknown for our exceeding happiness, or prayed for strength to be abstemious, persistent in work, and clear-sighted and constantly kind to others. But I was working so hard at technical details (roads, pavement and cleansing) that I had little strength left over for other reading or writing and was glad to let myself be absorbed in the mere enjoyment of light, air and colour.

Since we returned a fortnight ago I have been working for six hours a day, resorting the material back into structure so that we may begin to rewrite our first volume. . . .in the main we lead the student's life – at least I do – the rest being taken as recreation in the odd times left over from the working day.

Sidney Webb devised two educational 'ladders' for Londoners to climb – the system of scholarship leading from elementary through secondary to higher education and the part-time route of evening classes. His notion was that 'the great bulk of the population' would have access to the kind of schooling 'that their attainments and idiosyncrasies require'.

8 November. [41 Grosvenor Road]
. . . . Sidney has been busy drafting his scholarship scheme and getting it accepted by his Higher Education Committee. He has found his Progressive colleagues in a most kindly humour. . . .

We spent last Sunday at the Sydney Buxtons with Haldane and the Birrells, having endless discussions as to the future of the Liberal Party. It is clear that they are unrepentant in their determination to run into place on the old lines of 'economy' and 'freedom' of trade and 'anti-priest' bias. They refuse even to contemplate any other policy, dismiss all social reform from their minds except perhaps a revision of the incidence of taxation in favour of the small consumer.

They are not optimistic – look forward to a bare majority over the Irish and a tenure of one or two years – let us get a Front Bench is their cry. Haldane told us as we drove to the station early on Monday morning that there had been a move to exclude the 'Limps' last spring but that it had collapsed and the dominant note now was a Cabinet of all sections.

12 November. [41 Grosvenor Road]
Two days at Gracedieu with Mary Booth and her young folk. Charles Booth being absent I excused Sidney from coming. For the last few years there has been increasing friendliness between the two households; they and their children have dined here and I have once or twice been to their house in the afternoon to see Mary. So I thought I would accept the invitation and close the episode of estrangement.

Gracedieu has grown in magnificence since I was there fifteen years ago! Large reception rooms added to the old structure, three men servants and the rest to match, elegant luxury of a refined type is the note of the establishment. Mary and I slipt into the old intellectual intimacy, exchanged experience of life and opinions and gossip about common relations and friends. But alas! the old affection is, on my side, dead – so dead that it no longer hurts to be with her as it used to. I have a regard for her. She is the same strenuous polished kindly little woman as of old with a flow of clever talk about men and women, creeds and sentiments. She is an excellent wife and mother and a good housewife. But her purpose in life is the advancement of her family, a purpose that does not attract me. Moreover, I cannot help feeling that her return of friendliness to me has been brought about by our rise in the world's estimation. The young folk find my little dinners desirable entertainments and wish to claim me as an old friend and cousin, exactly as they wished to drop me twelve years ago. They are pleasant young persons – well educated and refined, honourable and passably philanthropic. But they are sybarites – intent on enjoying their personal existence and not much concerned as to the fate of the community they live in. Still, as the world goes, the Booth household must, I suppose, be counted on the side of good, though I distrust the effect of those large mixed establishments of overfed and under-occupied persons. The very morning I left Mary had discovered an intrigue of a low and deceitful character between her maid and one of the man servants, an intrigue which had entailed a long course of deceit on the part of the girls' maid as an accomplice of the guilty party. Not appetizing! It passes the wit of woman to keep such an establishment from demoralizing the inhabitants.

I am analysing all our material on vestries during the four morning hours, and reading eighteenth-century literature for two odd hours in the afternoon – altogether I find I can manage six or seven hours' study now as against the three or four hours of old days. I am splendidly well – all the result of abstinence in quantity, quality and frequency of food, combined with slow eating and sleeping in the open air. The less I eat the better I am. I doubt whether I have yet got down to the lowest level in abstemiousness and the highest in efficiency.

Lord Hobhouse (1819–1904), uncle and guardian of Henry Hobhouse, was a successful lawyer and judge who had been a member of the London School Board and an alderman of the L.C.C.

11 December. [41 Grosvenor Road]
Lord Hobhouse dead: a fine example of the cultivated and strenuous English gentleman who has chosen official life and open-eyed enlightenment as his path through the world. A touch of personal gratitude towards this courteous old man. He and Lady Hobhouse graciously beamed on our marriage and he always, in those early days of more or less social boycott, spoke with admiration and respect of 'Mr Webb' and thus won my heart. Henry inherits some £70,000 and the house in Bruton street, and Maggie already has visions of a peerage. The poorer members of the Hobhouse clan are left with small legacies, Lord Hobhouse evidently desiring to found a family or rather to enlarge the foundations of the Hadspen *ménage*. Stephen pitchforked into the Education Department by Lord Londonderry and Morant's favour. A good lad, and able – a worthy 'job' but a 'job'.

The war between Japan and Russia lasted from February 1804 to December 1905. The crushing Japanese victory made a great impact in Britain, especially on the advocates of imperial efficiency. The Webbs were even more impressed when they visited Japan in 1911.

22 December. [41 Grosvenor Road]
Off to Felixstowe for a three weeks' recess, during whch time we hope to finish off the Parish chapter to be typewritten. We might do indefinitely more research, but it is time to be getting on if we are ever to complete our whole work on English local government up to the present time. Moreover, it is necessary for Sidney's administrative work to increase his reputation by publishing a big work of research.

An outburst of jealousy among the leading Progressives at the scholarship scheme which has attracted much attention and is almost universally praised. Collins, Cornwall and Dickinson have not been making much of a success of their special functions, getting a good deal of odium for sins of commission and omission from Noncons and Church alike, Sidney on their instructions lying low. Then out he comes as chairman of the Higher Education Committee with his great scholarship scheme carefully thought out in detail with arguments showing that it is inevitable. They don't like to oppose it because the need for more teachers is urgent and the trend of opinion all in favour of increased facilities for the lower-middle class. They can't object to the detailed proposals because they don't know sufficient to suggest others to take their place, but it is offending the N.U.T., backing up the secondary schools and spending the rates. Moreover, as Collins naïvely remarked to the Council, 'If it is a success the credit will be Mr Webb's,' – he said it in a complimentary tone but it was clearly an uncomfortable thought. However, though it is adjourned, Sidney thnks it is certain to go through because of the general outside approval and because they cannot suggest an alternative. But he was a wee bit hurt at the lack of frankness and generosity on the part of the governing clique. I have given up trying to propitiate them as I don't find my cordiality makes any difference to their jealousy of Sidney's influence with the press and the powers that be. . . . Our amazing good fortune and perpetual happiness is an ample reward for these vexations.

Kate Courtney remarked the other day that she always wondered, in reading the published diaries or confidential writings of private persons, why they seemed so little concerned with the great questions of peace and war – so infinitely more important than their own little doings or narrow range of interests, solemnly recorded in their diaries. And I bethought me that there is hardly a reference to the Russo-Japanese war in these pages. The answer I gave on the spur of the moment, is, I think, the true one – 'The private person has no specialist knowledge, no particular or exceptional experience as to world politics. His thoughts and feelings would be a mere reflection of his morning newspaper and worthless both to him and to those who might some day read the story of his life.' And yet if one looks back on the past year and thinks how much one has brooded over the Far Eastern drama, how eagerly one has read each morning's news, how one has stumbled into foreshadowing the effect of the 'Rising Sun' on our western civilization, it is hardly fair to leave it unnoticed.

For instance, I watch in myself and others a growing national shamefacedness at the superiority of the Japanese over our noble selves in capacity, courage, self-control, in benevolence as well as in all that makes up good manners. They shame our Christianity, they shame our administrative capacity, they shame our inventiveness, they shame our leadership, and alas, they shame our 'average sensual man'. Perhaps it makes the matter worse that they have won not by the genius of one man, which might be an accident not likely to recur again, but on the intellectual, physical and moral qualities of the whole people. They seem both more scientific and more religious than ourselves, a nobler purpose and more ably contrived processes wherewith to carry out this purpose. Their success will alter not merely the balance of power, but the balance of ideas. It will tell against Christianity as the one religion, against materialistic individualism, against autocracy, against luxury, in favour of organization, collective regulation, scientific education, physical and mental training – but on the whole not in favour of democracy?

They have suddenly raised the standard of international efficiency, in exactly those departments of life that we Western nations imagined ourselves supremely superior to the Eastern races. How far this shock to self-esteem will go in English society, how far it will be neutralized by the vulgar delight of seeing our ally beat our enemy, remains to be seen. But for many a long day the Reformer will be able to quote on his side the innovating collectivism of the Japanese; the Idealist, the self-abnegation of all classes of the community in a common cause. Even in one's own daily life one is inclined towards greater persistency and more self-sacrifice.

So closes 1904 and this book.

VOLUME 25
∽ 1905 ∾

21 January. [41 Grosvenor Road]
Since we returned, ten days ago, from our recess at Felixstowe, I have been hard at work analysing all our 'select vestry' material and reading at the British Museum everything that bears on it, Sidney going on at the Poor Law pamphlets. . . .

But the main excitement is watching events in Russia, likely to prove the essential need for *consent* as an element in stable government. Japan is proving the superlative advantage of scientific methods in the international struggle for existence. How to combine the maximum of consent with the highest degree of efficiency is the problem before us in England, the average sensual man not wanting to be improved.

5 February. [41 Grosvenor Road]
I attended the crucial debate on the scholarship system. The two N.U.T. members attacked virulently; the Moderates, uncomfortable at finding themselves in such company, proposed their amendments in a halting fashion, the extreme Nonconformists objected to accepting any scheme based on the 'accursed Act', the official Progressives wavered. Sidney made a powerfully adroit speech and turned the scales, the party leaders supported him in a somewhat half-hearted fashion and the debate stood adjourned. But acceptance of the scheme is secured with a minor amendment in which Sidney concurs. Graham Wallas backed him up loyally and Sidney is supporting Wallas over the staffing of the voluntary schools – the two old friends are drawing closer together and have with them Bray and Harvey and some others. . . .

Sir Oliver Lodge (1851–1940) was a distinguished physicist who was also active in psychical research. He was at that time Principal of Birmingham University. Harley Granville-Barker (1877–1946) was an actor, dramatist and Fabian who became director of the Court Theatre in 1903 and, encouraged by the success of Shaw's *Candida* in which he appeared, put on a number of Shaw's plays. This theatrical experiment created an audience for a new kind of drama – the theatre of ideas – and Shaw, virutally unknown as a dramatist, leapt into prominence. The German-born Sir Julius Wernher (1850–1912) emigrated to South Africa and made a fortune in diamonds and gold before settling in London in 1884. He was on Haldane's 'Charlottenburg' committee planning the Imperial College of Science at South Kensington, to which he gave a foundation gift of £250,000.

8 February. [41 Grosvenor Road]
We have Sir Oliver Lodge staying here for two or three days. A delightful personality, large and fresh in his thought and feeling, but suffering from a bad fit of intellectual dissipation after a long life of specialism, made more acute by introduction to the Balfour, Elcho, Wyndham set, a fascinating temptation to an attractive person condemned to live in a provincial town. He is another instance of the fallacy that physical science is an outfit for the psychological and social

sciences. It never occurs to us economists and political science students to imagine that our long-standing study of the complicated structure and function of society fits us to be astronomers or physicists, but the physical science man plunges head foremost into the discussion of our questions, armed with the four rules of arithmetic and the instruments of a laboratory.

For his entertainment we had a little party consisting of the Bertrand Russells, Granville-Barker (the intellectual actor), Mackinder, Lion Phillimore, Wernher and Balfour. I begged the P.M. to talk to Bertrand and placed them next each other and they got on famously. I sacrificed myself during some part of dinner to the millionaire [Wernher] (who is endowing London University), Lodge, Granville-Barker; Sidney and the two charming ladies kept up a lively talk at the other end. There was a subtle antipathy of Balfour to Mackinder and Wernher, mere philistine materialist administrators he would feel. There was sympathy between him and Russell and Barker, and of course he and Lodge are affectionate friends and fellow 'synthetic philosophers'. Lodge got on with all the company; Mackinder and Wernher chummed up and walked away together; the intellectual young actor wrote me enthusiastically that he had walked home with the great man. Mr Balfour likes both 'the Webbs' – that is clear – finds them stimulating and attractive. Today I took our guest to lunch with the Courtneys to meet John Morley, the Spenders, George Trevelyan etc. John Morley eyed me suspiciously, but insisted on listening to my lively talk to Spender.

Beatrice included in her diary three extracts. One was a *Times* leader dated 12 February pointing out the moral lesson of the Russo-Japanese war – the iron fortitude, invincible determination and magnificent unity of Japan as against the 'hopeless disorganization of her antagonist'. It went on to say that it was 'part of our intense provincialism to look at the difference between creeds and trainings, and to conclude that those in which we believe must produce the best results'. The second was a letter signed by James G. Adderley of Oxford House, Bethnal Green, one of the East End settlements. He gives statistics of the extremes of luxury and poverty in London – twenty-eight out of every thousand citizens are paupers. He asserts that luxury in fact makes for poverty and appeals to his readers to lead simpler lives as a contribution to national stability. Beatrice also includes an advertisement for the 'Eustace Miles Individual Health Course for Men and Women'. Herbert Hensley Henson (1863–1947) was Canon of Westminster and Rector of St Margaret's 1900–12, Joseph Armitage Robinson (1858–1933) was a professor of divinity at Cambridge who became Canon and Dean of Westminster 1902–11.

20 February. [41 Grosvenor Road]
I have pasted these extracts in my diary because they are typical of three strong undercurrents of opinion, which are not as yet showing much on the surface of things – the rapid decay of the 'one true religion' notion; the assertion of the economic iniquity of luxury, and the growing consciousness that health is a question of physical abstinence and self-control. As to the first, it is astounding that the organ of conventional opinion should dare to call a faith in Christianity as the one true religion 'provincialism' – it opens up a vista of free thought that would have astounded the old militant secularist of 1870. But the phrase in *The Times* article represents a large current of opinion even inside the Church, a current which came to the surface in Scotland in the great controversy of last year, which is shown in England by the sayings of Henson, Armitage Robinson and others. Side by side with this latitudinarianism of creed is an awakening of faith in spiritual life, an intensity of aspiration towards communion with higher beings as yet unknown and unperceived by human intellect. A third and independent movement of opinion is the breaking of the idol of mere numbers and wealth in the Russo-Japanese war, the terrible object lesson of the failure even in the struggle for existence of the race which has lacked conduct, abstinence from physical pleasures, and trained intelligence in the bulk of its people. The 'champagne', the gross feeding, the women and gambling propensities of the Russian officers, their disorderly behaviour, their foolish talk, seems to be not remotely connected with their lack of initiative and even of courage. The whole picture is too uncomfortably like the description of Buller's army in South Africa to yield us much satisfaction. Of course the English officers were more respectable, and perhaps a shade more skilful, but there are more points of resemblance between them and the Russians than between them and the victorious Japanese.

To a mere onlooker it seems as if great events were taking place in the world and as if the next fifty or a hundred years may see changes in the conduct of life that are now undreamt of. It may be all a delusion. . . . But the hopefulness of the present movement lies in the co-operation of science with regard to the processes of life with religion in respect of the purpose of life, both alike, lit up by altruism. The old cry of religion – 'save your own soul' – is dead to rise no more. The comparatively new cry of pseudo-science – 'you have no soul, please your body' – is equally dead. Instead there is a new vision of the meaning of human life as a spirit escaping upwards by force of will and knowledge from mere animal impulses to a glorious unknown – a spirit not of one man, or of a few select men, but of all.

Meanwhile I find myself slipping back into conformity with the Church of England, accepting its prayers and rites as a child, not questioning their phrases or incidents but regarding them as representative for my race of the spirit of religion. . . .

29 February. [41 Grosvenor Road]
Sidney gleeful as to the acceptance of his scholarship scheme, the only piece of constructive work done as yet by the Education Committee of the L.C.C. . . .

5 March. [41 Grosvenor Road]
The Wallases and Bray came to dine last night and the three men sat for two hours discussing education policy, whilst I listened dreamily to Audrey's gentle chatter in the drawing-room. Sidney and Bray tried to get Graham to enter into a concordat – Sidney prepared to back him up with regard to the elementary education if he, Wallas, would back Sidney up in secondary and university matters. But Graham will not budge from his principle of 'starving out' the secondary schools under separate management. He will not agree to run both systems, provided and non-provided, side by side. Sidney, on the other hand, whilst ready to provide as many secondary and university institutions as the ratepayers will pay for, wants gradually to acquire sufficient control over all the others to raise their standard to the required level. . . . What is clear is that the present constitution of the L.C.C. as educational authority is transitional and unstable in the last degree. . . The next three years, with the parliamentary election to take some of the foremost Progressives into higher spheres, and the L.C.C. elections two years hence, to lose some Progressive seats, will clear off a good many of the present obstructions. But when exactly we shall feel free to go off for our eight months' trip to the Far East remains in dim obscurity – a vision of rest and refreshment at the end of many more months and years of sustained drudgery. I am beginning to hanker after a period of 'fallowness'.

9 March. [41 Grosvenor Road]
. . . . Suggested to Sidney this morning that we must not overlook the element of co-operation in government as part of the ideal to be

aimed at: mere efficiency, even if accompanied by consent, is not sufficient. Government must be considered as service and everyone should participate. He acquiesced but suggested that what we now considered as private functions ought to be governmental and therefore of the nature of service. Between these two suggestions we have to work out a middle line. . . .

Balfour was in an impossibly difficult position trying to hold together a party in confusion and divided over Chamberlain's protectionism. He was anxious to avoid both an appeal to the country and the enunciation of a policy which would put the party under the domination of the Tariff Reform League. A series of by-elections had shown the increasing popularity of the Liberals.

18 March. [41 Grosvenor Road]
All the news one hears (dining with Sydney Buxton, Haldane, Thesiger and others on both sides of politics) goes to show a stampede out of Chamberlain's camp. He himself is reported ill, much aged and dispirited. Austen [Chamberlain] is hanging on to the Chancellorship, eager to bring in a good budget next year, Balfour wishes to tide over another year for South Africa and the Education Act to become consolidated. Also as he knows he will be beaten, 'better later than sooner'. Meanwhile every day the protectionist proposals grow more stale and more 'unreal' – they are, properly speaking, not before the country, since the official head of the party, supposed to be in favour of them, refuses 'to put the question'. And Joe grows hourly older and iller and more resigned to subordinating his hopes to Austen's prospects. It is a pathetic sight, this rapid decline of the once powerful man, but I think it is a decline past retrieving. The end is not far off.

Meanwhile he is bestirring himself about Birmingham University. Mr Haldane dined with him alone and they concluded a sort of alliance to push forward government expenditure in that direction. Birmingham, its municipal organization and the growth of its social and intellectual life, will be his most substantial achievement. In this great work he has had disinterested purpose and accurate knowledge and he has attained what is wholly good.

31 March. [41 Grosvenor Road]
Another old friend passed away – Marie Souvestre. A brilliant woman, handsome, warm-hearted, the very soul of veracity, and keen-witted. A schoolmistress for nearly half a century, she must have

counted for much in the lives of many women coming from the best of the governing class of England, America, France and Germany. She was not only a schoolmistress: she was an *habituée*, during middle life, of intellectual society in Paris, Berlin and London: she had known most of the advanced politicians and thinkers springing from the professional and middle class. Twenty years ago, in York House days, I used to meet her at the Chamberlains, Harrisons, Morleys – it was she who introduced me to the Creightons. . . . A few weeks ago I visited her twice and thought I saw the hand of death on her face; she seemed quite as alive in spirit as when I first met her at Frederic Harrison's – and now where is she?

Veracity, an undeviating directness of intelligence, faithfulness and warmth of affection were her most delightful qualities; dignity of manner and brilliancy of speech her chief ornaments. An amazing narrowness of vision for so intelligent a person, a total inability to understand religion, a dogmatism that was proof against the spirit of scientific investigation, a lack of charity to feelings with which she did not sympathize – in short an absence of humility – was perhaps the most disabling of her characteristics. It narrowed her influence to those whom she happened to like and who happened to like her.

It is hard for those born in the modern England to understand the passionate hatred of ecclesiasticism – of religion – which seems to dominate French free-thinkers: it is so hard not to count it as an evil thing. Yet this feeling is not mainly evil – it has in it an element of idealism – of faith in noble qualities which were, far back in history, trampled under foot by organized Christianity, and which they still believe are a danger from the existing Church. . . . Marie Souvestre was not a wise woman – she was hard on the great mass of common people, occasionally even unjust. She always insisted, like Herbert Spencer, on being judge in her own case. She could not tolerate the idea that *she* might be wrong. And it was a strange irony that she was almost as ignorant of the persistent industry, patience and humility, involved in the scientific method, as she was of the religious impulse. . .

2 April. [41 Grosvenor Road]
Sidney is happier in his L.C.C. work than I have known him since the first Council. He has, in his special department of education, the maximum of power with the minimum of responsibility. He has no personal enemies on the Council, and the bulk of the Progressives,

feeling that they have behaved rather shabbily in keeping him out of all prominent places, are really anxious to oblige him on questions of policy. . . .

In *A Modern Utopia* H.G. Wells described a Swiss-style technocratic state ruled by a dedicated élite he called 'the Samurai', after the warrior-guardians of old Japan. Edward Talbot had just become Bishop of Southwark. Henry James (1843–1916) published his novel *The Golden Bowl* in England in 1905.

17 April. [41 Grosvenor Road]
Three or four weeks, day after day, spent either amassing new material at the British Museum for our chapter on the County or in analysing our twelve boxes of material at home. Some days I have spent a good six hours at work, seeing no one until Sidney returned in the evening, just going for a 'constitutional' after lunch or walking along the Embankment to call on Kate Courtney in the hour or so before supper. But most weeks we have had a thirteen-person dinner at home, dined out twice or three times, lunched casual persons on intermediate days, and on three occasions we have entertained at dinner the staff of the School, with gatherings of fifty to seventy students coming in afterwards. . . . Our life tends however to become more and more the student's life and to be less interrupted by social engagements – partly the pressure of completing these two first volumes disinclines me to accept 'dinners', makes me neglect 'calls', absolutely prohibit evening parties other than our own. With such persons as we do see, we find ourselves on the pleasantest of terms – the result of the privilege of living with a companion who knows neither malice nor envy, nor desire to excel, nor the remotest tinge of what the world calls snobbishness. Sidney is simply unconscious of all the little meannesses which turn social intercourse sour. He is sometimes tired, occasionally bored, but never unkindly or anxious to shine, or be admired, and wholly unaware of the absence of, or presence of social consideration. . . .

H.G. Wells came for the night: he had sent us his *Utopia*. 'The chapters on the Samurai will pander to all your worst instincts,' he laughingly remarked when I congratulated him. He is full of intellectual courage and initiative, and is now settling down to psychological novels – I fancy somewhat inspired by Henry James's late success.

A pleasant little dinner at the Talbots' on Saturday. The P.M., the Dean of Westminster, Lady Gwendolen Cecil [daughter of the late

Lord Salisbury] and ourselves. Mr Balfour's plaint: 'There is no need for the newspapers to tell me my faults, I know them all, but I can't alter them.' A long talk with the Bishop afterwards. Sidney hopeful about the future, he somewhat pessimistic. Lady Gwendolen Cecil, like her sister, Lady Selborne (whom we met at a large and fashionable dinner the other day, and with whom I talked much) has exactly the same philosophy as young Algernon Cecil [son of Lord Eustace Cecil and grandson of Lord Salisbury]. Utterly sceptical of any reform of society brought about by altering the environment of individuals – the boy brought up by drunken parents in the worst slum of London, Lady Gwendolen maintained, was as likely to turn out as satisfactorily as the most favoured person. 'It is surely a question of experience,' I suggested. 'Your experience of life leads to one conclusion, my experience leads me to another. But, in some subtle way, this reference to experience, as the test of our rival assumptions, did not satisfy her.

A surviving neighbour recalled that the Longfords servants nicknamed Beatrice and Sidney 'The Lovers', and himself remembers seeing them walk hand in hand round the Longfords garden.

11 May. [41 Grosvenor Road?]
A happy three weeks with the Playnes at Longfords. Wrote about one third of our part on the County, taking the two last days off for long rides in glorious weather – to Malmesbury one day, and then a lovely day in the Standish woods alone with my boy. We hid our cycles in the leaves at the top of the beech woods and wandered down, hand in hand, to the dear old field overlooking the house – the scene of childish sorrow and joy and all the stirrings and strivings of young womanhood. The valley was shrouded in heat mist, the broad surface of the Bristol Channel glimmering through the hills behind in faintest outline – these only to the eye of knowledge. Then a lovely walk wheeling our iron round the crest of the Cotswolds to the Beacon Hill overlooking a more glorious view of the greatest breadth of the Severn valley, bordered by the Malverns on one side and the Channel on the other. A ride back through the deep lanes of the valley – cottages, churches, and farms, that one knew long ago – even some familiar faces grown old and furrowed. A delicious ending to our Easter recess!

The Playnes are now our intimates in the family. Mary is religious and public-spirited, a gentle and wise elderly woman, the soul of all good effort in the neighbourhood. She is friends with Bill's wife – has won her over by persistent kindness. Arthur is a beneficent and pleasant elderly gentleman – irresponsible, it is true, but with no mean or poor motive left in his nature, a miracle of adult training by his wife. Bill is still commonplace – joyless, and finding as he advances in age that his life becomes less interesting. He too may change if Mary succeeds in converting his wife to the New Life. . . .

A long talk with H.G. Wells at Sandgate. Two articles of our social faith are really repulsive to him: the collective provision of anything bordering on religious or emotional training and the collective regulation of the behaviour of the adult. As to the latter we are not really at variance, for we would willingly accept his limitation of this intervention to all such behaviour as impinges on the non-adult – (heaven knows that little scheme would give us enough regulation of the adult and to spare). But he is obdurate as to education: no form of training must be provided out of common funds that he personally objects to. My plea for variety and experiment – for leaving the door open for new religions or morality by permitting those who believe in the old to have it provided for their children – [as well as] Sidney's plea for tolerance strikes a deaf ear. 'The child is not fit for emotional training until after adolescence,' he [Wells] dogmatically asserts; 'there is no justice in not giving one form of training,' he insists. But he went further than this. 'I don't believe in tolerance; you have got to fight against anything being taught anybody which seems to you harmful, you have got to struggle to get your own creed taught.' We all got hot and exaggerated in our arguments and were no nearer agreement when we parted.

I suppose it is inevitable that we who believe in extending the functions of the state in all directions should be keenly desirous of making this activity as catholic as possible; of safeguarding each new departure by deliberate provision for dissenters from the established view. Clearly the whole of liberalism in England is swinging into rigid conformity, both in the structure and formations of the social organism. As you cannot have each individual separately provided for according to his needs, therefore you must give identical treatment to all – seems their present dogma.

Alfred Standish Cripps was Blanche and William Cripps's second son and third child. Julia Faulder (1879–1921) was their second child who had married T.J. Faulder in 1904. Richard Harrison (1882–1950) was the fourth child and Henry Harrison, born 1887, was the sixth and youngest.

2 *June.* [41 Grosvenor Road]

The noble-hearted Blanche Cripps gone to her rest. Six months ago, faithful and devoted Fanny Hughes told me that Blanche had tried to strangle herself, that one night Fanny had missed her from bed, had run downstairs and found Blanche wandering about the drawing-room in a half-dazed condition looking for some instrument of death. Latterly she has seemed in good spirits, enjoyed the beauty of their new place in Argyleshire. On Wednesday evening, all the family were assembled at dinner to bid poor Standish Cripps (suffering also from melancholy suicidal mania) 'godspeed' before he left for New Zealand. Blanche seemed excited but said some beautiful words in a little speech. Before going to bed she insisted on ringing up on the telephone Julia Faulder, who had failed to come because of a severe headache, to say 'a sweet goodnight'. She followed Willie into his room and kissed him warmly. In the night, the two boys – Dick and Harry – were conscious that she was in their room bending over them and saying 'goodbye', 'be loyal to your father'. But they were so accustomed to strange words from her that they took no heed.

About four o'clock Willie, who was sleeping opposite Blanche and Fanny's room, possibly awakened by some noise, crossed over to get some water from his dressing-room. The door was locked: he hurried into her room, found her gone and Fanny fast asleep. They broke into the dressing-room by another door, and there was Blanche, robed in white, hanging from the shower-bath–still warm, but dead. The act had been carefully planned and was, in that sense, deliberate. 'God only knows,' she once said to Fanny, 'how I am tempted to kill myself. I feel impelled by a spirit stronger than my own.'

Blanche had a strange mind. She lived with great thoughts and tragic feelings. She was oblivious of the ordinary details of daily existence, disliked physical comfort, hated show, almost loathed riches. She was incapable of intellectual intercourse: she was either silent, or she spoke out her own thoughts, neither waiting nor caring for any reply from her companions. Whenever she could bring herself down to think of personal matters she was extraordinarily unselfish and generous. But since she was generally brooding on world propositions the net result of her life was not considerate. Her memory was so deficient that for years after father's death she used to ask me whether I was living at York House!

As a girl she was a prey to elemental passions, and as a wife and a mother she was bowed down by periods of world sorrow and religious melancholy. Possibly from an instinct for self-preservation, she incessantly occupied herself in restless fashion during the day, walking, fishing, sewing and lastly painting. 'Sketching' was her one absorbing delight – in the country she would have two or three large canvases going at once and rush from one to the other according to the light. Her pictures showed a weird talent, just wrong both in form and colour, but strangely and powerfully like what she tried to represent. They were 'impressionist' in spite of the laborious detail of her work, had in them the quality of an organic whole, a mad sort of consistency. She was a perpetual reader of Shakespeare and had been for years engaged in a futile task of translating Shakespeare into French, a language which she knew only in the schoolgirl way.

She was full of extravagant reverence for certain aspects of life: for age, for child-bearing, for death, for poverty, for all that belonged to the simple, natural man. . . . Hard labour and pain raised in her a spirit of exultation. Before she underwent a most dangerous and protracted operation some fifteen years ago, she was in a state of extraordinary happiness. In those fateful hours on Wednesday evening, when she had determined on the act, I can well imagine she was not miserable or even depressed. She was probably enjoying an exalted enthusiasm for death. Her vocation in the world would have been fulfilled by a splendid martyrdom. In the extremes of physical torture she would have died honoured and happy.

She was mated to a man with a nature almost as strange as her own. Willie Cripps has always been at first sight repellent, almost unclean-looking with the manners and conversation of a clever cad. He has no fixed principle: there is no action, however base, of which one would say unhesitatingly that Willie Cripps was incapable. Father, who had an extraordinary instinct about men, always disliked him, suspected him, and, in spite of his eventual success, never believed in him. And yet this man had, and even now, has undoubted qualities. A magnificent operator, an ingenious man of science, a first-class administrator, a born money-maker, he has stamped every episode in his career with success. . . . For twenty years he remained Blanche's romantic lover, worshipping her mad beauty and putting up with her innumerable and most aggravating mistakes. The day came when a woman who combined intellect, great artistic talent and considerable physical charm, crossed his path, and since that day he has been an erring husband, persistently inflicting pain on his wife by forcing her to receive this Italian singer [Julia Ravogli]. But throughout it all he has cared for Blanche, and provided in more ways than one for her happiness. Perhaps his worst side has been his persistent carelessness and selfishness towards his children, and his pitiful pursuit of social position across the happiness of his family and to the detriment of his professional skill. A great house in Scotland with fishing, shooting, motors, filled to overflowing with fashionable patients – earls, countesses, smart young men and the Italian singer, mixed up with professional friends and relations, has been his one relaxation from an untiring pursuit of gain. To Blanche it has been protracted pain and discomfort; to the children demoralizing and useless. He has been fully aware of this but has persisted. Will he persist?

When I saw him on Friday he was broken-hearted and grateful for any kind of affection. How long will this impression of her death last?

Sidney and I stayed three nights at Abbotsford last July, with Blanche and Fanny alone. Sir Walter Scott's rococo mansion with its sham towers and turrets, its furbished armour, its pretentious bookcases, and its stream of tourists was not an attractive home. Blanche effusively hospitable and apparently not unhappy. She was perpetually occupied standing in different parts of the garden for hours together, hard at work on great oil canvases, or striding off to see a gamekeeper's sick wife. . . . It was a mad life, unconnected with any consistent purpose. Now and again she would become ghastly white and be for minutes totally unconscious – a sort of epilepsy – crying in a strange voice, 'Willie, Willie,' as she came to. . . . She spoke little about herself, except to denounce the 'wicked feeling of jealousy'. Poor Blanche. What passed between her and Julia Ravogli when she visited her the afternoon before her death? Did she think that now that Willie had a grand new place he might be better with a new wife? And in her heroic mad way try to bring it about?

22 June. [41 Grosvenor Road]
A desolate fortnight in an old farmhouse lodging at Aston Magna. The beautiful countryside . . . was as soothing as I found it two years ago. But the little hamlet in which we lived had become, to my shaken nerves, intolerable with noise. . . Then weather was cold and windy: we could neither sit out nor bicycle. We worked and read and read and worked straight on end for the first three days, and then I collapsed into a restless and nervous incapacity. Always my mind reverted to the tragedy, not of Blanche's death – though that was horrible – but of her life. . . Then my thoughts would wander to the family, those young

men cursed with sleeplessness and melancholy, that young married woman also trembling on the brink, and those two happy natures – the youngest boy and girl – the only thoroughly sane ones of the family, on whom it had fallen to try to revive this dead mother for a whole hour by artificial respiration! Willie and Fanny called on them because they feared to call the others and tried to keep the facts from the servants. Over and over again my mind rehearsed the scene till I got dizzy with disgust.

Sidney was tender and consoling and now I am back at work on records I am recovering tone. Three days' complete holiday at Eastbourne ought to set me up.

26 June. [Beachy Head Hotel, Eastbourne]
Three delightful sunny days at Beachy Head, spending the whole day out-of-doors and the whole night in sleep, real good sleep. Now I feel fit for work again. . . .

Lord Lansdowne (1845–1927), was a Liberal statesman – Viceroy of India 1889–94, Secretary of State for War 1895–1900 and Foreign Secretary 1900–05. Ruth Cripps (1884–1978) was Alfred Cripps's eldest daughter and second child.

9 July. [41 Grosvenor Road]
Sunday at Parmoor. Alfred happy with his children but thoroughly disgruntled with politics. Tacking from Chamberlain towards Lord Lansdowne as leader. Tonight at Joe's great Albert Hall meeting, though, he took a large box to be filled by Ruth's friends, he himself arranged a dinner at the House to Lansdowne to ask some 'House of Commons men' to meet him. 'Some of us would like him as leader,' he confidentially suggested. With Balfour, and especially with Balfour's secretary, Sandars, I gather he is on the worst of terms, and if Balfour remains in the ascendant then Alfred has no chance of any move upward in the political sphere.

From our standpoint, apart from my genuine affection for the man, I am glad he has not succeeded. He is a persistent, able, almost a bitter enemy to any attempt to redress social inequality and raise the status of the manual worker. He delights in the freedom of the successful man to spend all he chooses on his own and his children's pleasures. . . . Twelve thousand a year he spends, each of his four boys costing him about £500. To earn this he gives a quantity of brainwork of very bad quality which leaves his mind tired but not sharpened – blunted, in fact. The one pleasant feature of the life is its charming kindness and courtesy to individuals – free-handedness – always ready to give to everyone and everybody and put the best construction on their doings. Even Blanche's tragic death he takes beneficently. 'I regard it simply as an illness – a disagreeable illness, but still merely an illness. Poor Blanche, she was always very kind to me,' he adds with a cheery tenderness. His boys, now three of them on the verge of manhood, are most agreeable lads, but slack and incapable of sustained effort. They come of energetic and ambitious stock, and these qualities may be brought out in their mature life, but at present they take their failure to get educated lightly and their pleasures seriously. He and Willie have gone to the two extremes in their treatment of their children, Willie harsh and niggardly, and Alfred tenderly and carefully indulgent. . . . With neither of them is there the faintest suspicion that there is any wrong-doing in the unlimited consumption of wealth by individuals without thought of making any return to the community. Such an idea would seem to Willie mere childish folly, to Alfred a dangerous heresy.

10 July. [41 Grosvenor Road]
The Progressives have turned Sidney off the party committee. Some of the Rump are very angry with him for entangling them in secondary education. The leaders are always civil to him, the rank and file find themselves accepting his proposals, but neither the leaders nor the ordinary members really like his policy and are vexed to find themselves pursuing it. So they try to keep him down *personally,* would I think be relieved to get rid of him. Sidney, meanwhile, is in the best of humours – his scholarship scheme is working admirably and forcing by its mere weight the Council either to subsidize existing secondary schools or to build and manage new ones. . . . When McKinnon Wood, I *think* sincerely, expressed his regret that he had been knocked off the party committee Sidney answered smilingly that he thought that 'there was really a cleavage of opinion between himself and the party, and that therefore it was well that this should be acknowledged; he was glad to feel at liberty to take his own line, which he could hardly do if he belonged to the inner circle.' Whereupon McKinnon Wood looked thoughtful and not over-pleased. They don't want to break with him.

Sir Cyril Jackson (1863–1924) was an educationist who was head of the Education Department of Western Australia 1896–1903; he then became chief inspector of the Board of Education in London until 1906 and a Progressive member of the L.C.C. in the following year. William Henry (later Lord) Beveridge (1879–1963) was an economist who was sub-warden of Toynbee Hall 1903–05, joined the civil service in 1908 and became Director of the L.S.E. 1919–37. Sir Albert Napier was a lawyer who later made a career in the Lord Chancellor's office: at this time he was private secretary to Cyril Jackson. Shaw's play *John Bull's Other Island* was first performed at the Royal Court Theatre on 1 November 1904. Beatrice took Balfour to the matinée performance on 10 November. The play was a great success – Balfour saw it five times – and did much to establish Shaw's reputation.

30 July. [41 Grosvenor Road]
Worked splendidly these last five weeks. . . Not dining out and not entertaining large parties makes all the difference to our efficiency especially in hot weather. . . .

One or two friends we have seen in a quiet way. A Sunday with Cyril Jackson of the Education Department, in his agreeable bachelor establishment at Limpsfield – to meet us, Masterman and Beveridge (a leading Toynbee-ite), and his secretary Napier, and a young friend of his about to become an Indian civil servant. This latter young man, whose name I have forgotten, struck us as typical of the coming civil servant. A 'double first', clean in looks and mind, strong-willed but unselfconscious, deprecating enthusiasm, critical of ideas and projects, and above all abstemious – given up tobacco, alcohol, meat. . . What his views are one could not tell, since he and Napier sat silent, listening to the torrent of discussion between Masterman, Beveridge and ourselves, with Jackson intervening as an official Conservative in a party of disputing Progressives. Masterman, an attractive journalist, combines being a religionist of the High Anglican order with sentimental and pessimistic radicalism. In theory he is a collectivist, by instinct an anarchist individualist – above all, he is a rhetorician. Beveridge, an ugly-mannered but honest, self-devoted, hard-headed young reformer of the practical type, came out well in comparison with Masterman; and from disliking him, as we had formerly done, because of his ugly manners, we approved him. There is no hope of the Liberal Party in either of these young men, but intense dislike of the Tories, and the usual anger with Balfour for remaining in [office?].

We have slipped into a sort of friendliness with Mr Balfour. He comes in to dinner whenever we ask him, and talks most agreeably. Perhaps our vanity is flattered by his evident interest in our historical and philosophical paradoxes, enjoyment of our conversation. I have not yet discovered any consistent attitude towards private and public life which comes to the surface in a dinner-party conversation. There is merely a rather weary curiosity as to other people's processes of reasoning and feeling, lit up, now and again, with a very real interest in human character where it is distinguished. The bulk of men bore him, whether regarded as individuals or as an electorate, or a Parliament, and all the common thoughts and feelings of common folk seem to him ineffably banal, fit only for the subject matter of Bernard Shaw's derisive wit.

I raised the question whether the derision embodied in *John Bull's Other Island,* derision unaccompanied by any positive faith or hope, counted for good. He seemed quite surprised at my doubt – thought it better to clear away humbug at any cost. I suggested that – though I personally loathed both the Irish and English Home Rule shibboleths – yet surely with many Irish Home Rulers and English Liberals these formulas embodied honest effort towards a better state of things? 'Question whether we may not be too intellectually aristocratic,' I urged, 'whether we may discourage right effort because it happens to express itself, not in bad grammar, because that is often picturesque, and, since Board Schools, somewhat unusual, but in fluffy thought and silly sentiment?' He acquiesced in his courteous way, but I could see he was not convinced.

Fyrish: two months – work, beauty, health. Left my diary, by mistake, behind.

The Haldane family home was at Cloan in Perthshire and Willie Cripps had taken Glendaruel as a shooting-lodge. In later years Beatrice thought she had been unfair to Julia Ravogli. Rosie Cripps (1885–1954) was the fifth child and second daughter of Blanche and Willie Cripps.

5 October. Grosvenor Road
On our way from Fyrish we stayed two nights at Mr Haldane's and four nights at Glendaruel. The pleasant impression of our stay at Cloan were rudely swept away by the nightmare of our visit to Glendaruel.

After a tedious journey of twelve hours we reached our destination to find a large house-party awaiting us and dinner deferred – Willie determined to show us gushing hospitality. To my intense disgust, there was the Ravogli woman, flaunted in the face of Willie's children still mourning for their mother. That was bad enough, but in the next few days I had to watch Willie philandering with Julia Ravogli, all of us conscious that it was passionate jealousy of the woman that was the occasion, if not the cause, of his wife's suicide a bare three months ago! The business was made almost more revolting by Willie's desire to talk sentimentally to me about Blanche and her 'nobility of nature'.

Puzzled as to what best to do, for the children's sake, I took refuge in cold but pleasant courtesy, withdrawing myself when possible from the general society, either with Rosie and the boys, or alone with Sidney. Poor little Rosie – her slim little figure draped in black, her white agitated face and sad eyes, flitted about uneasily in the background, desperately determined to ignore the Ravoglis but painfully frightened of her father's displeasure. The two boys were gloomy and taciturn and retired to the smoking-room when not shooting, afraid also to offend their father upon whom they are still dependent. . . . The luxurious establishment, run in the best style that money will buy, the beautiful valley and hillside, the whole set in exquisite, still October sunshine – all showed off the mockery, misery and sordidness of the whole business. Willie. . . . was an extraordinarily repulsive figure, a person in a nightmare. . . . The only element of satisfaction was the conviction that the children are not likely to be contaminated either by his wealth or by his philosophy of sensual egotism – the one is likely to be withheld from them, and the other is too disgusting in its outcome to offer any attraction. It is foolish to make resolutions which events may change. But unless driven to it by some urgent consideration of the children's welfare, never again do Sidney and I enter that man's house or welcome him in our home.

Felix Clay, an architect who specialized in school buildings, married Beatrice's niece Rachel Hobhouse in 1904. Louis Dausset was a French senator, a professor and a municipal councillor in Paris 1900–22. Arthur Henderson (1863–1935) was an iron-moulder who became a Labour M.P. in 1903; he was the organizer of the Labour victories in 1924 and 1929, and Foreign Secretary in 1929. George Peel (1868–1956) was a Treasury clerk who became a Liberal M.P. and a governor of the L.S.E. Mrs Craigie (1867–1906) was a novelist who wrote as 'John Oliver Hobbes'. Sir Albert Gray (1850–1928) was a legal official in the House of Lords.

14 October. [41 Grosvenor Road]
'Certainly revolting: but you must remember that you were tired and the atmosphere of such a house is wholly uncongenial to you and Sidney,' was Mary Playne's wise remark when I described the visit to

her. 'We must consult together and do what is wisest for the children.' So wrote Kate Courtney. 'The more passive we are the better. We cannot influence Willie for good, we had better not drive him into worse conduct by taking any decidedly hostile line,' represents the general feelings of the sisters, to which I suppose, Sidney and I will conform. I had one horrid nightmare of Willie trying to murder me – and then, with the hard work that waited me here, the whole matter passed out of my mind.

A flying visit to Hadspen for the silver wedding of the Hobhouses – that charming home presided over by Henry's dull but honourable spirit and Maggie's exuberant energies and good-humoured but somewhat vulgar sense; the four eldest children and Felix Clay, almost model young people, to meet the Playnes and Meinertzhagens. Then five days' hard grind at the manuscript records of the Bristol Corporation. . . . So we have settled strong and happy into the autumn's work.

A week or so disturbed by too much society. First the visit of the French deputies. We cut all the parties and I had not even to go to the dinners, while Sidney felt obliged to attend. But we had long talks with the brilliant journalist quartered on us, Dausset, who suffered our voluble bad French gladly for the sake of informing himself as to English society and English public opinion. In return he expounded to us the work of the Paris Municipal Council. . . Interesting to observe how intensely nervous all were about Germany – anxious to ascertain whether we genuinely intended to back them up in case of German aggression.

Mary Playne came up for ten days and knowing she liked to see folk I took the opportunity to ask people to dine. George Trevelyan and his wife, excellent and interesting young people with the charm of a strenuous and conscientious life and considerable talent, spent an evening alone with us. Among the young Liberals he is the most promising because he has some conviction and a fervent desire for more. He is to spend the next years of his life on a history of England 1790–1810 which is to be the glorification of Fox and rehabilitation of the French Revolution; one would think a somewhat conventional and banal task, a modernized replica of his father's. Still, he has enthusiasm and industry, and that is better than paradoxical orginality without these qualities.

On Sunday afternoon GBS and Granville-Barker dropped in and spread out before us the difficulties, the hopes, the ridiculous aspects of their really arduous efforts to create an intellectual drama. Granville-Barker has suddenly filled out – he looks even physically larger than a year ago. He has grown extraordinarily in dignity and knowledge of human nature. But he dislikes the absorption in mere acting and longs to mix with persons actually in 'affairs' or intellectually producing. GBS's egotism and vanity are not declining; he is increasing his deftness of wit and phrase but becoming every day more completely iconoclastic, the ideal derider. In the evening we dined with the Courtneys. On Monday John Burns and Mrs J.R. Green dropped in about 7 o'clock and stayed to share with Mary and ourselves half a pheasant! They talked 'at each other' – Alice raging against the Liberals, John raging against the priest. Incidentally Burns showed his dislike of the notion of a larger Labour Party and his rooted suspicion of even his present colleagues. Keir Hardie, Crooks and Henderson 'would all be out of Parliament' if he were Providence. It is pitiful to see the lack of good comradeship between these men.

On Tuesday there dined with us Wernher, the South African capitalist, a heavy, good-natured, public-spirited and scientific-minded millionaire, Lord Lytton, Bernard Shaw and Mrs Prothero (the mates of these three were ill) – a somewhat crooked party that was only straightened out by sheer energy on my part, into a comfortable affair. Wernher stumbled heavily along in his broken German, GBS scintillated, Mrs Prothero listened with Irish scepticism of Irish wit, Lord Lytton hung on GBS's words looking the beautiful, fastidious young artist and aristocrat – a party of interesting 'types' but not mixing well. Meanwhile I have got note after note from the Duchess of Marlborough who apparently has been seized with a whim to hear Sidney lecture and get us to dine with them afterwards. It would have been discourteous to refuse, so there was another evening of talk – the other guests being George Peel and Mrs Craigie. The Duke and Duchess corresponded exactly to the account given of them by the private secretary during our visit to Blenheim – somewhat futile young persons floating aimlessly on the surface of society, both alike quite unfit for a great position, swayed to and fro by somewhat silly motives, neither good nor bad. The little Duke is, I should imagine, mildly vicious; the Duchess has charm and I think goodness. I wondered how he came to be dragged by his wife to a technical lecture and into entertaining two dowdy middle-aged middle-class intellectuals, uncomfortably at a restaurant, for quite obviously they had come up to London on purpose. Was it GBS they were after? They reminded us of H.G. Wells's 'little white people' [the Eloi] in *The Time Machine*.

On Friday we had a really entertaining and useful party – Lord Milner, the Morants, the Albert Grays, Mackinder and C.A. Cripps. This was a real success – everyone was glad to meet the others and the conversation was sustained in subject as well as bright. I had a long talk with Milner after dinner. He has grown grim and, perhaps temporarily, bitter, obsessed too with a vision of a non-party government without having invented any device for securing it. His grimness may be the result of fatigue and lonely work, with a life among friends, and after rest it may work off.

His thesis is that the war itself, the dragging out of it, the unsatisfactory character of the settlement, the barely averted disaster – all were the result of the party system which forced half the political world to be against him. He is sufficient of a fanatic not to see that there was a genuine cleavage of opinion among the thinking people, that it was not merely a knot of cranks that disapproved his policy. He would take colonial affairs 'out of politics' but he does not suggest how. He is a strong man and an intensely public-spirited man, but he is harder and more intolerant, more distinctly the bureaucrat than when he left England. And he is sore, and bitter to opponents – not a good state of mind with which to enter politics. A little religion, or a purely intellectual pursuit, or perhaps some emotional companionship, is needed if he is to get back his sanity, his sense of proportion.

So ended our week's dissipation. On all but *one* day I managed to work, though the sleeplessness which always follows on talking late made the work of poor quality. . .

The smart world is tumbling over one another in the worship of GBS, and even we have a sort of reflected glory as his intimate friends. It is interesting to note that the completeness of his self-conceit will save him from the worst kind of deterioration – he is proof against flattery. Where it will injure him is in isolating him from serious intercourse with intimate friends working in other departments of life. Whenever he is free there is such a crowd of journalists and literary hangers-on around him that one feels it is kinder to spare him one's company, and that will be the instinct of many of his old friends engaged in administration, investigation or propaganda.

What a transformation scene from those first years I knew him: the scathing bitter opponent of wealth and leisure, and now! the adored one of the smartest and most cynical set of English Society. Some might say that we too had travelled in that direction: our good sense preserve us! Fortunately the temptation is at present slight and quite easily evaded. Curiosity about us is quickly satisfied and the smart ones subside, after one interview, into indifference. And Sidney steadily discourages my more sociable nature. 'By all means be courteous but keep clear of them,' is his perpetual refrain, in tone, if not in words. He is a blessed mate for me.

Chronology

1892   A general election in July results in a Liberal majority of 40 in the House of Commons. After their marriage on 23 July, the Webbs honeymoon in Ireland and Scotland. In October they settle in a flat at Netherhall Gardens, Hampstead. Sidney becomes chairman of the Technical Education Committee of the L.C.C.

1893   In January the Independent Labour Party is founded at Bradford. In February Gladstone introduces his second Home Rule Bill, but it is rejected by the House of Lords in September. Beatrice's sister Theresa dies in May, and the Webbs spend the summer at The Argoed with visits from Bernard Shaw and Graham Wallas. In October the Webbs move to 41 Grosvenor Road, and Sidney's article 'To Your Tents, O Israel' appears in the *Fortnightly Review* in November.

1894   In March Gladstone resigns as Prime Minister and leader of the Liberal Party. Lord Rosebery replaces him. The Report of the Royal Commission on Labour Disputes is issued; Sidney drafts its Minority Report. Shaw's play *Arms and the Man* is put on at the Avenue Theatre in April, and in May the Webbs' *History of Trade Unionism* is published. After a holiday in Italy the Webbs spend the summer at Borough Farm in Surrey, where they hear of the Hutchinson legacy and conceive the idea of founding the London School of Economics. In December the Progressives are defeated at the Westminster Vestry elections, and the Webbs spend Christmas with Alfred Cripps and the Courtneys at Parmoor.

1895   Lord Randolph Churchill dies in January. In March Sidney is re-elected for Deptford in the L.C.C. elections. Leonard

Courtney fails to be elected as Speaker of the House of Commons. W.A.S. Hewins is chosen as Director of L.S.E. in April. The Report of the Commission on the Aged Poor is published; Sidney writes the Minority Report. The Webbs spend Easter at the Beachy Head Hotel with friends, including Shaw and Wallas. At the general election in July the Tories are returned, with Lord Salisbury as Prime Minister. The Webbs spend the summer at The Argoed with Shaw; they cycle to Cardiff for the Trades Union Congress in September. The Webbs spend Christmas with the Trevelyans at Welcombe. The Jameson Raid takes place on 29 December.

1896   In February the offenders in the Jameson Raid are charged at Bow Street, and in May a Select Committee of the House of Commons is set up to enquire into the Raid. In April the Webbs holiday in the Lake District, where they hear from Ramsay MacDonald, who attacks the Webbs for misuse of the Hutchinson legacy. In May Leonard Courtney is threatened with blindness. The Webbs spend Whitsun at The Argoed, visit the Russells in June, and in August take a Suffolk rectory, where Shaw and Charlotte Payne-Towshend come to visit. In October the London School of Economics opens at Adelphi Terrace. The Webbs spend Christmas with Alfred Cripps at Parmoor.

1897   In February Beatrice addresses the women students at Girton and Newnham in Cambridge. In April Sir Alfred Milner is appointed High Commissioner of Cape Colony. In May Shaw is elected to the St Pancras Vestry. The Webbs take a house for three months with Charlotte Payne-Townshend, and Shaw visits them. A long strike of engineering workers begins in support of the Eight-Hour Day. In June Queen Victoria celebrates her Diamond Jubilee, and in July there is a Women's Jubilee Dinner. Following the publication of the report of the Enquiry into the Jameson Raid, there is a House of Commons debate in July. In November the Amalgamated Society of Engineers rejects the formula for settling the dispute. The Webbs spend Christmas at Parmoor.

1898   In January Graham Wallas marries Ada Radford. After the L.C.C. elections in March lead to a Progressive victory, the Webbs leave on a 'Sabbatical' journey to study local and national assemblies. They are in Washington when the Cuban war with Spain begins, and go on to Chicago and San Francisco. They arrive in Hawaii as the islands are annexed to the U.S., and go on to an extended tour of New Zealand and Australia, arriving home in December.

1899　In February the Webbs start work on the first of a series of volumes on the history of English local government. They engage Frederick Spencer as research secretary in March. In April Beatrice visits Bradford and Leeds on the first of their investigative tours. In September the Webbs visit Manchester, Liverpool and the Lake District. In October the South African war begins with the Boer invasion of Cape Colony.

1900　The Webbs in Devon for research. Boer victories are followed by the relief of Ladysmith in February and the relief of Mafeking in May. In February the Labour Representative Committee is formed to establish a Labour Party in Parliament. In July Beatrice meets Chamberlain at the House of Commons, and in August the Webbs go up to Tyneside for research, then visit the Trevelyans at Wallingford before taking a holiday at Bamburgh. In the 'khaki' election in October the Tories retain their parliamentary majority. The Webbs at Hadspen in December.

1901　Queen Victoria dies in January. Death of Mandell Creighton. Publication of Fabian Tract *The Education Muddle*. In March the Progressives win the L.C.C. election. The Webbs holiday at Lulworth, Dorset, in April and visit the Russells near Oxford in July. Sidney's article 'Lord Rosebery's Escape from Houndsditch' is published in the September issue of *Nineteenth Century*. The Webbs on holiday in Yorkshire Dales in September. Beatrice, in poor mental and physical health, becomes interested in food reform. In December the Webbs read *Anticipations* by H.G. Wells, which was published in November. Lord Rosebery makes an important speech at Chesterfield. The Webbs spend Christmas at Parmoor.

1902　In February the Webbs meet H.G. Wells. The Liberal League is formed. In March the Education Bill is introduced in Parliament. The Webbs are at Crowborough, Sussex, in April, and in May they stay with the Russells at Friday's Hill. The Boer War ends in May, and the permanent building for the L.S.E. is opened. In July Beatrice takes Alys Russell to

Switzerland. Lord Salisbury resigns and A.J. Balfour becomes Prime Minister. In August Edward VII is crowned. The Webbs on holiday at Chipping Campden in September. The Education Act is passed in December.

1903   The Webbs on holiday in Norfolk in January with the Shaws and Wallases. Beatrice visits Herbert Spencer at Brighton in February and in April the Webbs are at Longfords. In May Chamberlain advocates Imperial preference and tariff reform. The Webbs go for a holiday to the Cotswolds in June. Sidney is appointed to Royal Commission on Trade Union Law. In September the Webbs take a cycling holiday in Normandy, where they visit the Russells. Sidney writes 'London Education' in October for the *Nineteenth Century*. The London Education Act is passed. In November Hewins resigns as Director of the L.S.E. and is succeeded by Halford J. Mackinder. Herbert Spencer dies in December.

1904   War breaks out between Japan and Russia. In the L.C.C. elections in March Shaw is beaten at St Pancras. In April the Webbs visit Wells at Sandgate. In May they take a holiday in Hampshire near the Meinertzhagens. In July they start a three-month holiday in Scotland. In November Beatrice takes Balfour to see Shaw's play *John Bull's Other Island* at the Royal Court Theatre.

1905   Marie Souvestre dies in March. In May the Webbs spend three weeks with the Playnes at Longfords. They visit Wells at Sandgate. Blanche Cripps commits suicide in June. The Webbs spend a fortnight at Aston Magna and three days at Beachy Head. In August they go to Scotland for two months including a visit to Willie Cripps. The Russo-Japanese war ends with revolutionary outbreaks in Russia.

A Short Bibliography

The books listed below have for the most part been chosen because of their relevance and accessibility, at least in libraries: the few exceptions are references to particularly significant texts.

B.M. Allen, *Sir Robert Morant* (London, 1934).

Julian Amery, *The Life of Joseph Chamberlain* (Vol. IV), (London, 1952).

A.J. Balfour, *Chapters of Autobiography* (London, 1930).

R. Barker, *Education and Politics 1900–1951* (Oxford, 1972).

F. Bealey and Henry Pelling, *Labour and Politics 1900–1906* (London, 1958).

E.J.T. Brennan, *Education for National Efficiency: The Contribution of Sidney and Beatrice Webb* (London, 1975).

Harry Brown, *Joseph Chamberlain: Radical and Imperialist* (London, 1974).

Sydney Caine, *The History of the Foundation of the London School of Economics and Political Science* (London, 1963).

Ronald Clark, *The Life of Bertrand Russell* (London, 1976).

Peter Clarke, *Liberals and Social Democrats* (Cambridge, 1978).

H.A. Clegg, Alan Fox and A.F. Thompson, *A History of British Trade Unionism since 1889* (Oxford, 1964).

G.D.H. Cole, *British Working-Class Politics 1832–1914* (London, 1941).

Margaret Cole, *The Story of Fabian Socialism* (London, 1961).
    (ed.), *The Webbs and their Work* (London, 1949).

M. Creighton, *Life and Letters of Mandell Creighton* (London, 1904).

Blanche Dugdale, *Arthur James Balfour* (London, 1939).

Janet Dunbar, *Mrs GBS: A Biographical Portrait of Charlotte Shaw* (London, 1963).

361

Carol Dyhouse, *Girls Growing Up in Late Victorian and Edwardian England* (London, 1981).

Max Egremont, *Balfour* (London, 1980).

H.V. Emy, *Liberals, Radicals and Social Politics 1892–1914* (London, 1973).

R.C.K. Ensor, *England 1870–1914* (Oxford, 1936).

R. First and A. Scott, *Olive Schreiner* (London, 1980).

Peter Fraser, *Joseph Chamberlain: Radicalism and Empire 1868–1914* (London, 1966).

G. Gibbon and R.W. Bell, *History of the L.C.C. 1889–1938* (London, 1939).

G.P. Gooch, *Leonard Courtney* (London, 1920).

Elizabeth Haldane, *From One Century to Another* (London, 1937).

R.B. Haldane, *An Autobiography* (London, 1929).

José Harris, *Unemployment* (Oxford, 1972).

Frederick Harrison, *Autobiographical Memoirs* (London, 1911).

A.F. Havighurst, *Radical Journalist. H.W. Massingham* (Cambridge, 1974).

Archibald Henderson, *George Bernard Shaw: Man of the Century* (New York, 1956).

W.A.S. Hewins, *The Apologia of an Imperialist* (London, 1929).

S. Hobhouse, *Margaret Hobhouse and her Family* (London, 1934).

E. Hobsbawm, *Industry and Empire* (London, 1968).

Winifred Holtby, *Women and a Changing Civilisation* (London, 1935, rep. 1978).

James Hulse, *Revolutionists in London* (London, 1970).

B.L. Hutchins, *Women in Industry* (London, 1915).

Samuel Hynes, *Edwardian Occasions* (London, 1972).
The Edwardian Turn of Mind (Princeton, 1968).

Holbrook Jackson, *The Eighteen Nineties* (London, 1950).

Robert Rhodes James, *Rosebery* (London, 1963).

Roy Jenkins, *Asquith* (London, 1964).

Denis Judd, *Radical Joe* (London, 1977).

Stephen Koss, *Lord Haldane: Scapegoat for Liberalism* (New York, 1969).
Nonconformity and British Politics (London, 1975).
Asquith (New York, 1976).

Dan Laurence (ed.), *Bernard Shaw: Collected Letters 1874–1897 and 1898–1910* (London, 1965 and 1972).

Alan McBriar, *Fabian Socialism and English Politics 1884–1914* (Cambridge, 1962).

S. Maccoby, *English Radicalism 1886–1914* (London, 1953).

Norman and Jeanne MacKenzie, *The Time Traveller: A Biography of H.G. Wells* (London, 1973).
The First Fabians (London, 1977).

Norman MacKenzie, *The Letters of Sidney and Beatrice Webb* (Cambridge, 1978).

Philip Magnus, *Gladstone* (London, 1954).

John Marlow, *Milner: Apostle of Empire* (London, 1976).

David Marquand, *Ramsay Macdonald* (London, 1977).

Kenneth O. Morgan, *The Age of Lloyd George* (London, 1971).
Keir Hardie (London, 1975).

Margery Morgan, *The Shavian Playground* (London, 1972).

John Morley, *The Life of W.E. Gladstone* (London, 1903).

A.J.A. Morris, *C.P. Trevelyan 1870–1958* (London, 1977).

H.C.G. Matthew, *The Liberal Imperialists: The Ideas and Politics of a post-Gladstonian Elite* (Oxford, 1973).

M. Olivier, *Sydney Olivier* (London, 1948).

Elizabeth Pakenham, *Jameson's Raid* (London, 1960).

Thomas Pakenham, *The Boer War* (London, 1979).

Lord Parmoor, *A Retrospect* (London, 1936).

Hesketh Pearson, *GBS* (London, 1942).

E.R. Pease, *History of the Fabian Society* (London, 1916).

John Peel, *Herbert Spencer* (London, 1971).

Henry Pelling, *The Origins of the Labour Party* (London, 1953).
Popular Politics and Society in Late Victorian Britain (London, 1968).

Stanley Pierson, *British Socialists: The Journey from Fantasy to Politics* (London, 1979).

Philip Poirier, *The Advent of the Labour Party* (London, 1958).

John Ramsden, *The Age of Balfour and Baldwin 1902–1940* (London, 1978).

W.W. Robson, *The Government and Misgovernment of London* (London, 1939).

Kenneth Rose, *The Later Cecils* (London, 1975).

Andrew Rosen, *Rise Up Women! The Militant Campaign of the W.P.S.U. 1903–1914* (London, 1974).

Bertrand Russell, *Autobiography* (3 vols.) (London, 1967–69).

G.R. Searle, *The Quest for National Efficiency: A Study in British Politics and Political Thought 1899–1914 Imperialism and Social Reform: English Social Imperialist Thought 1895–1914* (Oxford, 1971).

B. Semmel, *Imperialism and Social Reform: English Social Imperialist Thought 1895–1914* (London, 1960).

Bernard Shaw, *Sixteen Self-Sketches* (London, 1949).

Brian Simon, *Education and the Labour Movement 1870–1920* (London, 1965).

Dudley Sommer, *Haldane of Cloan* (London, 1960).

Herbert Spencer, *An Autobiography* (London, 1904).

Peter Stansky, *Ambitions and Strategies* (London, 1964).

Barbara Strachey, *Remarkable Relations: The Story of the Pearsall Smith family* (London, 1980).

Ray Strachey, *The Cause: A Short History of the Women's Movement in Great Britain* (London, 1928, rep. London 1978).

E. Strauss, *Bernard Shaw: Art and Socialism* (London, 1942).

Alan Sykes, *Tariff Reform in Party Politics 1903–13* (Oxford, 1979).

Laurence Thompson, *The Enthusiasts* (London, 1971).

Paul Thompson, *Socialists, Liberals and Labour* (London, 1967).

Beatrice Webb, *Our Partnership* (London, 1948, rep. Cambridge, 1975).

Sidney Webb, *London Education* (London, 1904).

John Wilson, *CB: A Life of Sir Henry Campbell-Bannerman* (London, 1973).

Kenneth Young, *Arthur James Balfour* (London, 1963).

Index

The italic numeral *I* indicates that an earlier reference can be found in Volume I of the diary.

look at Art or letters & we deny ourselves
nothing that we really obtain — we are
— at any rate I am — self-indulgent — more
self-indulgent than we ought to be. But —
somehow or other when one wants
a thing one never finds time to
deny it to oneself.

Sad scenes at the Williams'. Opium
becoming a hopeless morphia & chloroform
drunkard, the little boy nervous & ailing,
Ross a slave to her husband, trying
to reconcile herself by having her own
way in the management of her child.
Mrs Thompson selected there as nurse
to both husband & child — Ross learning
to hate her out of jealousy — She
unendurably uncomfortable & wretched,
trying her best to keep the child in
health & the man from a suicidal
death. Poor little weak, jealous, misery
Ross — a pitiable spectacle —
struggling on bravely enough — but